VIETNAM IN IRAQ

More than most post-1970 conflicts involving US forces, the conflict in Iraq has been fought against a background of frequently invoked memories from the era of the Vietnam War. The essays in this book offer a series of perspectives on connections and parallels between the Vietnam War and the 2003 invasion of, and current conflict in, Iraq. In particular it examines the impact of the Vietnam analogy on the war in Iraq, assesses the military tactical lessons learned from the Vietnam War and explores the influence and persistence of its legacy in US politics, culture and diplomacy.

The book holds up to original interrogation some commonly held assumptions about historical analogy. Several distinguished authorities on the Vietnam War era, in particular, offer their thoughts on the value and applicability of Vietnam–Iraq parallels. If most contributions point out some obvious dissimilarities between the two eras, notably the transformed post-Cold War international environment, similarities, particularly those relating to the problems of cultural misunderstanding, are also apparent.

An original examination of a key debate in contemporary International Relations, this book will be essential reading for students and researchers in strategic studies, international relations and American politics.

John Dumbrell is Professor of Politics at Leicester University, UK. His most recent publications are *A Special Relationship: Anglo-American Relations in the Cold War and After* and *President Lyndon Johnson and Soviet Communism*, winner of the 2005 Richard E. Neustadt Book Prize.

David Ryan is currently a member of the Department of History at University College, Cork. His most recent publications are *The United States and Europe in the Twentieth Century* (2003) and *US Foreign Policy in World History* (2000).

VIETNAM IN IRAQ

Tactics, lessons, legacies and ghosts

Edited by John Dumbrell
and David Ryan

Routledge
Taylor & Francis Group

LONDON AND NEW YORK

First published 2007
by Routledge
2 Park Square, Milton Park, Abingdon, Oxon OX14 4RN

Simultaneously published in the USA and Canada
by Routledge
270 Madison Ave, New York, NY 10016

Routledge is an imprint of the Taylor & Francis Group, an informa business

© 2007 John Dumbrell and David Ryan editorial matter and selection;
individual chapters © the contributors

Typeset in Times by
HWA Text and Data Management, Tunbridge Wells
Printed and bound in Great Britain by
Antony Rowe Ltd, Chippenham, Wiltshire

British Library Cataloguing in Publication Data
A catalogue record for this book is available from the British Library

Library of Congress Cataloging-in-Publication Data
Vietnam in Iraq : tactics, lessons, legacies and ghosts / edited by
John Dumbrell and David Ryan.
p. cm. – (Contemporary security studies)
Includes bibliographical references and index.
1. National security–United States. 2. United States–Military policy.
3. Vietnam War, 1961–1975. 4. Iraq War, 2003– 5. United States–Foreign
relations–1945–1989. 6. United States–Foreign relations--1989– 7. World
politics–1945–1989 8. World politics–1989– I. Dumbrell, John, 1950– II.
Ryan, David, 1965– III. Title. IV. Series.
UA23.V44 2007
355'.033573–dc22   2006017344

ISBN10: 0–415–40562–9 (hbk)
ISBN10: 0–415–40563–7 (pbk)
ISBN10: 0–203–96765–8 (ebk)

ISBN13: 978–0–415–40562–1 (hbk)
ISBN13: 978–0–415–40563–8 (pbk)
ISBN13: 978–0–203–96765–2 (ebk)

FOR HEIDI, HANNAH AND LUCA

CONTENTS

CONTRIBUTORS

James M. Carter is an Assistant Professor of History at Texas A&M University – Corpus Christi. He received his PhD from the University of Houston in 2004. His areas of specialization are US foreign relations, the Vietnam War, and modern US political history. He has published editorials, essays and articles including, 'The Vietnam Builders: Private Contractors, Military Construction and the "Americanization" of United States Involvement in Vietnam', *Graduate Journal of Asia-Pacific Studies*.

John Dumbrell is Professor in the Department of Politics at the University of Leicester. He has published widely on US foreign policy and history including: *Vietnam and the Antiwar Movement*; *The Making of US Foreign Policy* with a chapter by D. Barrett; *The Carter Presidency: A Re-evaluation*; *American Foreign Policy: Carter to Clinton*; *A Special Relationship: Anglo-American Relations in the Cold War and After,* co-winner of the Cambridge University Donner Book Prize; and *President Lyndon Johnson and Soviet Communism*. He is currently working on a study of the international policies of the Clinton Administration.

Lloyd C. Gardner is the Charles and Mary Beard Professor in the History Department at Rutgers University and author of more than a dozen books on the history of US foreign policy, including *Approaching Vietnam* and *Pay Any Price: Lyndon Johnson and the Wars for Vietnam*. With Marilyn Young, he recently co-edited *The New American Empire*.

Richard Lock-Pullan is an RCUK Research Fellow in the Department of Political Science and International Studies at the University of Birmingham. He was formerly a Senior Lecturer at King's College, London based at the UK's Defence Academy. He is the author of *American Intervention Policy and US Army Innovation: from Vietnam to Iraq* and has published on US strategy, security, and military innovation in journals such as the *Journal of Strategic Studies*, *Contemporary Security Policy*, *War and Society*, and the *Journal of Military History*.

Matthew Masur is Assistant Professor of History at St Anselm College in Manchester, New Hampshire. He earned his doctorate in history from Ohio

State University in 2004 based on a dissertation on US–South Vietnamese relations, focusing specifically on cultural aspects of the 'struggle for hearts and minds' from 1954–63. He conducted research at several archives in the United States and was awarded a Fulbright-Hays Fellowship to complete his research at National Archives II in Ho Chi Minh City, Vietnam. He is currently revising his dissertation as a book manuscript.

Trevor B. McCrisken is Lecturer in American Politics and International Studies at the University of Warwick and Associate Fellow at the Rothermere American Institute at the University of Oxford. He is author of *American Exceptionalism and the Legacy of Vietnam: US Foreign Policy since 1974*, and co-author with Andrew Pepper of *American History and Contemporary Hollywood Film*.

Richard A. Melanson is Professor of National Security Strategy at the National War College, National Defense University in Washington, DC. He has published numerous books on US foreign policy including *American Foreign Policy Since the Vietnam War: The Search for Consensus From Richard Nixon to George W. Bush*; *Reevaluating Eisenhower: American Foreign Policy in the 1950s*; and *Writing History and Making Policy: The Cold War, Vietnam, and Revisionism*.

John Mueller is Woody Hayes Chair of National Security Studies, Mershon Center, and Professor of Political Science, Ohio State University. He is the author of several books, including: *The Remnants of War*; *Peace Prosperity and Politics*; *Policy and Opinion in the Gulf War*; and *War, Presidents and Public Opinion*.

Jon Roper is Professor and Head of the Department of American Studies at the University of Wales, Swansea. His publications include *The Contours of American Politics*; *The American Presidents: Heroic Leadership from Kennedy to Clinton*; *Democracy and Its Critics*; and articles in *The Journal of American Studies* and *Presidential Studies Quarterly*.

David Ryan is in the Department of History, University College, Cork, Ireland. He is author of several books and articles including *US–Sandinista Diplomatic Relations*; *US Foreign Policy in World History*; *The United States and Europe in the Twentieth Century*; and co-editor of *The United States and Decolonization*. He is currently working on a history of the Vietnam Syndrome and US intervention.

Marilyn B. Young is Professor in the Department of History at New York University. She has written and researched extensively on US foreign policy and US–Asian relations and most pertinently for this project is the author of *The Vietnam Wars, 1945–1990* and *Vietnam and America* (with Marvin Gettleman, Jane Franklin and Bruce Franklin), and *Reporting Vietnam: American Journalism, 1959–1975,* two volumes. *The Vietnam Wars* was the recipient of the Berkshire Women's History Prize.

ACKNOWLEDGEMENTS

The idea for this collection, and several of the contributions, originated at a conference organised by the Centre for Diplomatic and International Studies on 'Issues in American Foreign Policy' held at Leicester University in March 2005. The editors would like to acknowledge the financial assistance for the conference provided by the British International Studies Association.

David Ryan would like to acknowledge the generous support of the British Academy and the College of Arts, Celtic Studies and Social Sciences towards funding research in various Presidential Libraries and the National Archives and Records Administration.

Together the editors would like to thank Andrew Humphrys at Routledge for adopting the project and Marjorie Francois for her support throughout.

INTRODUCTION

John Dumbrell and David Ryan

'We must be wary both of the zealous ideologues who would overcommit us and of those who would withdraw us from meeting our legitimate responsibilities and interests', the National Security Advisor, Henry Kissinger wrote for the Staff Secretary in the concluding sections of a memorandum which responded to an article by Robert Nisbet in the *Wall Street Journal* early in 1971. The piece caused some concern and a flurry of analysis within the Nixon administration.[1] Nisbet in turn was reflecting on John Kenneth Galbraith's 'Who Needs the Democrats?' which pointed out that 'wars ... have come with devastating reliability' every time the Democrats are in power. Nisbet adopted William James's dichotomy of mind into the 'tender' and the 'tough', basically applying the tender to the intellectual Democrats, the tough to the realist Republicans. He argued:

> Among modern intellectuals, further, there is a frequently observed fondness for the uses of power, especially centralized, bureaucratized power in service to large-scale moral objectives. In a modern nation state, war is the supreme crisis, the highest expression of a complex of elements including love of large-scale undertakings involving masses of people, power, centralization, bureaucracy and chronic political moralism.[2]

As an antidote Kissinger advocated 'an intelligent tough-mindedness' that balances a realistic understanding of capabilities with rational aspirations.[3] The tender-minded who had taken the United States into Vietnam, Kissinger concluded in a development of the memo to the National Security Council, failed because they did not probe 'deeply enough into the substance of our options and emphasiz[ed] too much the formal structure of their thought. We got into Vietnam because we knew little about the foe, our allies or the terrain and the people over which we fought'. Castigating the Democrats of the early 1960s Kissinger argued that 'if we have learned to handle national security problems better today than ten years ago, I believe the credit must go to those who have stripped away moralisms that still suffocate our thinking ...'.[4]

The realism advanced by Kissinger seemed to stifle currents of other strong aspirations in US foreign policy. One of them, the urge to promote democracy abroad, is usually associated with the Democratic Party. However, elements

1

of democracy-promoting idealism, linked to the legacy of President Woodrow Wilson, also found their way into the later (primarily Republican) neo-conservative agenda, albeit in the context of a pronounced tendency to American unilateralism. This was coupled with a belief, shared by realists, that 'power is often necessary to achieve moral purposes'.[5] In the post-Vietnam period it was the Republican presidents who initiated two of the largest deployments of troops in 1990–1 and in 2003. There is of course another ten year parallel, roughly speaking. While a sense of realism and a knowledge of the limits of US power animated the decisions to end the Gulf War in 1991, those very limits chafed against the aspirations of certain strategic thinkers whose influence was coupled with power from 2001.

Concluding his book *Choosing War* on Vietnam, Fredrik Logevall argued that 'something very much like it could happen again' largely because of the 'continued primacy of the executive branch in foreign affairs'. Within the framework of President Johnson's priorities in 1964–5, war made sense. Logevall suggested 'a leader will assuredly come along who, like Johnson, will take the path of least immediate resistance and in the process produce disastrous policy – provided there is a permissive context that allows it'.[6] Vietnam, as Marilyn Young argues in this collection, provided a host of 'negative lessons' within the US political culture. It was the reference point for failure and defeat that had to be surmounted. The United States learned quickly from the wars in Vietnam. They rebuilt their military across the 1980s to a point where their conventional military power was pre-eminent. They learned the instrumental lessons that eased the use of that power within a culture that was now more reticent on matters of such engagement. The system was honed over time to ensure that US credibility and leadership remained resolute. There were readjustments in the balance of power between the Congress and the Presidency. But over time the 'moralism' too returned to strategic thinking, in the presidency of Jimmy Carter who was reluctant to assert power in such conflicts. With Reagan the Wilsonian current returned albeit applied in a limited fashion, but it was from this stream that the forty-third President, George W. Bush, supped, combining the proclivity of ills described by Nisbet above, to fashion a rhetorical strategy that mingled the 'tough' and the 'tender' in the 'balance of power that favors freedom'.[7] The permissive context was a consequence of the tragedies in New York, Washington and Pennsylvania in September 2001; the war in Iraq was still a war of choice. A war that resulted in occupation and the tentative transfer of formal authority if not power that might be counterproductive to the stated goals of the post-9/11 period, counterproductive to US interests and counterproductive to its power. The ghosts of Iraq will haunt US strategic thinking for the immediate to mid-term future; the lessons of Vietnam will be revisited; the legacies of both wars are and will be profound.

Lloyd Gardner dissects the often mystic chords of implicit intellectual intent. He examines the thinking and arguments underlying doctrines and strategies that have animated US policymakers during and after the Cold War but particularly focusing on the neoconservative loathing of certain realist aspects of US policy associated with Kissinger and the era of *détente*. The expediency adopted after Vietnam could not be allowed to replace a policy based on principle. As he writes:

'Realist arguments for restraint at the banks of the Euphrates appeared to neo-conservatives as unworthy of Reagan's promise to restore America in the Puritan image of a City on the Hill – not only unworthy, but positively dangerous in a world where, as President George W. Bush admonished audiences after 9/11, terrorists had access to weapons of mass destruction'. Containment, both actual and as philosophical guide, had to be transcended.

Marilyn Young examines the manner in which Vietnam has impacted on the current military and the resonances in US culture. In many respects it has become the focal point for failure amongst US politicians who sought to avoid the clutches of its reverberations. Above all, she writes, a lesson 'learned early and never forgotten: the most important battlefront is domestic'. Success depends in many ways on press manipulation, the executive ability to deceive and do so with unwavering conviction to constantly frighten the people to avert critical engagement. And while US troops fight in Iraq, Vietnam remains significant: in their tactics and their thoughts. Vietnam haunts the press coverage of this 'war'. Vietnam remains a presence 'in the American families who receive the bodies of the dead and the maimed and in the daily experience of Iraqis and Afghanis'.

Richard Melanson inspects the impact of the war in Iraq on the US foreign policy consensus. To do so he compares it with the impact of Vietnam. First he examines the Cold War consensus and the post-9/11 equivalent. He then demonstrates how Vietnam shattered the Cold War consensus and how the Iraq war has detrimentally weakened the post-9/11 accord. Finally, he traces the manner in which the presidents have tried to rebuild support for their efforts after public support has eroded.

Richard Lock-Pullan scrutinises the military lessons drawn from the Vietnam War and how they have exerted influence, particularly on the Army. He concentrates on the Army because of its lead role in the Iraq War. Vietnam significantly shaped the way the US understands war, what it does in Iraq and its understanding of counter-insurgency. As he quotes Hannah Arendt in what appears as ironic indictment, 'the means used to achieve political goals are more often than not of greater relevance to the future world than intended goals'. He then examines the limitations of the approach and the resulting impact.

James Carter then provides a comparison of the efforts of the private corporations that gained lucrative contracts in both Vietnam and Iraq. Vast proportions of the construction needs were given over to private corporations in a less than competitive environment often with significant rewards. He then compares the similar phenomenon in Iraq. In his analysis of state-building he suggests that the comparative approach sheds new light on both experiences, while Vietnam simultaneously provides significant lessons for Iraq. Despite this, he argues, the Bush administration is reluctant to address Vietnam's message.

David Ryan addresses the struggle for the 'hearts and minds' not only of the Iraqis but more pertinently of the American people. He argues that despite the fall of the Berlin Wall and the triumph in the Cold War, the loss in Vietnam remained a potent reference point for certain US strategists who sought to overcome the memories and constraints of the lessons produced after that war. While the instrumental lessons were sharpened across the decades through various tactics of intervention, US credibility remained problematical as the reluctance to commit ground troops was palpably obvious. Iraq provided an opportunity to exorcise many of the cultural limits on US strategists. In tragic irony it might have significant unintended and unforeseen consequences.

Jon Roper locates his discussion in the crisis for presidential power which emanated from the controversies of the era of the Vietnam War. He traces the evolution of presidential war-making from the early Cold War period. As do several of the contributors to this book, Roper acknowledges the diversity and ambiguity of Vietnam's 'lessons' for subsequent policymaking. He sees a central purpose of the administration of George W. Bush – especially of its more forthright and neoconservative elements – as the rescue of the American president from the putatively debilitating effects of the 'Vietnam syndrome'. Roper notes that, to the extent that presidents reject (or are allowed to reject) domestic and international constraints on their military decisions, they have to live with, and be judged by, the consequences. He also makes an important and original contribution to this debate, by identifying a Western European dimension to the 'Vietnam syndrome': the unwillingness of allies unconditionally and permanently to endorse a discretionary presidential power of military action.

Trevor McCrisken deals explicitly with the problem of analogies and 'analogy thinking' in foreign policy and international relations generally. Neither policymakers nor academic commentators can avoid 'analogy thinking'. Decision-makers are bound to raid their own experience in order to inform present difficulties. To do otherwise would be to denude the value of human experience. Yet, analogies often mislead. The Vietnam War, like appeasement of fascism in the 1930s for an earlier generation, shaped the outlook of all who lived through it. As McCrisken demonstrates, however, the Vietnam analogy must be subjected to constant interrogation. McCrisken offers important and subtle insights into the implications of seeing Iraq as 'Bush's Vietnam'. Despite the limitations of 'analogy thinking', McCrisken concludes that the famous 'lessons' of Vietnam – above all the fact that American international power is not limitless – still apply.

In our next chapter, John Mueller, a major and highly original contributor to contemporary debates about Washington's handling of the War on Terror, takes up a variety of issues, including the role of public opinion in both conflicts and debates about military strategy. Like McCrisken, he raises the thorny issue of 'acceptable costs', drawing on a well of relevant original research. His wider historical perspective is similarly original and striking. Mueller argues that the spectacle of America struggling against humiliation in Vietnam caused the Soviet Union to overreach internationally. In so doing, Moscow succumbed to an acute case of geopolitical indigestion. The upshot of the difficulties in Iraq, argues Mueller, may involve a replay of this process, with international terrorism the ultimate loser. Like Soviet communism, bin-Ladenism may simply fizzle out as a result of its own contradictions and inherent weaknesses.

Considering the rhetorical history of 'falling dominoes', Matthew Masur again draws attention to 'analogy thinking'. He examines the tendency – evident in

President George W. Bush's citing of parallels between the War on Terror and both the Cold War and the Second World War – to think in over-simplified analogical terms. Masur notes the potency of the anti-communist 'domino theory', usually associated with the era of President Eisenhower. The invasion of Iraq represented a kind of domino-theory-in-reverse, with a succession of 'free' dominoes raising themselves in the wake of the liberation of Baghdad. Masur cites detailed research on the US propaganda/public diplomacy war in Indochina in the 1950s to illustrate parallels with contemporary tropes. In Vietnam, official thinking maintained that no-one would freely choose communism; in Iraq, the public US line is similarly (argues Masur) that no-one freely chooses 'unfreedom'. Masur concludes with a fascinating review of academic and popular Vietnam War revisionism, relating it to current debates about Iraq.

In our concluding piece, John Dumbrell offers a general survey of Vietnam/Iraq parallels, revisiting and commenting anew on points raised in previous chapters. Many of the problems associated with the use of US international power in the 1960s – problems of local support, cultural insensitivity, the hazards of unsustainable commitment – reappear in the new century, albeit in an utterly transformed global context. Dumbrell focuses on two discrete areas: the role of the US Congress and relations between Washington and London. In the former case, he is struck by the degree to which Congress has acquiesced in the discretionary war power asserted by President George W. Bush. Contemporary legislative acquiescence mirrors, and to some degree even exceeds, the experience of the 1960s. In the case of US–UK relations, Dumbrell attempts to explain the divergent reactions to American wars on the part of Prime Ministers Harold Wilson and Tony Blair. Dumbrell also touches on parallels between the presidential elections of 1968 and 2004.

Turning points

Library shelves of books have been written about the political, cultural, social, military and international legacy of the Vietnam War. The controversies attending the 2003 Iraq invasion and its ugly aftermath already stimulate thoughts of the 'legacy' of the Iraq War. In such a context it is almost impossible to avoid Vietnam connections. Senator Barbara Boxer (Democrat, California) observed in December 2005: 'The war in Iraq is producing the greatest number of wounded and psychologically-impacted veterans since the Vietnam War – men and women who will return to their communities forever changed'.[8] American troop involvement in Iraq, as several of our contributors note, is not as intense as in Vietnam. However, the 'legacy' of the latter conflict may come to be felt in many unpredictable ways, not least in moulding the perceptions and international outlooks of an 'Iraq generation' (in the Middle East, Europe and elsewhere, as well as in the United States). In the short term, however, the future impact of the war has tended to be discussed primarily in terms of its possible impact on US foreign policy in the medium to long term.

A frequent theme in contemporary comment about the Iraq conflict is the possibility of the war generating a new 'syndrome': a new reluctance on the part of America's leaders and people to pay the price of an international engagement which can so easily cost precious blood and treasure. If it is right and proper that the 2003 invasion should engender caution, so it is troubling – for a host of American internationalists, from 2004 presidential contender John Kerry to sometime neo-conservative Francis Fukuyama[9] – to contemplate the possibility of national overreaction.

A common way of understanding the history of US international policy is to see it as being shaped by cycles. The US foreign policy tradition embraces various facets: Jeffersonian, Jacksonian, Hamiltonian and Wilsonian (in Walter Russell Mead's famous formulation);[10] isolationist and internationalist; unilateralist ('anti-entanglement') and mutilateralist; economic, geopolitical and democracy-promoting exceptionalist. These facets do not merely constitute policy content at any one time; they also rise and fall sequentially, usually in response to major policy reversals. G. John Ikenberry described the 2004 presidential contest as involving an explicit choice between unilateralism and neo-imperialism on the one hand (Bush's); and a more co-operative version of American hegemony on the other.[11] Wars do often represent turning points in international thinking and engagement. The Vietnam War unquestionably did see a (short-lived) reassertion of legislative authority, the emergence of a new public prudence about the use of military power, and a new caution at the top, embodied in figures as various as Caspar Weinberger and Colin Powell. The term 'isolationism' is extremely unfashionable in academic circles, and has become little more than a term of abuse. However, the Vietnam War did, for good or ill, usher in a kind of leftist isolationism, as well as a more generalised sense of caution. It affected profoundly the administration of President Jimmy Carter, as well as that of Ronald Reagan. Senator Stuart Symington, Democrat from Missouri, declared in the later stages of the Vietnam War that 'we should express less interest in South Asia and more in South St Louis'.[12] In the latter part of 2005, numerous comments were made to the effect that the US was prepared to fund a major war in the Middle East, but was unprepared to save New Orleans from the deprivations of Hurricane Katrina.[13] In his 2006 State of the Union Address, President George W. Bush hammered away against the 'false comfort of isolationism'. A Pew Center survey in October 2005 found 42 per cent of Americans in agreement with the proposition that the US 'should mind its own business internationally and let other countries get along the best they can on their own'. This represented a twelve point increase for such sentiment since 2002, and its highest level since the immediate post-Vietnam War era.[14]

Just as there was a policy reaction to Vietnam, so it is certain that there will be a policy reaction to Iraq. The 2003 invasion illustrated, at the very least, the perils of inadequate planning and over-confidence, as well as the problematic nature of committing troops to a major combat in which core national interests are not clearly and demonstrably at risk. It also illustrated the aloneness of the United States in such ventures. As John Mueller puts it, the experience of Iraq – more or less regardless of future developments in the Middle East – will lead to 'notable decreases in the acceptance of a number of beliefs' among US policymakers. Such beliefs include 'the notions that the United States should take unilateral military action to correct situations or regimes it considers reprehensible but which present no very direct or very immediate threat' and 'that it should and can forcibly bring democracy to nations not now so blessed'. A need to question such beliefs is the lesson of Iraq, just as it was the real lesson of Vietnam.

Notes

1 Henry A. Kissinger, Memorandum for the Staff Secretary, The White House, n.d. NSC Files, Subject files, box 378, press, TV, news 1970–1, vol. 1, Nixon Presidential Materials; see also Bruce Kuklick, *Blind Oracles: Intellectuals and War from Kennan to Kissinger*, Princeton: Princeton University Press, 2006.

2 Robert Nisbet, 'War, Crisis and Intellectuals', *Wall Street Journal* (New York), 25 January 1971.

3 Kissinger, op. cit.

4 Henry A. Kissinger, Memorandum for Staff Secretary, National Security Council, 18 February 1971, NSC Files, Subject files, box 378, press, TV, news 1970–1, vol. 1, Nixon Presidential Materials.

5 Francis Fukuyama, *After the Neocons: America at the Crossroads*, London: Profile Books, 2006, pp. 48–9.

6 Fredrik Logevall, *Choosing War: The Lost Chance for Peace and the Escalation of War in Vietnam*, Berkeley, CA: University of California Press, 1999, pp. 412–13.

7 Condeleezza Rice cited in Frances Fitzgerald, 'George Bush & the World', *The New York Review of Books* 49, no. 14 (26 September 2002), 80.

8 Barbara Boxer official website: http://boxer.senate.gov/news/record.cfm?id=249455, accessed 24 February 2006.

9 See Francis Fukuyama, *After the Neocons: America at the Crossroads*, London: Profile Books, 2006.

10 W. R. Mead, *Power, Terror, Peace, and War: America's Grand Strategy in a World at Risk*, New York: Knopf, 2004.

11 G. J. Ikenberry, 'A Liberal Leviathan', *Prospect*, October 2004, pp. 46–51.

12 Cited in J. Rourke, *Congress and the Presidency in Foreign Policy-Making*, Boulder, CO: Westview, 1983, p. 148.

13 See, for example, *Congressional Record*, 8 September 2005, E1804 (remarks of Congressman Bart Stupak of Michigan).

14 2006 State of the Union Address available on the White House website; 'The Isolationist Temptation', *The Economist*, 11 February 2006, pp. 47–8.

1

THE FINAL CHAPTER?

The Iraq War and the end of history

Lloyd C. Gardner

When the Berlin Wall came tumbling down on November 9, 1989, a novel argument popped up that 'history' itself had come to an end. Grasping what exactly the end of history meant depended upon *double entendre* – just the sort of wordplay the rising neo-conservative movement delighted in as the twentieth century closed. Of course there would still be plenty of events to fill the pages of *Foreign Affairs*, quipped Francis Fukuyama, its first and most famous publicist, but the central historical issue of the modern era had been resolved with the sudden collapse of the 'Evil Empire'. When the Berlin Wall came tumbling down, it produced an intellectual shockwave that Fukuyama and his followers rode like surfboarders at Big Sur. All viable systematic alternatives to Western liberalism had disappeared, he declared. What we may be witnessing, he added, was not just the end of the Cold War, 'but the end of history as such: that is, the end point of mankind's ideological evolution and the universalization of Western liberal democracy as the final form of human government'.[1]

Comparisons with George Frost Kennan's famous 1947 'X' article, 'The Sources of Soviet Conduct', were inevitable. Kennan had headed the State Department's Policy Planning Staff when he wrote the anonymous article that became the theoretical underpinning for the Cold War policy famously known as 'containment'. Fukuyama was Deputy Director of the Policy Planning Staff when he wrote his piece dividing the globe into historical and post-historical societies. His essay suited the remarkable ideological shift to the right with Ronald Reagan's election in 1980. Both men stressed the internal character of America's rival for global supremacy as the determining characteristic of the struggle. In that sense, neither was a 'realist' – however the term is defined – but rather a philosophic idealist. Kennan's reputation as 'realist' stemmed from his famous book, *American Foreign Policy 1900–1950*, that he himself described at times as a pot-boiler. What stands out in that book was his critique of America's traditional China policy as based upon unrealistic expectations, and needlessly aggravating to Japan.

Kennan, it will be remembered, had portrayed the Soviet regime as a product of Russian historical experience overlaid with a paranoid Leninist Marxism that could survive only by perpetuating a sense of permanent crisis. Even at the end of World War II, with its old enemies crushed, he argued, Moscow could never loosen its grip on Eastern Europe, or its absolute control at home, without destroying the only rationale for its continued repression of basic human rights, and, indeed, its very existence. Marxist ideology was a rotting fig-leaf of respectability it employed to cover its perpetual sins. Despite his condemnation of the Soviet system, however, Kennan counselled patience, and argued that 'containment' would promote the mellowing or even the break-up of Soviet power. Pursuing such a policy would impose terrific strains on the nation, he recognized, not least in the area of confidence in American ideals and institutions. But, in the end, it would provide a test of the nation's character, more than its atomic arsenal.

For neo-conservatives the arch-practitioner of *realpolitik* was not Kennan, however, but Henry A. Kissinger, whose primary error – in their view – was to base policy on expediency rather than principle. In so doing he supposedly allowed the United States to unilaterally 'disarm' morally and militarily as a result of failing to understand the nature of the Soviet system. Neo-conservatives believe, like Kennan ironically, that the internal structure or 'character' of a country determines its foreign policy, beyond all other issues of external pressure or circumstances. Understood as a commentary on containment, Fukuyama's argument sought to explain why Kennan's 'realist' code of operations was no longer relevant and should be abandoned lest it corrupt American ability to think clearly about its interests in the post-Cold War era.

Indeed, it was argued, realism had lost its value years earlier when Kissinger and Nixon reformulated containment as *détente* in the wake of the Vietnam War in order to obtain questionable arms control agreements that did little to improve American security, and, in fact, helped to sustain (and legitimize) a decrepit regime that had fallen behind in every area but missile throw weight. *Détente*, so the argument went, underestimated Soviet military strength even as it overestimated the stability of the Soviet political position at home and worldwide. Ronald Reagan's frontal assault on the 'Evil Empire' as lacking legitimacy startled 'realists' who had accepted the permanence of the Cold War, and left them theory-less when the Soviet Union collapsed in a heap of unfulfilled promises and shredded dogma. It should be noted here that since the essence of the confrontation for neo-conservatives was not the relative economic strength or political flexibility of the two systems, but the moral fibre of the competitors, the idea that neither side 'won' the Cold War, but rather that the United States had greater staying power, is, of course, abhorrent to them. As an indication of this view, Fukuyama's new book, *After the Neocons: America at the Crossroads*, implies the Johnson Administration's Great Society programme inhibited the nation from carrying on a foreign policy that would have hastened the Soviets' downfall. Neo-conservatives, he writes, saw the Great Society as imitative in some strange way of Russian 'social engineering' in the 1930s. A prime example was school bussing.

Reagan's supposed achievement sent realists scurrying here and there in vain after some alternative explanation to the end of the Cold War – and an operational code for the future. But Fukuyama-style arguments implied there would no longer be a need for theory, any theory. Unfortunately, cultural lag explained the failure to recognize containment's irrelevance and properly understand America's unique position in the world until 9/11. Thus, the argument continued, the first Gulf War a decade earlier had ended inconclusively because President George H. W. Bush refused to push on to Baghdad to remove the tyrant Saddam Hussein. Realist arguments for restraint at the banks of the Euphrates appeared to neo-conservatives as unworthy of Reagan's promise to restore America in the Puritan image of a City on the Hill – not only unworthy, but positively dangerous in a world where, as his son President George W. Bush admonished audiences after 9/11, terrorists had access to weapons of mass destruction (WMD). Indeed, to his harshest critics, the elder Bush had indicted himself for the failure in a comment to the American Society of Newspaper Editors on April 9, 1992:

> With the passing of the Cold War, a new order has yet to take its place. The opportunities, tremendous, they're great. But so, too, are the dangers. And so, we stand at history's hinge point. A new world beckons while the ghost of history stands in the shadows.

History's ghost, it was asserted, was none other than Saddam Hussein. The brutal tyrant might have been driven back from Kuwait, but he had been close to developing a nuclear weapon, readying himself to strike again at those foolish enough to leave him in power. During the brief Gulf War in 1991 Iraq had launched SCUD missiles with conventional warheads at the American airbase in Saudi Arabia, Dhahran, and at Israel. That was not all. He was also accused of poison gas attacks against the Iranians in the Iran–Iraq War, and more controversially against minority Kurds near the border. His regime was a repressive nightmare. It stood, a later National Security Adviser, Condoleezza Rice asserted, at the very centre of Middle Eastern ferment and disorder.

The United States had settled for a realist solution in Iraq in some ways not unlike the 1953 Korean War truce, which, it had now become painfully clear, spawned another dilemma with Kim Jong Il's nuclear ambitions. But there were regional counterweights to Kim – not so for an Iraq armed with WMD. And there was another issue flowing under the surface: Iraq's oil reserves, second only to those located in Saudi Arabia. Hussein was hardly fit to remain as custodian of that vital resource, especially since he had taken some unwelcome steps that endangered American interests. In the last days before 'Shock and Awe', Defense Secretary Donald Rumsfeld insisted that Iraq's oil had nothing – nothing at all – to do with the issues. But the would-be successor to Hussein, Ahmad Chalabi, whose Iraqi National Congress (INC) received hefty pay cheques from the Department of Defense, assured his benefactors that a new regime would not feel obligated to continue Hussein's policies that favoured other nations' companies and the euro market over the dollar. 'American oil companies will have a big shot at Iraqi oil', promised Chalabi. A senior INC official added, French and Russian companies 'would have to go as junior partners to Americans'.[2]

Chalabi's biggest fans were Richard Perle, chair of the Defense Advisory Board, and Rumsfeld aide, Under Secretary Paul Wolfowitz. Chalabi had studied at the University of Chicago with Albert Wohlstetter, the Godfather of the neo-conservative movement, whose influence on American defence strategy suggested that even the most tendentious mathematical assumptions rather than real-life experience with the Russians counted with the Pentagon. Wohlstetter introduced his student Chalabi to Perle at Chicago, a fateful meeting indeed. After Chicago, the Iraqi-exile founded the Petra Bank in Jordan, which grew to be the third largest in the country. His career took a sharp downturn, however, when he was accused of fraud, embezzlement, and currency manipulation, barely escaping before Jordanian authorities could arrest him. He was convicted *in absentia* and sentenced to twenty years at hard labour. The CIA picked him up, however, and made him the head of the Iraqi National Congress. And there he was, at hand and ready to brief the Department of Defense after 9/11. Chalabi's usefulness did not end with one or two appearances. He became an effective procurer of 'sources' for DOD/OSP (Office of Special Plans) efforts to 'supplement' and 'correct' the Intelligence Community's supposedly woefully inadequate reporting on WMD in Iraq – as the neo-conservatives saw it. Chalabi fell out of favour, alas, when it became apparent that he expected to be put into power much as General Douglas MacArthur had returned to the Philippines with Manuel Quezon in tow in 1945.

But Chalabi's story is really a sidebar to the end of history theoreticians. Years before, serving as an aide to Secretary of Defense Dick Cheney, Wohlstetter student Paul Wolfowitz had been the supervising author of a remarkable 46-page document, 'Defense Planning Guidance', that none too subtly picked up on complaints that the White House had stopped the war too soon. 'Our first objective', it declared, 'is to prevent the re-emergence of a new rival'. The United States must never again be put in the position that had existed in the Cold War; it must not be forced back into a 'historical' confrontation. 'We must maintain the mechanisms for deterring potential competitors from even aspiring to a larger regional or global role'. The choice of words here is interesting – a historical confrontation.

Beyond any challenge, read the paper, America had the material strength to start the world again; what it needed was 'the leadership necessary to establish and protect a new order' lest it be unable to deal with potential dangers to the nation's interests: Persian Gulf oil, proliferation of weapons of mass destruction, and terrorist threats. While Gulf War I had been fought under the imprimatur of the United Nations, in the future the United States would have to organize *ad hoc* coalitions that might not even outlive resolution of a particular crisis. 'World order is ultimately backed by the U.S.', it read, so, in the end, 'the United States should be postured to act independently when collective action cannot be orchestrated'.[3] The neo-conservative dislike of the United Nations had already become an obsession. It was almost as if Bush had diluted American power by acting as if it really mattered whether there was a UN imprimatur for his actions. Particularly if, as it seemed, one reason for not pressing on to Baghdad was world opinion.

Having spent so much time creating the Desert Storm coalition, and so much diplomacy at UN Headquarters in New York to ensure its 'legitimacy', White House displeasure when a leaked version caused a press furore was hardly to be wondered at. Orders were issued to tone down its more sweeping pronouncements, but the authors returned to the Pentagon eight years later to help with an even stronger statement of American prerogatives issued on September 17, 2002, this time as a White House document with a covering letter written by President George W. Bush.[4]

George H. W. Bush's failure to win re-election in 1992 was not, from the point of view of neo-conservative critics, a completely regrettable event. Not at all. Now there were fewer compunctions about party loyalty in commenting on the Iraq situation (or others), and free rein to go about the heady business of organizing a powerful pressure group to change the whole framework of arriving at specific decisions. The favourite model for such activity was the private 'Team-B' group that helped to derail arms control efforts in the immediate post-Nixon years. Conservative discontent with Nixon's efforts to put a cap on the arms race through the SALT process had led the Administration to create an extra-governmental Team-B, whose members promised to review CIA estimates and reveal where they fell dangerously short of an accurate estimate of Soviet ambitions and capabilities. It proved very effective, but it was the Soviet Union's intervention in Afghanistan that provided the tipping point that undid *détente,* and it was Jimmy Carter's creation of the Rapid Deployment Force that prefigured Donald Rumsfeld's strategy for Gulf War II.[5]

In the mid-1990s, meanwhile, a group of former policymakers and like-minded 'intellectuals' formed the Project for the New American Century. The PNAC manifesto declared the object of American policy was to gain absolute dominance in the Middle East:

> The United States has for decades sought to play a more permanent role in Gulf regional security. While the unresolved conflict with Iraq provides the immediate justification, the need for a substantial American force presence in the Gulf transcends the issue of the regime of Saddam Hussein.[6]

It did indeed, as the primary military base in the area was located in Saudi Arabia, where, it was feared, the presence of American military personnel caused the Saudi royal family headaches stemming from threats uttered by Osama Bin Laden and Al Qaeda. In the Gulf War, Saddam Hussein fired SCUD missiles at the Dhahran base without much effect. But in 1996 Osama's organization blew up a base facility housing Americans causing the loss of twenty lives and injuries to many more. Americans had been at Dhahran since 1945, but now it looked like Saudi hospitality might be wearing a bit thin. Removing Saddam Hussein, it was argued, would hopefully open the way to friendly cooperation with a new Iraqi government, a partner instead of a potential enemy, and thus provide a new home for advanced military operations. In January 1998 PNAC sent an open letter to President Bill Clinton urging him to seize the opportunity of Iraqi resistance to UN inspections to enunciate a new strategy to protect US interests and those of the country's allies around the world. Above all, the strategy should aim at the removal of Saddam Hussein's regime from power. It was a perfect moment for such an appeal because the Iraq imbroglio had reached one of its many crises points over inspections and sanctions. 'The policy of "containment" of Saddam

Hussein', it read, 'has been steadily eroding over the past several months ... we can no longer depend on our partners in the Gulf War coalition to continue to uphold the sanctions or to punish Saddam when he evades UN inspections'. The letter signers included Francis Fukuyama, Paul Wolfowitz and Donald Rumsfeld, and asserted that existing UN resolutions provided authority to take the necessary steps to protect the nation's vital interests. 'In any case, American policy cannot continue to be crippled by a misguided insistence on unanimity in the Security Council'. The ideas, and many of the words, came right out of the 1992 draft 'Defense Planning Guidance'. A primary objective of the letter was to ban the word 'containment' forever. Once that was accomplished presumably the rest would be easy.[7]

A month later there was a second letter signed by an even larger number of former Republican policymakers, including some who had signed the PNAC letter, but with the addition of a few from the Carter Administration to lend a bi-partisan gloss to what was essentially a neo-conservative project. One signer was Reagan Secretary of Defense Caspar Weinberger, who had struck a relatively cautious note on the use of American military policy in those years. Weinberger's ultimate judgment on his successors' policies is an intriguing question, however, as it appears to have emerged in the fictional guise of a 'thriller'. More about that later. This second missive zeroed in on Hussein's supposed arsenal of biological and chemical weapons and his alleged past use of poison gas in the Iran–Iraq War. 'It is clear that this danger cannot be eliminated as long as our objective is simply "containment", and the means of achieving it are limited to sanctions and exhortations'. Only a programme to effect regime change in Baghdad would bring the crisis to a satisfactory solution. While the first letter described the task as a difficult one, the second suggested that while that might be so, Iraq was 'ripe for a broad-based insurrection. We must exploit this opportunity'.

The letter ended with a set of recommendations apparently drawn from Ahmad Chalabi's Iraqi National Congress. Chalabi was convinced, and convinced others, that regime change was merely a matter of setting up a 'provisional government' in the south of Iraq near Basra, and supporting it with minimal armed forces until a 'rolling' *coup* could get under way that would rumble toward Baghdad and bowl over Hussein. CIA analysts who heard Chalabi's rant thought it was more likely to produce a 'Bay of Goats' than a new government. The letter recommended, nevertheless, recognition of a 'provisional government of Iraq based on the principles and leaders of the Iraqi National Congress (INC) that is representative of all the peoples of Iraq'. But that was only the beginning. From there the next step would be to establish a safe area where it could function and expand its authority over more and more territory. To insure its success would require little more than air strikes against Hussein's elite Republican Guard divisions which 'prop him up'.[8]

Such assertions betrayed profound ignorance about Iraqi political and cultural realities, as would become so painfully apparent in the months after March 2003. Bill Clinton's Iraq policy had endorsed regime change, but by most accounts he had serious reservations about the efficacy of outside aid to install an Iraqi

National Congress operation. In 1993, acting upon somewhat dubious evidence, Clinton had sent Tomahawk missiles against Hussein's national intelligence centre in retaliation for a supposed assassination attempt on former President George H. W. Bush, who was visiting Kuwait in something of a victory lap. The attack came at night when presumably few people would be inside the building, and succeeded in killing no important political figures, but at least one major Iraqi artist when a Tomahawk missed its target.[9]

In early 1998, Clinton only insisted that Iraq re-admit the UN weapons inspectors. 'If we fail to respond today, Saddam and all those who would follow in his footsteps will be emboldened tomorrow'. The stakes could not be higher. 'Some day, some way, I guarantee you, he'll use the arsenal'. The Iraqi leader finally agreed to allow the inspections to resume, but warned that the Gulf War sanctions on his country had to come to an end. American and British planes had enforced no-fly zones over Iraq ever since the Gulf War and the UN had imposed other military and economic sanctions that created intense hardships. But Saddam remained in power. The longer he did so, the more infuriating the situation became, especially to those who wanted a template resolution of the Iraq 'situation'.[10]

'We have to defend our future from these predators of the 21st Century', agreed Clinton. 'They will be all the more lethal if we allow them to build arsenals of nuclear, chemical, and biological weapons and the missiles to deliver them. We simply cannot allow that to happen. There is no more clear example of this threat than Saddam Hussein'. In fact, however, and as this quotation suggests, the intelligence about Iraq's weapons of mass destruction was being directed to the point of regime change two years before George W. Bush was declared president after a hotly disputed resolution of the Florida recount.

On October 31, 1998, Clinton signed the 'Iraq Liberation Act', which declared, 'It should be the policy of the United States to support efforts to remove the regime headed by Saddam Hussein from power in Iraq and to promote the emergence of a democratic government to replace that regime'. It authorized only about $100 million for this effort, and still stopped short of a full all-out authorization for military action, counting on the Iraqi dictator to provide an excuse for military action. That same day, Saddam Hussein ordered a halt to the inspections, but reversed himself on threat of attack in mid-November. The inspectors returned and carried out over 300 inspections. From that point on things become very murky. A report to the United Nations on Iraqi compliance was shaped 'at the margins' during discussions at the American UN mission in New York. And even before that, Clinton had issued secret orders to the Pentagon to launch the air attacks that bore the curiously memorable code name, 'Desert Fox'.[11]

Beginning on December 16, 1998, American and British planes began four days of attacks on Iraq that continued even as the Security Council discussed the re-shaped report submitted by Richard Butler, the Australian diplomat who headed the WMD inspection team. It was clear that no authorizing resolution could have been secured at that point because of opposition from France, Russia and China. Desert Fox thus became an appropriate code name for avoiding any commitment to UN sanctioned collective action, anticipating Washington policy decisions five years later.

Still, the real hawk in the Administration appeared to be Secretary of State Madeline Albright, who had repeated a clichéd criticism of President G. H. W. Bush's supposed initial reluctance to confront the Iraqi leader when he invaded Kuwait in a speech at Georgetown University. She began by stating that the United States had 'a vital interest in the security of the region's oil supplies', and for that reason had forged strong friendships with nations that respected international law in all its aspects. Then she zeroed in on the problem Iraq caused, saying 'we recognize that stability is not an import; it must be home grown. But we also know that circumstances may arise in which active American leadership and power are required'.

Having made the link between American interest in Gulf oil and respect for international law, Albright then reeled off all the things Iraq must do before sanctions could be lifted, including being willing to 'end support for terrorism and stop brutalizing its people'. These were deliberately vague requirements, but they made it clear destruction of weapons and weapons programmes was not enough; Iraq had to comply with a list that seemed to grow longer with each reading by an American official. Hussein's inability to meet all these demands was taken as a given:

> Is it possible to conceive of such a government under Saddam Hussein? When I was a professor, I taught that you have to consider all possibilities. As Secretary of State, I have to deal in the realm of reality and probability. And the evidence is overwhelming that Saddam Hussein's intentions will never be peaceful.

Lest anyone miss her point, she added, 'We do not agree with the nations who argue that if Iraq complies with its obligations concerning weapons of mass destruction, sanctions should be lifted'. Then she closed with a flourish, 'This is not, to borrow Margaret Thatcher's phrase, the time to go wobbly towards Iraq'. These were the very words, of course, that Bush I's neo-conservative critics seized upon throughout the Clinton years to suggest it had taken Thatcher's prodding to get him to act, and that he had not lived up to the Prime Minister's challenge in the months and years since Desert Storm.[12]

With the appointment of Colin Powell as Secretary of State and Condoleezza Rice as National Security Adviser, George W. Bush seemed to suggest, on the other hand, that his foreign policy would not be unlike his father's supposed realist orientation, as exemplified by his favourite adviser, Brent Scowcroft, who had mentored Rice in that Administration. He was said to be dead set against such supposed Clinton follies as Kosovo and 'nation building' in general. Such predictions turned out to be wrong, of course. Powell's struggle with Defense Secretary Donald Rumsfeld's bevy of under secretaries, assistant secretaries, and advisory boards was a loser from the beginning while Rice could hardly wait to shed her 'realist' cap and gown and don the evangelistic robes favoured by the Oval Office.

The standard narrative of the George W. Bush Administration places great emphasis upon his religious faith, and there can be little doubt about his views on such matters as abortion, stem cell research, and capital punishment. End of history talk resonated with the Southern Baptist ministries across racial lines, and with the myriad Protestant sub-denominations boasting a televangelist leader that have replaced familiar old-line brick churches on main street. The end of history would be understood in those groups in a somewhat different way but so long as things continued to point in the same direction, support for the president seemed assured. And then there was an 'X' factor. Bush would not shrink from Clinton's declared policy to rid Iraq of Saddam Hussein – however lukewarm the Democratic president had seemed about actual intervention – for he was the man Clinton had judged guilty of the attempted assassination of his father.

Condi Rice, meanwhile, talked about the tectonic shift that had occurred since the end of the Cold War, and the need to develop a new balance of power based on human freedom before the clay dried, and how the opportunity for creative thinking was as great as in the 1945–7 era when Harry Truman came up with the Marshall Plan, while Rumsfeld kept updating a memorandum that he had first started writing as early as March 2001. Rice was not entirely at ease with 'neo-conservatism' as a description of Bush's foreign policy, preferring the term neo-liberalism. 'It is, indeed, possible to see age-old problems in a new light. And, as an academic, may I suggest, to put aside age-old distinctions between realism and neoliberalism in thinking about the task ahead'. Realists downplayed the importance of values and the internal structures of states, she went on, emphasizing instead the balance of power as the key to stability and peace. 'Neoliberals emphasize the primacy of values, such as freedom and democracy and human rights, and institutions in ensuring that a just political order is obtained'. Call it neo-conservative or neo-liberal, the Bush Administration had – as she said – put aside age-old distinctions in favour of a foreign policy based almost solely upon the primacy of values.[13]

Early on in the Bush presidency both Colin Powell and Condi Rice had expressed the opinion that Saddam Hussein's regime had been put in a box by American policies. In a Cairo press conference on February 24, 2001, Powell did not waver in his criticism of Saddam Hussein's regime, and he urged that the sanctions be updated for better effect, but, he said, 'they have worked'. 'He has not developed any significant capability with respect to weapons of mass destruction'. Several times over in testimony before Congress on May 15, 2001, Powell used the 'C' word, concluding with: 'The Iraqi regime militarily remains fairly weak. It doesn't have the capacity it had 10 or 12 years ago. It has been contained'.

But Bush told the chronicler-of-our-time, Bob Woodward, that 9/11 changed all that. 'Keeping Saddam in a box looked less and less feasible to me'. He was a 'madman' who had 'used weapons of mass destruction in the past. *He has created incredible instability in the neighborhood*'. In a final word to Woodward, Bush indicated the real problem, 'The options in Iraq were relatively limited when you are playing the containment game'.[14]

No more 'containment game', then, but exactly when a final decision for war with Iraq was reached is difficult to determine as events unfolded over the next months. First there was the successful invasion of Afghanistan – the battleground of empires for centuries where, most recently, the Soviets had failed – that began on October 7, 2001. The Taliban regime had refused to give up Osama Bin Laden, and American forces came in force to find him. They toppled the Taliban (ironically former allies in the Cold War) with few casualties and with worldwide moral support. But they did not find Osama, even though he was surrounded at one point in a mountain area. When he remained 'at large' it became easier to convince the great majority of Americans not only that Iraq was behind the suicide attacks on the Twin Towers of the World Trade Center and the Pentagon, but also that he was linked somehow to Hussein because there was no one to contradict the assertions. Then there was the failure to find the culprit behind the anthrax letters sent to newspapers and the Capitol, which reinforced the notion that Saddam's agents were everywhere.

While Iraq became an obsession inside the Pentagon, for Rumsfeld and his good friend, Vice President Richard Cheney, the situation was a testing ground for a much wider vision of American hegemony – closely akin to the neo-conservative vision, but not identical to it. The implication of National Security Adviser Condi Rice's 2002 Johns Hopkins speech, for example, was that international stability rested on shared values, a point Rumsfeld and Cheney might not argue, but certainly wished to interpret on a case-by-case basis. What they *all* shared was that containment was a contaminated concept that produced indecisive results.

Anti-containment thinking meshed well into Rumsfeld's notions about the future of the American military as a kind of global police force with lily-pad launching bases worldwide. In 2002 a Special Operations Command (SOCOM) came into existence. That was the first step in the changeover to a military that could intervene inside supposedly failed states. Thus SOCOM offered an operational solution to the problem of the 'character' of places that had fallen out of the post-historical world like Afghanistan – but presumably anywhere, for example in Africa or Latin America. Today it would seem that Iran is SOCOM's main target. In a series of articles, the *Washington Post* detailed the results of Rumsfeld's campaign (it was about the only media source to do so), and outlined the implications for traditional views of the civil–military relationship. In January 2004 the *Post* reported that, 'Under Rumsfeld's direction, secret commando units known as hunter-killer teams have been ordered to "kick down the doors", as the generals put it, all over the world in search of al Qaeda members and their sympathizers'. A year later, the *Post* followed-up with an article on Rumsfeld's 'new espionage arm', the secret Strategic Support Branch, created, it was claimed, because the Defense Secretary wanted to end his 'near total dependence on CIA' for human intelligence (HUMINT). The article explained that Rumsfeld desired the ability to employ a range of methods from interrogation of prisoners to the recruitment of foreign spies including 'notorious figures' whose links to the US government might prove embarrassing if disclosed. But the espionage missions were also a partial cover, the article disclosed in oblique fashion, for activities described a year earlier in the newspaper. Assistant Secretary of Defense Thomas O'Connell, who oversees SOCOM, asserted that his boss had discarded the 'hide-bound way of thinking' and 'risk-averse mentalities' of previous Pentagon officials 'under every president since Gerald R. Ford'.[15]

There could hardly be a stronger assertion about the end of 'history' and the beginning of a path into uncharted territory. To the traditional historian, however, the creation of SOCOM reeked of past imperial experiences, and went beyond them. Algeria came to mind as the French used methods that would become well-known in Iraq at Abu Ghraib or at Guantanamo. Watergate and Iran-Contra were nowhere near as fraught with perils to the Constitution as what Pentagon officials called the 'Secret Army of Northern Virginia', falling into ranks under Donald Rumsfeld's stern gaze. Asked to describe a scenario where Strategic Support Branch might play a role, Secretary O'Connell happily obliged. 'A hostile country close to our borders suddenly changes leadership.... We would want to make sure the successor is not hostile'. Within a few weeks it emerged, in yet another *Post* article, that Rumsfeld wanted his Special Operations forces to enter a country and conduct operations without explicit concurrence from the US ambassador. In the Pentagon view, the article said, the campaign against terrorism is a war and requires similar freedom to prosecute as in Iraq. Chief of mission authority has been a pillar of presidential authority overseas, said an administration official familiar with the new tension between State and Defense. 'When you start eroding that, it can have repercussions that are ... risky'. Colin Powell's chief aide, Deputy Secretary of State Richard Armitage, instructed his counterterrorism coordinator J. Cofer Black to act as point man to thwart the Pentagon's initiative. 'I gave Cofer specific instructions to dismount, kill the horses and fight on foot – this is not going to happen'.[16]

But it is happening, if newspaper reports about the penetration of Iran are correct, with contingents of SOCOM making contact with various groups dedicated to the overthrow of the current Iranian regime. The State Department in the irony of ironies about US Middle Eastern policies, has been sending out officials to Los Angeles and elsewhere to find remnants of supporters of the Iranian monarchy, which American agents saved in 1953 only to see it toppled a quarter-century later by the mullahs.[17]

The only period during which a serious debate on the road to war in Iraq appeared to have taken place was during August–September 2002. The most dramatic utterance in that debate came from National Security Adviser Condoleezza Rice, previously termed the balance wheel in the Administration, in an 'anniversary' edition of CNN's *Late Edition* on September 8, 2002 with the always on the edge-of-your-seat Wolf Blitzer. Throughout the programme Rice kept tying 9/11 to Iraq's supposed WMD programme. 'Given what we have experienced on September 11', she began, 'I don't think anyone wants to wait for the 100 percent surety that he has a weapon of mass destruction that can reach the United States'. Set up beautifully by short video clips of Iraqi denials and one sceptic's demurral, Blitzer asked again – how close was Saddam to getting a weapon? Rice's answer dismissed the dissenters Blitzer had juxtaposed to her in a kind of set up: Tariq Aziz, Hussein's deputy Prime Minister, and former UN arms inspector Scott Ritter. They appeared to be mere dupes, while she used the most extreme fright tactics. 'The problem here is that there will always be some uncertainty about how quickly he can acquire nuclear weapons. *But we don't want the smoking gun to be a mushroom cloud*'.[18]

Rice's comment was also a stinging rebuke to Colin Powell, however, who had recently told British newscaster David Frost that it would be wrong to move without the UN cover that inspections would provide. American newspapers carried early excerpts from the BBC interview, noting that Powell 'trod carefully' because of 'possible disagreements' with other Administration officials. The story said that Powell was breaking his silence because of Dick Cheney's recent speeches in which the vice president had asserted that the idea of more weapons inspections was 'dangerous', in that it 'would provide false comfort'.[19]

Aiding in the campaign against the supposed passive containment holdovers was Prime Minister Tony Blair, who came to Camp David, and was introduced to the press by an ebullient President George W. Bush, 'It's awfully thoughtful of Tony to come over here . . . .because he's an important ally, an important friend'. Blair provided assurance that war on Iraq would not endanger relations with Europe – especially if he could act as go-between with continental Europe and bring those traditional allies along as well. Blair had his price, however, and it was somewhat higher than Bush really wanted to pay. The prime minister insisted that they must go back to the UN for his sake, to control Labour dissidents, who might hold up the military convoy to Baghdad before it got started. Blair's debating skills and circumlocution were on full display for the American press:

This is an issue for the whole of the international community. But the U.N. has got to be the way of dealing with this issue, not the way of avoiding dealing with it. Now, of course, we want the broadest possible international support, but it's got to be on the basis of actually making sure that the threat we've outlined is properly adhered to.[20]

Blair's enigmaphile countryman, Lewis Carroll, would have delighted in the prime minister's deft switchbacks. But a reporter's question cut through the murky grammatical trail: 'What is your actual target in Iraq? Is it weapons of mass destruction, or Saddam Hussein?'. Bush intercepted the question and answered regime change had been stated policy since 1998. Saddam Hussein had had more than a decade to keep his promise to get rid of weapons of mass destruction, and 'we're going to talk about what to do about it'. When they were alone, Bush told Blair that his wish had been granted, he would go back to the UN for one last time to get a resolution that would provide cover for his ally.

Blair also agreed at Camp David to take the lead in producing a 50-page intelligence dossier that the prime minister presented to parliament with great fanfare. The highlight, repeated by the prime minister several times over, was the bald assertion that Saddam Hussein had the capacity to strike Britain within 45 minutes of his orders! It also included a reassertion of the CIA-discredited claim that Saddam had purchased uranium in Niger. Pressed by the CIA to drop the claim, Blair's people insisted they had alternative sources aside from the forged letters that had first appeared a year and more earlier.[21]

Bush then used the British claim to bolster his arguments for war in pyramid-letter style. 'The British government', he said in his State of the Union message on January 28, 2003, 'has learned that Saddam Hussein recently sought significant quantities of uranium from Africa'. In between these trans-Atlantic bookend assertions Bush had delivered a strong speech to the UN in which he said he would work with the Security Council, 'But the purposes of the United States should not be doubted'. Two days later in his weekly five-minute radio talk to the nation, Bush declared that the UN must act or become 'irrelevant'. He also sent a resolution to Congress asking for the authority to use force. 'This is a chance for Congress to indicate support, a chance for Congress to say we support the administration's ability to keep the peace, that's what this is all about'.[22]

The White House also produced a new national security document that put Iraq into the broadest possible context, or neo-conservative framework. It sounded very much like the document Wolfowitz produced ten years earlier. 'Our forces will be strong enough to dissuade potential adversaries', the 2002 version reiterated the Wolfowitz brief, 'from pursuing a military build-up in hopes of surpassing, or equaling, the power of the United States'. Yet it was far more than an update of the 1992 document, setting forth positions on every major foreign policy question facing the nation, from AIDS in Africa to American refusal to submit its soldiers to investigations, inquiry or prosecution by the International Criminal Court. No such court could judge Americans, it asserted, because the nation stood apart and above all others in terms of its global responsibilities. 'In exercising our leadership, we will respect the values, judgment, and interests of our friends and partners. Still, we will be prepared to act apart when our interests and unique responsibilities require'. If there were disagreements 'on particulars' with its friends and allies, these will not be allowed to obscure 'our shared fundamental interests and values'. The best wordsmiths in the Administration had obviously worked over the language into the late hours of the night to satisfy the minimal requirements of diplomacy. Their task, difficult as it was, would have been impossible in the pre-9/11 world; but now the Administration and its supporters had fashioned out of the tragedy a new post-historical world, based upon a solipsistic vision of both past and future at which even John Winthrop would have blinked.

In this new world, Washington asserted the right of pre-emption to protect against future terrorist attacks, but there was something of a disconnect between the assertion and the reality of how terrorists actually operated from their bases. Bush tried to cover that omission in his cover letter, explaining that the danger emanated from 'weak states' as Afghanistan had demonstrated.

> The events of September 11, 2001, taught us that weak states, like Afghanistan, can pose as great a danger to our national interests as strong states. *Poverty does not make poor people into terrorists and murderers. Yet poverty, weak institutions, and corruption can make weak states vulnerable to terrorist networks and drug cartels within their borders.*[23]

These reflections were updated riffs on a classic conservative assessment of human nature that would have major influence if not on specific policy decisions then on the culture of the war on terror – and its implications for American values and democratic traditions. It also satisfied the need not to appear to be recommending a neo-liberal (although that description fitted some foreign aid programmes the United States had imposed on countries in Latin America and Asia through its control of the mechanisms of the IMF) programme at home. The short war in Afghanistan had presumably corrected the weak state there, although, it was argued, the United States paid no heed to British urgings that the opium poppy fields be attacked for fear of alienating Afghan Warlords who were a key part of the coalition of the willing in that struggle.[24]

Just at this moment the Russian Defense Minister Sergei Ivanov arrived for talks with Rumsfeld at the Pentagon. With the American Secretary of Defense standing close by, Ivanov said he believed that UN weapons inspectors could settle the issue without undue difficulty. We have had experience in that sort of business – both Americans and Russians, he said, a reference to Reagan's famous 'trust but verify' mantra during START negotiations. 'I think we can easily establish [whether] there exist or not weapons of mass destruction technology'.[25]

Rumsfeld did not interrupt Ivanov, but he told the House Armed Services Committee that Congress must act on Bush's recommendation before the UN Security Council took up the American-sponsored resolution. 'Delaying a vote in the Congress would send a message that the U.S. may be unprepared to take a stand, just as we are asking the international community to take a stand'. It might be the post-history world, but this was the classic Cold War White House ploy to put Congress over a barrel, first used with the 1947 Truman Doctrine. Bush added even more pointed friendly words of advice for Congressional incumbents seeking re-election. 'If I were running for office, I'm not sure how I'd explain to the American people – say, vote for me, and, oh, by the way, on a matter of national security, I think I'm going to wait for somebody else to act'.[26]

Bush also promised that there would be deadlines within the resolution being proposed at the UN. 'Our chief negotiator for the United States, our Secretary of State, understands that we must have deadlines. And we're talking days and weeks, not months and years'. The near use of the royal 'our' in Bush's description of Powell's role well portrays what had taken place: the realists had been put to rout. Rumsfeld now took the lead for the Administration in setting forth an opaque distinction between weapons 'inspectors', and weapons 'discoverers'. UN inspectors could not by any stretch succeed unless they were dealing with a cooperative regime; nobody could, for it would be asking the impossible with such a huge territory to cover. And yet, after the war began, Rumsfeld would insist that he knew the locations of the hidden WMD – with hardly a concern for any small matters of consistency.[27]

Eleven days into the war, on March 30, 2003, when the first flickers of doubt about the WMD began to sneak into the mainstream media, Secretary Rumsfeld answered a question posed by ABC News. 'We know where they are. They're in the area around Tikrit and Baghdad and east, west, south and north somewhat'. While he flatly denied other statements he had previously made in public appearances before the House Armed Services Committee the previous September concerning large stocks of clandestine weapons, Rumsfeld conceded that he might have over-reached just a bit (thus redoubling his inconsistency) about the location of the hidden WMD. 'I should have said, "I believe we're in that area. Our intelligence tells us they're in that area," and that was our best judgment'.[28]

He was adamant, moreover, that he had never said that Americans would be welcomed as liberators. 'There is no question but that they would be welcomed', he had told Jim Lehrer during the September 2002 period. 'Go back to Afghanistan, the people were in the streets playing music, cheering, flying kites, and doing all the things that the Taliban and the al-Qaeda would not let them do'. A year later on a particularly bloody day in Iraq, he was asked about that statement. 'Never said that', he cut the questioner short. 'Never did. You may remember it well, but you're thinking of somebody else. You can't find, anywhere, me saying anything like either of those two things you just said I did'.[29]

Instead of the Nixonian explanation that previous statements on a given subject were 'inoperative', Rumsfeld opted for flat denial – while seeming to point a self-exculpatory finger at 'others'. Vice President Cheney did not deny that on March 16, 2003, the day before the war began, he had said on Meet the Press, 'The read we get on the people of Iraq is there's no question but what they want to get rid of Saddam Hussein and they will welcome us as liberators'. Tim Russert commented dryly in an interview in September 2003, 'We have not been greeted as liberators'. Confronted with the videotape, Cheney refused to back off, 'Well, I think we have by most Iraqis. I think the majority of Iraqis are thankful for the fact that the United States is there, that we came and took down Saddam Hussein'.[30]

Cheney was no less unwilling to back down about the connections between Iraq, Al Qaeda, and 9/11, or the absent WMD. 'Where are they?' Russert asked. Well, replied Cheney 'the jury' was still out about what was known about the locations of the WMD. But, he said, one had to remember that he had had more than a decade to find places to hide the weapons. 'And I think that's what they did'. Then he shifted ground,

> So to suggest that there is no evidence there that he had aspirations to acquire nuclear weapons, I don't think is valid, and I think David Kay will find more evidence as he goes forward, interviews people, as we get to folks willing to come forward now as they become more and more convinced that it's safe to do so.[31]

When Kay reported to Congress a year later, of course, the WMD program began to disappear as justification for war, replaced by Hussein's innate evilness as one of the worst dictators of the era. He was, in other words, a transitional figure to Fukuyama's post-historical millennium, a sort of left-over from Rod Serling's 'Twilight Zone'. Cheney clung to the original argument, but Prime Minister Blair segued across the credibility gap with hardly a missed beat. 'If any part of the intelligence turns out to be wrong', he defended his actions in the

House of Commons, 'or if the threat from Saddam was different or changed from what we thought, I will accept this as I should, but let others accept that ridding Iraq of Saddam Hussein has made the world not just better but safer'.[32]

The transition was not so easy for others, for example, DCI George Tenet, who had at one point assured President Bush that Saddam's WMD were a 'slam dunk!'. The CIA's role in the build-up to the war was a curious one, as analysts had tried their best – under terrific pressure from Cheney who kept sending messengers over to Langley – to put some brakes on the White House rush to war. In a December 2002 Oval Office meeting, the president had sought the firmest commitment from Tenet that the DCI would stand behind the WMD intelligence. 'George, how confident are you?' Rising up from one of the couches, Tenet, an avid Georgetown fan, threw his arms in the air, 'Don't worry, it's a slam dunk!'[33]

In the aftermath of the 'Yellow Cake' imbroglio, National Security Adviser Rice put the blame squarely on Tenet. 'If the C.I.A., the director of central intelligence, had said, "Take this out of the speech," it would have been gone, without question'. Tenet's *mea culpa* appeared swiftly thereafter. In a public statement, the DCI 'confessed' that the Niger uranium tale 'did not rise to the level of certainty which should be required for presidential speeches, and C.I.A. should have ensured that it was removed'.[34]

It would be well, at this point, to recall just a few things about the origins of the Yellow Cake story, how it first surfaced in Italian and British intelligence reports, was discounted by the CIA, and then, after Bush and Blair met at Camp David in September 2002, resurfaced in the prime minister's intelligence briefing of Parliament – later dubbed by critics the 'Dodgy Dossier'. Months after he resigned Tenet was still falling on his sword in a talk at Kutztown State University in Pennsylvania, where he asserted the slam dunk analogy was the dumbest thing he had ever said. Administration spokesmen tried to follow the White House line as best they could, with the president finally telling ABC reporter Diane Sawyer,

> Diane, you can keep asking the question [about the missing WMD]. I'm telling you – I made the right decision for America because Saddam Hussein used weapons of mass destruction, invaded Kuwait. But the fact that he is not there is, means America's a more secure country.[35]

The 'intelligence made me do it' rationalization had proved untenable as the 2004 election campaign heated up. All sorts of commissions and inquiries could fiddle with the intelligence failures that had preceded 9/11 and the Iraq War, but it would not do for the White House to be seen as a passive recipient of faulty WMD reports. Instead, there had to be an affirmation that 'Operation Iraqi Freedom' contained the justification within itself for a war that grew more difficult in the months after Bush's famous landing on the *USS Abraham Lincoln*, on May 1, 2003, and declaration that 'Major combat operations in Iraq have ended. In the battle of Iraq, the United States and our allies have prevailed'.[36]

Comparing the 'battle of Iraq' with Normandy and Iwo Jima in World War II, Bush hailed the outcome as another instance of the 'decency and idealism that turned enemies into allies'. He thanked the armed forces of the United Kingdom, Australia and Poland for sharing in the hardships of war, for being the leaders in the 'Coalition of the Willing' when the UN Security Council had failed to act on a resolution specifically authorizing the use of force. The post-9/11 period had seen many references to the heroism of the 'greatest generation', the GIs who had fought against and overcome the Axis forces in World War II – books, films, TV productions. There was also renewed interest in the American Revolution and the 'Founding Fathers' as sources of inspiration.

How, then, did Iraq and the 'Coalition of the Willing' fit into this supra-historical narrative? The American army that fought in Iraq gave a second meaning to 'Coalition of the Willing'. Despite frequent newspaper references to 'GIs', especially at the beginning of the war, there were no GIs in Iraq. Conscription had ended with the Vietnam War. The American army in Iraq was now a 'volunteer' army, nearly half from the National Guard and Reserves. Recruitment goals for the regular army – until lowered by the Pentagon – went unmet from month to month, and re-enlistments were down by a third. One way the strength of the force was maintained was through 'stop-loss' orders that coerced soldiers to remain on active duty after their contractual enlistments expired – a back-door draft.[37]

But more informative about the fighting forces in Iraq were statistics about private contractors – previously called soldiers-of-fortune – who made up the second largest contingent in the 'Coalition of the Willing', narrowly outnumbering the 10,000 man British regulars as of December 2003. 'The private sector is so firmly embedded in combat, occupation and peacekeeping duties that the phenomenon may have reached the point of no return: the U.S. military would struggle to wage war without it'.[38]

Eager mercenaries, who could earn thousands of dollars a month, were recruited from many countries, especially in Eastern Europe and Latin America. One company, Blackwater USA, found Chile a particularly good recruiting ground for commandos who had received their military training in the days of Dictator Augusto Pinochet. El Salvador, to take another example, had sent 300 regular soldiers to stand in the ranks of the 'Coalition of the Willing', but twice that number worked for private companies doing everything from Kitchen Police (KP) duty to guarding oil installations and senior personnel. They came from far away Fiji, the Philippines and India. By March 2005 their numbers had doubled to 20,000 – more than twice the British contingent.[39]

Making money out of war is hardly a novel occupation, but in this instance it disguises the 'costs' of war – both in human and material terms. As recruiting difficulties continued to grow in the continental United States, the Pentagon upped enlistment bonuses and educational benefits. Taking a cue from the private firms, army recruiters turned to US territories in the Pacific, stretching from Pago Pago in American Samoa to Yap in Micronesia, 4,000 miles to the west, and found a bonanza. Army salaries have no difficulty competing with the average income in such places. 'You can't beat recruiting here in the Marianas, in Micronesia', said First Sgt. Olympio Magofna, who grew up on Saipan and oversees Pacific recruiting for the Army from his base in Guam. 'In the States, they are really hurting', he said. 'But over here, I can afford [to] go play golf every other day'.[40]

The overall numbers are small, but like the supposed oil reserves under the Alaskan wilderness, a proposed stop-gap for another seemingly intractable problem, worth it to policymakers with fewer and fewer options for maintaining the illusion that Iraq is the end of what World War II began. A few weeks before the 2004 election, writer Ron Suskind, who had helped former Treasury Secretary Paul O'Neill with his 'tell-all' memoirs, *The Price of Loyalty*, wrote about his own encounter with a Bush aide after he had written something else that displeased the White House. People like yourself, he told Suskind, were stuck 'in what we call the reality-based community', those individuals who believed that 'solutions emerged from your judicious study of discernible reality'. Suskind allowed that to be the case, murmuring something about enlightenment principles and empiricism. The aide cut him off.

> That's not the way the world really works anymore. We're an empire now, and when we act, we create our own reality. And while you're studying that reality – judiciously, as you will – we'll act again, creating other new realities, which you can study too, and that's how things will sort out. We're history's actors . . . and you, all of you, will be left to just study what we do.[41]

It seemed the rapture, as televangelists called it, had already come. But as the heady days of 'mission accomplished' and 'bring 'em on' disappeared from television screens, there was indeed a new reality confronting the nation. Mission accomplished became stay the course. After three years the number of casualties had risen to 2,300 deaths and over 16,000 wounded. Those were numbers for Americans only. 'Enemy' casualties were only estimates, because, as one general declared, 'We don't do body counts'. The infamous Vietnam 'body count' loomed over the war like a closing fist around American aspirations, and reminded people uncomfortably of the costs of empire. 'The mission in Iraq is tough', said Bush, 'because the enemy understands the stakes. A free Iraq in the heart of the Middle East will deliver a serious blow to their hateful ideology'.[42]

Less than 40 per cent believed, according to polls, that Bush really understood the stakes, and that instead of striking a blow at terrorism, Iraq had made the situation worse. Democrats seemed unable to find their way, on the other hand, to any solid position, fearful of acknowledging error in voting for the 2002 resolution and, struggling, as John Kerry did in the 2004 campaign, with weak-sounding 'I-did-and-I-didn't' non-answers to questions about the war.

Probably the most remarkable public segment of this ambiguous reality was the revolt of the conservatives. Rep. Walter Jones, Republican of North Carolina, whose district included the military installations at Camp Lejeune and Cherry Point, had claimed a small place on network News Hours with a successful effort in March 2003 to have the House dining hall change the name of 'French fries' to 'freedom fries', a gesture of contempt for French behaviour at the UN when 'America's oldest ally' led the charge against a resolution specifically authorizing military action. At the time most neo-conservatives cheered, because now it would be clear that the UN had become, as Bush suggested it would, irrelevant to American policy. Two years later after hearing from several war widows, Walter Jones had some long second thoughts about 'freedom fries' and those who had cooked up the war. He sighed, laying his cheek in his left hand, 'I wish it had never happened'. The nation had gone to war 'with no justification', Jones charged, and he demanded an apology from Richard Perle during testimony before the House Armed Services Committee. Perle would not oblige him, of course, and fell back to blaming bad intelligence. Perle claimed that the nation had been sucked into war by 'double agents planted by the regime' who succeeded because of the 'appalling incompetence' of the CIA. Jones was most unhappy with Perle's pirouette around the truth: 'I am just incensed with this statement'.[43]

Richard A. Viguerie, the veteran conservative direct-mail consultant, startled fellow Republicans even more than Walter Jones did with his statement that Mr Bush had 'turned the volume up on his megaphone about as high as it could go to try to tie the war in Iraq to the war on terrorism' before the election. 'I just don't think it washes after all these years'. In a category all by itself in terms of conservative commentary, there is the novel by Caspar Weinberger and Peter Schweizer, *Chain of Command: A Thriller*, published in June 2005. The plot concerns a *coup d'etat* attempt by a sitting vice president, determined to fight the war on terror with extra-legal methods, starting with a proposed 'Freedom From Fear' Act, and features among its political heroes, a southern senator very much like Sam Ervin of Watergate fame, or Robert Byrd, Bush's sometimes lonely opponent on the floor of the Senate. The novel does not denigrate the terrorist menace, but is framed as a cautionary tale about the misuse of foreign threats to achieve perfect 'security'.[44]

Weinberger, a former Secretary of Defense in the Reagan Administration, seems worlds apart from Donald Rumsfeld, who announced that the Pentagon would initiate a special commemoration on the fourth Anniversary of the September 11 attacks. 'This year the Department of Defense will initiate an America Supports You Freedom Walk'. The line of the march will begin at the Pentagon, he said, and end at the National Mall. Participants in this tribute would be invited to a special performance by country singer Clint Black. The key mid-level players in the planning for the Iraq War, OSP head Douglas Feith, Under Secretary Paul Wolfowitz, and the State Department's John Bolton, were no longer plying the corridors of power in Washington (at least not as they were when the Administration took office), and this fact was duly noted by the editor of *Foreign Affairs*, Gideon Rose. It suggested to him that the end of history missionary zeal and nonsense had reached its zenith and begun to recede – and it was safe for the 'realists' to come out and make their views known and so to manage the transition back to a foreign policy run by pragmatists, not fantasists. But, of course, the people in charge were American 'realists', not European *realpolitik* thinkers, like Condi Rice, now ensconced at State where Colin Powell had failed to stem the tide when it was at full flood. Rice would offer not different goals, wrote Rose on the *Times* op-ed page (a sure sign of Establishment approval), but a calmer and 'more measured path toward the same ones'. 'They still [Rice and the American-style realists] believe in American power and the global spread of liberal democratic capitalism'. But they sought legitimacy, not material dominance, and favoured cost-benefit analyses over ideological litmus tests and good results over good intentions.[45]

Rose noted in a final, half world-weary way, 'This is likely to play well—until domestic carping over the realists' supposedly limited vision starts the wheel of American foreign policy turning again'. How many more trillion-dollar wars the American empire can afford, whether led by the chameleon-like Condi Rice realists, or a resurgent group under a Bush successor, remains the key question. And, hey, we're far from out of the woods with this war.

History has caught up with us, and won't let go. The Iraqi project appears to be only the latest example of the colonial project that began when Europeans first sailed across the oceans to establish their dominance. The American embassy planned for Iraq, it is reported, 'will be the largest of its kind in the world, the size of Vatican City, with the population of a small town, its own defense force, self-contained power and water, and a precarious perch at the heart of Iraq's turbulent future'.[46] It is being built inside the 'Green Zone', the mammoth fortress-style centre of American operations, which also houses the new 'independent' government of Iraq. Iraqi postage stamps will no doubt carry the portraits of the new president and other leaders, if the quarrelling factions ever agree on their new leaders – just as Egyptian postage stamps once carried King Farouk's turbaned head in the 1930s – but it will be a long time before the stamps reflect real sovereignty.

Amidst all the news about the 'Battle of Crawford', pitting Cindy Sheehan against the Bush cavalcade in and out of 'Prairie Chapel' Ranch, the Texas White House, there appeared a startling new commentary from Francis Fukuyama, who had signed one of the letters to Clinton drafted by the authors of the Project for a New American Century. Fukuyama took the side of all those late-blooming-liberal critics who have now argued that the president ignored choices 'in keeping with American foreign policy traditions' – the very sorts of containment policies the neo-conservatives abominated as belonging to the historical era.

> We do not know what outcome we will face in Iraq. We do know that four years after 9/11, our whole foreign policy seems destined to rise or fall on the outcome of a war only marginally related to the source of what befell us on that day. There was nothing inevitable about this. There is everything to be regretted about it.

Fukuyama worries most about the re-birth of isolationism, the traditional scare word to ward off fundamental re-thinking of foreign policy objectives. He now calls himself a realistic Wilsonian – as things come full circle, but at a higher velocity. It is a measure of how profoundly Iraq has shaken the tree of American assumptions about the world – and itself.[47]

Fukuyama's new writings have apparently inspired several other past allies of the president to speak out. Representative Henry Hyde of Illinois, another conservative dissenter, may well have the last word on the end of history debate:

A few brief years ago, history was proclaimed to be at an end, our victory engraved in unyielding stone, our pre-eminence garlanded with permanence. But we must remember that Britain's majestic rule vanished in a few short years, undermined by unforeseen catastrophic events and by new threats that eventually overwhelmed the palisades of the past. The life of pre-eminence, as with all life on this planet, has a mortal end. To allow our enormous power to delude us into seeing the world as a passive thing waiting for us to recreate it in an image of our choosing will hasten the day when we have little freedom to choose anything at all.[48]

Notes

1 Fukuyama's essay, 'The End of History', can be found in the Summer 1989 issue of *The National Interest*. The liberalism Fukuyama was talking about, of course, was the pre-New Deal, nineteenth-century liberalism of nationalism and *laissez-faire*. Fukuyama paid great homage in the essay to free markets, not as the Marxist engine of capitalist striving, but as carriers of the ideals of liberalism.

2 Several sources deal with Chalabi's wooing of American oil interests. See, for example, Michael Renner, 'Post-Saddam Iraq: Linchpin of a New Oil Order', reprinted in Micah L. Sifry and Christopher Cerf (eds), *The Iraq War Reader: History, Documents, Opinions*, New York: Simon & Schuster, 2003, pp. 580–7; and Seymour M. Hersh, *Chain of Command: The Road from 9/11 to Abu Ghraib*, New York: HarperCollins, 2004, p. 183. The quotations are taken from these sources.

3 Excerpts from 1992 draft, 'Defense Planning Guidance', 'The War Behind Closed Doors', PBS, Frontline, http://www.pbs.org/wgbh/pages/frontline.

4 In parting company with many of his former neo-conservative associates, Fukuyama now regards the September 17, 2002 document as badly in need of revision, as it dangerously confuses preventive war with pre-emption. The lesson of Iraq should be that faulty intelligence can make for very bad decisions in this regard, based upon presumptions about the character of the Iraq regime. It thus becomes for argument whether the core neo-conservative argument has any validity at all, which seems to be Fukuyama's reason for writing his new book, *After the Neocons: America at the Crossroads*, London: Profile Books, 2006.

5 Anne Hessing Cahn, 'Team B: The Trillion-dollar Experiment', *Bulletin of the Atomic Scientists*, April 1993, 22, pp. 24–7.

6 Project for A New American Century, June 3, 1997 http://www.newamericancentury.org/statementofprinciples.htm

7 The letter can be found at http://www.newamericancentury.org/iraqclintonletter.html.

8 The letter, dated February 19, 1998, can be found at http://www.iraqwatch.org/perspectives/rumsfeld-openletter.

9 Seymour Hersh, 'Did Iraq Try to Assassinate ex-President Bush in 1993? A Case Not Closed', in Sifry and Cerf, op. cit. pp. 140–62.

10 The Clinton quotations in this paragraph and the one following are from Stephen F. Hayes, 'Democrats for Regime Change: The President Has Some Surprising Allies', *The Weekly Standard*, September 16, 2002. Hayes's purpose was to demonstrate that Clinton was the true author of regime change.

11 See Norm Dixon, 'Richard Butler – Servant of the UN or Washington?', reprinted at http://www.globalpolicy.org/security/issues/butler2.html. Dixon provides a catalogue of articles dealing with the strikes from the *Washington Post* and the *New York Times*.

12 Albright's speech, March 26, 1997, can be found at http://www.fas.org/news/iraq/1997/03bmd970327b.html.

13 A good example of Rice's post 9/11 rhetoric can be found in her speech to the Paul H. Nitze School of Advanced International Studies at Johns Hopkins University on April 29, 2002, http://www.whitehouse.gov/news/releases/2002/04.

14 Bob Woodward, *Plan of Attack*, New York: Simon & Schuster, 2004, p. 27 (emphasis added).

15 Gregory L. Vistica, '"Kick Down the Doors" Everywhere?' *The Washington Post National Weekly Edition*, January 12–18, 2004, p. 6; Barton Gellman, 'Secret Unit Expands Rumsfeld's Domain', *The Washington Post*, January 22, 2005.

16 Ann Scott Tyson and Dana Priest, 'Pentagon Seeking Leeway Overseas', *Washington Post*, February 24, 2005.

17 Steven R. Weisman, 'U.S. Program Is Directed at Altering Iran's Politics', *New York Times*, April 15, 2006.

18 Interview with Condoleezza Rice, September 8, 2002, CNN Late Edition, http://www.mtholyoke,edu/acad/intrel/bush/wolf.html (emphasis added).

19 Glenn Kessler, 'Powell Says Weapons Inspections Needed First', *Newark Star-Ledger*, September 2, 2002.

20 'President Bush, Prime Minister Blair Discuss Keeping the Peace', September 7, 2002, http://www.whitehouse.gov/news/releases/2002/09.

21 See Roger Morris, 'The Source Beyond Rove: Condoleezza Rice at the Center of the Plame Scandal', July 27, 2005, http://www.egp360.net/midnightride/morris_2005_07_24.shtml.

22 Matt Kelley, 'Bush Seeks OK for Military Force Against Iraq', September 19, 2002, Associated Press, http://www.salon.com/news/wire/2002/09/19/iraq_congress/print.html.

23 The National Security Strategy document of September 17, 2002, with the covering letter can be found at http://www.whitehouse.gov/nsc/nssall.html. I have added the italics.

24 See Richard Norton Taylor, 'The Rancid Relationship', The Guardian (London), March 23, 2006. See also Ron Suskind, 'Without a Doubt', The New York Times Sunday Magazine, October 17, 2004, downloaded from Truthout, January 31, 2005, http://www.truthout.org/docs_04/printer_101704A.shtml. Suskind discusses an encounter with a religious leader, Jim Wallis of the Sojourners, in the White House on February 1, 2002. The president seemed eager to greet Wallis to discuss the latter's book, *Faith Works*, but the conversation quickly turned in a direction Bush did not like or understand. Wallis said he told Bush, 'Unless we drain the swamp of injustice in which the mosquitoes of terrorism breed, we'll never defeat the threat of terrorism'. Bush looked quizzically at the minister. 'They never spoke again after that'. Wallis recounted the episode for Suskind, and then told him, 'When I was first with Bush in Austin, what I saw was a self-help Methodist, very open, seeking. What I started to see at this point was … a messianic American Calvinist. He doesn't want to hear from anyone who doubts him'. Suskind wondered, on the other hand, if a president trying to rally a country crying out for leadership in a crisis had time to entertain doubters. Still, Wallis's comments and fears had to do less with the immediate needs to respond to the nation's agony in the aftermath of 9/11 than with evidence of underlying assumptions and longer term policies, such as those that led to Abu Ghraib.

25 Taylor, ibid. Inside the Pentagon, Lt. Col. Karen Kwiatkowski, who would become a thorn in Rumsfeld's side after she retired and exposed the 'intelligence' operations of the OSP, observed the way the Iraq War was being plotted out in regard to information about WMD. In a press interview in 2004, Kwiatkowski said, 'We knew from many years of both high-level surveillance and other types of shared intelligence, not to mention the information from the UN, we knew what was left [from the Gulf War] and the viability of any of that. Bush said he didn't know. The truth is, we know [Saddam] didn't have these things. Almost a billion dollars has been spent – a billion dollars! – by David Kay's group to search for these WMD, a total whitewash effort. They didn't

find anything, they didn't expect to find anything'. Marc Cooper, 'Soldier for the Truth', *L.A. Weekly*, February 20, 2004, http://www.truthout.org/docs_04/022304B.shtml.

26 Matt Kelley, op. cit. 'President Bush Discusses Iraq with Reporters', September 13, 2002, http://www.whitehouse.gov/news/releases/2002/09.

27 See, for example, 'Secretary Rumsfeld Interview with Jim Lehrer', September 18, 2002, http://www.defenselink.mil/cgi-bin/dlprint.

28 Eric Rosenberg, 'Rumsfeld Retreats, Disclaims Earlier Rhetoric', Ocala Star Banner, November 9, 2003, http://www.truthout.org/docs_03/printer_1111031.shtml.

29 Ibid.

30 'Meet the Press, With Tim Russert', Transcript for September 14, 2003, http://msnbc.msn.com/id/3080244/default.html.

31 Ibid.

32 Patrick E. Tyler, 'Blair Tells Commons That Results in Iraq are More Important than Faulty Intelligence', *New York Times*, February 5, 2004.

33 Woodward, *Plan of Attack*, op. cit. p. 249. Woodward's source for this vivid scene might have been a tiny bit interested in protecting the president's reputation, as the justification shift needed a fall guy.

34 Rice and Tenet statements, *New York Times*, February 5, 2004.

35 Richard W. Stevenson, 'Remember "Weapons of Mass Destruction"? For Bush, They Are a Nonissue', *New York Times*, December 18, 2003.

36 'President Bush Announces Major Combat Operations in Iraq Have Ended', May 1, 2003, http://www.whitehouse.gov/news/releases/2003/05/iraq.

37 Sidney Blumenthal, 'This Pollyanna Army', *The Guardian* (London), January 27, 2005, http://www.guardian.co.uk/print/0,3858,5113021-103677,00.html.

38 Ian Traynor, 'The Privatisation of War', *The Guardian* (London), December 10, 2003, http://www.guardian.co.uk/print/0,3858,4815701-10355.

39 Jonathan Franklin, 'US Hires Mercenaries for Iraq Role', March 6, 2004, http://www.theage.com.au/cgi-bin/common; Danna Harman, 'Firms Tap Latin Americans for Iraq', *Christian Science Monitor*, March 3, 2005, http://www.csmonitor.com/2005/0303/p06s02-woam.html.

40 James Brooke, 'On Farthest U.S. Shores, Iraq is a Way to a Dream', *New York Times*, July 31, 2005.

41 Ron Suskind, op. cit.

42 Peter Baker, 'In Iraq, No Clear Finish Line', *Washington Post*, August 12, 2005.

43 Jones quoted in, 'The Education of Rep. Walter Jones', *The Carpetbagger Report*, May 26, 2005, http://www.thecarpetbaggerreport.co/wp-print.php?p-4297.

44 Adam Nagourney and David D. Kirkpatrick, 'Bad Iraq War News Worries Some in G.O.P. on '06 Vote', *New York Times*, August 18, 2005; Caspar Weinberger and Peter Schweizer, *Chain of Command: A Thriller*, New York: Atria Books, 2005.

45 Gideon Rose, 'Get Real', *New York Times*, August 18, 2005.

46 Charles J. Hanley, 'US Building Massive Embassy in Baghdad', the Associated Press, April 14, 2006, http://www.truthout.org.docs_2006/041606A.shtml.

47 Fukuyama, 'Invasion of the Isolationists', ibid., August 31, 2005.

48 Quoted in Martin Jacques, 'Imperial Overreach is Accelerating the Global Decline of America', *The Guardian* (London), March 28, 2006.

2

THE VIETNAM LAUGH TRACK

Marilyn B. Young

Right now, there is no 'Vietnam syndrome'. It's behind us. We know now that the American people are willing to go to war and to win. And, in the rest of the world, there is great respect not only for the power of the U.S. but for the Western values that we have been espousing for so long.

Representative Dante Fascell, chair of the
House Foreign Affairs Committee, 1991[1]

With a heavy dose of fear and violence, and a lot of money for projects, I think we can convince these people that we are here to help them.

Lt. Col. Nathan Sassaman, 2003[2]

I heard a man who had been in Abu Ghraib prison say: the Americans brought electricity to my ass before they brought it to my house.

Eliot Weinberger, 2006[3]

The guiding principle is to laugh for no reason. And that's one of the reasons it works so well for military families.

James 'Scotty' Scott, Colonel, retired, US Army, laughter training specialist
and chief Pentagon laughter instructor, 2006[4]

Vietnam is the great Satan of late twentieth-century American history, the Anti-Christ, the Bogeyman. If you don't watch out, politicians and military men for the past thirty years have told themselves and each other, Vietnam's gonna get ya. Whatever the war itself may have been, as history, war crime, graveyard for millions of Vietnamese and tens of thousands of Americans, ever since 1975 it has been the Book of Negative Lessons for the American government. Do not do as has been done and all will be well. One lesson was learned early and never forgotten: the most important battlefront is domestic. Victory is dependent upon the control and manipulation of the press, the capacity of the president and his men to lie consistently and with perfect conviction, the satisfaction, at least minimally, of consumer desires and the achievement of a delicate balance between frightening the people silly while not unduly inconveniencing them. Meanwhile, wherever American troops are at war, Vietnam is there: in the imagination of the troops, who know it through the movies, in the daily tactics of the US military, in the war reporting of young journalists, in the American families who receive the bodies of the dead and the maimed and in the daily experience of Iraqis and Afghanis.

Old wars are always in the imagination of troops going to new ones.[5] It was a commonplace of Vietnam War reporting that *Sands of Iwo Jima* inspired countless young men to join up to serve their country, defeat the enemy and raise the flag over Hanoi. The movie, released in 1949, was a conscious effort on the part of the Marines to promote the service, protect their share of the shrinking defence budget and remind the country just who had won the war in the Pacific. Built around an iconic image of victory, the raising of the American flag on Mount Surabachi, the movie starred John Wayne as its flawed but admirable hero. Marine recruiters claimed enlistments rose whenever the movie ran on TV. An Annapolis midshipman said he played a tape of the movie to his classmates once a week and got 'choked up every time'.[6] This is hardly surprising. Although Jeane Basinger has written about the unexpected subtext of *Sands* – the movie's affirmation of civilian rather than military values – what drives it is the male camaraderie of war, the inevitability of American victory, the sad death of one's elders, the triumphant survival of one's heroic young self, and over all, that gigantic flag waving in the breeze.[7]

Most Vietnam War films, like most of those made about WWI, were consciously anti-war. With the exception of *The Green Berets*, even films that did not explicitly reject the war – like *Hamburger Hill* and *The Deer Hunter* – could not be mistaken for recruiting posters. Yet if the movies of the Vietnam War did not recruit they did, surprisingly, inspire.[8] Anthony Swofford and his fellow Marines, awaiting deployment in Gulf War I, cheered on the helicopters in *Apocalypse Now* as they swooped down on a Vietnamese village, loudspeakers blaring Wagner, spurred on by the mad, eponymous Captain Kilgore. Vietnam War movies, Swofford wrote, 'are all pro-war, no matter what the supposed message…'. Whatever Kubrick or Coppola or Stone intended, their movies were 'pornography for the military man; with film you are stroking his cock, tickling his balls with the pink feather of history, getting him ready for his real First Fuck'.[9] Swofford's memoir about Gulf War I was made into a movie scripted by Bill Broyles, Jr, a Vietnam veteran, and released in the midst of Gulf War II, a war in which Broyles' son was serving his third tour of duty.[10] At the thematic heart of the movie, as it was of the book, is the Valkyrie scene from *Apocalypse Now* itself a dark homage to the ride of the Ku Klux Klan in *Birth of a Nation*.

Lawrence Weschler has spelled out the genealogy: 100 years after the premier of the first ride of the Valkyrie in Bayreuth, Coppola, Milius and Murch

> would begin work on their own shattering masterpiece, complete with its ironically inverted homage to Griffith, that horrific Valkyrie raid of choppers of the airborne cavalry, a scene that less than a generation later would be being deployed (pithed of all irony) to stiffen the resolve of an auditorium full of jarheads at Twentynine Palms Marine Base bound for a whole fresh war of their own, in a scene that, less than a generation after that, and in the

midst of yet another whole new war, would itself be forming the fulcrum, the very hinge, of yet another effort to nail down the whole self-immolating, self-devouring, agonizedly churning monster of a perplex.

As the editor of both *Apocalypse Now* and *Jarhead* told Weschler: 'at times I get to feeling like I'm inside my own Escher drawing'.[11]

John Crawford, Alpha Company, 3rd Battalion of the 124th Infantry, carried Tim O'Brien's *The Things They Carried* into war in Iraq. Not yet a veteran but planning ahead, when not on patrol Crawford is writing a short story about a veteran with bad memories of what happened to him in Iraq.[12] Relentlessly focusing on the American experience of making war, soldiers, filmmakers, memoir writers, essayists – even historians – hold their own hands and draw themselves.

And not just in books or movie houses. A report by John Burns recaptured the Vietnam War dispatches of reporters like David Halberstam as well as the movies made in the war's aftermath. Burns' dispatch bore the headline: 'Shadow of Vietnam Falls Over Iraq River Raids'. As the Marines moved upriver (the Euphrates, one had to remind oneself, not the Mekong) in SURCs (Small Unit Riverine Craft, rather than Swift boats), 'there were snatches of dialogue from Apocalypse Now'. A marine described the landscape around him as 'a Vietnam theme park', not Iraq, but not Vietnam either.[13] Rather a Disneyland where war happens.

The Marine was on to something. Iraq has become a Vietnam theme park and one the military and the public seem to wander through over and over again, a nightmare Groundhog Day.[14] From the very beginning there was talk of hearts and minds, although the talk yielded to another piece of Vietnam wisdom – 'Grab their balls and their hearts and minds will follow'.[15] Major John Nagl, a long-time student of the Vietnam War and author of *Learning to Eat Soup with a Knife: Counterinsurgency Lessons from Vietnam and Malaya*, lost interest in Iraqi hearts during his first tour of duty. 'I'm not really all that concerned about their hearts right now', he told a reporter.

> We're into the behavior-modification phase. I want their minds right now. Maybe we'll get their hearts later … Over time I'll start winning some hearts. Right now I just want them to stop shooting at us, stop planting IEDs [improvised explosive devices]. If they're not involved in these activities, they should start turning in the people who are.[16]

Hearts and minds talk never disappeared entirely, but it was side-lined in favor of Iraqification, on the model of Vietnamization in the latter years of the war. Well, perhaps not quite on that model, but something better, something that worked. Initially, things looked promising. In January 2005, Secretary of State Condoleezza Rice announced that 120,000 Iraqis had been trained and equipped, though no one challenged Senator Joseph Biden's observation that only 14,000 of them were reliable. In January 2006, Eliot Weinberger summarized subsequent developments: a marine general stated that Iraqis were starting to take care of things and American troops would soon begin to come home; an admiral said there were 145,000 combat-ready Iraqi troops; an Iraqi bureaucrat observed that perhaps as many as 50,000 of the 145,000 did not exist except for accounting purposes; Secretary of Defense Rumsfeld insisted that 130,200 had been trained and equipped, down from the 210,000 he had announced in 2004. Weinberger concluded: 'I heard the Pentagon announce it would no longer release Iraqi troop figures'.[17]

An equally intense effort is being made to train additional Iraqi police forces. There have been problems with the forces trained thus far. Many units are dominated by local militia whose loyalties are to their militia commanders. Marine Major General Stephen T. Johnson said that 1,200 Iraqi police officers were stationed in the troubled Sunni-dominated province of Anbar, although he acknowledged that none had been assigned to its major cities, Falluja and Ramadi. 'The ultimate goal', Lt. Col. Christopher Hickey emailed a reporter, 'is for the police to police'.[18]

Meanwhile, there are some intermediate goals. Police training is said to include 32 hours of instruction on human rights and the rule of law,[19] but the Special Police Commandos, under the operational control of Steve Casteel, formerly of the US Drug Enforcement Agency and Jim Steele, who led a unit of US Special Forces in El Salvador, receive instructions of a different sort. For Steele and Casteel, Iraq is not Vietnam but El Salvador, and it does not matter to them that their Special Police Commando unit is dominated by Sunnis trained, in another life, by Saddam Hussein. What mattered in El Salvador, what Steele and Casteel believed would matter in Iraq, was a readiness to inflict maximum violence against the insurgency, anyone who might be associated with it, even remotely, and anyone who failed to inform against it. Unmentioned in this search for the relevant analogy is the fact that the Saigon police force and the paramilitary Phoenix programme which targeted the 'infrastructure' of the insurgency in Vietnam were as handy at torture and brutality as anyone the Americans trained in Central America.

The Sunni-dominated city of Samarra, Peter Maass reported, was to be the 'proving ground' for the new El Salvador-based strategy. Maass visited the commandos there in March, 2005. He watched as 100 bound and blindfolded prisoners were slapped and kicked as they awaited interrogation. The interrogation room itself had a desk 'with bloodstains running down its side'. As the reporter was questioning a young Saudi prisoner about his treatment by his captors, he could hear the screams of a man being tortured next door. An American adviser with the commandos commented that he did not think Iraqis 'know the value of human life Americans have'.[20]

Nine months later, as US forces prepared to hand Samarra over to Iraqi police, it remained 'a major test for the U.S. military in Iraq, and one U.S. commanders… say they can't afford to fail'. The Special Police Commandos had withdrawn from Samarra in the spring and by July Major Patrick Walsh told a reporter, the city was once again becoming a 'neutral-to-bad-news story'. In August, the US Army engineers built an earthen barricade over eight feet high and six and a half miles long around the city (Operation Great Wall). Three checkpoints controlled all traffic into and out of town and the number of insurgent attacks subsided. To persuade Samarra's population of 200,000 to 'cooperate or we'll clear the city', Walsh spread the rumour that a major offensive was about to begin. In response, over half the population, along with half the police force, fled. There was a marked reduction in insurgent attacks, along with much of the active life of the city. As the US troops withdrew, an American observer thought the remaining Iraqi police force, barricaded in their Green Zone and temporarily reinforced by the return of the Special Police Commandos, might be able to defend themselves, though over half of them rarely showed up for work. With 'competent leaders', it would take two more years to build a local police force of 1,200.[21]

The Special Police Commando is Sunni-led; other death squads – the Mahdi army, the Badr Corps – are affiliated with Shi'a political parties. When asked if documented abuses by forces under the direct control of the Iraqi Ministry of the Interior would delay a US handover to Iraqi troops, Secretary of Defense Rumsfeld thought not. 'Obviously, the United States, does not have a responsibility when a sovereign country engages in something that they disapprove of', he said – which should be good news to the government of Iran and sovereign nations everywhere.[22]

Iraqification is only one of a mine-field of Vietnam references that appeared even before the quick and easy victory in Iraq yielded to the long, hard occupation. The Sunni Triangle recalled the old Iron Triangle, graveyard of so many Americans and Vietnamese; whenever members of the Bush administration, including the president, were caught in lies, they set off a small detonation and headlines about the 'credibility gap'; the slightly archaic reference to 'foes' as distinct from 'friends' returned, as in the classic Vietnam observation about the inability of American troops to distinguish between the two. The most common, appearing even before the invasion of Iraq, is 'quagmire' and one can hear the sucking noise it makes on any slow news day. R. W. Apple, who had reported the Vietnam War for the *New York Times,* wrote an article at the end of October, 2001, entitled 'A Military Quagmire Remembered: Afghanistan as Vietnam'.[23] There have been many since, including one by Max Boot, written in mid-November 2003, on the 'Lessons of a Quagmire'.[24]

The lesson Boot drew, that the US must focus on counterinsurgency, is the favourite of all Vietnam references and is rewritten on a regular basis by a variety of authors. Counterinsurgency rested on 'solid help from Iraqis', Boot wrote.

> Only locals can pick out the good guys from the bad. Also – and this is a more delicate matter – Iraqis would be able to try some of the strong-arm tactics that our own scrupulously legalistic armed forces shy away from.

Writing before the treatment of Iraqis in Abu Ghraib prison was common knowledge, Boot complained that American forces might be 'too Boy Scoutish for the rougher side of a dirty war'. Like the Vietcong, Iraqi guerrillas hoped to increase 'the cost of the conflict until the desire of the American public to continue the struggle is shattered'. The central question, Boot warned, was whether

America's 'will to sustain casualties [was] greater than our enemies' ability to inflict them. Upon that question will turn the future of Iraq'.[25]

Over the past three years, the desire of the American public to continue the conflict has indeed waned. To shore it up, selected policymakers and historians of the Vietnam War have been recalled to duty. The principle of selection is simple: the author must believe that the Vietnam War could have been won; *ergo* the Iraq War can be won. In the September/October 2005 issue of *Foreign Affairs*, Andrew Krepinevich, Jr, who had written a critical account of the Vietnam War, *The Army and Vietnam*, published an essay boldly entitled 'How to Win in Iraq'. The next month, Melvin Laird, Secretary of Defense in the first Nixon administration, whose silence since then misled many into thinking he had died, wrote 'Iraq: Learning the Lessons of Vietnam' for the same journal. At the same time, General John Abizaid, among many others, was reading *A Better War*, Lewis Sorley's 1999 account of how General Creigton Abrams had come close to winning the war in Vietnam by abandoning 'search and destroy' in favour of 'clear and hold'.[26]

It is worth looking at these new uses of an old lost war more closely. Krepinevich insists that withdrawal from Iraq would mean, as the Nixon administration claimed it would have meant in Vietnam (until, in 1973, it ordered US troops home), a bloodbath, a signal of America's weak will, and worse – the chaos following withdrawal from Iraq, Krepinevich warned, 'would drive up oil prices'. Instead of withdrawing, what the US needed was a 'real strategy built around the principles of counterinsurgency warfare'. Rather than hunt and kill insurgents all over the place, the military should concentrate on establishing security and providing services in certain key areas and then slowly, over time, expanding those areas of control. Krepinevich called it the 'oil-spot' strategy.

Daniel Ellsberg pointed out at the time, however, that Saigon, itself an eroding base of support for the Government of Vietnam, was 'pre-eminently the "oil spot" and almost the only one …'.[27] It was unclear then with what other spots Saigon could be connected. In Iraq, until very recently, the US has been unable to clear and hold even the five mile stretch of road that goes to the airport. But Krepinevich's faith in oil spots is undaunted. Without noting the prominent role Sir Robert Thompson, the architect of British victory in Malaya, played in advising the American military in Vietnam, Krepinevich cites Malaya as a model for the US in Iraq, as it was so often cited as a model for Vietnam. He does not discuss the terms of British victory: the herding of virtually the entire Chinese population of the country, some 400,000 to 500,000 people, into 400 closely guarded villages; the creation of a police state; the post-war violence and ongoing repression. Caroline Elkins, an historian of the British Empire, points out that 'repressive laws and undemocratic institutions, not peace and progress, were the primary bequest of the British to Malaya', a legacy underwritten by the tactics of counterinsurgency.[28]

But suppose Krepinevich is right and some oil spots could be secured and even expanded, the future he promises is on the grim side. His strategy requires a decade of total commitment on the part of the American people, the expenditure of 'hundreds of billions of dollars' and many more casualties. That is the price to be paid if the US wishes 'to achieve its worthy goals in Iraq'. Then Krepinevich puts it to the people as Boot did two years earlier: 'Are the American people and American soldiers willing to pay that price?'. The only way to find out would be for the Bush administration to present the people 'with a clear strategy for victory and a full understanding of the sacrifices required …'. And if Americans are not up to it? Well then the government must settle for the more modest goal of outmanoeuvring Iran and Syria and 'creating an ally out of Iraq's next despot'.[29] Krepinevich does not explain how the American people, far less American troops, are to make their wishes known in the absence of a parliamentary system. Through opinion polls? Desertion rates? The polls are down; recruitment rates, despite lavish bonuses, remain low. In the face of this, Krepinevich, like Max Boot and a host of others, has only one weapon, the bully's taunt: are you man enough to fight through to victory? Have you the *will*? We are back inside *Apocalypse Now*, channelling Joseph Campbell with Marlon Brando. Or maybe just upriver with Conrad in *Heart of Darkness*.

Melvin Laird's contribution to the debate was a spirited defence of the Nixon administration prompted by 'the renewed vilification of our role in Vietnam …'. Not only could the US have won in Vietnam, according to Laird, it *did* win the war in 1973; Congress then 'grabbed defeat from the jaws of victory' by refusing to fund the Saigon government so that it could continue the fight on its own. The shame of Vietnam, Laird insists, 'is not that we were there in the first place, but that we betrayed our ally in the end'. To be sure, both the Vietnam and the Iraq wars were 'based on intelligence failures and possibly outright deception'. It was worse in the case of Vietnam because intelligence lapses 'were born of our failure to understand what motivated Ho Chi Minh in the 1950s'. Had the US understood the 'depth of his nationalism, we might have been able to derail his communism early on'. Part of Bush's problem in Iraq has been his failure to 'market the mission'. There is a simple message to be communicated:

> Our troops are fighting to preserve modern culture, Western democracy, the global economy, and all else that is threatened by the spread of barbarism in the name of religion. That is the message and the mission. It is not politically correct, nor is it comforting. But it is the truth, and sometimes the truth needs good marketing.[30]

Krepinevich and Laird are in general agreement: Iraqification and/or spreading oil spots plus good marketing of a clear mission are all it takes to win in Iraq. On November 30, 2005, George W. Bush combined these elements, added a dash of Lewis Sorley's version of the Vietnam War and issued a 'National Strategy for Victory in Iraq'. In the future, the military in Iraq would refrain from driving insurgents out of cities and towns only to have them move back in the next day. Instead, having swept through a place, Iraqi troops would be left behind to hold it. As Lawrence Kaplan observed, this was good news: 'U.S. forces will no longer be fighting World War II all over again in Iraq …'. It was also bad news: 'tactical and operational concepts that were tested and found wanting in Vietnam', would be revived.[31]

The intersection of Iraqification and 'clear-and-hold' would seem to be the city of Tal Afar, 150 miles northwest of Baghdad. At the end of November 2005, Bush pointed to Tal Afar with pride. In contrast to the poor showing of Iraqi forces in the battle for Falluja in 2004, according to Bush, the assault on Tal Afar was led by Iraqi forces which had 'conducted their own anti-terrorist operations and controlled their own battle space – hunting for enemy fighters and securing neighborhoods block-by-block'. Moreover, these units had stayed on to 'help maintain law and order – and reconstruction projects have been started to improve infrastructure and create jobs and provide hope'.[32] Tal Afar could do with a bit of hope. American troops had conducted repeated, massive assaults against the city. The officer in charge of the most recent offensive was Col. H. R. McMaster, like Krepinevich a student of counterinsurgency and the author of *Dereliction of Duty: Lyndon Johnson, Robert McNamara, The Joint Chiefs of Staff, and the Lies that Led to Vietnam*. After several months, McMaster felt he had made enough progress to declare the city 'clearly contested, whereas before it wasn't'.[33] Indeed, by December 2005, Oliver Poole reported for the *Daily Telegraph*, 'there is no doubt that something has been achieved'. Sewers had been dug, shops destroyed by US troops, rebuilt, some 2,000 goats were distributed to local farmers and people cheered US convoys when they rumbled through the streets.[34]

Unremarked by Bush or by those intent on doing well in Iraq what they believe to have been done badly in Vietnam, is the substance of the demands made by the council of Nineveh (which includes Tal Afar) for an international inquiry into the treatment of the Sunni population of Tal Afar and the 'extreme use of force and the use of internationally forbidden weapons...'.[35] The council accused the Kurdish and Shi'a Iraqi security forces praised by Bush of perpetrating ethnic cleansing, the Kurds intent on annexing parts of the province, the Shi'a content to 'break the noses of the Sunnis'. McMaster and other American officers dismissed the complaints, saying they had 'impressed upon the army and police leadership the importance of fairness and the rule of law vis-à-vis the local population'. McMaster seems persuaded of the power of his pedagogy. An officer who had participated in the fighting around Tal Afar gave Seymour Hersh a somewhat different perspective: American troops:

> were placed in the position of providing a cordon of security around the besieged city for Iraqi forces, most of them Shiites, who were 'rounding up any Sunnis on the basis of whatever a Shiite said to them' with the 'active participation of a militia unit led by a retired American Special Forces soldier'.[36]

Vietnam cycles through Iraq in the person of men like McMaster and Krepinevich, Laird and Sorley, in movies like *Jarhead*, in the official language of tactics and the casual conversation of soldiers (hajis and ragheads rather than gooks; Indian country to name the world outside their bases), and in all the sentences beginning with 'another …'.[37] Old Vietnam hands return to the news programs, including Walter Cronkite, who remembers his 1968 call for US withdrawal as 'one of those [moments] that I'm proudest of …'. In January 2006, Cronkite went further, calling on current anchors to demand withdrawal from Iraq. The words he used 38 years ago would serve without a single change:

> To say that we are closer to victory today is to believe, in the face of the evidence, the optimists who have been wrong in the past. … It is increasingly clear to this reporter that the only rational way out then will be to negotiate, not as victors, but as an honorable people who lived up to their pledge to defend democracy, and did the best they could.[38]

The sop Cronkite offered then to the country's conviction that it always and ever meant well would serve today as well – all in the interests of an end to the occupation. But whereas President Lyndon B. Johnson, listening to Cronkite, told his aides, 'If I've lost Cronkite, I've lost Middle America', the response of the Bush White House would likely be an all-out effort to smear him.

Although conservatives frequently appeal to the morale and commitment of America's fighting forces as evidence that the US is doing the right thing in Iraq, those who fought in Vietnam are acceptable only insofar as they support administration policy. Otherwise they are subject to public accusations that their medals were unearned, their heroism mythical, and their opposition to the president shameful.[39] During the 2000 primary campaigns, questions were raised about Senator John McCain's behaviour as a prisoner of war; in 2004, an all-out attack was launched against John Kerry's military record, and when Max Cleland rose to his defence, he was mocked for having lost both legs and one arm in a 'non-combat' situation. Ugly, but then US election campaigns always are. Somewhat more surprising has been the attack on Rep. John Murtha after the Congressman's emotional appeal for the withdrawal of American troops from Iraq. On the floor of the House, a freshman Congresswoman, quoting a Marine constituent, accused Murtha of cowardice; in the week that followed, the circumstances in which Murtha had received his two Purple Hearts were called into question. Asked why Murtha's service record in 1967 was relevant to the current debate about Iraq, the head of Cybercast News Service replied: 'because the congressman has really put himself in the forefront of the anti-war movement. … He has been placed by the Democratic Party and anti-war activists as a spokesman against the war above reproach'.[40]

It is the case that Iraq is not Vietnam. It was not Vietnam in 1991 and it is not now. The history of Iraq, its demography, topography, resources, culture, and the nature of its resistance and insurgency are radically different from Vietnam. Vietnam haunts the war in Iraq in part because it has begun to smell like defeat but more significantly, I think, because the task the US has taken upon itself is similar: to bend a country about which it knows little, whose language and history are unknown to its soldiers, to its will. It is a haunting, rather than a serious engagement with the history of the Vietnam War or the direct application of lessons learned there, no matter how earnestly the Masters of Counterinsurgency claim they can do it better this time round. When accounts of the torture and general mistreatment of prisoners at Abu Ghraib and Guantanamo became public, they were instantly compared to the massacre of Vietnamese civilians at My Lai. The two situations had nothing whatsoever in common other than the public's fear that once again American troops had forgotten or mislaid the rules of war. The more exact comparison – to the treatment of political prisoners in Saigon's jails or in the infamous 'tiger cages' on Con Son Island – was never mentioned. Similarly, reports on the treatment of Iraqi civilians by US troops, at every point reminiscent of similar accounts during the Vietnam War, stand by themselves, their structural relationship to the past unmentioned and unmentionable.

One instructive example is the case of Lt. Col. Nathan Sassaman, an officer, according to Dexter Filkins, who had 'distinguished himself as one of the nimblest most aggressive officers in Iraq' and one who embodied 'not just the highly trained, highly educated officer corps ... but also the promise of the American enterprise itself'.[41] He is described as having had warm and friendly relations with the locals in the Shiite city of Balad in which he was stationed. Although Sassaman had had no training in nation-building or guerrilla war, 'he had quickly figured out what he needed to do: remake the area's shattered institutions, jump-start the economy and implant a democracy ...'. Sassaman's power in Balad was absolute. 'He could chart the future of a city, lock up anyone he wanted and, if trouble arose, call in an air strike'. He was, in his own words, 'the warrior king'.[42]

However excellent his relations with the Shi'a community were, his dealings with surrounding Sunni villages were less cordial.[43] In October 2003, as the insurgency gained strength, Maj. Gen. Raymond Odierno ordered the Fourth Infantry Division to 'increase lethality'. Sassaman was, apparently, eager to comply: 'When [he] spoke of sending his soldiers into Samarra, his eyes gleamed "We are going to inflict extreme violence"'.[44] As the insurgency intensified, so did Sassaman's reprisals. In November, after one of his men had been hit by an RPG (rocket propelled grenade) fired in the vicinity of the village of Abu Hishma, Sassaman, with the permission of his immediate superior, Col. Frederick Rudesheim, wrapped the village in barbed wire, issued ID cards (in English) and threatened to kill anyone who tried to enter or leave without permission. The explicit model for the treatment of Abu Hishma was Israel's treatment of the Palestinian insurgency in the occupied territories. In July 2003, Brig. Gen. Michael A. Vane, chief of staff for 'doctrine concepts and strategy', at the US Army Training and Doctrine Center, wrote of his trip to Israel to 'glean lessons from their counterterrorist operations in urban areas'.[45] In his own limited way, Sassaman used US firepower as it had been used in Vietnam. In response to a single mortar round, Dexter Filkins reported, he fired '28 155-millimeter artillery shells and 42 mortar rounds. He called in two air strikes, one with a 500-pound bomb and the other with a 2,000-pound bomb'. When his troops were fired on from a wheat field, Sassaman 'routinely retaliated by firing phosphorus shells to burn the entire field down'. Elsewhere in Iraq, the use of phosphorus shells was referred to as a 'shake and bake' mission.[46]

The results of these efforts pleased Sassaman: 'We just didn't get hit after that'. He did not say and the reporter did not ask about the effect on the human targets. Over and over again, Sassaman met resistance of any kind with massive force and taught his men to do likewise. Like the Vietnamese, the Iraqis, according to Sassaman and the troops under his command, understood only the language of force. In any event, it was the only language, other than English, any of them spoke.[47] Over the course of their tour, the men under Sassaman's command became increasingly punitive towards the Iraqis around them – any Iraqi, all Iraqis. When a shopkeeper gave passing troops the finger, they doubled back, searched his shop, drove him to a bridge over the Tigris and threw him in. 'The next time I went back, the guy is out there waving to us', a soldier told Dexter Filkins. 'Everybody got a chuckle out of that'.[48]

Sassaman's fall from grace involved his cover-up of the drowning of an Iraqi civilian by soldiers under his command. Two men, whose truck had broken down as they raced to reach home before the 11 p.m. curfew, had almost made it when they were stopped by American troops. They were searched, questioned and waved on, only to be stopped again, handcuffed, driven to a point ten feet above the Tigris, uncuffed and ordered to jump. The men begged not to be thrown into the river and indeed clung to the legs of the soldiers who, at gunpoint, pushed one of them in; the other jumped after him. Later, the soldiers claimed they had watched to make sure the men were OK – defined as 'doing good treading water', before taking off. One of the Iraqis, Marwan Fadhil, survived. His cousin, Zaydoon, did not. Their truck, Marwan reported, was where he'd left it – but the Americans had smashed it before going back to base.[49]

When Sassaman learned an investigation into the death would take place, he decided that 'throwing Iraqis into the Tigris was wrong but not criminal' and that drawing attention to it would 'whip up anti-American feeling'. On these grounds he initially decided to cover the incident up entirely. Later, Sassaman testified forcefully in defence of the two men held directly responsible for Zaydoon's death. It had been a mistake, he insisted, a 'bad call'. The soldiers were sentenced to six months and 45 days respectively; Sassaman was reprimanded and shortly thereafter decided to retire from the military.

Filkins's account of Sassaman's fall from grace was, on the whole, sympathetic to the dilemmas the officer and his troops faced. After all, Filkins asked, 'how much more serious was it to throw an Iraqi civilian into the Tigris, which was not approved, than it was to, say, fire an antitank missile into an Iraqi civilian's home, which was?'. Where was the line between a justifiable and a criminal use of non-lethal force? Like Krepinevich and Boot, Filkins stressed the lack of counterinsurgency training for both officers and the men they commanded. Towards the end of his essay, Filkins acknowledged that nearly 'every major counterinsurgency in the 20th century [had] failed', with the armies of the countries fighting them – the US in Vietnam, the French in Algeria, the Soviets in Afghanistan – utterly demoralized by the experience. Rather than question the advisability of entering into such conflicts, the response of the military – and of the media – has been an attempt to focus once more on counterinsurgency.

At the Army's Command and General Staff College, for example, courses on guerrilla warfare were not a required part of the curriculum.[50] Sensitive to such criticism, the military has made efforts to re-focus on counterinsurgency. Although the courses at the Command and General Staff College are not required, enrolment in electives on the subject has tripled in the academic year 2005–6 and the Army plans to introduce a new, required course of study on counterinsurgency. Work is also underway on a new manual on counterinsurgency, one which will include 'input' from the British army, 'which has had centuries of experience in places like Afghanistan and Iraq'.[51] In late January 2006, Lt. Gen. David H. Petraeus was described as 'spearheading' these efforts. Petraeus, whose 1987 doctoral dissertation for Princeton University was on the lessons of Vietnam, had commanded the 101st Airborne Division in Iraq before returning to run the US Army Combined Arms Center at Fort Leavenworth, Kansas. 'What we hope to have in Iraq', he told a reporter,

> is guys going over there with the broad skill sets to do everything from encouraging a sheik to participate in the political process to economic development to elections, to still being able to go out and get the bad guys, but in a way that is precise and exploits intelligence, and is sensitive to the culture.[52]

Meanwhile, as in Vietnam only less visibly, the air war in Iraq has intensified over time and there is considerable speculation that any withdrawal of US troops will involve – as was also the case in Vietnam – an increased reliance on bombing. The number of air strikes per month increased fivefold over 2005,[53] although in that same period the phrase 'air war' did not appear even once in any of the major US newspapers.[54] Indeed, as Seymour Hersh wrote for *The New Yorker* in December 2005, the air war was 'perhaps the most significant – and underreported – aspect of the fight against the insurgency'.[55] During the Vietnam War, the Air Force, Navy and Marines regularly gave journalists daily tallies of the number of sorties flown, the tonnage dropped and the names of targets. Press releases on the bombing in Iraq are infrequent, most often accompanying accounts of a major battle. For example, 500,000 tons were dropped on Falluja by one Marine air unit alone during the battle for the city in November 2004. There were no estimates offered of civilian casualties. One official told Hersh there was 'no sense of an air campaign, or a strategic vision. We are just whacking targets – it's a reversion to the Stone Age'.

Most of us think about the air war in terms of those killed, precisely or otherwise, by US bombing. Paul William Roberts, a freelance reporter in Iraq in the early days of the war, wrote of the bombardment of Baghdad for the *Washington Post* this way: 'A reddish-orange fog, aftermath of a sandstorm, hangs in the air, mingling with cordite, sewage, burning oil and fear. Every few minutes, there are bomb blasts, near or far …'. His book, *The War Against Truth*, reproduced the pages from his notebook on which the *Post* dispatch was based and gave a different picture of what being bombed is like:

Even the air is red with blood, choking on sewage, cordite, burning oil and my own fear. The bombs are getting <u>closer</u> ... the people look like lost souls in <u>Purgatory</u>. SHIT ... that was too close. Why? Why? Why? (This is madness – don't believe your leaders ... there's no justification for this...) **Fuck you, George Bush, you evil sonofabitch. ... <u>This</u> is** TERRORISM. This is SO bad, such a bad thing to do. The children are crying under the red sky. This is not LIKE hell—this IS **HELL.** The baby is dead. ... <u>they killed a baby</u> [typography as in original].[56]

A final thought: in Iraq, as in Vietnam, many people are convinced that only victory gives meaning to the (American) lives lost. To stop fighting short of victory is to render meaningless the deaths and maiming suffered thus far. More deaths, more grievous wounds are required to one end only: the making meaningful of the deaths and wounding already suffered. After the war, William Ehrhart asked a Vietnamese general what he thought of the Americans as warriors. After politely praising their bravery, the general named what he saw as their military shortcomings: fixed positions, dependency on air support, and ignorance of the country. 'Would it have mattered if we had done things differently?' Ehrhart asked. No, the general replied, 'Probably not. History was not on your side. We were fighting for our homeland. What were you fighting for?' Ehrhart answered, 'Nothing that really mattered'.[57] George Swiers, returning directly from the battlefield to San Francisco in 1970, remembered how he had 'set out to speak to his Fellow Americans. To share with them his hideous secrets, to tell them what went on daily *in their names*'. For a short time, the message Swiers and other veterans like him brought home to America, aka the Vietnam syndrome, served as a prophylactic against another Vietnam. In the decades that have passed since Swiers' return home, the hideous secrets have been forgotten, or worse, transformed into memories of virtue, sacrifice and service.[58]

Americans, the late Gloria Emerson wrote, have 'always been a people who dropped the past and then could not remember where it had been put'. This time, they've put it in Iraq.[59]

Notes

1 David Shribman, 'Victory in Gulf War Exorcises the Demons of the Vietnam Years', *Wall Street Journal* (New York), March 1, 1991.

2 Dexter Filkins, 'A Region Inflamed', *New York Times*, December 7, 2003.

3 Eliot Weinberger, 'What I Heard About Iraq in 2005', *The London Review of Books*, January 5, 2006.

4 Gregg Zorohya, 'Pentagon to Families: Go Ahead, Laugh', *USA Today*, January 14, 2006.

5 See Paul Fussell, *The Great War and Modern Memory*, New York: Oxford University Press, 2000, *passim*.

6 Garry Wills, *John Wayne's America*, New York: Simon and Schuster, 1998, p. 150.

7 The picture was taken by an Associated Press photographer, Joe Rosenthal. It is common knowledge that Rosenthal photographed the second instance of flag-raising on Surabachi, the first flag having been blown up by a Japanese grenade. It was not

his favourite picture. Rosenthal had landed with the Marines and hoped to take a picture that represented what he was seeing all around him. According to Frederick Voss in *Reporting the War*, as Rosenthal darted 'from shell crater to shell crater ... he spotted the bodies of two dead marines. In that moment, he conceived the idea for a photograph intended to evoke the essence of what he was witnessing. Thus, bringing the bodies of the two fallen men into his camera's focus, he waited for an advancing marine to come within view, and when one did, he took a picture that, in his estimation at least, embodied the "honest ingredients" of what the Iwo Jima story in its early phases was all about – the dead paving the way so that the living might follow'. That picture was never published. (Frederick Voss, *Reporting the War: The Journalistic Coverage of World War II*, Washington, DC: Smithsonian Books, 1994, p. 77.)

8   On the other hand, they may recruit. Anthony Swofford reflected on the way the scene of a badly wounded soldier in the mist of the famous Valkyrie ride in *Apocalypse Now* fades away and 'later, you don't remember him. It's Kilgore who you remember, at least if you're young and impressionable, with all his manly bravado. Him and those racing helicopters. Those are the images that have kids enlisting ...'. Lawrence Weschler, 'Valkyries Over Iraq', *Harpers Magazine* (New York), November 2005, p. 74.

9   Anthony Swofford, *Jarhead*, New York: Scribner, 2003, p. 7.

10 Broyles wrote a moving account of his war in Vietnam – and his return to the country after the war, *Brothers in Arms: A Journey from War to Peace*, New York: Knopf, 1986. He also wrote a hymn to the pleasure of war, 'Why Men Love War', *Esquire Magazine*, November 1984, pp. 55–65.

11 Lawrence Weschler, 'Valkyries Over Iraq: The Trouble with War Movies', *Harpers Magazine* (New York), November 2005, pp. 71, 66. Vietnam War movies have also instructed post-Vietnam generations as to what the war was 'really' like. Jean-Marie Fisher, the daughter of a veteran who committed suicide long after the war, told an oral historian that her 'biggest interest ... is everything that has to do with the Vietnam war. I'm reading lots of war books. I watched *Full Metal Jacket* and *Platoon*. It makes me see what my Dad went through ...'. See Penny Coleman, *Flashback: Posttraumatic Stress Disorder, Suicide, and the Lessons of War*, Boston, MA: Beacon Press, 2006, p. 5.

12 Christian Parenti, 'Stretched Thin, Lied to and Mistreated', *The Nation* (New York), October 6, 2003, pp. 11–14.

13 John Burns, 'Shadow of Vietnam Falls Over Iraq River Raids', *New York Times*, November 29, 2004.

14 In fact, it's worse. A short essay I wrote for the Middle East Research and Information Project (MERIP) could be republished today without most readers suspecting it referred to the old Iraq War rather than the new one. See 'This Is Not a Pipe: This is not Vietnam', *MERIP*, July/August 1991.

15 Variously attributed to General Patton, John Wayne and Chuck Colson.

16 For more on Nagl, see Peter Maass, 'Professor Nagl's War', *New York Times Magazine*, January 11, 2004 and Marilyn B. Young, 'Imperial Language', in Lloyd Gardner and Marilyn B. Young (eds) *The New American Empire*, New York: The New Press, 2005, pp. 32–49.

17 Eliot Weinberger, 'What I heard about Iraq in 2005', *London Review of Books*, January 5, 2006.

18 Eric Schmitt, '2000 More M.P.s Will Help Train the Iraqi Police', *New York Times*, January 16, 2006.

19 Ibid.

20 Peter Maass, 'The Way of the Commandos', *New York Times Magazine*, May 1, 2005.

21 Ann Scott Tyson, 'U.S. Seeks to Escape Brutal Cycle in Iraqi City', *Washington Post*, December 26, 2005.

22 Quoted in Spencer Ackerman, 'The Rise of Shia Death Squads', *TNR Online*, December 1, 2005, available online at: www.tnr.com.

23 R. W. Apple, *New York Times*, October 31, 2001.

24 Other essays around the same time also invoked Vietnam: Frank Rich, 'Why Are We Back in Vietnam?', *New York Times*, October 26, 2003; Craig Whitney, 'Tunnel Vision: Watching Iraq, Seeing Vietnam', Ibid., November 9, 2003; Max Boot, Ibid., November 16, 2003.

25 Max Boot, 'The Lessons of a Quagmire', *New York Times*, November 16, 2003.

26 David Ignatius, 'In Iraq, They're Revisiting Vietnam-Era Counterinsurgency', *The Daily Star*, November 8, 2005, online at http://yaleGlobal.yale.edu (accessed January 17, 2006).

27 Quoted in Noam Chomsky, 'The Menace of Liberal Scholarship', *The New York Review of Books*, January 2, 1969, available online at: www.chomsky.info/articles/19690102.htm.

28 Caroline Elkins, 'Royal Screwup', *The New Republic*, December 19, 2005.

29 All quotations from Andrew F. Krepinevich, Jr, 'How to Win in Iraq', *Foreign Affairs*, September/October 2005; available online at: www.foreignaffairs.org (accessed January 16, 2006).

30 All quotations from Melvin Laird, 'Iraq: Learning the Lessons of Vietnam', *Foreign Affairs*, November/December 2005; available online at: www.foreignaffairs.org (accessed January 14, 2006).

31 Lawrence F. Kaplan, 'Why Bush's New Document on Iraq Sounds Familiar', *TNR Online*, posted December 1, 2005; available online at: www.tnr.com (accessed January 16, 2006). See also Steven Metz, 'Unlearning Counterinsurgency', for critical comments on the simplistic approach to insurgency of the US military and civilian command; available online at: www.strategicstudiesinstitute.army.mil/newsletter/opeds/2004nov (accessed January 18, 2006).

32 George W. Bush, November 30, 2005, US Naval Academy; available online at: www.whitehouse.gov (accessed January 17, 2006).

33 Richard A. Oppel, Jr, 'Magnet for Iraq Insurgents is Test for U.S. Strategy', *New York Times*, June 16, 2005, p. A-5.

34 Oliver Poole, 'Iraqis in Former Rebel Stronghold now Cheer American Soldiers', *Daily Telegraph*, December 19, 2005; available online at: www.news.telegraph.com (accessed on January 18, 2006).

35 Ferry Biedermann, 'Tel Afar's Ethnic Tug of War Puts Iraq Army to the Test', *Financial Times*, FT.com, January 17, 2006. The Council is probably referring to the use of phosphorous bombs. The US government denied charges that it used napalm in the battle of Falluja, as was widely reported at the time and insisted that phosphorous shells were 'fired into the air to illuminate enemy positions at night, not at enemy fighters'. For government claims and their retraction, see George Monbiot, 'The U.S. Used Chemical Weapons in Iraq – and Then Lied About It', *The Guardian* (London), November 15, 2005; accessed online at: guardian.com, November 30, 2005.

36 Seymour Hersh, 'Up in the Air', *The New Yorker*, December 12, 2005.

37 Bob Herbert, 'From "Gook" to "Raghead"', *International Herald Tribune*, May 3, 2005. See also the ten-part documentary 'Off to War', in which a growing hatred for Iraq and Iraqis can be tracked over the 18 months the unit of the Arkansas National Guard unit remained in Iraq.

38 Glenn Garvin, 'Cronkite Urges News Anchors to Push Withdrawal', *Miami Herald*, January 16, 2006; available online at: www.miamiherald.com (accessed January 16, 2006).

39 The issue of troop morale is, as one might imagine, the subject of heated debate. See, for example, 'US Military "at Breaking Point"', BBCnews.com, January 1, 2006; and Dennis Ryan, 'Secretary Rumsfeld: "The Force is not Broken"', DCMilitary.com, January 27, 2006 (my thanks to Lloyd Gardner for the Ryan reference).

40 Howard Kurtz and Shailagh Murray, 'Web Site Questions Rep. Murtha's Vietnam War Medals', *Washington Post*, January 14, 2006. See also James Webb's angry op-ed piece 'Purple Heartbreakers' in the *New York Times*, January 18, 2006.

41 Dexter Filkins, 'The Fall of the Warrior King', *New York Times Magazine*, October 23, 2005. See also, 'Sassaman's Saga: the Fall of the Warrior King', October 27, 2005, www.gnn.com. Sassaman appeared in the documentary 'Battleground', directed by Stephen Marshall, and is the subject of a chapter cut from Anthony Lappe and Stephen Marshall's book, *True Lies*, New York: Plume, 2004. The chapter is reprinted on this GNN (Guerrilla News Network) website.

42 Ibid.

43 Filkins first reported on Sassaman in December 2003, see 'A Region Inflamed', *New York Times*, December 7, 2003.

44 The rest of the quotations are from Filkins' *New York Times Magazine* article unless otherwise stated.

45 Filkins, op. cit., December 7, 2003.

46 See also Paul Reynolds, 'White Phosphorus: Weapon on the Edge', November 16, 2005, www.bbcnews.com (accessed January 20, 2006).

47 There was a division of opinion on the efficacy of lethal as opposed to non-lethal force. Sassaman depicted Rudesheim as a 'desk man who didn't understand the needs of his men ...' and increasingly, according to Filkins, Sassaman ignored Rudesheim's orders. Major General Raymond Odierno, commander of the 4th Infantry division, on the other hand, had fewer compunctions. According to one of his deputies, 'Ray [Odierno] is saying, "Kill, kill, kill," And Rudesheim is telling us to slow down. It drove Nate [Sassaman] crazy'. At the checkpoint to Abu Hishma, Capt. Todd Brown told a reporter how important it was to understand the 'Arab mind. The only thing they understand is force – force, pride and saving face'. Filkins, op. cit. p. 66.

48 Not everyone laughed. Specialist Ralph Logan protested this and other harsh and humiliating tactics. And some of the men had a remarkably clear-eyed view of why the US was in Iraq. Sgt Robert Hollis, for example, told Marshall and Lappe that the war was about 'globalization. It's about expansion of markets. We have to stabilize new and emerging markets in order to secure resources. ... when America says liberation. We mean capitalism. Can you tell mothers and brothers and sisters that your sons and daughters are dying for capital goods? No, you cannot. You have to make sure you tell them you are fighting for a noble cause. No mother wants her son to die making the world safe for Big Macs' (see 'Sassaman's Saga', op. cit.). Filkins, op. cit.

49 Filkins, op. cit.

50 'When the Vietnam War ended, the Army tried to pretend it never happened', a retired Special Forces officer told Filkins. But see Andrew J. Bacevich, who argues that the turn away from counterinsurgency was not an oversight. Rather, for the post-Vietnam officer corps, 'the starting point for retrieving professional legitimacy lay in avoiding altogether future campaigns even remotely similar to Vietnam'. See *The New American Militarism: How Americans Are Seduced by War*, New York: Oxford University Press, 2005, p. 42.

51 Thomas E. Ricks, 'Lessons Learned in Iraq Show Up in Army Classes', *Washington Post*, January 21, 2006.

52 Ibid.

53 Ellen Knickmeyer, 'U.S. Airstrikes Take Toll on Civilians', *Washington Post*, December 24, 2005.

54 'Tomgram: Dahr Jamail on the Missing Air War in Iraq', www.tomdispatch.com, January 5, 2006 (accessed January 6, 2006).

55 Seymour Hersh, 'Up in the Air: Where is the Iraq War Headed Next?' *The New Yorker*, December 12, 2005.

56 Paul William Roberts, *The War Against Truth: An Intimate Account of the Invasion of Iraq*, Vancouver, BC: Raincoast Books, 2004, pp. 3–4.

57 Quoted in Marilyn B. Young, *The Vietnam Wars, 1945–1990*, New York: HarperCollins
    1991, pp. 327–8.
58 Ibid., p. 325.
59 Ibid., p. 319.

3

UNRAVELING THE DOMESTIC FOREIGN POLICY CONSENSUS

Presidential rhetoric, American public opinion, and the wars in Vietnam and Iraq

Richard A. Melanson[1]

The Vietnam War traumatized much of America, greatly weakened the Cold War domestic consensus, and left a legacy that largely discouraged presidents from Gerald Ford to Bill Clinton from undertaking major ground combat. Whereas George Bush did employ a US-led coalition to forcibly eject Saddam Hussein from Kuwait in 1991, Operation Desert Storm's goal was strictly limited to restoring Kuwaiti sovereignty in the aftermath of a classic act of aggression. The Iraq War that was initiated in 2003 (Operation Iraqi Freedom) has divided the American public more deeply than any conflict since Vietnam, significantly eroded the domestic consensus that arose in the wake of 9/11, and threatens to leave a legacy that will deter future presidents from seeking to forcibly impose regime change on other nations.

This chapter has three aims: (1) to articulate the axioms of the Cold War consensus and its post-9/11 counterpart; (2) to show how the wars in Vietnam and Iraq significantly weakened each consensus; and (3) to indicate the ways in which presidents attempted to win back public support for these conflicts after it had begun to erode.

The axioms of the Cold War and 9/11

The slippery yet important concept of domestic consensus contains three components—policy, procedural, and cultural. In the US context *policy* consensus involves substantial public and elite agreement about the grand strategic design of American foreign policy; *procedural* consensus refers to presidential–congressional understandings about the respective tasks to be performed by these branches of government; while *cultural* consensus entails broad, grassroots agreement about an appropriate set of public and private values linked to America's international role.[2] Until gravely weakened by the Vietnam War, for about 20 years commencing shortly after World War II, American foreign policy was characterized by a relatively stable policy, cultural, and procedural domestic consensus.

Seven axioms characterized the Cold War *policy* consensus:

1 The United States alone had both the material power and moral responsibility to create a just and stable international order.
2 Because of the interdependent nature of the world, US security interests were global and indivisible.
3 Soviet and Soviet-inspired aggression and subversion constituted the primary threat to world peace.
4 The strategy of containment represented the best way to halt further Soviet and Soviet-inspired aggression.
5 The United States must possess a substantial nuclear arsenal to help deter Soviet or Soviet proxy attacks on America and its allies.
6 A stable, open world economy required American leadership.
7 The survival of international organizations like the United Nations and alliances such as NATO necessitated the leadership of the United States.

Central to the *procedural* Cold War consensus was a series of votes in Congress from 1945 to 1964 highly supportive of major presidential initiatives. American membership in the United Nations, NATO, the OAS, ANZUS and SEATO, aid to Greece and Turkey, the Marshall Plan, ratification of the Japan Peace Treaty, the Korea Defense Pact, the Formosa (Taiwan) Security Pact, the Nuclear Test Ban Treaty, and regional resolutions covering the Middle East, Berlin, Cuba, and Indochina all received at least 70 percent of congressional votes with several, including the Gulf of Tonkin resolution, claiming virtually unanimous approval. Occasionally this procedural consensus wavered, as for example when Truman decided against seeking a declaration of war against North Korea, but, on balance, the consensus held. It especially flourished during the Eisenhower administration with the help of congressional joint resolutions whereby the president sought to win public and congressional support for proposed actions in order to deter the Soviets and their allies from doubting the seriousness of US commitments. In short the procedural consensus rested on the widely shared conviction that the president was the ultimate authority in making foreign policy and in deciding if threats required the use of force.

The Cold War *cultural* consensus was grounded in the notion of an 'American way of life' celebrating the 'nuclear' (the term was used without irony) family of male breadwinner, full-time housewife, and a home packed with such consumer conveniences as TV dinners and frost-free refrigerators. While some leftist social critics ridiculed the alleged stifling conformity and intolerance of a 'nation of sheep', vulnerable to McCarthyite excesses, Cold War Americans tolerated a peacetime draft and a defense burden representing 9 percent of the gross national product and almost half of the federal budget. There appeared to be a symbiotic relationship between this consensus and those broadly shared axioms about US foreign policy. A genuine ethic of sacrifice seemed to suffuse American society and led the normally circumspect George Kennan to ask his fellow citizens to be grateful to a Providence which, by 'providing this ...implacable [Soviet] challenge, has made their entire security as a nation dependent on their pulling themselves together and accepting the responsibilities of moral and political leadership that history plainly intended them to bear'.[3]

The domestic divisiveness spawned by the Vietnam War deeply eroded, but did not completely destroy, the Cold War consensus. A substantial majority of the American people continued to believe that containing communism remained an important foreign policy goal, but the public grew notably more skeptical after Vietnam about the desirability of using military force and economic assistance to stop Soviet and Soviet-backed expansionism. Foreign policy no longer dominated public opinion polls and would not do so again until after the 9/11 attacks. Moreover, the *structure* of public opinion changed. The 'followership' model of the Cold War which featured a layer of political leadership (sometimes referred to as the 'foreign policy establishment') that largely agreed on the ends and means of US foreign policy, an 'attentive public' that followed this leadership, and a mostly inert 'mass public' generally uninterested and uninvolved in international affairs, but nevertheless hostile to communism, was destroyed by the Vietnam War.[4] In its place arose a more complex and ideological structure of opinion. Four distinct attitude clusters about foreign policy emerged among both the political elites and the broader public. *Isolationism* remained one outlook and found considerably more support with the mass public than the elites. For example, in the quadrennial polls of the Chicago Council on Foreign Relations (CCFR) done between 1974 and 1986, isolationism attracted about one-quarter of the mass public but only between 2 and 7 percent of the opinion leaders.[5]

But internationalists had divided according to their attitudes about communism, the use of force abroad, and relations with the Soviet Union. There were now two identifiable groups of internationalists: *hardliners* and *accommodationists*.[6] The first group, believing that the Cold War still raged, supported the continued containment of the Soviet Union, overt and covert aid to anti-leftists in the Third World, and a well-funded defense establishment. It saw considerable validity in the domino theory, believed the Soviet Union to be expansionist, and was convinced that the United States must be willing and able to employ its military power unilaterally in pursuit of its interests. Not surprisingly, this group portrayed the international system in East–West terms: totalitarianism versus democracy, communism versus capitalism, repression versus freedom.

Accommodationists argued that for a variety of reasons—the Sino–Soviet split, the Vietnam quagmire, the diffusion of global military and economic power, Third World nationalism, the emergence of complex, transnational interdependence—the world of the 1970s had fundamentally changed from that of the 1940s and 1950s. They rejected the domino theory as a dangerous, self-fulfilling prophecy, viewed the Soviet Union as primarily defensive in its goals, and were deeply skeptical about the utility (and morality) of US military force in peripheral areas. They viewed the international system more as a global unity beset by common problems, and in need of multilateral solutions, than as the arena of zero-sum superpower competition. Thus the arms race, natural resource depletion, environmental degradation, and international economic inequality were perceived as the most pressing problems. For them the Cold War was all but over. Yet both hardliners and accommodationists bestowed on the United States primary responsibility for implementing their respective agendas and both approached foreign policy in highly moralistic ways. Those who held the fourth foreign policy outlook—the *traditional internationalists*—supported active American involvement in world affairs and favored that combination of militant and cooperative, unilateral and multilateral approaches reminiscent of the pre-Vietnam internationalist paradigm.[7]

In the CCFR surveys from 1974 to 1986 the mass public divided quite evenly and consistently into each of these four attitude clusters. In contrast, almost all of the opinion leaders were internationalists of one stripe or another, though relatively few held hardliner outlooks (5 to 13 percent). For example, in 1974 about 54 percent had accommodationist attitudes, while just under 40 percent evinced traditional internationalist beliefs. In the ensuing surveys the proportions gradually reversed so that by 1986 traditional internationalists accounted for almost 60 percent of the elites, whereas the accommodationists had fallen to about one-quarter.[8]

To win elite support for their foreign policies post-Vietnam presidents were obliged to construct coalitions comprising at least two of the three internationalist groupings. Although a traditionalist–accommodationist coalition was in theory the most readily available alliance, the rising visibility and influence of hardliners among opinion leaders in the late 1970s and early 1980s made it difficult for presidents to ignore this group. Indeed, the backbone of Ronald Reagan's support came from it, as would that of George W. Bush 20 years later. Furthermore, the much higher proportions of hardliners and isolationists among the mass public meant that post-Vietnam presidents, in fact, risked the loss of broader support if they overlooked these constituencies. The end of the Cold War, on the other hand, increased the number of accommodationists at the expense of the hardliners until the attacks of 9/11.

The Vietnam War also did much to alter significantly the Cold War procedural consensus. Important structural changes in Congress made it much more difficult for presidents to strike and enforce deals by working with a handful of senior legislative leaders. Stripped of many of their old privileges and prerogatives by the reform movement of the early 1970s, these leaders found it more difficult to deliver votes on presidential foreign policy initiatives. Moreover, the proliferation of committees and subcommittees dealing with various aspects of foreign policy vastly increased the number of legislators whose support needed to be curried.[9] Congress as a body, largely because of Vietnam and Watergate, no longer automatically trusted presidents and their advisors to provide accurate information, one major result being a dramatic increase in the size of Capitol Hill staffs. Far from simply providing foreign policy information to legislators, who in earlier days had been wholly dependent on executive sources, these staffers frequently functioned as powerful advocates of positions opposed by the White House. The preferred Cold War era device of the joint congressional resolution was replaced by an extended, yet fitful, series of efforts by Congress to limit the foreign affairs prerogatives of the president. Beginning with senatorial attempts in the early 1970s to restrict Nixon's ability to wage war in Southeast Asia, they soon came to involve both houses of Congress in issues that included arms control, human rights, arms sales, covert operations, and the deployment of US armed forces abroad. In short, the procedural consensus of the early post-war decades largely evaporated and in its place emerged a protracted, inconclusive struggle between presidents who resented this so-called legislative micromanagement, and a Congress that had grown deeply suspicious of alleged presidential attempts to subvert the Constitution. The results often bordered on chaos.

Finally, the stable, white, middle-class, nuclear family composed of working father and housewife mother and cemented by such values as patriotism, anti-communism, and civic-mindedness provided the Cold War consensus with cultural stability, if only as a unifying myth. No doubt this model remained compelling for millions of Americans in the post-Vietnam era. But it should be obvious that the old cultural consensus was deeply shaken by successive challenges to its domination. Racial conflict, the civil rights movement, and the youthful counterculture of the 1960s; the sexual revolution and women's movement; large-scale immigration from Asia, Central America, and the Caribbean; the emergence of a drug culture; growing public fears of violent crime; and the aging of the American population constituted but a few of the phenomena that in many ways transformed Cold War America. At the very least they muddied the notion of a single, preferred American 'way-of-life' by forging alternative lifestyles and emergent, competing social structures. On balance, these social changes probably made foreign policy issues less dominant and increased the importance of newer concerns like child day care, the homeless, crime, education, and the environment. The end of military conscription, which had been widely accepted by Americans in the 1950s and early 1960s as a necessary sacrifice in the struggle against communism, had the effect of further distancing foreign policy concerns for most Americans, and neither presidents nor Congress showed any interest in reinstating it even after 9/11.

The horrific events of September 11, 2001 unleashed a series of strategic and tactical responses by the United States government that for a short time reconstructed a foreign policy consensus not unlike that of the Cold War. Its policy component rested on five axioms:

1 The United States was uniquely qualified to use its overwhelming military power and its moral stature to create a stable international order.
2 In light of the interdependent nature of the world, US security interests must necessarily be global.
3 Terrorism with a global reach constituted the primary threat to American security.

4 An offensive strategy designed to eradicate Al Qaeda and its allies was the best way to achieve homeland safety.

5 The United States would rely on international institutions like the United Nations in the global war on terrorism only if they supported America's foreign policy goals.

After decades of challenging presidents on a host of foreign policy initiatives from Central America to Somalia and the Balkans, Congress reacted to 9/11 by deferring to executive authority to a degree not seen since the mid-1960s. The creation of the Department of Homeland Security and the rapid congressional passage of the USA Patriot Act, suggested that both the executive and legislative branches considered September 11 a watershed event worthy of dramatic responses. International economic issues, which had been a focus of the post-Cold War era, largely were again relegated to 'low policy' as a new 'national security state' re-emerged to fight Al Qaeda on several continents. For example, defense spending soared from $332 billion in fiscal year 2002 to almost $436 billion in fiscal year 2004 after remaining nearly constant during the 1990s, while outlays for homeland security almost doubled during the first three George W. Bush years. According to one observer, 'In fundamental ways that have gone largely unrecognized, Congress has become less vigilant, less proud and protective of its turf, and less important to the conduct of American government than at any time in decades'.[10]

In the wake of the September 11 attacks Attorney General John Ashcroft offered an ambitious proposal to give law enforcement personnel additional tools to uncover and dismantle domestic terrorist operations. The USA Patriot Act, as it was dubbed, passed the Senate 98-1 and the House 357-66. What little opposition emerged in the House came from civil libertarians on the right and the left who worried about privacy issues.

In addition, President Bush issued executive orders in January 2002 that defined captured Al Qaeda and Taliban fighters as 'enemy combatants' rather than prisoners of war. Bush argued that Al Qaeda was not a party to the Third Geneva Convention and could not enjoy its benefits. The state of Afghanistan had signed this Convention, but the administration contended that the Taliban did not qualify for prisoner of war status because they did not wear distinctive uniforms recognizable from a distance; they did not carry their arms openly; and they failed to conduct their operations in accordance with the laws and customs of war. Consequently the Defense Department incarcerated these 'enemy combatants' at Guantanamo Bay, Cuba and other locations for an unspecified time period. While civil libertarians in the US and Britain complained about these decisions, the administration contended that these detainees would be treated in accordance with the Geneva Convention 'to the extent practicable and consistent with military necessity'.[11] More than 9,000 detainees were being held overseas with no legal rights, no access to lawyers, and, in some cases, subject to physical and psychological abuse. Unknown numbers were subjected to 'renditions', whereby suspects were secretly flown to third country prisons for various forms of interrogation. Yet it was not until after the situation in Iraq began to deteriorate in mid-2003 that domestic critics began to protest these tactics or to question certain provisions of the Patriot Act.

Shortly after September 11 Bush also created the White House Office for Homeland Security and named Tom Ridge, the Republican governor of Pennsylvania as its director. But many in Congress believed that the office deserved Cabinet status in order to give Ridge the power necessary to prevent future attacks. For months the administration resisted, but in June 2002 Bush pre-empted Congress and announced the creation of the Department of Homeland Security and nominated Ridge to be its secretary. The result was a 180,000-employee department with a $29.4 billion budget for fiscal year 2004. Moreover, this mammoth organization melded twenty-two agencies and offices of wildly differing histories, cultures, and responsibilities. Ridge's charge was daunting—to secure American borders, skies, and ports—and the public appeared ready to hold Ridge accountable for any lapses or failures. The federal government had once again been transformed into a 'national security state' that was perhaps even more intrusive in its domestic reach than its Cold War counterpart.

Americans were justifiably frightened by the Al Qaeda attacks on the World Trade Center and the Pentagon, and this fear was briefly transformed into a cultural consensus that included such elements as hostility toward Islamic fundamentalism, a reverence toward the American military, and an apparent willingness to make genuine sacrifices to help win the global war on terrorism. In response, President Bush offered a mixed message. While emphasizing the vulnerability of the homeland to further assaults—and advertising it with a highly visible color-coded alert system—he simultaneously urged Americans to get on with their lives and ignore the threat posed by Al Qaeda.

Polls conducted on September 10, 2001 indicated that thirty-nine percent of the public considered economic issues to be the most salient ones facing the nation, while *one* percent believed that terrorism was the most important. These results mirrored those of surveys taken over the preceding decade. Two days later, 64 percent were convinced that terrorism posed the greatest threat to America, while only 20 percent saw economic problems as paramount. President George W. Bush declared a war on terrorism with a global reach and on October 7 announced the commencement of air strikes against the Taliban regime in Afghanistan which for several years had harbored Osama bin Laden and other Al Qaeda officials. Many commentators declared that these events marked the end of the post-Cold War era in American foreign policy and the start of a twilight struggle against radical Muslims determined to destroy this nation and those who shared its liberal democratic values.

Yet by the spring of 2004, 36 percent of likely voters considered the economy and jobs to be the single most important issue, and 17 percent believed it was terrorism. While these results certainly did not mark a full return to the survey results of the post-Cold War era, they did signify an important shift away from opinions expressed in the immediate aftermath of the September 11 attacks. According to an ABC*Washington Post* poll conducted in February 2002 the public had become evenly divided about whether the economy or terrorism constituted the primary national problem. On the other hand, were the United States to suffer another devastating blow to the homeland, elite and mass opinion would doubtless change again. In short, it remains unclear whether the events of September 11 will prove to be as historically enduring as Pearl Harbor or the Vietnam War.

Indeed, after a short period in which the public appeared willing to follow the president in a manner reminiscent of the Cold War, its partial disillusionment in the aftermath of the invasion of Iraq seemed to reopen the post-Vietnam fissures among internationalists. Republican supporters of the president held 'hard line' views of the world, while most Democrats and a growing number of independents, tended to embrace the tenets of 'accommodationist' internationalists.

Why, by the early autumn of 2005, had a majority of the American people turned against the war in Iraq? In assembling a broad coalition of sympathetic states to wage Operation Enduring Freedom, George W. Bush appeared to follow in the footsteps of his father during Operation Desert Shield/Storm. Particularly in Europe where sentiment for America after September 11 was palpable and widespread, but also among leaders in states as diverse as the Philippines and Russia, the administration received an outpouring of support that mirrored its popularity at home. It eventually accepted offers of troops from almost 20 countries. President Bush's public approval ratings that had hovered around 50 percent before the attacks soared to 90 percent in their aftermath mirroring the support enjoyed by the elder Bush immediately after the first Persian Gulf War. A steady erosion occurred during 2002, however, as the electorate grew concerned about a persisting economic recession, and by year's end had returned to levels only slightly higher than those before 9/11. Nevertheless, it still strongly backed his handling of the global war on terror until the summer of 2004.

On the other hand, international support for the administration's foreign policy began to plummet in the wake of the president's 'axis of evil' State of the Union Address of January 29, 2002, for until then it had led friendly nations to believe that Washington's sole priority was in defeating Al Qaeda and preventing future attacks. Yet in his speech Bush averred that the United States must:

> prevent regimes that sponsor terror from threatening America or our friends and allies with weapons of mass destruction. Some of these regimes have been pretty quiet since September 11. But we know their true nature. North Korea is a regime arming with missiles and weapons of mass destruction, while starving its citizens. … Iran aggressively pursues these weapons and exports terror, while an unelected few repress the Iranian people's hope for freedom. … Iraq continues to flaunt its hostility toward America and to support terror. The Iraqi regime has plotted to develop anthrax, and nerve gas, and nuclear weapons for over a decade. This is a regime that has already used poison gas to murder thousands of its own citizens ….[12]
>
> States like these, and their terrorist allies, constitute an axis of evil, arming to threaten the peace of the world … . They could attack our allies or attempt

to blackmail the United States … . We'll be deliberate, yet time is not on our side. I will not wait on events, while dangers gather. I will not stand by, as peril draws closer and closer. The United States of America will not permit the world's most dangerous regimes to threaten us with the world's most destructive weapons.[13]

Bush's assertion that Iraq, Iran, and North Korea constituted a triple threat to America, much like the 'Axis' powers of World War II, had struck some observers, especially in Europe, as hyperbole, made worse by Bush's injection of 'evil' to describe this motley trio. They had long been concerned about Bush's routine injection of religious discourse into his speeches on foreign policy, especially in those instances when he spoke of American freedom as 'God's gift'. He had, of course, skillfully blended the rhetoric of FDR with that of Reagan to create his hydra-headed monster, and the metaphor proved somewhat less controversial domestically. In fact, its rhetorical excesses aside, the president had essentially renamed the threats that the Clinton administration had dubbed 'rogue' and 'outlaw' states. Nevertheless, Bush's penchant for describing a Manichaean world of good and evil struck some observers as an unwelcome return to language of the Cold War. Even more controversial, however, was Bush's assertion that the United States reserved the right to launch preventive attacks upon looming threats before they had become 'clear and present dangers'. In response, several states, including Pakistan and India, claimed the same right and threatened to initiate nuclear strikes if they felt less than fully secure. International legal scholars scurried to find precedents for such a doctrine, and predictably, failed to reach a consensus. Yet, in another sense, George W. Bush had only stated the obvious: the United States would never again wait to be attacked. The real issue was whether or not the states constituting the 'axis of evil' posed threats that required preventive action.

Shortly after the 'axis of evil' speech, National Security Advisor Condoleezza Rice and Secretary of State Colin Powell (though the latter harbored deep, private reservations about a preventive attack on Iraq) began to appear regularly on the Sunday TV talk shows. Rice, for example, contended that 'the world will be much safer when the Iraqi people have a regime that they deserve, instead of the regime that they have. It is hard to imagine Saddam Hussein ever doing the kinds of things that he needs to do to make others feel secure around him'.[14] In other words, even a new round of UN inspections, which had been halted in 1998, would prove fruitless. Though Powell continued to quietly support the continued containment of Iraq, Vice President Dick Cheney, especially, argued that new inspections would prove to be a colossal waste of time that would enable Saddam to build even more weapons of mass destruction. And despite a notable lack of evidence, the Vice President and the former Director of Central Intelligence (DCI) James Woolsey, repeatedly attempted to link Al Qaeda to Saddam Hussein. On the other hand, the then current DCI, George Tenet, warned Congress that an invasion of Iraq would spur more terrorism by transforming Saddam Hussein into a martyr and even tempting him to transfer some of his WMD to Al Qaeda. Nevertheless, sometime during the spring of 2002 Bush reached the conclusion that war was inevitable.

On October 7, 2002 in a speech in Cincinnati, he presented his arguments to the American people. First, 'by its past and present actions, by its technological capabilities, by the merciless nature of its regime, Iraq is unique'. Second, the danger of the threat 'is already significant, and it only grows worse with time'. Third,

> we know that the regime has produced thousands of tons of chemical agents ... ballistic missiles with a likely range of hundreds of miles ... [and] has a growing fleet of manned and unmanned aerial vehicles that could be used to disperse chemical or biological weapons across broad areas.

Fourth,

> over the years Iraq has provided safe haven to terrorists like Abu Nidal ... and Abu Abbas. We know that Iraq and Al Qaeda share a common enemy— the United States of America. We know that Iraq and Al Qaeda have had high-level contacts that go back a decade. Some Al Qaeda leaders who fled Afghanistan went to Iraq.

Fifth,

> the evidence indicates that Iraq is reconstituting its nuclear weapons program....Iraq has attempted to purchase high-strength aluminum tubes and other equipment needed for gas centrifuges, which are used to enrich uranium for nuclear weapons.... [I]t could have a nuclear weapon in less than a year.

Sixth, Bush asserted, having experienced the horrors of September 11, 'America must not ignore the threat gathering against us. Facing clear evidence of peril we cannot wait for the final proof—the smoking gun—that could come from a mushroom cloud'. Finally, Bush repeated a challenge he gave to the United Nations a few weeks earlier,

> Failure to act would embolden other tyrants, allow terrorists access to new weapons and new resources, and make blackmail a permanent feature of world events. The United Nations would betray the purpose of its founding, and prove irrelevant to the problems of our time.[15]

Interestingly, Bush concluded his remarks by likening America's alleged current vulnerability to that of 1962 after the Soviets placed missiles in Cuba and approvingly quoted President Kennedy's contention that 'neither the United States of America, nor the world community of nations can tolerate deliberate deception and offensive threats on the part of any nation, large or small'. In essence, President Bush had cleverly conflated the presumed threat from Saddam Hussein with Al Qaeda's attacks of September 11 and the Cuban Missile Crisis.

n March 19, 2003 President Bush addressed the nation to announce the ......nencement of combat operations against Iraq. Citing 35 nations who were providing 'crucial support' for what would be called Operation Iraqi Freedom (or OIF) the president explained that his goal was 'to disarm Iraq, to free its people and to defend the world from grave danger'. He assured the American people that 'we come to Iraq to respect its citizens, for their great civilization and for the religious faiths they practice. We have no ambition in Iraq, except to remove a threat and restore control of that country to its own people'.[16] In the wake of this speech domestic public support for war jumped from 59 percent on March 11 to 71 percent. Its approval of Bush's handling of the Iraq situation rose from 55 percent to 64 percent during the same time period.[17] Both of these levels held steady throughout the spring. We need not recount the details of the ensuing war except to note that it proceeded swiftly and extraordinarily well.

On May 1, 2003, in one of Karl Rove's most dramatic stagings, the president landed in a fighter jet garbed in a flight suit on the deck of the USS Abraham Lincoln at sea off the coast of San Diego to announce the end of combat operations in Iraq. Against the backdrop of huge banners that proclaimed 'Mission Accomplished,' Bush celebrated the heroism demonstrated by 'coalition' forces (though it had, in fact, been almost exclusively an Anglo-American enterprise) and contended that

> the liberation of Iraq is a crucial advance in the campaign against terror. We've removed an ally of Al Qaeda .... And this much is certain: No terrorist network will gain weapons of mass destruction from the Iraqi regime, because the regime is no more.

He assured the nation that 'our commitment to liberty is America's tradition— declared at founding; affirmed in Franklin Roosevelt's Four Freedoms, asserted in the Truman Doctrine and in Ronald Reagan's challenge to an evil empire'.[18]

The erosion of the 9/11 consensus

In retrospect, this dramatic appearance as the 'Top Gun' president probably signified the high-water mark of Bush's Iraq policy, though that cannot yet be stated with certainty. The post-combat or 'Phase Four' part of Operation Iraqi Freedom was fraught with problems from the beginning. Despite massive efforts, inspectors failed to find any weapons of mass destruction. Why, then, had Saddam boasted of possessing WMD, threatening to use them if invaded? It appears that he had done so in order to bolster his domestic standing, and perhaps deter Iran, by seeming to be tough, and, ironically, administration officials fell for the ruse. Bush continued to counsel patience, citing that Iraq was a large country and that weapons would be found, but it gradually became evident that US pre-war intelligence had been grossly flawed as none were uncovered. It had been so, in part, because senior officials in the Defense Department chose to rely on information fed to them by Iraqi exiles, especially the Pentagon's favorite, Ahmad Chalabi, and, in part, because of dubious intelligence from the CIA. Hence, the administration's main public rationale for launching a preventive war against Iraq had been destroyed. Yet, interestingly, until 'post-combat' conditions in Iraq seriously deteriorated during 2004, much of the public proved willing to forgive Bush for what proved to be false claims, perhaps because the administration had shifted the rationale for the war, by now emphasizing Saddam Hussein's massive human rights violations and the historic opportunity to build a democratic Iraqi state.

Moreover, remarkably little planning had been done about rebuilding Iraq after the war. While a small group at the State Department had tried to wrestle with this admittedly complex task through the Future of Iraq Project, Bush had given the Defense Department the task to oversee post-war planning, and it chose to ignore State's work. Indeed, General Jay Garner, US Army, retired, who would briefly lead early reconstruction efforts, asserted that he was told by Secretary of Defense Donald Rumsfeld to ignore the Future of Iraq Project.[19] Instead, the Defense Department concentrated on preparing for two contingencies, a humanitarian crisis reminiscent of Kosovo, and Saddam's burning of oil wells, which he had done in Kuwait in 1991. Yet, neither of these things occurred. Rather, widespread looting of hospitals, museums, libraries, and other public places broke out in cities across Iraq, and US forces proved incapable of controlling it for weeks, because they had been stretched very thin. That, in turn, had occurred because Rumsfeld and Deputy Secretary of Defense Paul Wolfowitz had rejected Army Chief of Staff Eric Shinseki's strong recommendation that as many as 400,000 troops would be needed to pacify Iraq. Rumsfeld had originally favored deploying as few as 75,000 forces in order to demonstrate that light, mobile 'transformed' units were superior to the traditional, heavier ones that the Army had used for decades, but eventually agreed on a figure of about 175,000.[20] The result had been a rapid military victory followed by a prolonged period in which basic services such as electricity could not be restored, and secure conditions could not be achieved. By the summer of 2003 an insurgency apparently composed of Saddam supporters, Sunni dissidents, Iraqi nationalists, Shiite 'extremists', and foreign fighters erupted and by late 2005 had claimed more than 2,000 American and about 30,000 Iraqi lives. On July 16 the head of the Central Command (CENTCOM), General John Abazaid, acknowledged that the coalition now faced 'a guerrilla-type campaign'.[21] Even the capture of Saddam Hussein in December 2003 failed to quell these deadly attacks that frequently featured horrific suicide bombings. The administration tried, at first, to downplay the severity of the insurgency, but as more and more lives were lost, including the chief UN administrator, Sergio Vieira de Mello, two members of the Governing Council (or Coalition Provisional Authority) and more than 100 Iraqi political and religious leaders, the seriousness of the situation became increasingly obvious. Moreover, saboteurs were successful in repeatedly attacking Iraqi oil pipelines, so that exports frequently ran at only about 20 percent capacity.

Wolfowitz and other Defense Department officials had predicted before the war that American forces would be welcomed by cheering Iraqis as liberators. These predictions were not entirely unjustified, especially in the Kurdish north and to a lesser degree in the Shiite south. Moreover, American audiences were no doubt gratified to watch live television pictures of gleeful Sunnis toppling a huge statue of Saddam in Baghdad (albeit with some assistance by US Marines). L. Paul 'Gerry' Bremer III, a foreign service officer named by Bush to replace Jay Garner as the reconstruction czar, faced enormous challenges, and soon requested additional funding. In September 2003, President Bush submitted to Congress a supplemental budget request for $51 billion to support ongoing military operations in Iraq as well as $20 billion more to rebuild the Iraqi economy. In July the United States and Britain had installed a 'Coalition Provisional Authority (CPA)', composed of a broad array of indigenous notables, which proved of dubious legitimacy and questionable competency in the view of many Iraqis. As the months passed and as the insurgency intensified, anti-American sentiment became palpable, and the 'liberators' were increasingly seen as 'occupiers'. Even worse, in the spring of 2004 the *Washington Post* began showing lurid photos of naked Iraqis being tortured by American guards at Abu Ghraib prison in Baghdad. While the Pentagon had apparently known about these incidents for several months, little had been done to correct the abuses until they were exposed by the media. Such revelations no doubt contributed to growing Iraqi suspicions about US intentions. A secret poll commissioned by the CPA in May 2004 and leaked to the press in June revealed that more than 50 percent of those surveyed believed that they would be more secure if US forces withdrew and that all Americans behaved like the prison guards at Abu Ghraib. Ninety-two percent considered coalition troops to be occupiers, and confidence in the CPA had fallen to 10 percent from 47 percent in November 2003.[22]

In view of these unanticipated events it should not be surprising that the American people gradually became more critical of the administration's Iraq policies. As late as December 2003, a Gallup poll indicated that 65 percent thought that the war had been worth fighting, while 33 percent did not. Two months later, opinion for the first time was evenly divided about whether the war should have been undertaken, probably in large part because of the testimony of CIA weapons inspector, David Kay, and Secretary Powell, that suggested the probability that no WMD had been in Iraq at the time of the invasion.[23] By June 2004 a *Washington Post*/ABC News survey showed that fewer than half of the public—47 percent believed that the war had been worthwhile. Fifty-two percent thought that it should not have been launched, and the public was sharply split about whether the security of the United States had been enhanced as a result of Operation Iraqi Freedom with 51 percent asserting that it had been strengthened.[24] By October 2005 only 30 percent approved of Bush's handling of the war and 55 percent believed that he had no plan to achieve victory. Moreover, support for the Iraq War and the global war on terror tended to erode together. Bush, after all, conflated the threats from Al Qaeda and Iraq, and the American people responded in kind. By late 2005 a majority of Americans also disapproved of the Bush administration's handling of Operation Enduring Freedom, though by smaller majorities than was the case with Operation Iraqi Freedom. In short, disillusionment about Iraq had begun to weaken the 9/11 consensus.

Efforts to remobilize public support

Faced with mounting domestic criticism and increased violence in Iraq, the Bush administration persisted for many months to simply urge Americans to 'stay the course' much as President Johnson had done in Vietnam. But, as this strategy proved less and less effective, it accelerated its timetable for conducting Iraqi elections and turning more of the fighting over to Iraqi forces. In 2005 elections were held to convene a constituent assembly charged with writing a constitution, to ratify that document, and to elect a parliament. Although voting results reflected the deep sectarian divisions of the country, Washington hailed them as proof of great progress. Of course, in 1966 and 1967 the Johnson administration had supported a series of elections in South Vietnam in order to enhance the democratic legitimacy of the Saigon government and had similarly celebrated the results. President Bush and his advisors also decided that the 'Iraqification' of the conflict was essential to allow the return of American troops. This policy, of course, mirrored President Nixon's 'Vietnamization' plan that gradually withdrew US forces from South Vietnam and slowly quelled domestic dissent.

On November 3, 1969 Nixon had tried to dismiss anti-war critics with his 'silent majority' speech praising the patriotism of those many Americans who quietly supported his policies in the face of a 'new class' of 'neo-isolationists' who would allegedly abandon historic US commitments to freedom and democracy. This speech afforded Nixon crucial time to implement his Vietnamization strategy. After offering a highly misleading history of the roots of America's intervention in Vietnam, Nixon attempted to distance himself from Johnson's conduct of the war by claiming that since becoming president he had begun to undertake a 'long overdue change in American policy'. Despite North Vietnam's intransigence in the face of a series of diplomatic initiatives, Nixon reminded his audience that more than 60,000 US combat troops would soon be withdrawn because of the enhanced fighting ability of the South Vietnamese Army. He concluded with a plea to the 'silent majority' to support his strategy of diplomacy, Vietnamization, and gradual, orderly withdrawal. If that majority showed patience, Nixon promised to 'end this war in a way that will bring us closer to that great goal to which Woodrow Wilson and every American president in our history has been dedicated—the goal of a just and lasting peace'.[25]

Public response to the 'silent majority' speech proved overwhelmingly positive, and substantial majorities in both houses of the Democratic-controlled Congress evinced support for Nixon's Vietnam policy. Perhaps emboldened by this reaction, in April 1970 the president ordered US troops to enter parts of Cambodia in order to locate the headquarters of the Viet Cong. He defended this escalation of the war by asserting that 'if when the chips are down, the world's most powerful nation … acts like a pitiful, helpless giant, the forces of totalitarianism and anarchy will threaten free nations and free institutions throughout the world'.[26] Claiming that 'it is not our power but our will that is being tested', he mentioned great decisions made by previous presidents and noted that 'in those decisions, the American people were not assailed by counsels of doubt and defeat from some of the most widely known opinion leaders of the Nation'. Rejecting the advice of those who had allegedly urged him to 'take the easy path ... blame this war on previous administrations ... and ... bring all of our men home immediately', Nixon contended that he

> would rather be a one-term president and do what I believe is right than to be a two-term president at the cost of seeing America become a second-rate power and to see this Nation accept the first defeat in its proud 190-year history.[27]

In contrast to his November speech this address was greeted with howls of protest and culminated in the tragic killing of four students at Kent State University by members of the Ohio National Guard. Nixon belatedly realized that the public would only support him if he refrained from widening the war and continued to withdraw American troops.

In October 2005 President Bush escalated his rhetoric and began to liken radical Islam to communism: 'Like the ideology of communism, our new enemy pursues totalitarian aims. Its leaders pretend to be an aggrieved party, representing the powerless against imperial enemies'. Moreover, they 'seek to end dissent in every form and to control every aspect of life and to rule the soul itself .... And Islamic radicalism, like the ideology of communism, contains inherent contradictions that doom it to failure'. And thus, 'Our commitment is clear: We will not relent until the organized international terror networks are exposed and broken and their leaders are held accountable for their acts of murder'.[28] Later that month he further elaborated this comparison by claiming that like communists, radical Islam's aim was to create a vast empire of repression, in this case one that would stretch from Iberia to Indonesia. Yet these rather incendiary words did little to move the public, and its approval of Bush's handling of the Iraq War continued to fall.

Then in November and December 2005 President Bush offered a series of addresses that did more than intone Americans to 'stay the course'. Instead, he unveiled a 'National Strategy for Victory in Iraq' that the White House posted on its webpage in conjunction with a presidential speech at the United States Naval Academy on November 30. This 35-page document purported to lay out a plan to defeat the insurgents, build a democratic Iraq, and allow for the gradual, orderly withdrawal of US forces. It was, in large measure, the work of Peter D. Feaver, a political science professor and public opinion expert, recruited from Duke University by the administration in June as a special advisor to the National Security Council for the explicit purpose of remobilizing public support for the war. For thirty years the prevailing academic orthodoxy had contended that a direct correlation existed between rising US casualties and decreasing levels of public support. Based on a 1973 study of Korea and Vietnam by John Mueller, a political scientist then at the University of Rochester, this finding had been largely accepted by presidents since Gerald Ford.[29] But Feaver and his colleague at Duke, Christopher Gelpi, challenged this contention after reviewing more recent polling data and concluded that Americans would back a conflict with increasing casualties if they believed the cause to be important and, more crucially, if they thought it would ultimately succeed.[30] In other words, a war fought for vital interests that showed good prospects for victory would attract and retain public backing.

Bush's October speeches likening the fight against radical Islam to the Cold War and prophesying a vast new totalitarian Caliphate if left unchecked certainly attempted to portray the stakes as vital to America's survival. His subsequent addresses also directly bore the imprint of Feaver's influence—indeed Feaver appears to have written large sections of the president's Annapolis speech. Against a curtained backdrop festooned with the slogan 'Plan for Victory', Bush proceeded to use the word 'victory' no less than 15 times. During the next two weeks President Bush discussed various elements of his 'victory plan' in speeches to the Council on Foreign Relations, the Philadelphia World Affairs Council, and the Woodrow Wilson International Center for Scholars. These venues were noteworthy, for in the preceding several months Bush took care to speak about Iraq exclusively before friendly military audiences, much as Johnson had been forced to do as criticism mounted over Vietnam. This rhetorical barrage culminated in a nationally televised address from the Oval Office on December 18 in which the president appeared to be uncharacteristically humble in admitting that 'much of the [prewar] intelligence turned out to be wrong' and that 'the work in Iraq has been ... more difficult than we expected'. Yet he reassured the American people that the world was safer without Saddam Hussein and that his administration had put in place a strategy to create a democratic Iraq 'that can defend itself, that will never again be a safe haven for terrorists, and that will serve as a model of freedom for the Middle East'. And 'in all three aspects of our strategy—security, democracy, and reconstruction—we have learned from our experiences and fixed what has not worked'. Disparaging 'defeatists who refuse to see that anything is right', Bush vowed that 'to retreat before victory would be an act of recklessness and dishonor and I will not allow it'.[31]

In the aftermath of these speeches and the Iraqi parliamentary elections, approval of Bush's handling of Iraq increased by ten points to 46 percent—the highest point of his second term. The belief that the United States was making significant progress in establishing a democratic government there jumped from 47 percent in November to 65 percent. And those who approved of Bush's performance on terrorism rose to 56 percent.[32] Yet John Mueller remained unimpressed, contending that he did not believe that presidential speeches or a well-publicized 'victory plan' could produce more than a fleeting improvement in public support—'As costs go up, support goes down'.[33]

Hence it remains unclear the degree to which Operation Iraqi Freedom has unraveled the 9/11 consensus. The unexpected difficulties encountered after Saddam's collapse, at the very least, have undermined much of the public's tolerance for future forcible regime changes and has put enormous burdens on the US military. And although both houses of Congress were controlled by the Republicans, Bush was forced to redefine his torture policies against suspected terrorists, accept hearings into the allegedly illegal domestic wiretaps by the National Security Agency, and compromise on the extension of certain provisions of the USA Patriot Act. A secure and democratic Iraq no longer dependent for its security on US troops would doubtless restore the stability of the 9/11 consensus, yet the outbreak of a civil war in that deeply divided nation would lead to a further erosion.

Notes

1 The views expressed in this article are solely those of the author and do not represent those of the National War College, the National Defense University, or the United Sates Department of Defense.

2 The following section on the Cold War consensus draws heavily on Richard A. Melanson, *American Foreign Policy since the Vietnam War: The Search for Consensus from Richard Nixon to George W. Bush*, Armonk, New York: M. E. Sharpe, 2005, fourth edition.

3 George F. Kennan, 'The Sources of Soviet Conduct', *Foreign Affairs*, July 1947, p. 868.

4 William Schneider, 'Public Opinion', in Joseph S. Nye, Jr (ed.), *The Making of America's Soviet Policy*, New Haven, CT: Yale University Press, 1984.

5 See for example, John E. Rielly (ed.), *American Public Opinion and U.S. Foreign Policy 1987*, Chicago, IL: Chicago Council on Foreign Relations, 1987, p. 11.

6 Eugene R. Wittkopf, *Faces of Internationalism: Public Opinion and American Foreign Policy*, Durham, NC: Duke University Press, 1991, pp. 25–6.

7 It should be noted that Wittkopf identifies two dimensions of opinion—involvement versus non-involvement and cooperation versus militancy. Some commentators, including William Chittick, have suggested a third dimension is needed to capture the full range of opinion—unilateralism versus multilateralism. See, for example, William O. Chittick, Keith R. Billingsley, and Rick Travis, 'Discovering the Structure of Foreign Policy Beliefs: From Flatland to Spaceland', unpublished paper, 1994. My reading of Wittkopf's data leads to the conclusion that accommodationists tend to have multilateral inclinations, while hardliners are more comfortable with unilateral initiatives. I agree with Chittick that some portion of Wittkopf's isolationists are, in fact, unilateralists. But none of this should obscure the main point: the Vietnam War contributed to the erosion of the Cold War consensus by fragmenting internationalists into at least three identifiable attitude groups.

8 Wittkopf, ibid., p. 140.

9 See, for example, Cecil V. Crabb, Jr, and Pat M. Holt, *Invitation to Struggle: Congress, the President, and Foreign Policy*, 2nd edn, Washington, DC: Congressional Quarterly Press, 1984, p. 39.

10 Robert G. Kaiser, 'Congress-s-s-s', *Washington Post*, March 14, 2004, p. B1.

11 *New York Times*, January 29, 2002, p. A1.

12 This was a reference to Saddam's gassing of the inhabitants of a Kurdish town in 1988.

13 George W. Bush, 'The President's State of the Union Address', January 29, 2002; available online at: http://www.whitehouse.gov/news/news/releases/2002/01/20020129-11.html.

14 Quoted in Ivo H. Daalder and James M. Lindsay, *America Unbound: The Bush Revolution in Foreign Policy*, Washington, DC: Brookings Institution Press, 2003, p. 131.

15 George W. Bush, 'Denial and Deception', Cincinnati, Ohio, October 7, 2002; available online at: http://www.whitehouse.gov/news/releases/2002/10/print/20021007-8html.

16 George W. Bush, 'President Bush Addresses the Nation', March 19, 2003; available online at: http://www.whitehouse.gov/news/releases/2003/03/print/20030319-17.html.

17 ABC/*Washington Post* poll, March 18, 2003.

18 George W. Bush, 'President Bush Announces Combat Operations in Iraq Have Ended', May 1, 2003; available online at: http://whitehouse.gov/news/releases2003/05/iraq/20030501-15.html.

19 David Rieff, 'Blueprint for a Mess', *New York Times Magazine*, November 2, 2003, p. 47.

20 'Frontline' interview with James Fallows, January 28, 2004, www.pbs.org/wgbh/pages/frontline/shows/invasion/interviews/fallows.html.

21 *The New York Times*, July 17, 2003, p. A1.

22 'Poll of Iraqis Finds Stark Picture of Anti-American Sentiment', *Wall Street Journal Online*, June 17, 2004; available online at: http://online.wsj.com/article_print/0,,SB108747121603439895,00.html.

23 *Christian Science Monitor*, February 13, 2004, http://www.occupationwatch.org/article.php?id=3054.

24 *Washington Post*, June 21, 2004, p. A1.

25 Richard Nixon, 'Vietnam Address', November 3, 1969.

26 Richard Nixon, 'Address to the Nation on the Situation in Southeast Asia', April 30, 1970.

27 Ibid.

28 George W. Bush, 'Address to the National Endowment for Democracy', October 6, 2005; available online at: http://www.washingtonpost.com/wp-srv/politics/administration/bushtext_100605.html.

29 John Mueller, *War, Presidents, and Public Opinion*, New York: John Wiley, 1973.

30 *New York Times*, December 4, 2005, A1.

31 George W. Bush, 'President's Address to the Nation', December 18, 2005; available online at: http://onlinewsj.com/article_print/SB113495783455026067.html.

32 Results of an ABC/*Washington Post* poll, December 19, 2005. http://abcnewsgo.com/Politics/print?id=1421748.

33 *New York Times*, December 4, 2005, p. A1.

4

IRAQ AND VIETNAM

Military lessons and legacies

Richard Lock-Pullan[1]

Comparing the Vietnam War to the intervention in Iraq is fraught with difficulties because the wars are so different. For example, in terms of scale the US commitment in Vietnam was much greater both in troop numbers (half a million to 140,000), and deaths (58,000 to 2,300); the terrain of Iraqi desert is very different to Vietnamese delta, highlands and paddy fields; the political environment of the Cold War contrasts with the War on Terrorism; the war in Iraq was against the ruling regime rather than propping it up; and the nature of the insurgency that US forces face is disparate compared to the one faced in Vietnam. However, it is an issue worth examining because of the fear of the US entering another Vietnam 'quagmire',[2] and because the Vietnam War has been so influential in shaping how the military has prosecuted operations in Iraq.

This chapter will examine how the lessons drawn from the experience of the Vietnam War have influenced how the US military, and the Army in particular, understand war and how this has shaped what it does in Iraq, and how this creates its understanding of counter-insurgency (COIN). The concentration is on the Army because it is the lead force in the essentially ground war in Iraq, and, as Hannah Arendt notes, 'the means used to achieve political goals are more often than not of greater relevance to the future world than intended goals'.[3] Second, there are legacies that are highlighted to explain the blind-spots and limitations of the US Army's approach, even though the legacies are filtered through the changes and experiences the Army has undergone since its withdrawal from Vietnam in 1973.

The main themes of analysis will cover the lessons of the Vietnam War on how to fight wars with the need to: set clear objectives; win wars rapidly and decisively; use overwhelming force; and focus efforts on enemy forces. This has created a reliance on technology. The legacies of the importance of avoiding casualties and rejecting the roles of nation-building and civil protection, which leaves the Army ill-prepared for the non-conventional stages of war, will be shown to create difficulties that are a product of the very lessons above and a rejection of potential lessons from Vietnam that never received consensual agreement. Fundamentally the argument is that the lessons and legacies of the Vietnam War have led to a greater effectiveness by the US in prosecuting main-force conventional warfare, but this very success has undermined the ability to handle the more complex insurgency phase of the war. There is an irony here that needs to be explored as these were the very lessons that should have been learnt from the experience in Vietnam and are now coming to the surface – too late in America's war in Iraq.

Lessons

At its simplest level the 'lessons' of Vietnam are those perceptions of the war that received consensual agreement and were then enacted. To understand the lessons that the Army drew from the war one must appreciate General Westmoreland's (the MACV [Military Assistance Command Vietnam] commander in Vietnam till 1968) point when he says: 'The military quite clearly did the job that the nation asked and expected of it'.[4] Often heavily criticised from within the Army, Westmoreland actually expresses a broader consensus of Army thought on this point.[5] For the Army, the tactical success that it enjoyed in Vietnam did not lead to victory, therefore the loss of the war lay outside of the military and on a more strategic level. The painful and costly quagmire of a protracted conflict was home-grown and lost in Washington, DC, not in Vietnam.

The mainstream mindset concerning the lessons of the war and how the politicians lost it was laid out by Colonel Harry Summers in his influential book *On Strategy: A Critical Analysis of the Vietnam War*.[6] It was written for the Army under the auspices of the Army Vice-Chief of Staff as part of the Army War College's examination of the conflict. Summers saw the Vietnam War in conventional terms and made much of Clausewitz's dictum that 'war was the continuation of politics by other means' prosecuted by a trinity of 'people, army, and government', though that was an incorrect reading of Clausewitz, and actually fitted the model of the US constitution – Congress, military and the President.[7] General Meyer, the Army Chief of Staff, endorsed Summers' analysis by ordering its publication in 1981 and distributing copies to all Army general officers (whilst reformer Newt Gingrich sent copies to all members of the US Congress).[8] It provided a template for the Army's broad understanding of strategy and the Vietnam War. *On Strategy* was still on CGSC (Command and General Staff College), Army War College and the Chairman, Joint Chiefs of Staff reading lists throughout the 1990s.[9] It is still in print.

The wider influence of Summers' book, and the mindset it embodies, can be seen in the attitude of the Secretary of Defense during the Reagan years, Caspar Weinberger. He made a crucial speech in November 1984[10] outlining his 'doctrine' for the use of force by the US and, as one critic pointed out, 'Weinberger's speech may be read as almost a summary of conclusions of official military summaries of the lessons of Vietnam'.[11] His speech writers were influenced by Summers' book.[12] Weinberger outlined six criteria of which two will be examined here – in committing troops 'we should have clearly defined political and military objectives' and that 'we should do so wholeheartedly, and with the clear intention of winning'. Both of these were critiques of the practice of war in Vietnam and became intertwined as a 'mindset' concerning how to prosecute war.

Objectives

For the Army the key aspect of the failure in Vietnam was that the politicians were not sufficiently clear about what the aim or the objectives of the war there were – the objectives were never 'precisely delineated'.[13] In the view of Westmoreland's Deputy,

> In Vietnam, we, the United States, never decided firmly and collectively on operational objectives. And without operational objectives we went on and fought hundreds of successful tactical operations. We inflicted 800,000 KIA [Killed in Action] on the North Vietnamese and the Viet Cong and wounded a million, to no good end. We never achieved freedom of operational maneuver simply because we never decided which objectives we needed to take, and many of them were in North Vietnam.[14]

The lack of clear political objectives meant the Army was unable to take the initiative and to plan a coherent campaign.

The role of clear objective setting was underpinned by the Army developments in the 1980s where it had developed a concept of war that articulated three 'levels' of warfare. The national level of decision making is 'strategic', the lowest level of war is 'tactical' battles, and in-between are campaigns which joined the battles together to fulfil the strategic aims – it was named the 'operational' level. The new thinking was tested in the first Gulf War and seen to be vindicated.[15] The emphasis on clear objectives as a key battlefield condition can be seen in policy statements such as the 1995 *National Military Strategy* which reasserted the principle of 'Clear Objectives: Decisive Force'. The principle was explained as: 'In any application of force, military objectives will be clearly defined to support our national political aims in the conflict. We intend to commit sufficient force to achieve these objectives in a prompt and decisive manner'.[16]

The institutionalisation of the Army's strategic lessons from Vietnam are somewhat ironic as Weinberger's speech in 1984 was made to counter the pressure from the Secretary of State, George Shultz, for the military to take a larger role in the fight against terrorism – for example, by attacking training camps.[17] Shultz was not arguing for a return to the Limited War ideas of the Vietnam era, but looked to integrate military and diplomatic power far more closely. Shultz saw that US policy required the necessary tools for coercive diplomacy, and that the murkiness of many politico-military situations created a need to subordinate military 'effectiveness' to political objectives.[18] The aims of policy and not the means should shape policy options.

Others, such as Andrew Krepinevich, saw the Army 'lessons' as actually erecting barriers to avoid fighting another Vietnam War: 'the result has been that instead of gaining a better understanding of how to wage counterinsurgency warfare … the Army is trying, through the six tests enunciated by Secretary Weinberger, to transform it into something it can handle'.[19] Krepinevich's book, *The Army and Vietnam*, was 'the flip side of Summers' book',[20] and was highly critical of the

Army's organisational learning during the Vietnam War and its lack of doctrinal development for the unconventional war it fought there. The book stressed that the US Army fought the wrong type of war in Vietnam by ignoring counter-insurgency. Ironically, a key Army study made the same point as Krepinevich.[21] This highlights an important aspect of the learning and the conclusions that were drawn from the Vietnam War – many in the Army saw that the nation had simply fought the wrong war there.

For proponents of counter-insurgency the understanding of war by the likes of Summers removes the political aspects of war and leaves them as the politician's responsibility – the Army is left with a role of countering enemy forces. The militarised response to terrorism, announced by the President with the 'War on Terrorism', follows this pattern. The state-centric emphasis of the administration, targeting the regime and its security forces, gives the Army a clear and defined strategic role, and the administration's policy is based on the premise that the challenges were 'essentially military in character and that military power alone can deliver victory'.[22] The use of force by the US would thus be based on the concerns of the Army and these would set the criteria for their use. For example, General Tommy Franks' briefing to the President in December 2001 concerning the invasion of Iraq had a list of needs that 'put the president on notice that the military had certain expectations, that the success of any operation would be contingent on others meeting those stated conditions. At the same time it could be seen as a list of demands'.[23]

The need for clear objectives generated three imperatives to guide the planning and conduct of the Iraq campaign: to topple the regime, find and neutralise weapons of mass destruction, and prevent Saddam setting fire to the oil wells or dumping it in the Gulf, whilst keeping the casualties to a minimum.[24] Associated with these was the aspiration to deliver humanitarian aid as quickly as possible. The plan required establishing land-based control over Iraqi territory. It focused on the military target of defeating the regime – a militarised objective – rather than on what to do following that. This model of strategy struggles to work effectively once things move away from the Army's preference for conventionally fighting enemy forces. This has now left the administration with a military goal rather than a strategy in Iraq and it has not yet settled on a strategy for defeating the insurgents.[25]

Part of this problem is due to the fact that the thinking behind the prosecution of war was focused on rapidly overwhelming the enemy – the whole point of Weinberger's emphasis on being 'wholehearted'.

Overwhelming/decisive force

After the Vietnam War there was clear attention on winning wars in a decisive manner, rather than being bogged down in another Vietnam-like situation. It was a 'New American Way of War' as the US switched from a slow and ponderous build up of forces and resources, as in World War Two, to a more focused and qualitatively-based approach that looked to rapidly overcome opponents in a short time with few casualties.[26] General Colin Powell became associated with this approach as he had been a clear proponent of 'overwhelming force', whereby the sheer scale of US forces would aid victory and leave the outcome in no doubt. He was a product of the Vietnam officer generation, and had been Weinberger's influential Military Assistant and the Chairman of the Joint Chiefs of Staff during the first Gulf War.[27]

The first Gulf War saw the application of overwhelming force, as did the invasion of Panama in 1989. The first Gulf War showed that 'Establishing the battlefield conditions necessary for winning big, winning quick, and without casualties is one of the primary lessons from the war'.[28] For many, however, the heavy forces needed for this approach were extremely slow, expensive and inflexible – they were also of questionable political utility. By the time the end of the Cold War was a decade old the Army's reliance on heavy forces was in serious doubt, especially after Kosovo. As Michael Vickers puts it, 'the United States Army found itself face-to-face with irrelevance and declared it had "gotten the message" … and embarked upon on a new initiative to create lighter, more mobile forces'.[29] General Shinseki, the Army Chief of Staff, launched the Army onto the path of transformation, aiming to make the Army a deployable force capable of meeting the strategic challenges.[30] The Army began to field the new 'Stryker brigades' as part of the effort to bridge its light and heavy forces in line with the developing Army ideas.[31]

However, Donald Rumsfeld as Secretary of Defense had a different focus. He aimed for a military force that was heavy enough to defeat conventional forces, but was agile enough to defeat asymmetric threats found in most environments. It was a vision of a rapidly deployable, fully integrated joint force that was capable of reaching distant theatres quickly, striking them swiftly and with devastating effect.[32] Transformation has become a key aspect of the military debate in the US, and Rumsfeld has been criticised for his emphasis on technology rather than troops.[33]

Concerning Iraq, the extent to which either the post-Vietnam era thinking of 'conventionally overwhelming the opposition', or the 'transformed' Rumsfeld idea of concentrating on fast moving, lighter forces (especially Special Forces and high technology), shaped the intervention is, in many respects, a non-debate. The transformation envisaged had not yet begun in earnest and is five years away at least, and the lighter configurations of forces such as the 'Stryker brigades' are geared to lighter opposition than the Iraqi Republican Guard.[34] However, where it does matter is that Rumsfeld has been criticised for not providing sufficient troops to do the job asked of it.[35] In a broader perspective it is clear that the US military has focused on greater precision and qualitative strength, so the emphasis is now on developing a decisive force which overwhelms by quality rather than quantity. The conventional campaign was not simply a question of numbers swamping the opposition, but of fast tempo and scale of effort, which itself tied in with a key Vietnam era lesson.

Fight to win

Weinberger made it clear that there should be a clear intention of 'winning' when troops are committed. This may seem obvious as countries do not fight to lose, but often they actually fight for the *status quo* or to stabilise situations – armies do not just fight to win by destroying enemy forces. The lessons from Vietnam have led to a focus on 'winning' and a rejection of 'gradualism'.

There is little doubt that in conventional terms the Army's entry into the Vietnam War was ragged, as the first advisory phase was followed by an 'Americanisation' of the war and the commitment of half a million US troops from 1965; the policy 'slunk in on cat's feet'.[36] Even though 'gradualism' was a concept borrowed from nuclear doctrine – with the idea of escalating costs to the opponent to change their behaviour – the use of the Army actually was closer to crisis management than coercive diplomacy.[37] As one Army Captain, the future SACEUR (Supreme Allied Commander, Europe) General Wesley Clark, put it in 1975, 'gradualism represented an unhappy attempt to combine military art and diplomacy'.[38] For critics like Summers who saw the Vietnam War as essentially a conventional war, once troop levels had been escalated in 1965, policy should have been refocused to reflect that change.[39] Escalation of wars can 'ebb and flow',[40] but the Army looked to avoid an incremental involvement and aimed for a decisive, rapid and overwhelming start to hostilities so they could be brought to a rapid and successful end. It was a clear lesson from the 'quagmire' of Vietnam and it also matched the conventional developments the Army had undergone since 1973.[41]

The focus on winning with clear objectives and overwhelming force is seen very clearly in the prosecution of the invasion of Iraq.[42] The basic idea was to 'shock' the Iraqis into surrendering by dominating, rather than seizing, territory south of Baghdad, before establishing points for a final attack on the capital city and home of the regime. An initial air strike failed to kill Saddam Hussein but the raid showed very clearly that the war was about decapitating and removing the Hussein regime.

The ground campaign was the embodiment of post-Vietnam thinking, as it looked to create fast, multiple crises for the regime to deal with, a rolling attack generating constant overwhelming pressure along several lines of operation. The idea being to have the regime collapse as they tried to cope with the overload. There was thus stress by the US on operational fires, manoeuvre, sabotage, disarray in the inner circle and supporting the opposition. The emphasis was on tempo; the relative speed of the US over its adversaries. The original plan had been for simultaneous southern and northern invasions, but the vote in Turkey forbidding the US from using Turkish territory as a base from which to invade Iraq, eliminated the northern front as an approach for ground forces.

The operation was, unlike Vietnam, joint and multi-national, and, unlike the first Gulf War, used Special Forces extensively. The plan had V Corps swinging up along the western side of the Euphrates, whilst the Marines (1 MEF) would push through the east in the heavily populated Tigris and Euphrates valleys. The British division was to take Basra in the south. North of Baghdad the ground force role was to be taken up by Special Forces – they were given responsibility for almost two-thirds of Iraq, having to protect the western flank of the Coalition and open a second front in the north, using Kurdish support but avoiding a Turkish intervention in the region. The war was thus fought on various fronts simultaneously.

The speed of advance was impressive. In less than a week US forces made a huge advance into enemy territory, and the final advance on Baghdad came from a series of concurrent operations where the Third Infantry Division drove through the Karbala Gap and the First Marine Division crossed the Tigris at An Numaniyah.[43] On the eastern side the Marines destroyed Fedayeen resistance in the cities, whilst on the western side V Corps had a five-pronged assault. The outskirts of Baghdad were probed, and the combined air and ground attacks rendered most of the Republican Guard units defending the city very ineffective. The US used 'thunder runs' of high speed armoured sorties with air support to capture the city, taking the airport, then pushing into the centre of the city, with the Marines driving in from the east. By April 6, 2003, members of the regime were fighting their way out of the city. A mere 44 days after operations began, the President declared on May 1, 2003, 'Major combat operations are over'.[44] For the Army it was a clear victory and they planned to start pulling out of Iraq within 60 days.

It was a quick, fast, focused attack – there was no slow build up and enemy forces were targeted and destroyed. The speed of the invasion was not simply a rejection of the gradualism and coercive model from Vietnam at the strategic level of political-military planning, but was also a product of how wars should be fought at the operational (campaign) level and tactical level. The Iraq invasion showed that by having clear objectives and a clear start to hostilities it was able to implement a new way of war developed since the Vietnam War.

Force on force

The 'new' way of war, however, still stood in the tradition of focusing on the enemy armed forces, aiming to destroy them. In Vietnam, Westmoreland had been clear that his role was 'seeking, fighting, and destroying the enemy'.[45] The Army under Westmoreland, therefore, focused on bringing the North Vietnamese to battle, especially after the success in 1965 of Ia Drang.[46] But once this was not conclusive this meant, 'We will have to grind him down. In effect, we are fighting a war of attrition, and the only alternative is a war of annihilation'.[47] During the 'big-unit' period of 1965–7, the US Army developed the idea of mass sweeps, which were to be known under the blanket term 'search and destroy'. This and later developments were an attempt to regain the initiative in a conventional war, but were still reliant on 'excruciating direct military pressure'.[48]

The propensity of the American Army to fight conventionally was recognised by the North Vietnamese, so it dispersed potential Vietnamese targets.[49] Without having the initiative, the US response to the North Vietnamese strategy was to use its technological and firepower advantage: 'helicopter gunships, free fire zones, defoliants, napalm and bombing were used. This reliance on unrestrained firepower devastated large portions of the nation the United States was ostensibly trying to save'.[50] In Iraq, fast attrition against the key aspect of the regime was fundamental. However, one of the key features of Vietnam soon returned.

Legacies

Technology

The sheer technological and logistical dominance of US forces in Iraq makes it, as in Vietnam, far more sensible for the enemy not to face them conventionally but to slide back into the populace and fight from there, making the reliance on firepower and technology in conventional war become huge weaknesses in the American prosecution of the war. The approach has also, like Vietnam, made the accommodation of counter-insurgency operations by the Army far harder. In fact the destructiveness of the very invasion, which many thought would be a largely unopposed liberation, created some of the key difficulties, as in Vietnam. Basically, the 'technowar' production approach in Vietnam was inapplicable to the enemy's strategies.

The shadows of the 'technowar' thinking that were seen so clearly in the Vietnam War have returned in Iraq as the instrumental technologically-based approach to warfare becomes predominant. However, as Gibson observed of the Vietnam War, there was a deep structural logic of how it was conceptualised and fought; but it was a closed, self-referential universe.[51] The problem with this is that in war the world of values, norms and traditions is more important than simple instrumental action. As Michael Howard observes, 'Military forces are shaped not only by weapons with which they are armed, but by the social background from which they emerge and the political function for which they are intended'.[52] Technology is a means to an end, not an end in itself, and the political, social and cultural aspects of war need to be kept in balance. Many civilians and officers in the post-Vietnam reform movement recognised this and saw that people and ideas come before hardware, but this thinking has faded in influence.

Part of what has led to the re-emphasis on technology in Iraq is the success of the first Gulf War. After Vietnam the Army had focused far more on out-thinking the enemy but technology was seen as key to the success in defeating Hussein in 1991. This view was supported by the 'technoeuphoria' during the war and the image of it as 'computers at war', which reinforced an exclusively technological approach to the lessons of the war.[53] It heralded the great promise of a Revolution in Military Affairs (RMA) which focused on technological proficiency and information dominance. For example, the Pentagon currently has an Office of Defense Transformation and they have determined that 'Network Centric Warfare (NCW) is the core concept that guides the transformation of the US military. NCW is the embodiment of Information Age warfare'.[54]

The emphasis on technology missed the fact that from the mid-1970s it was *social* and technological forces that eventually brought industrialised and massed warfare of World War Two-style to an end and initiated the revolutionary process, replacing mass destruction with 'precision destruction'.[55] The innovation was thus not only in technology but in the changed understanding of warfare, with a move away from simply destroying the enemy's forces to an emphasis on manoeuvre and out-thinking the opponent, and this shift produced a new theory of victory.[56]

However, the reliance on technology is enhanced by the Vietnam legacy of casualties, where it became a public index of American failure in the war. The public aversion post-Vietnam is enhanced by the broader social trend that is reluctant to have casualties because of the increased value given to life – the 'post-heroic' age.[57] The public reluctance is reinforced by junior officers' experiences in Vietnam, who were appalled by the waste of life sanctioned by senior officers.[58] Casualty avoidance is thus vital in perpetuating domestic US support and is inherent in the post-Vietnam officer generation. One can see this clearly in Iraq where avoiding US casualties is a key 'centre of gravity' for the US forces and thus the target of insurgents' efforts.[59] Countering the threats to US troops' lives, with force protection measures and the use of heavy firepower, aids domestic support at home but undermines the very effort to win the popular support necessary in Iraq. The Army thus returns to the practice of fighting a conventional war dependent on high levels of firepower and technology, which was Krepinevich's basic criticism of the Army's prosecution of the war in Vietnam. In his terms, it creates a prevalent 'Army concept'; a 'focus on mid-intensity, or conventional, war and a reliance on high volumes of firepower to minimize [US] casualties'.[60] Firepower is crucial in winning wars but can actually aid the losing of the peace, and in Iraq the US is still prepared to generate a lot of Iraqi casualties to keep its own to a 'manageable' level; 58,000 deaths was a lot of citizens to lose in a war of choice in Asia, but the Vietnamese deaths inflicted also contributed to the loss of the war.

The avoidance of the social and political aspects of war in the Revolution in Military Affairs is part of a broader divergence between social and military values.[61] And Vietnam was the point of this crucial rift and has led to the more socially isolated understanding of warfare. As Lawrence Freedman observes, the Revolution in Military Affairs (RMA) after the first Gulf War was actually critically affected by the lifting of the limits on the prosecution of war due to the end of the Cold War, not just technological developments. The social aspects of war mean that in future wars would not just be about information dominance but 'territory, prosperity, identity, order, values – they all still matter, and provide the ultimate tests of a war's success'.[62] After the first Gulf War nowhere was this borne out more clearly than in the intervention in Somalia, which showed the key limitations of looking at military problems as simply technical issues. The Army successfully re-asserted the Weinberger doctrine,[63] and the separatist thinking of hiving off political and social concerns from the prosecution of war was still prevalent in Army doctrine as it went into Iraq and had to face the post-war insurgency.

Winning the peace

Unlike the conventional lessons drawn from the Vietnam War, the perception of the war as unconventional, and its associated lessons, never reached consensus in the US Army.[64] Many of the legacies of the Vietnam War are to do with lessons that were identified in Vietnam but never came to fruition in the mainstream Army.

'Winning the peace' after a conventional war, and in an insurgency, is a political task rather than solely a military one. The military has to underpin the political efforts and provide the basic security to allow political developments to take place. A lack of appreciation of this can undermine and nullify the political efforts to generate a peaceful and stable situation. Thus it should be held in mind that there is a civilian lead to prosecuting the war and Iraq is very much 'Rumsfeld's war' as he tasked the combatant commander, General Franks. Rumsfeld has been criticised for ignoring military advice on troop levels needed to restore order; dismissing State Department plans for reconstruction; failing to cope with the initial looting; disbanding the Iraqi Army; and the torturing of prisoners.[65] Nevertheless, in Iraq the conventionally focused US Army has faced a serious problem in handling the shift to the counter-insurgency role and many of its efforts have actually been counterproductive. For many this was the lost opportunity of the Iraq intervention – a stunning conventional victory that was not capitalised upon.[66]

It must also be kept in mind that the insurgencies in Vietnam and Iraq are very different. In Vietnam it was:

> a classic, peasant-based, centrally directed, three-stage Maoist model insurgency, culminating in a conventional victory. ... In Iraq, small, scattered, and disparate groups wage a much smaller-scale war of ambushes, assassinations, car bombings, and sabotage against U.S. and other coalition forces and reconstruction targets ... nor do these insurgents have an explicit set of war aims.[67]

The focus of this section is thus on how the conventional Army handles operations against unconventional opponents.

Ill-prepared

The US Army in Vietnam was ill-prepared for counter-insurgency. The initial US military advisory effort focused on creating a South Vietnamese military force that was conventional in tactics and equipment and patterned after the standard US organisation.[68] However, in 1968 after the Tet Offensive, the Army replaced its commander, Westmoreland, with General Creighton Abrams who immediately changed the tactics and theatre strategy. He focused on population control, used different measures of success, and improved the South Vietnamese capability. He also, rather more controversially, attacked bases in Cambodia and Laos – all in a period of diminishing support and resources. It was a successful change in approach, as 'the U.S. and South Vietnam were able for the first time to gain a real measure of control in the countryside'.[69]

However, having learnt these key lessons the Army soon expunged them. After the war the Army was in such a poor state it was clear that it did not wish to fight a war like that again and that to rebuild itself it needed to focus on its basic mission

– conventional war in Europe.[70] It closed down its civil aid programmes and Special Forces. When it did have to address these issues in the 1980s it focused on having soldiers as trainers rather than participants. This mindset continued with the Army's focus remaining on main force conventional warfare in Europe. Congress, in frustration, created a separate Special Forces Command in 1987.

It was only in 1993 that 'Operations Other Than War' began to reach some prominence in doctrinal terms, mainly because there was uncertainty about the Army's role in the post-Cold War world. The inclusion of a chapter on 'Operations Other Than War' in the Army's keystone doctrine manual was itself the subject of much debate at the four-star generals' conference considering the manual. For example, General Joulwan was a firm advocate of moving the Army and the doctrine away from a conventional warfare focus, with its emphasis on mechanised infantry and tank battles, towards the interagency-type operations that had been conducted by Southern Command against drugs.[71]

The doctrine the Army went to war in Iraq under, namely the 2001 manual,[72] had four types of operations (offence, defence, stability and support). It had one term, 'stability', to cover peacekeeping through to counter-terrorism, but this innovation hardly equips the Army to cope with the ambiguous area between war and other operations, especially to cope with the scenarios that 'can be more challenging than in situations requiring offensive and defensive operations'.[73] This is reflective of a broader trend of not giving enough emphasis to roles that are not mainforce conventional ones. For example, at the most basic level the Army did not, for all the huge technical developments, establish a dedicated training centre or specialised organisation to prepare and train its forces to conduct peacekeeping operations. It is thus still down to the individual unit to prepare itself for the operation.[74] At a higher level the Pentagon has no single organisation to coordinate its response to asymmetric threats. Remarkably it was only in 1998 that the US military created programmes specifically for urban capabilities, and currently the emphasis is on asymmetric warfare.[75] The lack of conceptual understanding is shown by the Army's creation in 2004 of an 'Asymmetric Warfare Group' to assess the tactics used to exploit US vulnerabilities, especially how to deal with the threat of IEDs (Improvised Explosive Devices) which are a particular problem in Iraq and driving the changes.[76] However, many Vietnam era lessons are being re-learnt due to the experience in Iraq.

Nation-building

For commentators such as Record and Terrill, state building is the relevant analogy with Vietnam.[77] (Sustaining domestic public support is the other.) Whilst in South Vietnam the US had an unhappy experience of propping up a corrupt government with ineffective security forces, in Iraq the US is starting from scratch as, after the invasion, there was no viable government or domestic security apparatus. Both cases require legitimate governments and effective security forces to protect them. The experience of Vietnamization, the building up of Vietnam's own security forces, should be followed now with Iraqification.[78] The Army's reluctance to be involved in Vietnam style 'nation-building' haunts the post-invasion situation, marred as it was by the experience in 1990s peacekeeping and the growing emphasis on force protection over operational effectiveness. As the former US Army officer Ralph Peters complained, this undercuts the nature of the Army, 'as they maneuver to avoid roles in "nonmilitary" problems, they betray the trust placed in them by the citizens they are pledged to protect. A military's reason for being is to do the nation's dirty work'.[79] This has left the Army ill equipped and lacking in crucial experience.

However, it has also not taken on the experience that it has had. For example, as in Panama in 1989, there was extensive looting after the regime had fallen, which in the case of Iraq seriously damaged the infrastructure from which to rebuild. There was also an underestimation of the post-war security challenges, leading to a lack of constabulary forces.[80] The Army should have been aware of this from its own experience, rather than seeing its role as winning the war and others winning the peace.

Rather than draw on its own experience, the Pentagon is drawing upon Israeli practice.[81] Critics have shown that the British approach of tighter Rules of Engagement mean that they only fire when attacked, using minimum force, and only at identified targets; the Israeli experience is very different. The British aim to generate popular support whilst the Israelis, through house demolitions, snipers and targeted assassinations, aim to suppress attacks, even though it can be utterly counterproductive to popular support initiatives.[82] However, policing Gaza and the West Bank is very different to Northern Ireland. The US has little experience because it has chosen not to engage in operations that lie between war and humanitarian assistance – this limitation is compounded by broader factors nonetheless.

As one study put it, 'The strategic plan for the military aspects of the 2003 war in Iraq has been lauded as brilliant. But neither the U.S. military nor U.S. civilian agencies have a corresponding capacity to plan for postwar reconstruction'.[83] Basically the poor reading of the likely outcome complicated the situation in Iraq, as it was hoped the Coalition would be seen as liberators. It was also assumed the Iraqi police and military forces would remain intact. These misperceptions, the conventional mindset, coupled with the lack of security for reconstruction firms, means that the rebuilding of Iraq as a viable country and state is a long way off. Not only that, but foreign terrorists are drawn into Iraq to engage in insurgency,[84] which 'draws' terrorism away from the US but creates a series of readily available American targets and feeds the new type of terrorist. The invasion produced the opposite effect to the intended one of pacifying Iraq and leading to it becoming a democratic state and of protecting Americans from terrorism.

Civil protection

Fundamental to nation-building is providing security to the populace. During and after Vietnam there has been a traditional resistance within the Army to the unconventional task of civil protection. As Richard Betts says,

Resisting civilian unconventional war doctrine, military leaders recognized the military complexity of the war but insisted on dividing the labor, leaving the politics to the civilians and concentrating themselves on actual combat. ... To these soldiers, mass operations were natural and congenial and could be recommended and pursued with more confidence and energy than the bizarre tactics of the Green Berets.[85]

During the Vietnam War, the Marines, as opposed to the Army, developed 'civic action' programmes to live and work out of villages, and these efforts were a world away from the Army's ideas.[86] For example, the Combined Action Platoons (CAP) were a key feature of the Marines' more strategically relevant approach. They integrated rifle squads into Vietnamese forces and lived in villages. They aimed to secure 'real estate' and provide secure roads rather than indicate success by the 'body count' of enemies killed.[87]

The clearest proof of Army resistance to this key lesson was that counter-insurgency roles were given to the revived Special Forces rather than integrated into general operations.[88] This is apparent in Iraq where the focus has been on destroying the enemy, not defeating it. Traditional COIN is concerned with defeating the insurgent through a variety of means, especially of 'winning hearts and minds' and moving support towards the government. Destruction does not do this and comes at a cost. For example, after the November 2004 assault on Fallujah it was reckoned that 36,000 houses were demolished, 9,000 shops disappeared, 65 mosques were destroyed, as well as 60 schools – in addition, the US forces destroyed one of the two bridges out of the city, both train stations, two electricity stations, three water treatment plants, the whole sanitation system and the communication network. Hundreds of women and children died in the assault.[89] It is reckoned that Iraqi casualties since the invasion now number between 30,000 and 100,000 overall.[90]

The US Army has failed to see that the use of excessive force, as conventional thinking would dictate, can actually undermine the very support needed to win the peace rather than the war. The emphasis on attrition 'through the destruction of the insurgent' sees the population as a distraction, if not a target for repression. Ultimately, as the British Brigadier Aylwin-Foster notes, 'U.S. Army personnel were too inclined to consider offensive operations and destruction of the insurgent as the key to a given situation, and conversely failed to understand its downside'.[91] Though the US military has been criticised for having a 'pathological resistance' to this type of warfare, some isolated units are attempting to work closely with the local culture and structures to provide a greater degree of security.[92]

During the Vietnam War the key shift in thinking was the move from 'search and destroy' to pacification, namely winning the population over to the government cause. The establishment of the Civil Operations and Rural Development Programme (CORDS), headed by Ambassador Robert Komer, addressed this limitation.[93] The previous separation of political and military responsibilities meant there was a growing need for synchronisation of the political and military arms of national strategy,[94] especially as the Communists had a brilliant strategy during the war.[95] There was an emphasis on working at the local level to provide security. It incorporated personnel from the CIA, USIA (United States Information Agency), AID (American Agency for International Development), the State Department, the White House and all the military services and Komer reported directly to Westmoreland and later Abrams. There were civil-military advisory teams in all 250 districts and 44 provinces. However, it came too late in the war.[96] There are signs that the lessons are beginning to percolate into the mindset of the current military.

General Schoomaker, the Army's Chief of Staff – namely, its most senior officer – is distributing a book to senior officers to which he wrote the foreword; John Nagl's *Learning to Eat Soup with a Knife: Counterinsurgency Lessons from Malaya and Vietnam.* In Schoomaker's terms it is an examination of how the British and American armies faced the challenge 'to transform to meet the demands of a different kind of war than the one they had planned for'.[97] Nagl is a Lieutenant Colonel in the Army and served in Iraq from September 2003 to September 2004. His basic argument is that the British Army was more successful at counter-insurgency because it had a learning culture, whereas the American Army did not. The speed of learning in Iraq and the publication of such pieces as the British Brigadier Aylwin-Foster's highly-critical article in the US Army's *Military Review*, are signs of organisational health as it takes on serious self-criticism.[98]

The self-criticism has gone so far as to revive Vietnam era policies, such as Andrew Krepinevich's advocacy of the 'oil spot' strategy.[99] Basically, the aim is to provide security for the Iraqi people in certain areas and then, like an oil spot spreading out, broaden the secure areas out. It is counter to the prevalent focus on hunting down and killing insurgents. The strategy was applied in Malaya by the British and advocated in Vietnam. There is evidence that at the lower levels Army officers are starting to apply this thinking.[100] However, to be really effective it needs to be applied at a much higher level, especially as there is a need to draw down the troop numbers in Iraq, raising again the question of whether there are sufficient troops for a successful strategy to be implemented in Iraq.

Understanding war

At the heart of the Army's difficulty in Vietnam and Iraq, is its concept of war – not so much for what it has in, but what it leaves out. Michael Howard criticised the Western powers' understanding of counter-insurgencies thirty years ago, and it is still pertinent:

> the inadequacy of the sociopolitical analysis of the societies with which we were dealing ... lay at the root of the failure of Western powers to cope more effectively with the revolutionary and insurgency movements. ... Of the four dimensions of strategy [operational, logistical, social and technological], the social was here incomparably the most significant.[101]

This goes back to Colonel Charles Callwell, who pointed out in 1896 that 'small war' operations by regular forces against irregular ones (who will not meet them in open ground) are different to wars against regular forces, because the moral effect is often more important than beating the armies.[102] Principles governing regular warfare may be wholly inapplicable in this environment. For example, the demands to use minimum force are a crucial component. How this is handled is dependent upon the military organisation's culture.[103]

A key figure in the US military community who has been pointing this out for a decade is the former Marine Commandant General Krulak. He gave a clear example of the changing nature of warfare that the Army needs to address, and the challenge that Iraq now embodies. He called it the 'three block' war.[104] Basically, land forces have to cope simultaneously with warfighting, peacekeeping and humanitarian aid happening concurrently and within blocks of each other. In addition to this, there is the rise of the 'strategic corporal' where the responsibility for the decisions that have a strategic effect are moving much further down the chain of command. Being fast and decisive with full spectrum dominance does not resolve this problem or address this type of operation.

As Iraq shows, these broader skills are necessary in modern main force war as well as in the more humanitarian work. The accusations and trials for torture of US forces raise very large questions concerning the professional standards of some small parts of the Army in these circumstances. Young men and women in this very stressful environment need to be trained, physically and mentally, for its rigours. The culture of winning wars, strategic thinking premised on achievable objectives, and a highly conventionalised Army face huge problems with the intractableness of urban conflicts and cultural wars. The cost of not training for this and avoiding the issue of the social and cultural aspects of warfare is seen clearly in Iraq. This should not be seen as an optional extra but is inherent to the nature of war and strategy. The lack of utility of the post-conflict US policy is partially due to the lack of utility of the Army, which is itself due to a gap in capability and concepts, and that is a product of a particular self-understanding. As retired Colonel Douglas Macgregor notes, in terms of logistics and force design the Army's deployment to Iraq showed that it still thinks in terms of WWII models.[105] The Army is heavily bureaucratic and needs to be more flexible, both in the tasks it undertakes and changing its role within conflicts. Its fixation with 'big war' means it is still very poor in language training and policing skills, even though it has been in Iraq for years. These shortcomings need to be addressed to allow the broader policies to come into effect[106] – defeating insurgencies is, ultimately, a political task of garnering popular support.

Conclusion

It is necessary to remember that the differences between Vietnam and Iraq far outweigh the similarities. This chapter has focused on how the mindset of the military, and the Army in particular, has shaped the approach to the invasion of Iraq. The important lessons concerning the need for clear objectives, the need to win, and the rejection of gradualism have shaped the overall campaign, and have left the US ill-prepared for nation-building and civic protection. These lessons and the lack of counter-insurgency learning have left the military with a far more complex situation in dealing with insurgents. It is here that lessons that were learnt during Vietnam and subsequently discarded are being revived. Vietnam is thus not being repeated in Iraq but there are many parallels. As the former Secretary of Defense Melvin Laird puts it, 'The war in Iraq is not "another Vietnam." But it could become one if we continue to use Vietnam as a soundbite ignoring its true lessons'.[107]

As Iraq shows, the US and its Army is still better at winning battles than wars and it still struggles to win the peace. It has an over-reliance on one operational concept regardless of the strategic situation. This is then exacerbated by the poor interagency process and the directions from the National Security Council.[108] At a more conceptual level, the terms and concepts provided by the Army's 'lessons of Vietnam' shape how the practice of strategy is perceived and the options on offer to the administration – the tools of the policy shape the policy.

Having been so successful in avoiding the full range of 'lessons from Vietnam' for so long, the Army and the nation are now paying the price as they cope with the problem of how to handle an increasingly intractable war, and the associated fear of an Iraq syndrome – 'the renewed, nagging and sometimes paralyzing belief that any large-scale U.S. military intervention is doomed to practical failure and moral iniquity'.[109] The tools of policy need to change as does the associated understanding of strategy.

This highlights the importance of Army reform. The professionalism developed after the Vietnam War opened the Army to new vistas of thought and practice but its legacy was to restrict its further development and hinder America's military response to the new strategic environment. That needs to change, even if much of it is too late. The Army cannot split the political away from its responsibilities, and its thinking needs to reflect this. It needs to integrate political and military aspects of conflicts far more closely to see and address the ambiguity that lies at the heart of strategy and modern warfare.

Strategy, like virtue, is a product of the society from which it emerges; it reflects an understanding of past experiences, current dilemmas and future aspirations, and these tensions and different understandings need to be kept in communication. For strategy this means that there is a need for political consensus building and an overall strategic direction, and the military providing the means to fulfil this, with the politics permeating every level of military expertise; relying on militarised objectives will not do. The aims and the means cannot therefore be separated as in Weinberger's doctrine; neither does it mean that the past can be used to hobble developments. This understanding of strategy is a long way from the current position of seeing strategy as a managerial task – where setting political objectives and having the clear means to achieve them is sufficient. Strategy is inherently unstable, and coherence is generated by not treating the aims and means of policy as separate steps in a formula, but as part of a broader communal understanding of the past, present and future – and that lies in the realm of politics not military capability. And politics lies at the heart of counter-insurgency.

Notes

1 I would like to thank Drs David H. Dunn, Rod Thornton and David Ryan for their very helpful comments on an earlier draft of this chapter.

2 J. Record and W. A. Terrill, *Iraq and Vietnam: Differences, Similarities, and Insights*, Carlisle, PA: Strategic Studies Institute, 2004, p. vii

3 H. Arendt, *On Violence*, New York: Harcourt Brace, 1970, p. 4.

4 W. Westmoreland, *A Soldier Reports*, New York: Dell, 1976, p. 562.

5 R. Buzzanco, *Masters of War: Military Dissent and Politics in the Vietnam Era*, Cambridge: Cambridge University Press, 1996, pp. 9–11.

6 H. Summers, Jr, *On Strategy: A Critical Analysis of the Vietnam War*, Novato, CA: Presidio, 1982.

7 E. Villacres and C. Bassford, 'Reclaiming the Clausewitzian Trinity', *Parameters*, 25/3, 1995, p. 10.

8 H. Summers, Jr, *On Strategy II: A Critical Analysis of the Gulf War*, New York: Dell, 1992, p. 132.

9 For example, see the 'Chairman, Joint Chiefs of Staff Professional Military Reading List' in *Joint Chiefs of Staff. Joint Pub. 1: Joint Warfare of the US Armed Forces*, Washington, DC: GPO, 1991, pp. 71–2 and the 1995 edition, Appendix B.

10 The speech is given in an appendix to his autobiography. See C. Weinberger, *Fighting for Peace: Seven Critical Years in the Pentagon*, New York: Warner, 1990, pp. 433–45.

11 S. Daggett, 'Government and the Military Establishment', in P. Schraeder (ed.) *Intervention into the 1990s: U.S. Foreign Policy in the Third World*, 2nd edn, Boulder, CO: Lynne Rienner, 1992, p. 428.

12 The information on the speech writers is drawn from confidential interviews by the author.

13 W. Clark, 'Gradualism and American Military Strategy', *Military Review*, 60/9, 1975, p. 7.

14 W. DePuy, 'Infantry Combat', in L. Gilmore and C. Conway (eds) *Selected Papers of General William E. DePuy*, Fort Leavenworth, KS: Combat Studies Institute, 1994, p. 453.

15 R. Lock-Pullan, *US Intervention Policy and Army Innovation: From Vietnam to Iraq*, London: Routledge, 2006, pp. 77–108, 140–51.

16 Department of Defense, *National Military Strategy of the United States of America*, Washington, DC: GPO, 1995, p. 305.

17 For the views of the protagonists and its context, see Weinberger, op. cit., pp. 159–61, 163–5, 401–2, and G. Shultz, *Turmoil and Triumph: My Years as Secretary of State*, New York: Macmillan, 1993, pp. 646–51.

18 C. Gacek, *The Logic of Force: The Dilemma of Limited War in American Foreign Policy*, New York: Columbia University Press, 1994.

19 A. Krepinevich, Jr, *The Army and Vietnam*, Baltimore, MD: Johns Hopkins University Press, 1986, p. 275.

20 R. Spector, 'U.S. Army Strategy in the Vietnam War', *International Security*, 11/4, 1987, p. 131.

21 Department of the Army, *A Study of Strategic Lessons Learned in Vietnam*, 8 Vols, McLean, VA: BDM Corporation, 1979.

22 S. Halper and J. Clarke, *America Alone: The Neo-Conservatives and the Global Order*, Cambridge: Cambridge University Press, 2004, p. 2, see also pp. 31–5.

23 B. Woodward, *Plan of Attack*, New York: Simon and Schuster, 2004, p. 63.

24 W. Murray and R. Scales, Jr, *The Iraq War: A Military History*, London: Belknap/Harvard University Press, 2003, pp. 89–90.

25 A. Krepinevich, Jr, 'How to Win in Iraq', *Foreign Affairs*, 84/5, 2005, pp. 87–104.

26 F. Hoffman, *Decisive Force: The New American Way of War*, London: Praeger, 1996.

27 D. Roth, *Sacred Honor: The Authorised Biography of General Sir Colin Powell*, London: HarperCollins, 1994.

28 R. Helms, *The Persian Gulf Crisis: Power in the Post-Cold War World*, Westport, CT: Praeger, 1993, pp. 162, 168.

29 M. Vickers, 'Revolution Deferred: Kosovo and the Transformation of War', in A. Bacevich and E. Cohen (eds) *War Over Kosovo: Politics and Strategy in a Global Age*, New York: Columbia University Press, 2001, p. 204.

30 R. Dunn, 'Transformation: Let's Get it Right This Time', *Parameters*, 31/1, 2001, pp. 22–8.

31 US Army, 'Army Completes Stryker Brigade Certification', http://www.army.mil/features/strykeroe/ (accessed February 1, 2006).

32 See D. Rumsfeld, 'Transforming the Military', *Foreign Affairs*, 81/3, 2002, p. 28 and *Military Review*, 83/3, May–June 2002, pp. 8–27, 68–9. http://usacac.leavenworth.army.mil/CAC/milreview/index.asp (accessed September 5, 2002).

33 See F. Kagan, 'A Dangerous Transformation', *Wall Street Journal OnLine*, http://www.opinionjournal.com/extra/?id=110004289 (accessed November 14, 2003).

34 A. Cordesman, *The Iraq War: Strategy, Tactics, and Military Lessons*, Washington, DC: CSIS Press, 2003, pp. 160–8.

35 L. Freedman, 'Rumsfeld's Legacy: The Iraq Syndrome', Washingtonpost.com, January 9, 2005. www.washingtonpost.com/ac2/wp-dyn/A58318-2005Jan8 (accessed January 17, 2005).

36 H. McMaster, *Dereliction of Duty: Lyndon Johnson, Robert McNamara, The Joint Chiefs of Staff, and The Lies That Led to Vietnam*, New York: HarperCollins, 1997, pp. 323, 334.

37 W. Simons, 'U.S. Coercive Pressure on North Vietnam, Early 1965', in A. George and W. Simons (eds) *The Limits of Coercive Diplomacy*, 2nd edn, Boulder, CO: Westview, 1994, pp. 133–73.

38 Clark, 'Gradualism and American Military Strategy', op. cit. p. 3.

39 Summers, *On Strategy*, op. cit. p. 173.

40 E. Cohen, 'Dynamics of Military Intervention', in A. Levite, B. Jentleson and L. Berman (eds) *Foreign Military Intervention*, New York: Columbia University Press, 1992, pp. 261–84, and L. Freedman, 'Escalators and quagmires: expectations and the use of force', *International Affairs*, 67/1, 1991, pp. 15–31.

41 Lock-Pullan, *US Intervention Policy and Army Innovation*, op. cit.

42 Murray and Scales, *The Iraq War: A Military History*, op. cit.

43 Ibid., pp. 184–233 for a narrative of the later phase of the campaign.

44 White House, 'President Discusses National Economic Security in California, May 2, 2003'. http://www.whitehouse.gov/news/releases/2003/05/20030502-7.html, (accessed May 5, 2003)

45 Westmoreland, *A Soldier Reports*, op. cit. pp. 198–9.

46 Krepinevich, *The Army and Vietnam*, op. cit. pp. 168–72.

47 Ibid., p. 296.

48 J. Ewell and I. Hunt, Jr, *Sharpening the Combat Edge: The Use of Analysis to Reinforce Military Judgment. Vietnam Studies*, Washington, DC: GPO, 1974, pp. 76–8, 83.

49 P. MacDonald, *Giap: The Victor in Vietnam*, London: Fourth Estate, 1993.

50 J. Sweeney (ed.) *A Handbook of American Military History: From the Revolutionary War to the Present*, Boulder, CO: Westview, 1996, p. 252.

51 J. Gibson, *The Perfect War: Technowar in Vietnam*, Boston, MA: Atlantic Monthly, 1986.

52 Michael Howard, *The Franco–Prussian War*, London: Rupert Hart-Davis, 1961, p. 8.

53 C. Gray, *Postmodern War: The New Politics of Conflict*, London: Routledge, 1997, pp. 36–50, 248.

54 Office of Defense Transformation, *Network Centric Operations Conceptual Framework Version 1.0*, November 2003. http://www.oft.osd.mil/index.cfm (accessed January 10, 2004).

55 A. Latham, 'Re-Imagining Warfare: The "Revolution in Military Affairs"', in C. Synder (ed.) *Contemporary Security and Strategy*, London: Macmillan Press, 1999, pp. 230, 210–35.

56 S. Rosen, 'New Ways of War: Understanding Military Innovation', *International Security*, 13/1, 1988, pp. 134–68.

57 E. Luttwak, 'Where Are the Great Powers? At Home with the Kids', *Foreign Affairs*, 73/4, 1994, pp. 23–8, and his later 'A Post-Heroic Military Policy', *Foreign Affairs*, 75/4, 1996, pp. 33–44.

58 D. Kinnard, *The War Managers*, Wayne, NJ: Avery, 1985.

59 A. F. Krepinevich, Jr, 'How to Win in Iraq', *Foreign Affairs*, 84/5, 2005, pp. 87–104.

60 Krepinevich, *The Army and Vietnam*, op. cit. p. 5.

61 For example on the divergence, see S. Sarkesian, J. Williams and F. Bryant, *Soldiers, Society and National Security*, London: Lynne Rienner, 1995, p. 9.

62 L. Freedman, *The Revolution in Strategic Affairs. Adelphi Paper 318*, London: Oxford University Press/RIIA, 1998, p. 78.

63 Lock-Pullan, *US Intervention Policy and Army Innovation*, op. cit. pp. 169–72.

64 R. Downie, *Learning From Conflict: The U.S. Military in Vietnam, El Salvador, and the Drug War*, Westport, CT: Praeger, 1998.

65 Freedman, 'Rumsfeld's Legacy: The Iraq Syndrome', op. cit.

66 N. Aylwin-Foster, 'Changing the Army for Counterinsurgency Operations', *Military Review*, November–December, 2005, pp. 2–15. http://usacac.leavenworth.army.mil/CAC/milreview/download/English/NovDec05/aylwin.pdf.

67 Record and Terrill, *Iraq and Vietnam*, op. cit., p. 2.

68 J. Collins, Jr, *The Development and Training of the South Vietnamese Army 1950–1972. Vietnam Studies*, Washington, DC: GPO, 1975.

69 R. Spector, *After Tet: The Bloodiest Year in Vietnam*, New York: Free Press, 1993, p. xvi.

70 R. Lock-Pullan, '"An Inward Looking Time": The US Army 1973–7', *Journal of Military History*, 67/2, 2003, pp. 483–511.

71 Downie, *Learning From Conflict*, op. cit. p. 217.

72 Department of the Army, *FM 3-0, Operations*, Washington, DC: GPO, 2001.

73 Ibid., pp. 9–15.

74 B. Bankus and W. Flavin, 'Training US Army Peacekeepers', *Small Wars and Insurgencies*, 15/1, 2004, pp. 129–39.

75 A. Hills, *Future War in Cities: Rethinking a Liberal Dilemma*, London: Frank Cass, 2004, pp. 42–7.

76 E. Grossman, 'Army To Create "Asymmetric Warfare Group" To Prepare For New Threats', *Inside the Pentagon*, July 8, 2004. http://www.oft.osd.mil/index.cfm (accessed July 10, 2004).

77 Record and Terrill, *Iraq and Vietnam*, op. cit., pp. vii, 32–47.

78 M. Laird, 'Iraq: Learning the Lessons of Vietnam', *Foreign Affairs*, 84/6, 2005, pp. 24, 22–43.

79 R. Peters, *Fighting for the Future: Will America Triumph?* Mechanicsburg, PA: Stackpole Books, 1999, p. 28.

80 B. Crocker, 'Iraq: Going it Alone, Gone Wrong', in R. Orr (ed.) *Winning the Peace: An American Strategy for Post-Conflict Reconstruction*, Washington, DC: Center for Strategic and International Studies, 2004, pp. 267–8.

81 A. Finlan, 'Trapped in the Dead Ground: US Counter-insurgency Strategy in Iraq', *Small Wars and Insurgencies*, 16, 2005, pp. 1–21.

82 Ibid.

83 Crocker, 'Iraq: Going it Alone, Gone Wrong', op. cit., p. 266.

84 See for example, BBC News, 'Iraq is al-Qaeda battleground', July 29, 2004. http://news.bbc.co.uk/1/hi/uk_politics/3935755.stm, (accessed July 29, 2004).
85 R. Betts, *Soldiers, Statesmen, and Cold War Crises*, Cambridge, MA: Harvard University Press, 1977, p. 138.
86 D. Avant, *Political Institutions and Military Change: Lessons From Peripheral Wars*, Ithaca, NY: Cornell University Press, 1994, pp. 76–101, and Krepinevich, *The Army in Vietnam*, op. cit., pp. 172–7.
87 M. Peterson, *The Combined Action Platoons: The U.S. Marines' Other War In Vietnam*, Westport, CT: Praeger, 1989, p. 123.
88 F. Kelly, *U.S. Army Special Forces 1961–1971. Vietnam Studies*, Washington, DC: GPO, 1985.
89 Oxford Research Group, 'Learning From Fallujah: Lessons identified'. www.oxfordresearchgroup.org.uk/publications/books/fallujah.pdf (accessed February 5, 2006).
90 Iraq Body Count website: http://www.iraqbodycount.org/index.php?PHPSESSID=9a4b695f76f6f87899c7fd615bde9054&submit3=Enter+Site, and BBC News, October 29, 2004, http://news.bbc.co.uk/1/hi/world/middle_east/3962969.stm (accessed February 10, 2006).
91 Aylwin-Foster, 'Changing the Army for Counterinsurgency Operations', op. cit., p. 4.
92 G. Jaffe, 'On Ground in Iraq, Capt. Ayers Writes His Own Playbook', *Wall Street Journal*, September 22, 2004, p. A1.
93 Robert Komer wrote an important critique of Vietnam: *Bureaucracy at War: U.S. Performance in the Vietnam Conflict*, Boulder, CO: Westview, 1986.
94 Department of the Army, *A Study of Strategic Lessons Learned in Vietnam*, Omnibus Executive Summary, VI 11.
95 B. Palmer, Jr, *The 25 Year War: America's Military Role in Vietnam*, New York: Da Capo, 1984, pp. 180–1.
96 J. Nagl, *Learning to Eat Soup with a Knife: Counterinsurgency Lessons from Malaya and Vietnam*, Chicago, IL: University of Chicago Press, 2005, pp. 164–6.
97 Ibid., p. ix
98 Aylwin-Foster, 'Changing the Army for Counterinsurgency Operations', op. cit.
99 A. F. Krepinevich, Jr, 'How to Win in Iraq', *Foreign Affairs*, 84/5, 2005, pp. 87–104.
100 N. Wadhams, 'U.S. troops in Iraq Adopt Oil Strategy', Associated Press, February 1, 2006. http://rempost.blogspot.com/2006/02/us-troops-in-iraq-adopt-oil-strategy.html, (accessed February 8, 2006).
101 M. Howard, 'The Forgotten Dimensions of Strategy' in his, *The Causes of War*, London: Unwin, 1984, p. 108.
102 C. Callwell, *Small Wars: Their Principles and Practice*, 3rd edn, Lincoln, NB and London: University of Nebraska and HMSO, 1906/96, pp. 21, 42.
103 R. Thornton, 'The British Army and the Origins of its Minimum Force Philosophy', *Small Wars and Insurgencies*, 15/1, 2004, pp. 83–106.
104 C. Krulak, 'The Strategic Corporal: Leadership in the Three Block War', *Marine Corps Gazette*, 83/1, 1999, pp. 18–22.
105 D. Macgregor, *Transformation Under Fire: Revolutionizing How America Fights*, Westport, CT: Praeger, 2003.
106 R. Kaplan, *Imperial Grunts: The American Military on the Ground*, New York: Random House, 2005, especially pp. 307–70.
107 M. Laird, 'Iraq: Learning the Lessons of Vietnam', *Foreign Affairs*, 84/6, 2005, p. 24.
108 Crocker, 'Iraq: Going it Alone, Gone Wrong', op. cit., pp. 263–85.
109 Freedman, 'Rumsfeld's Legacy: The Iraq Syndrome', op. cit.

5

'A NATIONAL SYMPHONY OF THEFT, CORRUPTION AND BRIBERY'

Anatomy of state building from Iraq to Vietnam

James M. Carter

Before becoming vice president, Dick Cheney once bragged about the omnipresence of his former company, Brown & Root, in the conduct of US foreign policy, saying, 'the first person to greet our soldiers as they arrive in the Balkans and the last one to wave good-bye is one of our employees'.[1] Although speaking specifically about the firm's role in the Balkans crisis of the 1990s, Cheney's comment reflected a larger phenomenon that has grown exponentially over the years since. That phenomenon is the United States government's reliance upon private corporations to meet its foreign policy objectives. Today, hundreds of private corporations operate under contract with the government to provide services too numerous to count. Their presence mushroomed in the years following the end of the Cold War. Now, hundreds of companies specializing in tasks once carried out by military personnel compete for federal contracts supporting the US military operations around the world. From 1994 to 2002, the US government signed over 3,000 contracts worth an estimated $300 billion with private firms.[2] Today in Iraq, more than 150 companies work under government contract as part of the Bush administration's effort to build a new, modern, democratic state in the Middle East.

Though the United States has relied increasingly upon the private sector to achieve foreign policy objectives in recent years, their use is not at all a new phenomenon.[3] Leading to escalation of the war in Vietnam during the mid-1960s, the administration of Lyndon B. Johnson quietly authorized a consortium of four large corporations to put in place an enormous modern military construction programme that would transform southern Vietnam and 'modernize' its physical infrastructure. Their effort, which they and others termed 'the construction miracle of the decade', prevented the collapse of the American project by making southern Vietnam militarily defensible. Importantly, it did not make success in the state building effort any more likely. Furthermore, the 'no bid' deals provoked sharp criticism as investigations turned up an environment of inefficiency, waste, fraud and corruption that fatally handicapped larger policy aims.

Viewed through the lens of state building, Iraq today and Vietnam decades ago share more than they differ.[4] A comparative analysis of the two sheds light on both, while the Vietnam experience also yields important lessons for Iraq. Ironically, officials in the Bush administration are loath to consider the Vietnam experience as they attempt state building in Iraq even though that earlier example provides the best lessons they are likely ever to get.

In this chapter, I will examine and draw comparisons between the state building experiences in Iraq and Vietnam. Throughout I use the term 'state building' rather than the more common nation building because, in both examples, a nation already existed before American involvement. The United States sought to build a completely new state in the southern half of Vietnam and now seeks the rebuilding and transformation of the crumbled state of Iraq. The building of a state, borrowing from the American experts in both examples, involves a physical process of constructing and piecing together some of the attributes of modern states (usually Western states such as the United States); and though it involves a military component, in the final analysis, political imperatives and 'winning the hearts and minds' prove the key determinants. In both cases, private contractors play a significant role in creating the necessary physical infrastructure to sustain US policy. Also in both cases, their absence would substantially limit America's freedom of action and the overall American position. Consequently, my discussion of state building and war profiteering will centre on the relationship between US state building efforts and private corporations in carrying out policy objectives.

Iraq, private contractors and the windfalls of war

In Iraq today, many private companies operate under contractual agreement with the US government to carry out dozens of tasks. The corporations are there, in large measure, to take part in a vast state building effort. Over the past 15 years much of Iraq's infrastructure, physical and other, has been neglected, destroyed through warfare and/or pilfered and looted in an atmosphere of relative lawlessness and desperation. Twelve years of international sanctions also reduced Iraq to a traditional state in terms of its agricultural, communications, transportation, public health and educational infrastructure.[5] Years of neglect as a desperate regime clung to power and funnelled its limited resources toward maintaining itself and away from maintenance of the nation also contributed to the erosion and decay of a modern state.[6]

Following the rapid American invasion and conquest of Iraq in March 2003, post-war planners and experts were quickly flown into neighbouring countries to await a modicum of safety before entering Baghdad to begin their work in stabilizing and rebuilding a ravaged country. Within weeks, the federal government began granting contracts to American corporations to rebuild Iraq's infrastructure. According to the Center for Public Integrity's investigation, those with the best relationship to government officials quickly found themselves on an inside track with greater access to the enormous sums of money pouring into Iraq. As of September 2003, Vice President Dick Cheney's old company Halliburton, and subsidiary Kellogg, Brown & Root, had received almost one-quarter of a billion dollars in payment for work done so far, with much more to follow. The total contract value stood at $2.3 billion.[7] In less than a year, additional federal contracts brought their total to more than $11 billion.[8] Among other tasks, the companies were and are responsible for the rebuilding of Iraq's oil producing infrastructure.

Halliburton (and subsidiary KBR), though by far the largest contractor in Iraq, is only one of many dozens of similar corporations contracted for billions in reconstruction projects. Bechtel Group, another corporation with solid government connections, signed contracts with the government valued at $2.8 billion. Washington Group International, another well connected firm with an interesting history in the federal contracting business which I will explore in some detail below, signed on for around $500 million for Afghanistan and more than $3 billion for work in Iraq. Blackwater USA contracted to provide an array of security services valued at $21 million. DynCorp, the private corporation charged with creating and training an Iraqi police force, contracted for around $93 million. Vinnell Corporation (Northrop Grumman), tasked with training the New Iraqi Army (NIA), signed on for $48 million. Fluor Corporation, a construction giant with some 50,000 employees in 25 countries spread across six continents, contracted for projects totalling $3.7 billion in logistics support. CH2M Hill, a Colorado-based firm handling construction and engineering tasks, signed on for over $1.5 billion; and American International Contractors, Inc., specializing in an array of construction services, signed contracts valued at $1.5 billion. Still, these are just a few of the more than 100 corporations contracted for work in Iraq and Afghanistan in 2003.[9]

By late summer, independent experts estimated that one-third of the $3.9 billion cost of the on-going conquest and occupation of Iraq was devoted to private contractors. The flood of money to post-war Iraq (and Afghanistan) continued to grow. In November 2003, the Bush administration pushed for and Congress appropriated $18.7 billion to cover the initial costs of reconstruction and logistics work for Iraq. The pace of the work surprised nearly everyone, including officials at the Pentagon, who quickly found themselves inundated with not only requests and bids, but also complaints and accusations of cronyism, fraud and corruption. Officials quickly established a central office to oversee the letting of contracts saying, 'the work in Iraq is moving at such an incredible pace that we needed one office to oversee everything'.[10] At the same time, representatives from hundreds of companies flocked to a Pentagon conference for contractors held in Arlington, Virginia to hawk their particular wares and solicit work from the federal government. Lest we assume these corporations were eager to do their part to stamp out global terror, one excited conference attendee and prospective bidder pointed out, 'there is just so much money that we can tap into. It's just wonderful to have this opportunity'.[11] Before the year was out, more than 150

US corporations had received contracts worth some $50 billion for work in Afghanistan and Iraq.[12]

These companies (as well as numerous subcontractors) are currently scrambling to build and rebuild the infrastructure destroyed over the past dozen years. They are working on a police network, a military force, a communications grid, transportation system, an integrated media system, the oil production and transportation system, water and sewage treatment systems and ports. The number of those working for the contractors is estimated at between 50,000 and 75,000. That would make the numbers working for private contractors in Iraq alone greater, by more than two to one, than the military forces making up what the Bush administration calls the 'coalition of the willing'.[13] The contractor employees seem even more willing for reasons one can guess.[14]

Many of the activities and practices of these private and largely unaccountable corporations have been the object of sharp criticism from the public, certain media outlets and from congressional watchdogs.[15] The way in which the contracts are let, for example, has led to accusations of favouritism, cronyism and conflicts of interest among government officials with close ties to the military industry. Dick Cheney is only the most well-known and visible of these.[16] Contracts awarded to Halliburton, KBR and Bechtel raised congressional eyebrows because the contracts were awarded on the basis of an existing and past relationship with the federal government and were not open to any outside bidding process. In some cases, corporate representatives sat in on meetings at which they discussed the terms of the contract the company was about to receive, thus obliterating the line between the federal government and private firms.

Additionally, the contracts through which these deals are codified are known as 'cost-plus-award-fee'. This type of contract stipulates that the government will pay for all costs associated with the job as well as an additional award fee based on performance. Most of them are arranged through either the US Defense Department or the Agency for International Development and investigating officials have been unable to gain access to them in order to better understand the process. Although made illegal amid the revelations of WWI profiteering, this particular contractual device was decades ago revived and now flourishes in Iraq and Afghanistan. The cost-plus-award-fee arrangement permits rising profits as costs rise; all a contractor has to do to increase the former is to increase the latter. Consequently, curbing the costs of the work or project becomes disadvantageous to a corporation that might otherwise be keen to reduce costs in the interest of greater profits. Through these contracts, private corporations have realized windfall profits by taking advantage of the relative urgency, chaos and uncertainty of war. Despite clear evidence of fraud, mismanagement, corruption and kickbacks, the Bush administration steadfastly refused to make the system transparent and congressional committees of jurisdiction have also repeatedly refused to launch serious and public investigations.[17]

Congressman Henry Waxman, by far the most visible figure investigating and calling for greater scrutiny of the whole process, has written that the Bush administration intends to reward a few hand-picked companies by awarding 'individual contractors monopolies over different sectors of the Iraqi economy'.[18] By spring 2004, there were some 2,300 reconstruction projects planned, and none of the contracts for them was subject to competitive bidding.[19] Evidence of corruption, kickbacks, bribery and waste also abounds.

One journalist recently wrote that 'June 2004 has emerged as a month when both money and accountability were thrown out the window'. June 2004 was, not coincidentally, the month for the official transfer of authority from the United States to the Iraqis, the dissolution of the American-run Coalition Provisional Authority (CPA). Referring to the unregulated atmosphere then prevailing in Iraq as 'something like a *Barneys* warehouse sale in the Wild West', the *Los Angeles Times* disclosed official documents exposing a frenzied effort to rush contracts and otherwise log jammed projects through the system hurriedly to beat the deadline for the transfer of power. On just one day in late May, officials pushed through more than $1.5 billion in spending for projects. More than 1,000 contracts were signed in the month of June alone, roughly double the usual monthly figure. Two-thirds of those were signed without following standard procedures.[20] Investigators have found refurbished schools and hospitals in a state of disrepair. Many projects remain incomplete or not begun. In some places, piles of materials await the start of projects and, in others, workers wait for materials. Relying on officials' statements, the *New York Times* reported that even the oil and power infrastructure 'are in worse shape than during the regime of Saddam Hussein'. American officials in Iraq during this period concede that the frenetic atmosphere led to unimaginable waste and corruption. In more than one instance, occupation officials were given large amounts of cash, $6.75 million in one case, and told simply to get rid of it by the end of the month. Iraq was awash in cash, more than 360 tons of shrink-wrapped bricks of $100 bills. Some Americans in Baghdad even played football with bricks of it to fight boredom.[21]

Those who worked closely with the firm Custer-Battles have now come forward to report shocking levels of bribery and kickbacks totalling untold millions. Halliburton (and subsidiary KBR) accepted bribes for handing out subcontracts from their posh villa in Kuwait, digs they had staked out well before the invasion of Iraq even began. With the invasion quickly over and the occupation begun, KBR began vastly overcharging the US government to transport fuel into Iraq and to provide meals to soldiers. The profiteering in this case climbed to more than $150 million. Vinnell Corporation did such an apparently poor job of training Iraqi forces that the entire first battalion walked off the job, and the US Army had to take over. Employees from the security firm CACI International were deeply entangled in the prisoner abuse scandal at the Abu Ghraib facility. These and other companies remained virtually unaccountable for a time. By late 2005, however, a US district court handed out the first formal indictments for instances of money laundering, bribery, wire fraud, conspiracy and interstate transportation of stolen property. American officials working for the Coalition Provisional Authority, investigators soon discovered, had accepted bribes of hundreds of thousands of dollars to steer government contracts worth more than $13 million to particular companies. The conspirators kept this hidden by writing bids not exceeding

$500,000. Any contract beyond that amount would be reviewed by higher level officials.[22]

Overall, the rebuilding or state building in Iraq moves sluggishly along. A disproportionate share of money committed to Iraq is in fact devoted to dealing with military and security needs and related construction and not to the (re)building campaign. Large-scale military campaigns launched against Fallujah and Najaf aimed at defeating an increasingly sophisticated insurgency garner inordinate energies as well as media coverage. Relatively little reconstruction aid has actually been spent. Of $18.4 billion in the 2004 supplement, only $3.6 billion was committed to relief and reconstruction efforts (about 35 percent of the goal). Of this figure, only $2.1 billion had been obligated.[23] As of late 2005, Congress had approved $20.9 billion for the reconstruction of Iraq. Of that figure, $12 billion had been spent.[24] Additionally, estimates of the costs of increased security run from 22 to 36 percent of each rebuilding project. Violent attacks and a growing broad-based resistance to the American presence have continued to grow since 2003. Military officials report dozens of attacks daily on US forces and Iraqis who cooperate with them. From May to September 2005, insurgent attacks killed more than 3,000 in Baghdad alone.[25] During 2006, the target of the violence shifted away from the Americans as Sunni insurgents attacked Shiites and Shiite death squads attacked Sunnis. Serious and thoughtful observers began to speak in very sober terms of full-scale civil war in Iraq.

Reflecting the increased violence throughout Iraq, in March 2005, the Agency for International Development (AID) cancelled two power generator projects to move $15 million to ramp up security. Other projects have been cut for the greater emphasis on security issues. These mounting costs have resulted in millions in reconstruction aid shifting away from rebuilding projects. Relatively optimistic estimates contend that 1,887 of 2,784 projects have been completed. These include power stations, water treatment facilities and police stations. In many cases, however, completed projects remain unusable. Five of the newly constructed electrical substations, built at a cost of $28.8 million, sat idle because no system to distribute the power had been built. Others are hastily built and then neglected for lack of trained personnel or equipment availability and quickly fall into disrepair. Inspectors also found millions had been squandered and wasted or completely lost.[26] Despite successful building projects here and there, auditors and inspectors generally report on the failure to rebuild Iraq's physical infrastructure. Despite the more than $5.5 billion committed to restoring the electricity service, according to a July 2005 Government Accountability Office (GAO) report, 'power generation was still at lower levels as of May than it had been before the U.S. invasion in 2003'.[27]

Even on those features of state building for which money has been spent and some work done, the results are mixed at best. An independent investigator who travelled to Iraq to see the progress, found supposedly rebuilt schools with leaky roofs, no working sewage system, flooded playgrounds, unreliable electricity, missing and broken equipment and peeling paint. All across Iraq's cities, the electrical grid is notoriously unreliable and due to a rise in the incidence of cholera, kidney stones and diarrhoea, people do not generally trust that the water is potable. With hospitals and clinics still lacking adequate medicines, equipment, funding and staffing, the nation's public health infrastructure also remains critically fractured.[28]

The US occupation authorities have as their central task the reversal of years of downwardly spiralling public health trends. A young population (half are under 18 years of age), Iraqis are also saddled with high infant and childhood mortality rates, high general, chronic and acute malnutrition rates and an elevated rate of infectious disease.[29] These conditions hit the young particularly hard. Chronic illness, such as high blood pressure and cholesterol, is much more prevalent among women and the elderly. More than 220,000 Iraqis live with chronic illness directly attributed to war. So far the current war in Iraq has exacerbated these trends. A recent study concludes,

> the proportion of chronically disabled in population groups that are not normally soldiers – namely women, children below nine and elderly above 60 – is larger in the ongoing war than in the first Gulf war, and was in turn larger in the first Gulf war than in the Iran–Iraq war.[30]

Despite the seeming omnipresence of private contractors, remarkably little has been done to rebuild the physical infrastructure of the ravaged nation and to reverse these ominous trends.

In general, the situation in Iraq seems no closer to conclusion than a year ago. Even the ends of US involvement there have become less and less clear. Uncertainty persists in the political realm, alongside widespread violence. With incidents of violence and insurgent attacks on a sharp rise during all of 2005, American officials in May offered the quite candid assessment that the US military will likely have to stay on in Iraq for 'many years' and one US officer believed the US 'could still fail' in Iraq.[31] There is also a sharp divide between reports out of the country and the often upbeat and sanguine official statements emanating from officials of the Bush administration. In December, although typically loath to respond to sagging public opinion polls, the president announced a 'Plan for Victory' in Iraq that was long on platitudes of freedom, security, liberty and victory, but revealed little new insights or innovations.[32] Indeed, in a number of ways the situation in Iraq is looking increasingly similar to the United States' long and tragic involvement in Vietnam.

Private contractors, war profiteering and state building in Vietnam

By the time Lyndon Johnson took the oath of office shortly following John Kennedy's death late in 1963, the United States had for nearly a decade been trying to build a new state below the 17th parallel in Vietnam.[33] The American mission in southern Vietnam included specialists in civil police, public administration, public finance, military, counter-espionage, propaganda, industry, agriculture and education. Private contractors also built or rebuilt hundreds of miles of roadways and dozens of bridges, dredged hundreds of miles of canals and built airfields and deep draft ports to receive a continuing and growing volume of economic and military aid.[34] They built roads connecting all parts of Vietnam to Saigon, which they promised would result in greater access for both government officials and peasants to sell their crops to a larger market. They trained and equipped a rapidly expanding military force to keep Ngo Dinh Diem in power and they began to piece together a paramilitary security force and a Vietnamese Bureau of Investigation (VBI) modelled on the American FBI. They even inaugurated an identity card programme to catalogue the identity and keep track of every Vietnamese in the interest of maintaining security.[35] By the early 1960s, the United States government had poured into this project over $2 billion. The project failed. That is, the new nation of South Vietnam never emerged from all of the effort. Instead, a powerful insurgency spread over the whole of southern Vietnam and seized the initiative in the contest over who would control Vietnam's future. Further, southern Vietnam, and Saigon in particular, remained badly fractured politically as well as socially and economically.[36]

Shortly after toppling their most stable and long-term client, Diem, in November 1963, American officials proceeded to further militarize US involvement in Southeast Asia. From around 23,000 American troops in Vietnam in 1964, the number increased the following year to 185,000, and again the next year to over 385,000. American force levels peaked at around 543,000.[37] This expansion of the direct US military role in Vietnam set the stage for a Herculean military construction project.

By all accounts a traditional society, southern Vietnam had no infrastructure to receive this influx of military aid. All of southern Vietnam had only three airfields capable of landing jet aircraft. Its national airline, 75 percent government owned, consisted of twelve aircraft, none of which was jet propelled.[38] Tan Son Nhut, the Saigon airfield serving as the principal hub, received some of the military aid, but could not begin to keep pace with the flood of materiel. Of all the supplies destined for southern Vietnam, over 90 percent arrived by sea. Saigon, in fact, was one of only two ports with deep draft berthing. Other port facilities such as those at Da Nang, Nha Trang and Hué could handle far less capacity. Over the next year, almost half of all military cargo and 90 percent of all AID cargo passed through the port at Saigon. The congestion became legendary as ships and barges often waited a period of weeks or even months for dock space to off load. In past years, though recognized periodically as an obstacle, this underdeveloped infrastructure was not nearly the problem it soon became. A congressional team explained the importance of the port situation following a series of investigative trips there in 1966: 'Vietnamese port capacity is the chief factor bearing on the amount of assistance – both military and economic – that the United States is physically capable of providing to Vietnam'.[39]

Significantly escalating the American presence in Vietnam thus required substantial physical development. Such a large-scale military construction programme would have meant tens of thousands of engineer forces being sent into Vietnam earlier than politically feasible. The president believed, and continued to worry over it even after deciding on escalation, that such a move would provoke unwanted and damaging domestic criticism. Consequently, the administration breathed new life into a several year old $15 million construction contract awarded to a two firm consortium made up of Raymond International and Morrison-Knudsen (RMK). Morrison-Knudsen, a construction giant based in Boise, Idaho, recently became Washington Group International following a merger. The Vietnam consortium, of which it was the lead sponsor, had handled military construction needs since 1962.[40] The Boise firm dominated the arrangement, receiving 40 percent of the profits. In the early 1960s, its involvement in Vietnam had been somewhat limited by the relatively limited nature of the American role. The engineers carrying out the work believed entering 1964 they would soon leave Vietnam and they had begun to scale down their presence anticipating that departure. The mood quickly shifted beginning in the summer as orders for new work began to arrive at their offices. Before year's end the number of new projects had mushroomed.[41]

By spring, construction allocations climbed to over $150 million and RMK could hardly keep pace.[42] The projects numbered over 100 concurrently at the peak of construction. Suppliers in the US could hardly keep up either and backlogs of three to six months became commonplace. Caterpillar Tractor Company's annual report to shareholders intoned, '1965 was another recording-breaking year and only the physical limitations of production capacity kept sales and profits from being higher'.[43] Because so much of the work had to be completed prior to escalation, the consortium knew of the imminent American expansion well before most others. At the same time, the scale of the work, the pace of the projects and the funds allocated provided some early indication of things to come.

Construction projects quickly spread across much of southern Vietnam and involved bases, ports, ammunition dumps, airfields, radio installations, refugee camps, barracks, fuel depots, hospitals and warehouses. By May, the consortium had more than doubled its workforce from the 1964 level, hiring several hundred American construction workers and 11,000 Vietnamese, largely as non-skilled labourers.[44] Several months later, the orders still ran far ahead of the capacity of RMK alone. One exasperated MK official explained, 'all we knew was that they wanted a lotta roads, a lotta airfields, a lotta bridges, and a lotta ports, and that they probably would want it all finished by yesterday'.[45] In early August, RMK brought onboard two other large American construction firms, Brown & Root and J. A. Jones Construction, to form the RMK-BRJ. This consortium, frequently called the largest construction entity ever, became the sole contractor for the federal government for construction projects in Vietnam.[46] The consortium, renaming itself The Vietnam Builders in 1966, played a key role in the American presence in Vietnam and ingratiated itself there just as much as the US military or the other exponents of the American mission.

At its peak, the consortium's workforce numbered slightly more than 51,000, with around 47,000 Vietnamese, Koreans, Filipinos and others, and 4,000 Americans overwhelmingly in supervisory and management roles. Within these numbers, however, this workforce changed a great deal. Over the life of the contract the Builders employed between 180,000 and 200,000 Vietnamese.[47] A high rate of turnover, the demands of the work and the fluidity of a war environment in general gnawed away at cohesion and unity of purpose that the private contractors relied upon in their constant race to make deadlines and increase the pace of work on hundreds of simultaneous projects across southern Vietnam. Workers endured an intense work environment including injuries, kidnappings and killings. Some of the most troubling labour unrest, which the Builders' own self-evaluation termed a 'minor civil war', began not out of grievances between labour and management, but out of the general opposition to the regime.[48] Despite these and other considerable obstacles, the Builders benefited from a large pool of labour. Because of the very limited nature of Vietnamese home production and industry, these labourers were unlikely to be siphoned off to other attractive industry and/or factory jobs locally. Nevertheless, Builders management understood the need to attract workers given the omnipresent war climate.[49]

Despite all that had been built up during the second half of 1965, it was really just the beginning of a much greater construction project. Construction achieved a pace of $1 million of work-in-place-per-*day* by late summer. The contractors expected to (and did) achieve $40 million of work-in-place-per-month in the fall.[50] Construction materials competed with an increasing flow of commodity aid, food aid, military aid and all other imports for limited dock space, deep draft berthing and airfields. Once the needed materials did arrive, a reliable transportation system would have to then disperse the right supplies and equipment to the right job site out of the many hundreds then underway.[51] The Builders also required the simultaneous construction of their own camps, demanding still more resources of labour, time, materials and a system of efficient and rapid supply.

During the life of the contract, the Vietnam Builders moved 91 million cubic yards of earth, used 48 million tons of rock product, and nearly 11 million tons of asphalt. They built six ports with 29 deep-draft berths, six naval bases, eight jet airstrips 10,000 feet in length, 12 airfields, just under 20 hospitals, 14 million square feet of covered storage, and 20 base camps including housing for 450,000 servicemen and family. In short, they put on the ground in southern Vietnam nearly $2 billion (or $8.8 billion adjusted) in construction of various kinds of facilities and infrastructure. Only when assessed in full measure does one begin to appreciate why those involved referred to their work as 'the construction miracle of the decade'.[52]

The emphasis on preparation for war meant a diminution in emphasis on nation building. While southern Vietnam's military-related infrastructure, roads and bridges, ports and airfields, became modernized, the war destroyed hamlets, villages and farmland, turned peasants out as refugees and generally disrupted the countryside in an overwhelmingly agrarian society. The resulting mass movement and forced urbanization exposed the absence of infrastructure in the urban environments as well. Access to decent housing, jobs and job training, health care and education, and measures to combat poverty and protect against vice and crime were notably absent. At the height of the war, the regime in Saigon spent less than 1 percent of its enormous US aid budget on public health. Incidences of cholera, dysentery, diarrhoea and malnutrition ballooned into a public health crisis. The number of orphans also shot up, reaching well over 10,000. The war also produced approximately 100,000 casualties each year, an estimated 30,000–50,000 amputees awaiting prosthetics they would likely never receive, and 4 million refugees out of a population of 14 million.[53]

Tragically, the American aid programme also contributed to the obstacles to state building as it inundated southern Vietnam with an array of consumer goods, equipment and people. The avalanche of goods and the resulting economic inflation, in fact, became one of the chief preoccupations of the American mission, officials back in Washington and congressional investigators. In 1966, the United States sent to Vietnam $793 million in economic aid and $686 million in military aid. The level of aid dropped slightly in fiscal year 1967, but rose again to nearly $2 billion for 1968. Merchandise imports alone accounted for $650–$750 million of this aid package for each of those years.[54] This influx of troops, equipment, money and other goods in large quantities critically undermined the building of an indigenous economic base even without the flood of people.[55] At the same time, such infusions also created many opportunities for corruption, which became rife throughout the aid program. Congressional investigators found that an alarming quantity of aid goods never reached their intended target but were diverted into the thriving black market that operated as a kind of shadow economy throughout much of the war.

At home just as in Vietnam, Johnson fought to control inflationary pressures. Those pressures mounted as the war in Southeast Asia increased in scope and intensity. The soaring demands on the construction industry certainly meant rising profits but also threatened rising prices.[56] Congress became sharply critical of Johnson's handling of the Vietnam situation, warning his policies threatened to over-heat the domestic economy and drive prices up. By the late 1960s, well known Senators such as J. William Fulbright (D-Ark.), Mike Mansfield (D-Mon.) and Edward M. Kennedy (D-Ma.) joined war critics Ernest Gruening (D-Ak.) and Wayne Morse (D-Or.), becoming much more outspoken on the costs of the war for both the Americans and the Vietnamese. Fulbright began publicly asking very difficult questions of the Johnson administration. Mansfield had come to believe that the war was essentially un-winnable and not worth fighting, and Kennedy investigated and reported on the millions of Vietnamese made refugees by the war.[57]

In the House as well, a delegation embarked on an investigative trip to Vietnam in spring 1966. Their efforts yielded the first comprehensive investigation into all aspects of US policy in Vietnam. Committee members quickly discovered a failed state building project. As an unidentified US official in Vietnam told investigators, 'running parallel with the war is a national symphony of theft, corruption, and bribery'. Investigators turned up an alarmingly inefficient and counterproductive aid programme. As the war progressed, problems in the programme became more pronounced and more difficult to solve. The conclusions of that investigation, carried out by the House Committee on Foreign Operations, constituted the most damning indictment by Congress of the overall program to date.[58]

During the whole of the war, the black marketing of American goods created a substantial underground economy. One of the most visible manifestations of this economy could be found by visiting what was tellingly termed 'PX Alley' (Post Exchange). PX Alley consisted of a several-block area of the city devoted to dozens of individual stalls or kiosks lining both sides of the street and selling American consumer goods such as Lucky Strike, Salem, Kent and Winston cigarettes, radios, hair spray, razor blades, Styrofoam coolers, soap, US Army K rations, blankets and Campbell's Soup among dozens of other well-known American commodities. Though technically illegal, not to mention detrimental to larger objectives of American aid, this very visible and widespread phenomenon continued unabated for years. Nor was this market limited to PX Alley. The resale of American goods flourished and they could easily be found all over Saigon and in other cities as well. In many instances goods destined for the PX actually showed up on the black market before they had been stocked on the shelves at the US military facility. The exchange rate for these diverted black market goods ranged from 160–200 to 1.

The deputy director of the AID mission believed 'this is the most serious problem that exists for the U.S. Government in Vietnam today'. The availability of American goods and the diversion of those goods into the black market economy created 'a vast number of profiteers'. In the course of congressional investigations, officials discovered substantial diversion of goods and numerous warehouses full of tons of items being hoarded to drive up local prices. Investigation also turned up a large camp that acted as a depot for receiving pilfered American aid goods. This camp contained such commodities as 1,500 tons of rice, 6,000 pieces of galvanized sheet metal and 1,000 gallons of kerosene. The US military seized American pharmaceuticals from the insurgents half a dozen times in as many months.[59]

Importers could bring in essentially anything they thought they could sell internally or easily export. These importers, who had to obtain a special licence from the regime, enjoyed considerable advantages over domestic producers. They could avoid the 'competitive bidding' process by simply applying for a licence to import commodities valued at slightly under $10,000. Any import order for less than this amount did not have to go through the more rigorous and potentially competitive process, but was simply approved and the transaction moved through the pipeline. These transactions, which one congressman termed an 'invitation to steal', could be simply handed out to friends and associates and were, by design, beyond the reach of the AID. For fiscal year 1966, approximately 85 percent, or 25,000 transactions, of all licences issued came in below $10,000 and a large number of them amounted to $9,900.[60] Investigators found that despite the AID's knowledge of these importers and of the substantial diversion of commodities to the VC and the black market, there still existed no system to check on the honesty, the integrity, past patterns of good or bad behaviour or the political background of importers. The regime disqualified and blacklisted only 23 of the 2,000 importers. Even then, for 20 of those 23, officials only disqualified them following the congressional investigation.[61]

Legitimate opportunities to work and to earn a living were limited and much of Vietnam was wracked by war rendering it politically and economically profoundly unstable. Bribes, kickbacks and petty theft became a common method to supplement one's income. Corruption characterized the system at every level, not just among civil servants and lower level representatives of the regime, but among politicians, businessmen and military officers as well. According to the AID, 'there was an inordinate amount of corruption – by any standard'. 'The amount of corruption was far beyond that which could be tolerated under the grease-the-wheel theory'. On the American side, too, corruption ran rampant in the black market, in currency manipulation scandals, theft and more. Corruption ate into the programme's effectiveness, its legitimacy, its members' morale and its ability to carry out the ultimate aims of the United States. The AID's final comprehensive report concluded, 'there is little question that corruption ... was a critical factor in the deterioration of national morale which led ultimately to defeat'.[62]

There are many explanations for the pronounced level of corruption. Ultimately, congressional investigators and others concluded that a psychology of abundance had emerged years earlier and continued to govern thinking on spending and oversight of the aid programme. Because so much emphasis had been placed on accomplishing the military objectives in southern Vietnam, the costs of the project became at best secondary. As those costs soared, as inflation became a serious problem, as the economy haemorrhaged, and as criticism of the serious deficiencies built into the programme mounted, officials in Vietnam simply papered over the problems. Mission officials in Vietnam actively discouraged audits which might reflect poorly on the programme. Reports were either shelved or records discarded. Congressional investigators complained repeatedly that no paper trail existed to follow up on allegations of fraud, and that mission representatives simply could not provide answers to even the most basic questions. Illinois Representative Donald Rumsfeld, a member of the House investigative team, expressed his frustration over this problem:

> I want this record and you gentlemen to know how disappointed I was at the discussions in Vietnam with AID personnel. Invariably the reason [our questions] could not be answered was because of the lack of records, the lack of audits, the lack of procedures whereby this information would be available ... I got the feeling ... that the information is not available ... It is distressing for a ... member of a subcommittee to be attempting to come to grips with these problems, and to be repeatedly told that necessary and basic information is not available.[63]

The US aid economy was rife with corruption, graft, waste and outright fraud. Even some of its built-in, intentional features actually undermined the larger objectives. While the Commodity Import Program (CIP) continued to more or less effectively prevent galloping inflation, it also prevented local production and created enormous opportunity for pilferage and piracy. Countless millions of tons of commodities and supplies of all kinds wound through the labyrinth of the black market, providing profit-taking opportunities for numerous clandestine operators. Local businessmen were shielded from punishment by the lack of effective records, audits and investigations, among other protections. Even American GIs, many of them gone AWOL, found the opportunities too great to pass up. Just one such well organized ring of 50 US servicemen netted as much as a quarter of a million dollars a month in 'one of the largest black market/currency manipulation rings in Saigon', according to one study. Theft in these cases involved illegally obtaining and then selling US money orders and military pay certificates (MPCs) on the black market often at astonishingly disparate exchange rates.[64] Congressional investigators could not even determine the precise level of corruption. They could only guess at the amount of capital being hurried out of Vietnam and into safer accounts elsewhere. Some suggested that the black market in currency manipulation was a billion dollar business.[65] Whatever the precise volume of the theft, the economy of southern Vietnam continued to haemorrhage as both Americans and Vietnamese bled the aid programme dry.

Congressional watchdogs also specifically criticized the way in which the growing volume of aid, both construction/military and economic, was distributed in Vietnam. Officials within the AID and within Congress believed that at least part of the reason for the ineffectiveness and inefficiency of the US programme to create the new nation south of the 17th parallel stemmed from an extraordinary level of corruption, waste and profiteering. House Republican leader Gerald Ford specifically pointed out the contradictions of US state building policies in Vietnam saying, 'Americans must pay more and more to make powerful Saigon interests richer and richer and the Vietnamese people more completely dependent on us. This is just the opposite of our declared purpose of building a free and independent South Vietnam'.[66] As many, including Ford, had now come to realize, very little of the enormous US aid package actually went toward economic development and/or state building. At the same time, a few corporations, well-placed officials of the Saigon regime, and various opportunists hoarded vast sums for themselves and their friends.[67]

Illinois Representative Donald H. Rumsfeld (R) inveighed against the corruption associated with the little-known corporate involvement in Vietnam. In Congress, he charged the administration with letting contracts which 'are illegal by statute'. He criticized in particular the infamous 'President's Club',[68] to which Brown & Root head George R. Brown, one of the principal Vietnam contractors, had given tens of thousands of dollars in campaign contributions. Rumsfeld pushed for full investigation into the whole affair saying,

> under one contract, between the U.S. Government and this combine [RMK-BRJ] it is officially estimated that obligations will reach at least $900 million by November 1967 … why this huge contract has not been and is not now being adequately audited is beyond me. The potential for waste and profiteering under such a contract is substantial.[69]

The contracts that so troubled Representative Rumsfeld were the so-called cost-plus-award-fee type that allowed for greater profits as the costs of the work rose. The award fees over and above these costs ensured even greater profits. Morrison-Knudsen, as the contract's lead sponsor enjoyed 40 percent of the profits; the other three in the consortium split the remainder evenly. Needless to say, the companies made hundreds of millions for their work in Vietnam.[70] Neither Rumsfeld's nor other critical voices over the next several years effected much change.

As investigation uncovered waste and corruption in Vietnam, the war ground on, inexorably preventing ultimate success for the larger project of creating a new, modern, democratic nation below the 17th parallel. For the United States, the war in Vietnam finally ended rather ingloriously in 1973, and the sovereign nation state of 'South Vietnam' still had never become a reality. Instead, much if not most of southern Vietnam lay in ruins, torn asunder by years of warfare extending back to the late 1940s. The North finally completely eliminated the remnants of the Saigon regime, reuniting the country in 1975. The Vietnam Builders' contract expired in 1972. During the consortium's final days, an out-going General Manager wrote, 'There are no more pyramids to build. We have just about completed the largest construction effort in history'.[71] Despite this enormous project to put in place an integrated, modern physical infrastructure, the United States failed to achieve its objectives in Vietnam. The effort to invent 'South Vietnam' contained deep structural problems that stretched back many years. The war proceeded alongside the physical transformation of southern Vietnam into a defensible territory while the features of a new and independent state, such as they existed at all, completely atrophied.

Conclusion

What comparisons can be drawn between Iraq today and Vietnam decades ago and what lessons can be learned?

The once discernable line between the private sector and the public-military sector has continued to erode. In the case of Vietnam, the federal government relied upon a consortium of just four large firms for nearly all of its military construction needs. It selected those firms quite purposefully without any semblance of an open, competitive atmosphere. The firms were large and formed a collective reach and resource base unmatched by any competitors. In the case of Brown & Root, political connections also served them very well. Lyndon Johnson chose private contractors to somewhat quietly put in place an immense military infrastructure to allow for a greater American military role. Construction engineers and military planners quickly began to put in place an infrastructure complete with airfields, military bases, deep draft ports, primary and secondary roadways, dredged canals, an electrical grid, water, fuel and oil storage facilities, barracks and hospitals. The project immediately consumed enormous sums of money and untold manpower, both American and Vietnamese. Indeed, this massive military construction project, aimed at greater security and making Vietnam defensible, siphoned critical resources away from state building. This was a dilemma that Lyndon Johnson explicitly recognized.[72] The private consortium allowed the president to escalate to a major war in Vietnam. It could accomplish a great many tasks quickly and efficiently. It could not, however, solve the greater crises of state building. It could only temporarily mask those problems.

In Iraq, the level of corporate involvement, measured in either numeric terms or scale of the work responsibility, is at least as great as in Vietnam. Private firms now carry out a range of tasks that, up until very recently, the military did for itself. The line separating the military role from the private corporate role is faint, to say the least. Corporations are charged with a vast rebuilding effort that is central to the larger aims of US policy in Iraq. In some cases, employees of private firms such as KBR who have no experience or training in combat find themselves in active combat zones at an operational level. In other cases, company employees are themselves ex-military and use their specific training and skills in a combat setting for pay. More generally, the rise of what author P. W. Singer has termed the Privatized Military Firm (PMF) also erodes the line between traditional military personnel whose virtue has always been the public trust and the privatized soldier for hire whose interest is profit.[73] Both cases seem to suffer a critical lack of coordination and oversight that weakens the pursuit of larger policy aims amid a diffusion of corruption and mismanagement.

At the same time, corporations such as Halliburton (KBR), Lockheed-Martin, Boeing, Bechtel, DynCorp, Northrop-Grumman and hundreds of others have become relatively permanent fixtures in Pentagon circles. From logistics, supply, research and development, training and security, to food preparation, base building, maintenance and transportation, the American military relies heavily upon the private sector. The full effect of these relationships cannot at this point be fully known. There is little doubt that such a role for private contractors and the blurring of the line between them and the military impacts on both the domestic and foreign policy realm.

In this context, is US involvement in Afghanistan and Iraq a harbinger of things to come or the culmination of post-Cold War developments? Either way, it is a manifestation of a powerful American militarism and an omnipresent military–industrial complex.[74] That oft-used label once referred to the symbiotic relationship between the public military and the private arms makers. The concern, as President Dwight Eisenhower described it in his famous 1961 speech,[75] was that the latter would come to have inordinate influence in the public realm. This depiction of that relationship seems almost quaint nowadays.

The Vietnam experience demonstrates the longevity of this trend. Corporations have long been deeply involved in the exercise of US foreign policy. Further, large, well placed firms who regularly win government contracts have for decades assiduously cultivated their relationship with the government. Three of the four firms making up the Vietnam Builders ranked in the top ten of 400 US construction and service companies contracted with federal government for 1966. All of them actually increased their ranking as a result of their work in Vietnam. Morrison-Knudsen moved from number 5 to 3; Brown & Root moved from number 7 to 2; J. A. Jones from number 25 to 17. The final company of the consortium, Raymond

International, ranked tenth among companies doing business outside the United States.[76]

Many of the corporations winning government contracts during the Vietnam War continue to win contracts for work in Afghanistan and Iraq. In 1966, the top 400 firms winning contracts with the government included Bechtel Corp. (at number one), Brown & Root, Morrison-Knudsen (now Washington Group International), The Ralph Parsons Company and The Fluor Corporation, all in the top ten. Other corporations currently contracted in Afghanistan and Iraq appearing on the list include the Foster Wheeler, Perini, and Vinnell Corporations. It should also be understood that government contracts for carrying out the war in Vietnam were not limited to just these few firms. Five-hundred and twenty-three firms signed contracts for various tasks/services related to the war. The top 62 held contracts worth over $100 million each. Familiar names such as American Machine and Foundry (AMF), Alcoa, Eastman Kodak, Bulova Watch Company, Magnavox, General Motors, McDonnell Douglas, Lockheed, DuPont, Boeing and Honeywell all won contracts. It seems unnecessary to even point out that corporations came to see long-term, open-ended US foreign policy commitments such as Vietnam as business opportunities. As one General Motors executive told an interviewer in 1968, 'we want to be known as a car and appliance manufacturer, not a merchant of war ... but we also want to be ready to profit from the apparently endless series of brushfire wars in which the U.S. seems to involve itself'.[77] So great were the ties between the government's war in Vietnam and American corporations that a drawdown of forces in the early 1970s caused alarm for its potential harmful impact on the US arms/military industry and on the US economy generally.[78]

A significant corporate role in the execution of the government's foreign policy objectives, far from being a new phenomenon, is part of a very lengthy and complex tradition. The advocates of war in the private sector have long profited from its conduct.[79] Do they now also influence the coming and process of war itself for that reason? For these mighty corporations to sustain themselves, ensure continued profits and stable share prices, and maintain their competitive advantage, they push for greater military spending, and an increased role in the world in support of the military and preparations for war. Moreover, the relationship between corporate, government and military officials and the revolving door of employment opportunities between them deepens and perpetuates these connections. Seen this way, US foreign policy interventions such as invasions, peace-keeping, sanctions enforcement and state (re)building all become job security. This institutionalization of war profiteering alters its historic meaning. Corporations once had to rely on the existence of the specific conditions of warfare for contracts and an opportunity for profits. The Cold War re-created these war conditions, albeit in the absence of outright warfare between the rival states. And although the post-Cold War period yielded a less than favourable environment, those more favourable conditions have now returned in the guise of an open-ended, multi-front, geographically shifting and somewhat ambiguously defined 'war on terror'.[80]

Notes

1 Cheney quoted in, Tom Ricks and Greg Schneider, 'Cheney's Firm Profited From "Overused" Army', *Washington Post*, September 9, 2000.

2 P. W. Singer, 'War, Profits, and the Vacuum of Law: Privatized Military Firms and International Law', *Columbia Journal of Transnational Law*, 24(2), Spring 2004, p. 522. See also Singer, *Corporate Warriors: The Rise of the Privatized Military Industry*, Ithaca, NY: Cornell University Press, 2003. For a brief survey of the global activities of the Privatized Military Firms (PMFs), see pp. 9–17.

3 For a general history of war profiteering, see Stuart D. Brandes, *Warhogs: A History of War Profits in America*, Lexington, KY: University Press of Kentucky, 1997.

4 Such comparisons have, not surprisingly, become something of a national pastime. Of course, so have the refutations of them. See, J. Record and W.A. Terrill, *Iraq and Vietnam: Differences, Similarities and Insights*, Strategic Studies Institute, May, 2004; John Dumbrell, 'The Iraq and Vietnam Wars: Parallels and Connections', unpublished paper presented to the Society of Historians of American Foreign Relations Annual Conference, June 2005, University of Maryland and the National Archives and Records Administration, College Park, Maryland. By April 2004, President Bush felt compelled to publicly reject comparisons between Iraq and Vietnam, calling the idea a 'false analogy' that sends the wrong message both to the more than 100,000 US troops in Iraq and to the insurgents.

5 In 1990, Iraq ranked 50th among the nations of the world according to the United Nations Development Programme's Human Development Index. By 2003, its rank had slipped to 126th. See *Iraq Living Conditions Survey, Volume II: Analytical Report*. United Nations Ministry of Planning Development Cooperation, Baghdad, Iraq, 2005, p. 57; see especially 'The Iraqi Health System – From Success to Breakdown in One Decade, ibid., p. 82.

6 Anthony Arnove (ed.), *Iraq Under Siege: The Deadly Impact of Sanctions and War*, Cambridge, MA: South End Press, 2000. See also, 'Iraq Country Analysis Brief', US Department of Energy, November, 2004. http://www.eia.doe.gov/emeu/cabs/iraq/html (last accessed May 4, 2005). The United Nations Iraq Living Conditions Survey describes a substantially dilapidated, but nevertheless present, modern national infrastructure including a sewage system, potable water system and an electrical grid.

7 The Center for Public Integrity, 'Winning Contractors: U.S. Contractors Reap the Windfalls of Post-war Reconstruction', October 30, 2003. http://www.publicintegrity.org (last accessed April 19, 2005). As early as summer 2003, there were an estimated 20,000 contract workers in Iraq. See Michael Dobbs, 'Iraq: Halliburton Reaping Huge Profits: One in Three Military Dollars Spent Goes to Contractors', *Washington Post*, August 28, 2003; Elizabeth Becker, 'Details Given on Contract Halliburton Was Awarded', *New York Times*, April 10, 2003; Stephen J. Glain and Robert Schlesinger, 'Halliburton Unit Expands War-Repair Role', *Boston Globe*, July 10, 2003. The Center for Public Integrity's recently published investigation into the role of private contractors in both Afghanistan and Iraq reveals that over 70 American companies had contracted close to $8 billion in government contracts to rebuild Afghanistan and Iraq. They also shared ongoing and close relations with the federal government and provided more in campaign contributions to George W. Bush than any other official over a 12 year period.

8 Andre Verloy and Daniel Politi, 'Halliburton Contracts Balloon', The Center for Public Integrity, August 18, 2004. Michael Dobbs, 'Halliburton's Deals Greater Than Thought', *Washington Post*, August 28, 2003. By this time, over 150 companies had signed contracts with the federal government for work in Afghanistan and Iraq worth some $51 billion. For more background on Halliburton, see Jeremy Kahn, 'Will Halliburton Clean Up?', *Fortune*, March 30, 2003. See also Pratap Chatterjee,

'Cheney's Close Ties to Brown and Root', Corpwatch, March 20, 2003. http://www.corpwatch.org (last accessed February 22, 2005).

9 Karen DeYoung and Jackie Spinner, 'Contract for Rebuilding of Iraq Awarded to Bechtel', *Washington Post*, April 18, 2003. Elizabeth Becker and Richard A. Oppel, Jr, 'U.S. Gives Bechtel a Major Contract in Rebuilding Iraq', *New York Times*, April 17, 2003. Richard A. Oppel, Jr, 'Bechtel, the U.S. and Iraq: An Old Link', *New York Times*, April 19, 2003. For a list of the corporations and their contract values, see The Center for Public Integrity, Windfalls of War project at http://www.publicintegrity.org/wow/ (last accessed April 19, 2005).

10 Sue Pleming, 'U.S. Plans 24 New Contracts for Iraq by February', Forbes.com, November 18, 2003. http://forbe.com/newswire/2003/11/18 (last accessed May 4, 2005).

11 Sue Pleming, 'Heady Days for Contractors in Race for Iraq Deals', *Forbes.com*, November 20, 2003. http://www.forbes.com/iraq/newswire/2003/11/20 (last accessed April 26, 2005).

12 Daniel Politi, 'Winning Contractors – An Update', The Center for Public Integrity, July 7, 2004. http://www.publicintegrity.org/wow/ (last accessed April 19, 2005). See also Corpwatch's Top Military Contractors at http://www.warprofiteers.com (last accessed May 4, 2005).

13 Max Boot, 'Different Rules for Contractors Put Military at Disadvantage', *The Sun-Herald*, April 5, 2005. www.sunherald.com (last accessed May 4, 2005).

14 Contractors such Kellogg, Brown & Root offer substantially higher salaries that are tax free to induce Americans to go and work amid the dangers in Iraq. See Michael Serazio, 'Gambling on Iraq', *The Houston Press*, December 2–8, 2004, pp. 21–8. By 2005, 412 contracted workers and other civilian workers had died in Iraq. Around 147 of them were Americans. James Glanz, 'U.S. Inquiry Cites Missteps in Iraqi Reconstruction', *New York Times*, October 30, 2005. As expected in such a fluid environment, the estimates of injuries, deaths and suicides vary from source to source. See also, John Ward Anderson and Steve Fainaru, 'U.S. Confirms Killing of Contractors in Iraq: Four Were Slain by Angry Mob Last Month', *Washington Post*, October 23, 2005. 'Roadside Bomb Kills Four American Contractors in Basra', *New York Times*, September 7, 2005.

15 Andrea Buffa and Pratap Chatterjee, 'Houston, We Still Have a Problem', Corpwatch, May 17, 2005. http://www.corpwatch.org (last accessed May 18, 2005). A much more detailed examination of Halliburton can be found in, 'Houston, We Still Have a Problem: An Alternative Annual Report on Halliburton', May, 2005, produced by Pratap Chatterjee of Corpwatch.

16 Lee Drutman and Charlie Cray, 'Cheney, Halliburton and the Spoils of War', *Citizen Works*, April 4, 2003. http://corpwatch.org/issues/PID.jsp?articleid=6288 (last accessed February 22, 2005). Pratap Chatterjee, 'Cheney's Former Company Wins Afghanistan War Contracts', Corpwatch, May 2, 2002.

17 Edward Epstein, 'Congress Curious About Iraq Deals', *San Francisco Chronicle*, May 20, 2003. http://sfgate.com/cgi-bin/article.cgi?f=/c/a/2003/05/MN148811.DTL (last accessed February 22, 2005). Erik Eckholm, 'The Billions: Top U.S. Contracting Official Calls for an Inquiry in the Halliburton Case', *New York Times*, October 25, 2004. On the illegality of the cost-plus-award-fee contract, see Kaufman, *The War Profiteers*, pp. 118–19. Letter to Lt. Gen. Robert Flowers, US Army Corps of Engineers from Representative Henry Waxman, March 26, 2003. Letter to Rep. Henry Waxman from Robert Flowers, April 8, 2003. Letter to David M. Walker, Comptroller General of the United States, General Accounting Office from Rep. Henry Waxman and Rep. John Dingell, April 8, 2003. Letter to Lt. Gen. Robert Flowers from Rep. Henry Waxman, April 10, 2003 and April 16, 2003. Letter to Les Brownlee, Acting Secretary of the Army from Rep. Henry Waxman, May 29, 2003. Letter to Honourable Donald Rumsfeld from Rep. Henry Waxman, April 30, 2003. Letter to Henry Waxman from

Robert Flowers, May 2, 2003. Letter to William H. Reed, Director, Defense Contract Audit Agency from Rep. Henry Waxman, February 12, 2004. Letter to Honourable Joseph E. Schmitz, Inspector General, US Department of Defense from Rep. Henry Waxman, February 24, 2004. Letter to David J. Lesar, President, Chairman, and CEO, Halliburton from Rep. Henry Waxman, February 27, 2004. For specific details on Halliburton's contract abuses of the public trust, see Letter to Democratic Members of the House Government Reform Committee from Rep. Henry Waxman, March 10, 2004. All letters/correspondence available in PDF format at http://www.house.gov/ waxman/news_letters.htm (last accessed May 13, 2005). See also my editorial, 'Is Congress AWOL on Iraq?', *History News Network*, March 7, 2005. Available at http:// hnn.us/articles/10477.html (last accessed October 17, 2005).

18 Letter to Rear Admiral (ret.) David J. Nash, Director, Iraq Program Management Office from Rep. Henry Waxman, December 18, 2003.

19 Statement of Rep. Henry A. Waxman, Ranking Minority Member, Committee on Government Reform. Hearing on the Complex Task of Coordinating Amid Chaos: The Challenges of Rebuilding a Broken Iraq, March 11, 2004.

20 T. Christian Miller, 'Rules and Cash Flew Out the Window', *Los Angeles Times*, May 20, 2005. See also Craig S. Smith, 'Poor Planning and Corruption Hobble Reconstruction of Iraq', *New York Times*, September 18, 2005.

21 Miller, 'Rules and Cash', op. cit. and Ed Harriman, 'Where Has all the Money Gone?', *London Review of Books*, 27(13), July 7, 2005. 'Iraq was Awash in Cash. We Played Football with Bricks of $100 bills', *The Guardian* (London), March 20, 2006.

22 Letter to Honourable Joshua Bolten, Director, Office of Management and Budget from Rep. Henry Waxman, September 30, 2003. Statement of Rep. Henry A. Waxman, Contracting Abuses in Iraq, October 15, 2003. Letter to Honourable Tom Davis, Chairman, Committee on Government Reform, from Rep. Henry Waxman, January 23, 2004. Letter to Honourable Joseph E. Schmitz, Inspector General, US Department of Defense from Rep. Henry Waxman, January 16, 2004. Memorandum for Corporate Administrative Contracting Officer, Defense Contract Management Agency San Antonio (DCMAW-GEHC), Defense Contract Audit Agency, January 13, 2004. Neil King, Jr, 'Halliburton Tells Pentagon Workers Took Kickbacks to Award Projects in Iraq', *Wall Street Journal*, January 23, 2004. Max Boot, 'Different Rules for Contractors', op. cit. P. W. Singer, 'War, Profits, and the Vacuum of Law', op. cit., p . 525. David Phinney, 'Contract Quagmire in Iraq', Corpwatch, April 27, 2005. David Phinney, 'Halliburton Bribery Scandal Deepens', Corpwatch, March 29, 2005. http://www.corpwatch.org/print_article.php?&id=12158 (last accessed May 4, 2005). Neela Banerjee, '2 in House Question Halliburton's Iraq Fuel Prices', *New York Times*, October 16, 2003. 'Army Eyes Halliburton Import Role in Iraq', *The Associated Press*, November 5, 2003. 'Audit: KBR Lost Track of Government Property in Iraq', *The Associated Press*, November 26, 2004. James Glanz, 'U.S. Should Repay Millions to Iraq, a U.N. Audit Finds', *New York Times*, November 5, 2005. Erik Eckholm, 'Showcase: Rebuilding of Basra Progresses, But It's Harder Than Expected', *New York Times*, January 19, 2005. James Glanz, 'American Faces Charge of Graft for Work Iraq', *New York Times*, November 17, 2005. Charles R. Babcock and Renae Merle, 'U.S. Accuses Pair of Rigging Iraq Contracts', *Washington Post*, November 18, 2005.

23 As a 2004 study warns, however, '*even "obligated" does not mean that Iraqis are seeing any real progress in terms of actual project completions*' (emphasis in original). See Anthony H. Cordesman, 'Nation Building in Iraq: A Status Report', Center for Strategic and International Studies (CSIS), Washington, DC, March 25, 2004, p. 8. Michael R. Gordon, 'Nation-Building in Iraq: Lessons from the Past', *New York Times*, November 21, 2003.

24 Peter Baker, 'Bush Cites Setbacks in Rebuilding By the U.S.', *Washington Post*, December 8, 2005.

25　Ellen Knickmeyer, 'Baghdad Neighborhood's Hopes Dimmed by the Trials of War; Some Who Welcomed Americans Now Scorn Them', *Washington Post*, September 27, 2005. Craig Smith, 'Poor Planning and Corruption Hobble Reconstruction of Iraq', *New York Times*, September 18, 2005.

26　James Glanz, 'U.S. Inquiry Cites Missteps in Iraqi Reconstruction', *New York Times*, October 30, 2005.

27　Renae Merle and Griff Witte, 'Security Costs Slow Iraq Reconstruction, Contract Excesses Also Hamper Progress', *Washington Post*, July 29, 2005. An important indicator of rebuilding and a gauge of potential political trends is the fact that the average unemployment rate is 50–65 percent. See 'Administration is Shedding the "Unreality" that Dominated Invasion, Official Says', *Washington Post*, August 14, 2005. Spencer Ante, 'A Hole in Bush's Iraq Exit Strategy', *BusinessWeek Online*, April 19, 2005. http://www.businessweek.com/bwdaily/dnflash/apr2005/nf20050418_5596. htm (last accessed December 12, 2005).

28　Pratap Chatterjee, *Iraq, Inc.: A Profitable Occupation*, New York: Seven Stories Press, 2004, pp. 73–92. 'Investigation Reveals Reconstruction Racket in Iraq', Corpwatch, February 4, 2004. http://www.corpwatch.org/press/PPD.jsp?articleid=9849 (last accessed November 14, 2005).

29　*Iraq Living Conditions*, op. cit., chapter 3.

30　*Iraq Living Conditions*, op. cit., p. 85.

31　John F. Burns and Eric Schmitt, 'Generals Offer Sober Outlook on Iraqi War', *New York Times*, May 19, 2005. On the emphasis on military conditions and warfare, see Sidney Blumenthal, 'Far Graver than Vietnam', *The Guardian*, September 16, 2004. Eric Schmitt and Thomas Shanker, 'Pentagon Sets Steps to Retake Iraq Rebel Sites', *New York Times*, October 8, 2004.

32　Scot Shane, 'Bush's Speech on Iraq War Echoes Voice of an Analyst', *New York Times*, December 4, 2005. According to one of the researchers for the document, 'Plan for Victory', it is not a 'strategy document from the Pentagon about fighting the insurgency ... .The Pentagon doesn't need the president to give a speech and post a document on the White House Web site to know how to fight the insurgents. The document is clearly targeted at American public opinion'. The author is a political scientist at Duke University. See 'National Strategy for Victory in Iraq', http://www. whitehouse.gov/infocus/iraq/iraq_strategy_nov2005.html (last accessed December 6, 2005). The document itself bares a striking resemblance to Vietnam, down to its use of language such as 'clear and hold' operations to root out insurgents.

33　Despite the fact that the effort below the 17th parallel in Vietnam was the most ambitious, sustained nation building project the US had ever undertaken, very little literature exists specifically dealing with this topic. Of that which has been written, see especially Robert Scigliano, *South Vietnam: Nation Under Stress*, Boston, MA: Houghton-Mifflin Company, 1963; David L. Anderson, *Trapped By Success: The Eisenhower Administration and Vietnam, 1953–1961*, New York: Columbia University Press, 1991; and John Ernst, *Forging a Fateful Alliance: Michigan State University and the Vietnam War*, East Lansing, MI: Michigan State University Press, 1998.

34　Immediately following the Geneva Conference's Final Declaration in 1954, the United States began pouring money and expertise into southern Vietnam to build a modern, democratic state below the 17th parallel. Dozens of specialists and technicians, from civil police, public administration, public finance, military, counter-espionage, propaganda, industry, agriculture and education immediately descended upon Saigon, the southern city made the capital of the whole project. These experts, along with the US government and military installed Ngo Dinh Diem who then used American aid to remove all viable opponents, crackdown on dissidents, forcibly eliminate the political opposition and to physically transform southern Vietnam. See MSUG Final Report, Michigan State University Vietnam Advisory Group Papers, Michigan State University Archives and Special Collections (henceforth *MSUG Papers* with appropriate filing information). United States Operations Mission (USOM), *Vietnam Moves Ahead*, Annual Report for Fiscal Year 1960. Committee on Foreign Relations, U.S. Senate, 86th Congress, 1st Session, *The Situation in Vietnam*, July 30 and 31, 1959.

35 Report of Comprehensive Work Plan to USOM and Vietnamese Government, *MSUG Papers*, Vietnam Project, Correspondence, Ed Weidner, 1954, box 628, folder 102. Letter to Arthur Brandstatter (Head, Department of Police Administration) from Howard Hoyt (Deputy Advisor, Police), July 5, 1955, *MSUG Papers*, Vietnam Project, Police Administration, Arthur Brandstatter Correspondence, 1957–61, box 681, folder 10. For detailed reports on the establishment and evolution of the police system, see *MSUG Papers*, Vietnam Project, Police Administration, PSD/ICA/W Monthly Reports (Bound), 1957–60, box 679, folders 63, 66 and 69 for specific field reports on a variety of locations around southern Vietnam.

36 See James M. Carter, 'Inventing Vietnam: The United States and State-making in Southeast Asia', Dissertation, University of Houston, 2004.

37 George Herring, *America's Longest War: The United States and Vietnam, 1950–1975*, 4th edn, New York: McGraw Hill, 2002, p. 182.

38 AID Administrative History, LBJL, 424. United States Economic Assistance to South Vietnam, 1945–75, Agency for International Development (henceforth, USEASV), Washington, DC, 1975, vol. II, p. 408. Carroll H. Dunn, *Base Development in South Vietnam, 1965–1970*, Washington, DC: Department of the Army, 1972, pp. 7–12.

39 An Investigation of the US Economic and Military Assistance Programs in Vietnam, October 12, 1966, House of Representatives, 89th Congress, 2nd session, Report No. 2257, 64. See also, Memorandum for Mr Robert Komer, Subject: Report of Special Mission – Port of Saigon, Vietnam, June 14, 1966, NSF, Komer-Leonhart File, box 20, LBJL.

40 Contract No. *NBy-44105*, 'Raymond-Morrison-Knudsen Joint Venture Contractor for Airfields and Communications Facilities, Vietnam', US Navy Bureau of Yards and Docks, January 19, 1962, *RMK-BRJ Papers*.

41 A. H. Lahlum, *Diary of a Contract*, Saigon, July 1967, *RMK-BRJ Papers*, p. 22. Originally, the private consortium consisted of Raymond International and Morrison-Knudsen. In August 1965, Brown & Root and J. A. Jones Construction were both added in order to gain greater reach and access to greater resources commensurate with an expanded American military role and related construction needs in Vietnam. All documents referred to as *RMK-BRJ Papers* were obtained from the companies involved and came in no discernable order or arrangement. They are all in the author's possession.

42 'Military Construction in South Vietnam', The Em-Kayan Magazine, November 1963, pp. 8–9, *RMK-BRJ Papers*. Captain Charles J. Merdinger, 'Civil Engineers, Seabees, and Bases in Vietnam', *U.S. Naval Institute Proceedings*, No. 807 (May 1970), p. 261. The rate of work taking place was measured on a work-in-place-per-month basis (WIP). At the end of 1964, the WIP figure stood at $1.7 million. By the next spring, it had leapt to over $4 million. As plans for expansion continued, the amount of work expanded, to an eventual peak of more than $65 million WIP.

43 'War Slows Equipment Deliveries', *Engineering News-Record*, February 17, 1966, p. 23 and 'Leading Contractors Exploiting Industrial and Overseas Booms', *Engineering News-Record*, May 19, 1966, pp. 32–4.

44 The Vietnamese workforce was increased from 4,900 to 11,000, a leap of nearly 125 percent. As of April 1965, according to the *Diary of a Contract*, op. cit., 'every day some new and bigger phase of work was received and no diminishing of this trend was foreseen', *Diary of a Contract*, *RMK-BRJ Papers*, pp. 27–8. 'Work Increases as War Expands', *Engineering News-Record*, May 13, 1965, pp. 25–8. 'Construction Expands in South Viet Nam', *The Em-Kayan Magazine*, June 1965, p. 7, *RMK-BRJ Papers*.

45 John Mecklin, 'Building by the Billion in Vietnam', *Fortune*, September 1966, p. 114.

46 Letter from MK to Raymond Intl, Brown & Root and J. A. Jones, 'Joint Venture Agreement', August 16, 1965; Letter from Lyman Wilbur (Morrison-Knudsen) to H. C. Boschen (Raymond International, Inc.), August 25, 1965, *RMK-BRJ Papers*. Carroll Dunn, *Base Development*, 1972, p. 27. Lieutenant David L. Browne, 'Dust and Mud and the Viet Cong', *U.S. Naval Institute Proceedings*, No. 811 (September 1970), pp. 53–7. Commander W. D. Middleton, 'Seabees in Vietnam', *U.S. Naval Institute Proceedings*, No. 774 (August 1967), pp. 55–64, 60.

47 *Diary of a Contract*, op. cit., pp. 148, 153. 'Work Increases as War Expands', *Engineering News-Record*, May 13, 1965, pp. 25–8. This article's author reported the Vietnamese were 'small men' and they 'often weigh only 90 lb or so, and look like children at the wheel of a big bulldozer or truck. Some are strong enough for only four or five hours a day of such work'. The article offers no explanation of how the same Vietnamese ever became such efficient and productive farmers in this climate that exhausted the American soldier.

48 See, *inter alia*, Evaluation of Contractor's Performance, 1 April 1966–30 September 1966, *RMK-BRJ Papers*, III-b-1, VI-c-1 to VI-c-4. *Jones Construction Centennial: Looking Back, Moving Forward*, Charlotte, NC: Laney-Smith, 1989, p. 154. 'U.S. Ally in Vietnam: Civil Works', *Engineering News-Record*, May 5, 1966, pp. 17–20. For much more detail on these matters see James M. Carter, 'The Vietnam Builders: Private Contractors, Military Construction, and the "Americanization" of US Involvement in Vietnam', *Graduate Journal of Asia-Pacific Studies*, 2(2), 2004, pp. 44–63. See also, 'Toward Negotiations', *TIME Magazine*, April, 1966.

49 'VN Incentive Program Launched', *The Viet Nam Builders*, 1(19), November 1, 1966, p. 1.

50 'Construction of Military Facilities by RMK-BRJ is Changing Face of South Viet Nam', *The Em-Kayan Magazine*, 25(6), August 1966, pp. 12–13. To date, the Builders had paved 1,260 acres in airfields alone, imported 1,628 miles of water pipe and poured enough cement monthly to pave 35 miles of four-lane highway. Chairman's Memo, 'Subject: Impressive Achievements in South Viet Nam', *The Em-Kayan Magazine*, 25(10), December, 1966, p. 1.

51 *Diary of a Contract*, op. cit. pp. 148, 154.

52 The contract extended to 1972, though the most intense period of construction was achieved during 1966–8. Combined Completion Report, Basic Report, schedule XIII, pp. 1–3, *RMK-BRJ Papers*. 'RMK-BRJ, The Vietnam Builders, "The Construction Miracle of the Decade"', *RMK-BRJ Papers*. *Diary of a Contract*, op. cit. The combined result of these many projects made the defence of a piece of territory possible. Overall logistics capacity, from airfields to sea ports, increased many times over during this brief period. The network of canals and rivers, of roads, primary, secondary and tertiary, also expanded many times over. This expanded capacity made possible the prosecution of a major war. By the middle of 1968, the United States deployed over 530,000 troops. The forces defending the Saigon regime, principally the ARVN (Army of the Republic of Vietnam), numbered 562,000 by the end of 1966. This force level, which needed also to be highly mobile and swift, required an immense and efficient logistics grid. Document in author's possession.

53 'Civilian Casualty and Refugee Problems in South Vietnam', Subcommittee to Investigate Problems Connected with Refugees and Escapees, 90th Congress, 2nd session, May 9, 1968, pp. 2, 4. Richard Eder, 'U.S. Refugee Plan for Vietnam Set', *New York Times*, August 31, 1965. American officials even approached agencies of the United Nations for help with the crisis. See Richard Eder, 'U.S. Seeking U.N. Aid for Vietnamese Refugees', *New York Times*, February 15, 1966.

54 Douglas Dacy, *Foreign Aid, War and Economic Development: South Vietnam, 1955–1975*, New York: Cambridge University Press, 1986, p. 200. *USEASV*, op. cit., vol. I, p. 8.

55 *USEASV*, op. cit. vol. I, p. 107.

56 On the Vietnam War and its impact on US politics and the economy, the British periodical *The Economist* maintained consistent and insightful coverage during the period. See, *inter alia*, 'Congress Turns Cautious', *The Economist*, April 23, 1966; 'Frustrations of Consensus', *The Economist*, April 30, 1966; 'Taxing Questions', The Economist, March 19, 1966; 'There's a Better Way than LBJ', *The Economist*, May 20, 1967; 'Paying for the War', *The Economist*, August 12, 1967.

57 *The Vietnam Hearings*, with an introduction by J. William Fulbright, New York: Vintage Books, 1966. 'Refugee Problems in South Vietnam and Laos', Subcommittee to Investigate Problems Connected with Refugees and Escapees, U.S. Senate, 89th Congress, 1st session, July, 1965 and 'Civilian Casualty and Refugee Problems in South Vietnam', Subcommittee to Investigate Problems Connected with Refugees and Escapees, 90th Congress, 2nd session, May 9, 1968.

58 An Investigation of the U.S. Economic and Military Assistance Programs in Vietnam, October 12, 1966, House of Representatives, 89th Congress, 2nd session, Report No. 2257.

59 An Investigation of the U.S. Economic and Military Assistance Programs, op. cit. pp. 17, 22, 26–37. See also, Herring, *America's Longest War*, op. cit. pp. 196–8.

60 'Improper Practices, Commodity Import Program, U.S. Foreign Aid, Vietnam,' Hearings before the Permanent Subcommittee on Investigations of the Committee on Government Operations, U.S. Senate, 90th Congress, 1st session, April 25–27, 1967, part I., pp. 2–4, 91. *USEASV*, vol. II, pp. 461–2.

61 An Investigation of the U.S. Economic and Military Assistance Programs in Vietnam, 1966, op. cit., p. 16. Commodity Import Program for Vietnam (Follow-up Investigation), U.S. House of Representatives, Committee on Government Operations, 34th Report, October, 1970, p. 9.

62 *USEASV*, vol. I, pp. 224–6. For corruption within the US mission, see Fraud and Corruption in Management of Military Club Systems, Illegal Currency Manipulations Affecting South Vietnam, Hearings before the Permanent Subcommittee on Investigations of the Committee on Government Operations, United States Senate, 91st–92nd Congress, September 1969–March 1971, parts I–VIII.

63 An Investigation of the U.S. Economic and Military Assistance Programs in Vietnam, op cit., pp. 56, 62–3.

64 William Allison, 'War for Sale: The Black Market, Currency Manipulation and Corruption in the American War in Vietnam', *War and Society*, 21(2) (October, 2003), p. 146.

65 Fraud and Corruption in Management of Military Club Systems, Illegal Currency Manipulations Affecting South Vietnam, op. cit., September 30, 1969, part I, p. 2.

66 Felix Belair, Jr, 'Rep. Ford Scores the "Other War"', *New York Times*, October 9, 1967.

67 *USEASV*, vol. I, pp. 224–6.

68 Though the Presidents Club membership was only about 800, it had given more than $1 million to the Democratic Party. See Fred Graham, 'Johnson Denies Any Favoritism in the Award of U.S. Contracts', *New York Times*, August 25, 1966.

69 Remarks by Donald Rumsfeld found in, 'Construction Activities in Vietnam', *Congressional Record*, August 18, 1966, pp. 19, 920 and in *Congressional Record*, August 30 and August 31, 1966, pp. 21, 303–21, 304. Fred P. Graham, 'Johnson Denies Any Favoritism in the Award of U.S. Contracts', *New York Times*, August 25, 1966. In May 1966, the contract changed from a cost-plus-fixed-fee (CPFF) type to a cost-plus-award-fee (CPAF) type.

70 Although the precise figures were and remain difficult to pin down in part due to lack of record keeping and transparency.

71 John B. Kirkpatrick (Former General Manager, RMK-BRJ), Joint Venture, Saigon, Vietnam, 'Subject: End of Viet Nam Construction Program', *The Em-Kayan Magazine*, June, 1972.

72 Memorandum for the President: Basic Policy in Vietnam, January 27, 1965, National Security Files (NSF), Memos to the President, McGeorge Bundy Papers, box 2, LBJL. McGeorge Bundy meeting notes, January 27, 1965, McGeorge Bundy Papers, Notes on Vietnam, 1964–5, LBJL.

73 Singer, *Corporate Warriors*, op. cit. p. 204. See also, Ken Silverstein, *Private Warriors*, New York: Verso, 2000, chapter 5.

74 Chalmers Johnson, *The Sorrows of Empire: Militarism, Secrecy, and the End of the Republic*, New York: Henry Holt & Company, 2004. Andrew J. Bacevich, *The New American Militarism: How Americans Are Seduced by War*, New York: Oxford University Press, 2005.

75 Eisenhower's famous military–industrial complex speech is available at: http://coursesa.matrix.msu.edu/~hst306/documents/indust.html (last accessed on June 5, 2005). Although less well known, Eisenhower himself earlier advocated the creation of the military–industrial complex he later deplored. See Seymour Melman, *Pentagon Capitalism: The Political Economy of War*, New York: McGraw-Hill Company, 1970, Appendices A and B, pp. 231 and 235 respectively.

76 'War Slows Equipment Deliveries', *Engineering News-Record*, February 17, 1966. 'Leading Contractors Exploiting Industrial and Overseas Booms', *Engineering News-Record*, May 19, 1966.

77 Economic Priorities Report, Council on Economic Priorities, Washington, DC: 1971. General Motors executive quotation is from *The Sunday Times* (London), April 21, 1968.

78 See also *Economic Impact of the Vietnam War*, The Center for Strategic Studies, Georgetown University, Washington, DC, 1967, particularly chapter 4 and The National Economy and the Vietnam War, The Research and Policy Committee of the Committee for Economic Development, New York: 1968, pp. 49–60.

79 See source in note 3.

80 Ken Silverstein, *Private Warriors*, op. cit., chapter 1. Chalmers Johnson, *Sorrows of Empire*, op. cit., chapters 6, 7 and 8. Commenting on the shift in US global strategy during the dozen or so years following the end of the Cold War, Johnson writes, 'without a superpower enemy, the first hints of the openly-proudly-imperial role it would take on in the new century emerged .... The United States now assumed ... responsibilities for humanitarian intervention, the spread of American-style "market democracy" via globalization, open warfare against Latin American drug cartels and indigenous political reform movements, the quarantining of "rogue states", leadership of an endless "war on terrorism", and finally "preventive" intervention against any potentially unfriendly power' (pp. 21–2).

6

'VIETNAM', VICTORY CULTURE AND IRAQ

Struggling with lessons, constraints and credibility from Saigon to Falluja

David Ryan[1]

When Secretary of State Madeleine Albright took office in 1997 shortly after President Clinton's second electoral victory, she told one of her early audiences that her reference point was Munich not Vietnam. Indeed she would invoke Munich again two years later as the United States moved toward intervention in Kosovo.[2] The intended implication suggested that the lessons of Vietnam had inhibited US policymakers on questions of intervention; it was time to revert to more satisfactory instructions and narratives associated with the 'good war', to eschew appeasement and stand up to aggression. Indeed President George H. W. Bush and others before him had invoked Munich as an antidote to the operative constraints of the Vietnam analogy[3] and perplexingly President Reagan used the Munich analogy while simultaneously assuring Congress that there was no thought of sending American boys to Central America; it remained unclear whether the United States was standing up or standing down.[4] For some policymakers US credibility and resolve had been questioned for far too long. The importance of credibility during the Cold War was obvious. The US's 'stature as a world power, a psychological dimension of international relations' was at stake. The prospect of failure in Korea, Vietnam or the Gulf might undermine allied confidence in US leadership and 'embolden unfriendly powers'.[5] After Vietnam concerns on credibility were even more acute. President Richard Nixon talked of the 'pitiful, helpless giant' as the war demonstrated that a superpower could be defeated. If the United States wanted to remain an activist superpower based on its traditional approach to international relations it was imperative to limit the lessons of Vietnam and the emerging Vietnam syndrome. Vietnam demonstrated that while the superpowers might have been able to destroy the world they could not control it.[6] Power usually has invited resistance.[7] The Soviet challenge had been relatively clear and containment soon became the operative framework within which Washington would limit its reach;

111

but changes in the Third World, whether revolution or nationalism, or both, were much more problematic. In many cases there lingered a sense of doubt on how best to confront such forces and on whether the United States *could* win. Further cultural doubt sometimes lingered in certain cases on whether the United States *should* win. After Vietnam such misgiving became even more acute. In the current situation, to overcome the cultural analogies of Vietnam, Washington would need to win the 'hearts and minds' of not just Iraqis, but also the American people.

The tactical lessons that ensured the ability to sustain intervention as a military option over time became closely associated with the Powell Doctrine, the use of overwhelming power to win decisively and quickly. Named after Colin Powell, who served in Vietnam, rose to prominence in the Reagan administration and served in principal capacities during the Gulf War of 1991, the Clinton administration and of course as Secretary of State in President George W. Bush's first term, the doctrine evolved to a point where, given US technological proficiency, it almost found a method of intervention that was acceptable in US culture. The doctrine had become an incredibly important solution to the dilemma of how to reconcile US credibility and the credibility of their power after the loss in Vietnam with US commitment, resolve, reliability, leadership, decisiveness and its image around the world.[8] It was restrictive. Overwhelming power would be used only after four criteria were met. The criteria stemmed selectively from the lessons of Vietnam and almost directly from the principles of November 1984 enumerated by the then Secretary of Defense Caspar Weinberger. First, objectives were clearly defined centred on identifiable national interests; second, public and Congressional support had to be assured; third, success had to be a strong likelihood; fourth, there had to be an exit strategy that left US credibility intact.

If these criteria were present, Washington could opt for the use of force. The demonstrations of such power might requite lingering doubts associated with defeat in Vietnam, but those who resisted US hard power around the world also learnt that conventional confrontation with US forces was pointless; opposition would be irregular. Broadly speaking, US tacticians focused on the instrumental lessons of Vietnam; despite the more fundamental strategic lessons on intervention, hegemony, and the need to recognise the limits of US power and influence, certain strategists were inclined to reconstruct policies of preponderance that the United States had initially built after the Second World War.[9] Yet now the use of the military as an instrument of power had to account for the impact of the Vietnam syndrome; strategists sought methods of continued intervention that would demonstrate the United States had not been detrimentally affected by the experience in Vietnam and that it remained steadfast in its orientation. The Vietnam syndrome had to be contained. If the 'tragedy of great power politics' was and is that all states seek opportunity to alter the distribution of global power in their favour,[10] the tragedy of the Bush administration is that rather than accepting positive aspects of the Vietnam syndrome and the instrumental lessons shaped to conform to the limits of its cultural toleration, it sought to overturn the overriding guidelines that had emerged over the decades since the late 1960s, and reassert US power. Iraq provided the opportunity. In its implementation, the limits of US power and credibility, the appeal of its leadership and the strategic basis for its continued dominance were severely questioned.

While various executives sought continued preponderance, it was clearly the case that at times US culture was unwilling to pay the price and bear the burden of such adventures.[11] The democratic restraint on the executive's ability to exclusively construct strategy was considered a hindrance and exposed a point of supposed weakness. If the Vietnamese leadership, especially Pham Van Dong, recognised that the strategic point of vulnerability lay within the United States, in the reluctance of its people to support sustained wars of choice where success was elusive, and if in the post-heroic age the Vietnam syndrome represented a modicum of democratic influence over executive options in making war, the strategies of intervention represented a compromise between the various presidencies and the parts of US culture and its population that were wary of the motives for war. The use of proxy force as in the *contras* in Nicaragua, the *mujahedin* in Afghanistan or the use of technology through airpower largely provided presidents with vehicles of intervention that operated within the constraints of the syndrome. The apotheosis of instrumental lessons after Vietnam was implemented in Kosovo in 1999, where NATO and the Clinton administration's response was largely confined to the use of airpower, keeping US personnel at 15,000 feet above harm's way. Slobodan Milosevic did capitulate but only after intensified repression during the period of exclusive aerial bombing. Moreover, not one US fatality was incurred in Kosovo, prompting Michael Ignatieff to suggest that with precision war through airpower the democratic constraint on the executive through the conduct of seemingly 'virtual war' might be removed.[12] For other observers outside Western circles Kosovo also demonstrated that Washington was still reluctant to fight on the ground; its will and credibility were still open to question. Furthermore, Saddam Hussein survived the war of 1991; without a significant change in US tactics he could possibly survive another such attack. The fault with the Rumsfeld approach to war was that, in the discerning words of Robert Singh, 'the Powell Doctrine was less an exercise in timidity than an object lesson in judicious calculation ...'.[13] Yet for some that very caution represented an intolerable constraint on executive licence. As early as 1968, Albert Wohlstetter, University of Chicago academic and an influential Cold War strategist, who ultimately influenced Paul Wolfowitz, argued, 'of all the disasters of Vietnam the worst may be the "lessons" that we'll draw from it'. He feared that Americans might prefer to avoid intervention in the future rather than searching for more reliable tools of engagement. 'In effect', Bacevich suggests, he 'feared that Vietnam might induce a populist challenge to elite control of strategy'.[14] The war in Iraq, in the slipstream of 9/11, provided the opportunity to overcome such constraints and move beyond the use of exclusive airpower, to demonstrate that the United States was not sundered by a memory, that its force was credible, and that the domestic point of vulnerability had been addressed.

The ends of victory

The lessons of Munich exercised considerable influence at the origins of the Cold War and the Korean War; they were pertinent for Presidents Kennedy and Johnson on Cuba and Vietnam.[15] After 9/11 the familiar message was abundantly clear. US resolve was soon invoked and the credibility attached to that resolve created a further national interest and yet another commitment. The implicit message of Munich, updated by George W. Bush, was that failure to stand up to the aggression would as in the past 'encourage further aggression by undermining the credibility of all commitments'.[16] The demonstration of resolve was pivotal after 9/11 as Bush prepared the country for war, a long war; a war that would define the administration and the contemporary meaning of US policy.

The meaning of US power and the fundamental purpose of its foreign policy was central to neoconservative thinking.[17] Coincidental with the end of the Cold War, Francis Fukuyama, a former employee of the US Department of State, published 'The End of History' in *The National Interest*. The argument had widespread appeal. History had come to an end. US-style liberal democratic capitalism represented the teleological terminus of the great American journey towards this *particular* end of history.[18] The confidence and certainty of this argument that in symbolic form represented the culmination of the great orthodox or traditional meta-narrative of US history, diplomacy and foreign policy, of the march of freedom and the progress of democracy, spawned a line of triumphal histories of the Cold War over the 1990s.[19] Yet, despite the obvious victory in the Cold War (a conflict that in and of itself had eroded the traditional notions and feelings of victory by obviating any meaningful triumph short of mutual destruction), another niggling yet fundamental narrative remained important in US culture and collective memory. The memories associated with the US loss in Southeast Asia remained pertinent and a powerful inhibiting factor to the exercise of US power. The confidence of the nation was not so secure; its identity tarnished. All administrations since the defeat in Vietnam and the ignominious, catastrophic and confused retreat off the rooftops of US buildings in Saigon, soon to be Ho Chi Minh City, dealt with the impulse and strategic imperative to restore and demonstrate US credibility around the world. Such was the disquiet; President Bush Sr attempted to pre-emptively mitigate the effects of Vietnam on his administration. In his inauguration speech on January 20, 1989, he observed that: 'the war cleaves us still. ... But friends, that was begun in earnest a quarter century ago. Surely the statute of limitations has been reached'. He then argued that 'the final lesson of Vietnam is that no great nation can long afford to be sundered by a memory'.[20] The dissatisfaction of defeat dented the confidence of the culture shaped by a multitude and supporting narratives of victory. The 'culture of defeat' had to be reversed.[21] The fall of the Berlin Wall did not requite the post-Vietnam frustration.

Administrations struggled from the 1970s onward with the question of intervention and the restoration of the triumphant aspect of US identity. President Ford reverted to a spectacular and unnecessary use of force in the *Mayaguez* incident of May 1975; President Carter avoided intervention; Reagan restored the rhetorical narrative of triumph and exceptionalism while using proxy forces to pursue US 'victories' in Nicaragua, Afghanistan and elsewhere. The Gulf War of 1991 was supposed to reverse that US inhibition in war, that fear of losing US troops abroad in undefined conflicts where national interests were not obvious, and American popular support was wanting; that Vietnam syndrome. It was imperative to demonstrate at that crucial point, that moment, when the Soviets were preoccupied with the collapse of their outer empire and the imminent implosion of the inner empire, when the United Nations authorised the use of force and there was broad support behind the US-led action.[22] Iraq provided an opportunity as well as a conventional war in a desert not a jungle. That devastation and destruction of Iraqi forces and civilians over the early months of 1991 temporarily restored the US confidence in the victory culture, though as Saddam Hussein survived the war, and reasserted his own power through retributive destruction of the Shia uprising in the south, the exuberance faded. Moreover, when Syria asserted its presence in Lebanon shortly after, US resolve was again open to question. American feelings of victory were compromised and compounded still further by President Clinton's indecisive use of force in Bosnia, Somalia and Haiti, and the total absence of a US presence as the genocide unfolded in Rwanda. Victory through the use of airpower in Kosovo in 1999 confirmed to some that ground troops were still considered superfluous, echoed later in the book and film *Jarhead*.[23] The evolution of technology had assisted their reassertion of power since Vietnam; yet the collective memories, that democratic inhibitor, limited the latitude of foreign policy strategists in Washington.

The 9/11 attacks temporarily changed the context. The level of death and symbolism of the destruction temporarily obviated the Vietnam syndrome as the immediacy of war loomed. Internal administration disputes on the scope and extent of the retribution and pursuit of justice and war limited the initial military concentration in Afghanistan. Al Qaeda was quickly conflated with the Taliban, though the conflation of the terrorists with the tyrants would take another few months, facilitated by the Manichaean Presidential rhetoric which echoed throughout US culture. Still, the operations in Afghanistan, though relatively swift, were reminiscent of a combination of the Powell and Reagan doctrines: overwhelming airpower combined with the disproportionate use of indigenous ground forces, primarily through the Northern Alliance. Such an approach was necessary against a cacophony of warning on the failed Soviet and British ventures in that territory. Contemplation of an even more limited pursuit of al Qaeda, requiring negotiation of Afghani terrain smacked too much of the metaphorical quagmire, albeit dry, dusty and mountainous. Still, Afghanistan provided a sense of limits; in the words of Schivelbusch, 'to nominate another nation as a terrorist or rogue state so as to locate the spectre of terrorism within a concrete territorial enemy, a target'.[24] Expiation in Afghanistan invoked the traditional response of war against another nation. The Taliban fell with relative speed, and dispersed into the country. After Afghanistan, Charles Krauthammer caught a certain influential mood:

The elementary truth that seems to elude the experts again and again—Gulf War, Afghan War, next war—is that power is its own reward. Victory changes everything, psychology above all. The psychology in the region is now one of fear and deep respect for American power. Now is the time to deter, defeat or destroy other regimes in the area that are host to radical Islamic terrorism.[25]

Iraq offered another opening through conflations of terrorists with tyrants and nightmares of the assumed presence of weapons of mass destruction and the continued actual presence of Saddam Hussein. It offered location, a target and another opportunity to remove much of the cultural inhibition on war. According to polls, most Americans celebrated the victory of 2003, the swift application of force with ground troops, 'while a significant minority saw the world's most powerful military machine decimating a small, weak country and were ashamed'.[26]

We are familiar with the narratives associated with the rush to war, the endless conflations in Bush's rhetoric on the 'terrorists and the tyrants', the absence of weapons of mass destruction, the initial absence of links between al Qaeda and Iraq, and the ambitions to bring democracy to Iraq and the wider region. The terrible irony of the current situation in Iraq derives from the combination of first, the long held will to victory, held by some, after Vietnam; second, their focus throughout the 1990s on Iraq as unfinished business; and third, their desire to overcome the Vietnam syndrome and demonstrate an ability to put US troops on the ground, albeit fewer in number, augmented by the developments of the Revolution in Military Affairs, though as one US officer put it, 'Basically, we've got all the toys, but not enough boys'.[27] Yet the very presence of US troops, their rules of engagement, their offensives, and the resulting deaths of civilians may well be counterproductive, sustaining and expanding the support for the various insurgencies.[28]

Historical lessons are largely used in a constructivist fashion for contemporary needs and particular purposes.[29] The lessons of Vietnam cut both ways in the US and international discourses. US inhibition created opportunities and fashioned the tactics of certain opponents. The 'catastrophic' victory in Iraq represented the culmination of a yearning for triumph, which soon unfolded and unwound in the face of various forms of resistance from Falluja, Najaf and elsewhere over the subsequent months and years. Initially, Bush seemed to be riding high on the back of not only the victory in Afghanistan, but also the psychological boost derived from it. Iraq as an example would produce a demonstration effect. The confidence of American opponents would be shattered, their actions inhibited. Henry V experienced the euphoria of such a demonstration at Agincourt in 1415. Bush, according to John Lewis Gaddis, got a taste of that by the end of 2001.[30] That sense of victory was reflected in the grandiose visions that emerged in 2002, primarily contained in Bush's National Security Strategy[31] and in the idea to 'democratise' the Middle East over the next generation. The sentiment of predominance left traces within some administrations since Vietnam. The explicit and implicit narratives of a desire to recreate preponderance can be traced backward from the NSS of September 2002, which indicated that 'Our forces will be strong enough to dissuade potential adversaries from pursuing a military build-up in hopes of surpassing, or equaling, the power of the United States'. The military priorities included the need to 'dissuade future military competition; deter threats against U.S. interests, allies, and friends; and decisively defeat any adversary if deterrence fails'.[32] The desire for the restoration of unquestioned primacy of US power was also clear in the leaked 1992 *Defense Planning Guidance* document that sought to 'discourage' advanced industrial nations 'from challenging our leadership or seeking to overturn the established political and economic order'. Moreover competitors must be deterred 'from even aspiring to a larger regional or global role'.[33] Earlier still Reagan's National Security Council worried about the 'loss of U.S. strategic superiority' in the post-Vietnam context, not just because of perceived Soviet advances, but also because of 'the increased political and economic strength of the industrial democracies [in Europe]...'[34] Post Iran-Contra, Robert McFarlane, formerly National Security Advisor, reflected predominant administration beliefs in hearings before Congress:

> We had just witnessed a five year period where the Soviet Union tried out a stratagem of sponsoring guerrilla movements that would topple moderate regimes, and install their own totalitarian successor, and they had phenomenal success ... in Angola, Ethiopia, South Yemen, Cambodia, Afghanistan, Mozambique, [and] Nicaragua. ... If we could not muster an effective counter to Cuban-Sandinista strategy in our own backyard, it was far less likely that we could do so in the years ahead in more distant locations. ... We had to win this one.[35]

As reflected in McFarlane's vision there was this deeper desire to stem the perception of the United States as the 'helpless giant' in the face of this arc of revolutionary activity. The metaphor of the arc suggested a certain unity and teleological direction, if not even instruction reminiscent of the domino theory, which had to be addressed. From the early 1970s to the Reagan era there were 14 successful revolutions. The various rebellions had disparate aims, objectives, motivations and ideologies that were too easily conflated in some strategic thinking.[36]

The domino theory was largely discredited during the 1960s with the Sino–Soviet hostility, and the wars between Vietnam and Cambodia and then Vietnam and China in 1978 and 1979 respectively. Yet, from early in the 1970s Noam Chomsky utilised the domino theory in a different sense in Congressional testimony before the Senate Committee on Foreign Relations. He contended that:

> National independence and revolutionary social change, if successful, may very well be contagious. The danger is what Walt Rostow, writing in 1955, called the 'ideological threat', specifically, 'the possibility that the Chinese Communists can prove to Asians by progress in China that the Communist methods are better and faster than democratic methods.'

While the 'domino theory in military terms was always entirely senseless', the domino theory in terms of example had an element of plausibility and caused a level of concern in Washington.[37] The disparate, instrumental and constructivist lessons that others took from the US experience in Vietnam suggest a widespread and deep impact on various tactics. Already one sees reactions to Iraq in the Hugo Chávez government's decision to create a two million strong reservist army following Condoleezza Rice's description of Venezuela and Cuba as 'sidekicks' to Iran, at the onset of what she called an 'inoculation strategy' against the country. Venezuelan General Alberto Muller Rojas argues that if the United States invaded Venezuela, which is what they generally expect, 'the only way we could repel such an attack would be a full scale guerrilla war against the foreign aggressors'.[38] But more importantly as far as the scope of this chapter is concerned and especially given the tendency to lump many of these diverse forms of opposition to US policy together, there was and is a cumulative worry that the effects of further defeat or the loss of credibility could have widespread implications. Once the commitment had been made, especially in 2003 with troops on the ground, persistence, staying the course, demonstrating the will and so forth became potent narratives that could not be avoided. This is not to suggest parallels with Vietnam, more to suggest the deep political impact of that war on the current situation.

The demonstration effect was certainly important. Not in the sense that Iraq would provide a model of development for other countries, more in the sense that as a defined 'rogue' state it provided a symbol of resistance. After the conventional phase of the war in 2003, the continued insurgency also demonstrated the limits of US power. Military analysts decried the discourse of doubt and early exit strategies, even as the White House advanced such programmes through accelerated training schemes for the Iraqi army and police forces. Militarily the US casualties were considered within acceptable bounds, sustainable. But the battleground, as Pham Van Dong had earlier recognised, was also within the United States. Here Bush had to reconcile the growing domestic pressure for a withdrawal of US forces with the maintenance of US credibility. By mid-2005 Bush explained that the war in Iraq and the wider war on terrorism and the casualties incurred therein were 'worth it' because the results would be decisive. The terrorists would be left 'emboldened, or defeated'. Freedom in Iraq would become a model for the region, and the failure of that project would send similar inverse messages.[39]

The Vietnam syndrome is not and was not only limited to the American psyche, or its collective memories, but was and is also utilised elsewhere. Utilitarian, constructivist and often lacking deep parallels, the mere reference to Vietnam or associated words or phrases were often enough to spread doubt or question resolve. For instance, in early 1981 soon after President Reagan was inaugurated, a series of documents were produced on 'Why El Salvador Isn't Vietnam'. After some discussion tracing all the differences between El Salvador and Vietnam, Richard Allen, the National Security Advisor's advice to peer principals was to 'try not to mention the word Vietnam; even its use may tend to validate the thesis'. Vietnam was to be substituted in public discourse with the phrase 'previous historical situations'.[40]

It was certainly the case that there was widespread use of the Vietnam analogy both within Washington and by US opponents to stem the proponents of intervention. The Sandinistas were well aware of the structural breakdown and the political space created after Vietnam. In their exchanges with US officials the costs of intervention were alluded to. Moreover, the Sandinistas worked the Hill to influence the debate on *contra* aid. More pertinently, in both 1990 and 2002–3, Saddam Hussein utilised the Vietnam syndrome in his flawed decision making. He told an Arab Summit in February 1990 that all he had to do was act boldly and the Americans would do nothing.[41] He apparently really did not expect Bush to go to war in 1990. Days before the Iraqi invasion of Kuwait, he told US Ambassador to Iraq, April Glaspie, that 'yours is a society that cannot accept 10,000 dead in one battle'.[42] In 2003 Hussein was reportedly convinced that US operations would be confined to the use of airpower and that like 1991 he could sit it out and survive; despite the devastating consequences for Iraqis. In March 2002, as Washington's attention returned to Iraq as the location to advance the war on terrorism, Deputy Prime Minister Tariq Aziz warned that, 'it was not the jungle that allowed the Vietnamese to win but determination. The Iraqis will fight in every street and every house'.[43] Echoed later in the year with the metaphorical taunt: 'let our streets be our jungles, let our buildings be our swamps'.[44] When Shia leader Moqtada al-Sadr's newspaper was closed and a close deputy arrested, widespread violence broke out across the Shia dominated south and in the Sunni town of Falluja in the west. Hundreds died as the US used both overwhelming air power and sent US troops in; Sadr needled US politicians: 'Iraq will be another Vietnam for America and the occupiers'. [45]

It was as if these men had found the 'point of vulnerability in the American mind'. The commitment might be fragile; their ability to stay the course could be questioned.[46] Washington was also cognisant of the impact of Vietnam. President Bush Sr's leaked 1990 NSD-26 argued that: 'In cases where the US confronts much weaker enemies, our challenge will be not simply to defeat them, but to defeat them decisively and rapidly'.[47] Moreover, on the eve of the coalition bombardment in 1991, President George H. W. Bush indicated that this would *not be another Vietnam*; 'we don't need another Vietnam. … No hands are going to be tied behind backs … It will not be a long, drawn-out mess'.[48] The experience of Lebanon 1983 too augmented the Vietnam syndrome, partially expiated in Grenada. NSD-26, in words of prescient importance, argued that

> For small countries hostile to us, bleeding our forces in protracted or indecisive conflict or embarrassing us by inflicting damage to some conspicuous element of our forces may be victory enough, and could undercut political support for US efforts against them.[49]

Similarly in the 1990s, in 1993 and 1999, there were frequent references to the Balkan Vietnam, a possible quagmire the United States might be dragged into, developing fears of the inability to extricate itself or the number of casualties which ensured that the war was fought primarily from several thousand feet above the metaphors.

This point is central to the struggle. President Bush's rhetoric is filled with the familiar post-Vietnam vocabulary: commitment, resolve, will and determination, US credibility and leadership. He had learnt well. The commitment to Iraq is not just about the country, its territorial integrity, its political stability and the imposition of a constitutional democracy, and the defeat of the insurgencies and the terrorists. It is also about the US forces' ability to stay the course; and its demonstration effects. This much was clearly recognised by Bush in the Veterans Day speech of November 11, 2005.[50]

Back in 1972, Leslie Gelb, then of the Brookings Institute, who had left service in government and later was co-author of *The Irony of Vietnam: The System Worked* (1979), testified to the US Senate that the story of US entry into the Vietnam War was not one of misguided descent into 'unforeseen quicksand'. He explained,

> it is primarily a story of why U.S. leaders considered that it was vital not to lose Vietnam by force to communism. Our leaders believed Vietnam to be vital not for itself but for what they thought its loss would mean internationally and domestically.[51]

The cognition of the implications of loss permeated strategic thinking, though it was often unclear whether it was US national interests or those of the particular politicians and their credibility that were at stake. Early in his administration President Nixon, in conversation with Singapore's Prime Minister Lee Kwan Yew, identified the 'high stakes' in Asia. A precipitous withdrawal would be disastrous for Asia and Europe, 'But, the most serious effect would be in the United States. When a great power fails, it deeply affects the will of the people'.[52]

The terrible irony, as Fredrik Logevall amply demonstrated in his 1999 work, was that the war in Vietnam was a war of choice, like that of Iraq in 2003. Both were unnecessary and could have been avoided. He concludes, 'there is this, finally, to say about America's avoidable debacle in Vietnam: something very much like it could happen again'. The central lesson related to the primacy of the executive branch and within the branch of a few individuals at the exclusion of the bureaucracy, in pursuit of immediate political advantage rather than 'long-term national interests'. 'A leader will assuredly come along who, like Johnson, will take the path of least immediate resistance and in the process produce disastrous policy—provided there is a permissive context that allows it'.[53]

Lessons

The range of lessons after the Vietnam War was plentiful. Culturally there was an initial inclination to turn off the war and turn away from its meaning and significance. Policymakers to a large extent also tried to limit the range of instruction, to contain the emerging Vietnam syndrome. Yet, Wolfgang Schivelbusch observed in his study of defeat that it was remarkable 'how briefly the losing nation's depression tends to last before turning into a unique type of euphoria'. There was the scapegoat of the old regime, or the old *realist* premises of US policy under Nixon and Kissinger, augmented by the Watergate scandal and Congressional investigations of CIA abuses by the Church and Pike Congressional Committees. Schivelbusch's broad observations suggest, 'the more popular the revolt and the more charismatic the new leadership, the greater the triumph will seem'.[54] While Carter certainly departed from the realism associated with Nixon and Kissinger, his popularity proved short lived. Still, President Carter reinvested US policy with a moral tone, centred on non-intervention and human rights. Fukuyama wrote much later that 'after Vietnam ... a very different view emerged that was reflected in the words of President Jimmy Carter, who believed that the West lived in "inordinate fear of Communism"'. Yet, he continued, 'Neoconservatives after Vietnam simply continued to bear the torch of the earlier Cold War view about communism as a unique evil'.[55] The rest of the Carter quotation from 1977 indicated that the United States embraced any dictator that shared that fear. The point was about confusing traditional US values and strategic objectives. Carter, albeit in a very inconsistent manner, sought some distance from the most odious regimes that abused human rights consistently. Yet Reagan rejected Carter's reservations, transformed the atmosphere within the United States, resituated Vietnam within the narrative of the just cause and rekindled the US relationship with a range of dictatorships that still shared that sense of fear or provided other strategic opportunities. Hence, the initiatives to improve relations with Saddam Hussein's Iraq in the early 1980s facilitated by Donald Rumsfeld as Special Envoy to the Middle East.

Earlier, after Vietnam, Henry Kissinger attempted to limit the impact of the Vietnam lessons. In memoranda for President Ford, he wrote:

> It is remarkable, considering how long the war lasted and how intensely it was reported and commented, that there are really not very many lessons from our experience in Vietnam that can be usefully applied elsewhere despite the obvious temptation to try. Vietnam represents a unique situation, geographically, ethnically, politically, militarily and diplomatically. We should probably be grateful for that and should recognize it for what it is, instead of trying to apply the 'lessons of Vietnam' as universally as we once tried to apply the 'lessons of Munich'.

Recognising that the battleground was largely domestic, Kissinger opined that 'tenacity of the American people and the ultimate failure of our will' were instrumental in the US defeat and that the United States was unable to engage in protracted war. Americans would not long support a war that jarred with their traditional attitudes.[56] The Iraq War had to be about more than the negative reasons associated with the pursuit of WMD or links between Saddam Hussein and al Qaeda; the positive framework of democracy promotion in Iraq and perhaps the region was imperative, despite the long history of support for authoritarian regimes in the Middle East.

These more ambitious goals invited resistance. Moving away from the Vietnam syndrome required a series of steps. Militarily, Washington needed to demonstrate that it could place large numbers of troops on the ground in distant lands. Politically, it would need to pacify and reconstruct Iraq to demonstrate that the exit strategy was more than just the way out for the United States; that they left something worthwhile rather than the chaos that prevailed after 2003. And of course, they would need to win over the American people to support executive decisions on intervention.

There is little sign of positive progress to date. Vietnam continues to be used throughout US culture, politics and foreign discourse. The analogy remains potent despite the differences between Vietnam and Iraq outweighing the similarities.[57] Vietnam references have a cumulative effect and become especially significant during periods in which US casualties are more extensive: in November 2003 when 82 Americans were killed, in April 2004 (135), and November 2004 (137), a period during which Senator Kerry was questioned over his Vietnam experience during the presidential campaign; also in January 2005 (107) and during April 2005 on the anniversary of the US withdrawal from Vietnam, or at least the anniversary of the symbolic end as US helicopters left rooftops in April 1975, rather than the official end with the signing of treaties in 1973. The debate on Iraqification was haunted by the ghosts of that collapse and imminent total defeat of the venture. This time US credibility related to its ability to stay the course, and exit with a degree of stability, prosperity and democracy in Iraq if not the entire region. That broad agenda starkly contrasts with the lessons of Vietnam that US objectives had to be limited, defined, supported by the American people and Congress, and achievable.

In 1975 State Department analysts wrote in a memo forwarded to Kissinger:

> Having been badly burned in Viet-Nam, the American people now appear to have quite different, and more limited, visions of our proper role in the world and our ability to influence events. In a sense, a control mechanism has evolved within our society which is likely to prevent for the foreseeable future any repetition of a Viet-Nam style involvement. The danger may therefore be not that we will ignore the lessons of Viet-Nam, but that we will be tempted to apply them too broadly, in East Asia and around the world. … It is tempting to say, as many do, that we should either use our power totally or not use it at all.[58]

The instrumental lessons that took US tactics in the direction of 'overwhelming power' across the late 1980s and the beginning and end of the 1990s in Panama, the Gulf and Kosovo, exemplified the extent to which total power could be used within culturally acceptable bounds. Carter largely decided that he would not use US military power, at least in terms of conventional intervention, whereas Reagan's predilection to use proxy forces provided a path between Carter's non-intervention and the Vietnam syndrome. In both cases credibility remained a problematic issue in the minds of policymakers that harboured desires for more assertive power. Kissinger warned Ford,

> In the end, we must ask ourselves whether it was all worth it, or at least what benefits we did gain. I believe the benefits were many, though they have long been ignored, and I fear that we will only now begin to realize how much we need to shore up our positions elsewhere once our position in Vietnam is lost. We may be compelled to support other situations much more strongly in order to repair the damage and to take tougher stands in order to make others believe in us again.[59]

The pervasive impact of Vietnam relating to clear objectives, assured success, domestic support and an exit strategy was not initially lost on the Bush administration, but after 9/11 Bush had no problem convincing American audiences that national interests were at stake and the response needed to be broad and sustained.

But the parameters of the breadth of the response were problematical; support waned as the administration broadened its scope beyond the seemingly obvious connections to 9/11. In the process the administration ignored most of the salient post-Vietnam guidelines. Renewed to his position as Secretary of Defense, Donald Rumsfeld reassessed the criteria for intervention in March 2001. Updating the thinking that permeated the meetings that dealt with the *Mayaguez* incident of May 1975, Rumsfeld wanted a more vigorous US presence in the world. He argued that the United States must be 'willing and prepared to act decisively to use the force necessary to prevail, plus some'. They must 'act forcefully, early ...'. Political difficulties had to be acknowledged; 'dumb down' versions of the missions should not be advanced to gain public support. Exit strategies should not be linked to dates providing opponents with the option to 'simply wait us out'. While most of the instruction since Vietnam suggested inaction unless crucial criteria were fulfilled, Rumsfeld considered the costs of such inaction: 'Just as the risks of taking action must be carefully considered, so, too, the risk of inaction needs to be weighed'.[60]

Clear objectives

The opportunity to move against Saddam Hussein resulted from the political fallout of 9/11 coupled with a proclivity to use a Manichaean framework to narrate the meaning of the events and the US response. Bush could thus conflate the so-called War on Terror, through rhetorical signifiers with the long held desire to rid Iraq of Saddam Hussein and a corner in the neoconservative mind of an inadequacy, of which Hussein was a reflection. In the process, the desire to assert US power coupled with the opportunity of a relatively vulnerable regime, the injunction to pursue clear objectives was lost.

Objectives were unclear from the start. Beyond regime change there was little positive planning for the post-war period. The specific military mission and its objectives were achieved with relative ease. The broader objectives relating to the stabilisation of Iraq let alone those of the war on terrorism remained vague, undefined and therefore difficult to achieve. On the wider 'war' on terrorism Bush's rhetorical explanations were exceedingly broad and at times echoed the universal rhetoric of the early Cold War period, sustained until Vietnam and the Nixon administration replaced such talk with a recognition of limits.[61] But it was precisely these 'realist' limits that had to be overcome. The attacks of 9/11 were not just related to the specific grievances in Bin Laden's rhetoric, but also in Bush's response conflated with US values and ideals, their way of life. Bush early on informed the audience at the National Cathedral, 'In every generation, the world has produced enemies of human freedom. They have attacked America, because we are freedom's home and defender. And the commitment of our fathers is now the calling of our time'. And days later at the joint session of Congress,

> Either you are with us, or you are with the terrorists. (Applause). ... This is not, however, just America's fight. And what is at stake is not just America's freedom. This is the world's fight. This is civilization's fight. This is the fight of all who believe in progress and pluralism, tolerance and freedom.[62]

Such conflation hopelessly extended the definition of the US objectives. Terrorists, not just the specific terrorist groups but theoretically all terrorists, tyrants and rogue nations would be the focus of the 'long war' eventually articulated in the Quadrennial Defense Review of early 2006.[63] The conflation and the confusion over the definition of opponents, like that of the conflation of nationalism and communism at certain junctures in the Cold War, involve similar ambition, overextension and ultimately the need to recognise limits.

The clear division between Colin Powell and Pentagon officials, especially Rumsfeld and Paul Wolfowitz, on the military objectives was played out early after 9/11. Powell's position was initially influential: that should the mission be defined too broadly, beyond the scope of Afghanistan, allies would drop off. But Iraq was already on the agenda. Rumsfeld was given to citing Eisenhower to the effect: 'if a problem cannot be solved, enlarge it'.[64] While Iraq did provide a target long sought after by the neoconservatives, it was quite certain that the shifted focus would alienate some allies, inflame the anti-American sentiment regionally and more broadly, and provide an opportunity and recruiting ground for terrorist movements.[65]

Nevertheless, conflation continued through the Axis of Evil rhetoric of January 2002 and the West Point speech linking the 'terrorists and tyrants' in common cause, repeated frequently after that. The rhetorical association of Hussein and al Qaeda permeated US official discourse. Polling evidence indicates that the strategy was initially successful as many Americans shared these beliefs until the situation began to deteriorate in Iraq. In 2004, for instance, Americans believed that the war in Iraq was assisting the war against terrorism; that it demonstrated the power of the US military; and confirmed that the United States supported democracy promotion. US opinion departed from opinion elsewhere. Distinctions between the war in Iraq and that on terrorism were more pronounced, Washington was considered less trustworthy as a result of the war in Iraq and 'even U.S. military prowess is not seen in a better light as a result of the war in Iraq'.[66] Official objectives in Iraq were largely based on illusion, bypassing the post-Vietnam admonition on accurate and honest intelligence. The pursuit of WMD was largely based on a fiction; the attempt to inhibit the connections between the terrorists and the tyrants facilitated the creation of conditions in which such connections became apparent. And democracy promotion would always be a double-edged sword, potentially destabilising and alienating long-time regional allied authoritarian regimes.[67]

The specific Pentagon objectives were more focused but they were still partly fuelled by illusion. Eight objectives were identified for Iraq: to end the Hussein regime; to eliminate WMD; to capture or drive out the terrorists; to collect intelligence on terrorist networks; to collect intelligence on WMD; to secure the country's oil fields; to end sanctions and deliver humanitarian relief; and finally to assist Iraq to establish representative government and secure its territorial integrity. While several objectives were unnecessary and the last two have proved quite problematical, the broader US objectives relating to ambitions of unrivalled power challenged post-Vietnam injunctions.

Strong likelihood of success

Success obviously relates to the objectives sought. Bush's characterisation of the war as a 'catastrophic success' captures the disjunction between the limited military objectives and the fact that there was little planning for the post-war situation.[68] The Vietnam analogy is most pervasive on the question of US endurance and its ability to stay the course, which is closely related to the casualties incurred.

As a result of significant casualty phobia after Vietnam the various administrations devised strategies to avoid such losses. Given Rumsfeld's March 2001 memorandum on the use of ground troops, President Bush prepared Americans early on Afghanistan and Iraq. He used the necessary language that signalled US resolve and determination:

> I will not settle for a token act. Our response must be sweeping, sustained and effective. … You will be asked for your patience, for the conflict will not be short. You will be asked for your resolve, for the conflict will not be easy. You will be asked for your strength because the course to victory may be long.[69]

Despite the preparation of the country and the assumed effects of 9/11, the Vietnam analogy remained culturally potent, especially as casualties mounted.

Naturally there was considerable doubt and concern throughout. During the autumn of 2002 these concerns were rehearsed in the debate on the likely Iraqi war tactics. Hussein's officials had already repeatedly laid out the scenario most likely to invoke the ghosts of Vietnam and memories of Hue, when in 1968 US and South Vietnamese forces tried to take the city back from the Northern forces and suffered over 600 fatalities and thousands of casualties within weeks. While the Iraqis were keen on advancing scenarios of protracted and devastating urban warfare, Rumsfeld was keen to suggest the war would be decisive and short, 'I can't say if the use of force would last five days or five weeks or five months, but it certainly isn't going to last any longer than that. It won't be a world war three'. Though close associates talked about a fourth World War. Hussein had reduced the size of his military after 1991 to create a more loyal force. While open warfare in the desert would be avoided, critics of Rumsfeld argued, the remnants of Hussein's army were caught between the Iraqi population and the external invading forces. They had no where to go and a fight for the regime's survival was their only option; a conventional fight, however, it would not be.[70]

On the eve of the war Saddam Hussein stepped up the rhetoric exhorting his people to fight the invading forces, again suggesting that urban warfare would be widespread and that the US would lose its patience and perhaps withdraw. Iraq's defence minister, General Sultan Hashim, warned that the Americans would have to 'pay a heavy price in blood' by fighting in Baghdad. In mocking tones he suggested that the US forces could go to the North of Iraq, 'they can even go onto Europe. But in the end, to achieve their objective, they will have to come to the city. The city will fight them. They say a land fights with its own people'. Bush simultaneously warned Americans that the fight would be tough and that they were just at the beginning of it, as strategists took the lessons from across the 1990s and warned the public that the war could not be won by airpower alone, that decisive action on the ground was necessary too to achieve political objectives. But even before this, before the bombs started to fall and the troops began to move into Iraq, there was widespread talk in the region, especially in Lebanon, on the prospects for the resistance; something that had not entered US calculations. Washington expected a popular Iraqi welcome, which of course was not to be. Iraqi exiles predicted strong resistance. Days before the Western invasion, Robert Fisk reported, an exile in Lebanon suggested that the Americans would not be left alone, 'Iraqis are tough people. They won't accept American occupation. They have never accepted foreign occupation'.[71]

The early illusion of Iraq miscalculated the extent of resistance. Iraq could be pulled off. If success was assured, the price of intervention might be tolerated. It was a tremendous irony that the United States could go to war precisely because of the absence of the link between Iraq and al Qaeda and the absence of WMD. Had they existed, the fear of a prolonged or a devastating war would have been unthinkable. To exorcise the ghosts of Vietnam required a crushing victory as in 1991, but also something a little more permanent and ultimately conclusive. If Iraq had sufficient WMD they would have provided a logical deterrent to US intervention. The Bush administration had authorised the use of nuclear weapons in Iraq provided Hussein used his WMD, but such scenarios were unlikely. Iraq was a do-able operation; 'it is precisely because he [Hussein] is not now a real threat to the US, nor a real ally of al-Qaida, and nor, probably, in possession of useable weapons, that war is feasible', Woolacott wrote in 2002.[72]

Domestic support

After Vietnam strong domestic support was deemed essential. Media coverage and media containment were crucial throughout the 1980s and 1990s, especially on US casualties, but also on unnecessary civilian casualties and bombing errors that produced adverse reaction.[73] Rumsfeld wanted to reverse this and be more direct about US casualties, but the Bush administration avoided the issue. Bush was heavily criticised for not attending funerals, and the media was restricted in its use of photography depicting US casualties and returning coffins draped in the flag. It was also imperative to limit the depiction of Iraqi civilian casualties. Obviously, the Iraqis and many others had learned, just as the Vietminh had in the 1960s, that one of the points of vulnerability for a democratic society was its public's opinion and their support for the war. Hussein and his commanders, as noted above, specifically intended to engage in a warfare that would erode the US will to persist, and of course the diverse elements of the insurgency continue that strategy.

The positive perceptions of the US military effort declined over the long term. Initially 93 percent of respondents to Pew polls indicated a positive view of operations, down to 63 percent in January 2004 and further eroded to 54 percent in early 2005. Opposition to the decision to go to war has also been rising steadily. And as the conflict drags on opinions on Bush's handling of the war have steadily declined.[74]

One sees greater use of and manipulation of the Vietnam analogy during periods of increased casualties. In April 2004 as operations intensified in Falluja and Najaf with the considerable rise in casualties (135 as opposed to roughly half that in the same month in 2003), increasingly Iraq was portrayed as a 'quagmire'. 'Iraqification' became the palliative, but that process too proved to be a double-edged sword. A hasty exit, or the appearance of it, would also draw parallels to Vietnamization, where the priority was more on exit than the pursuit of strategic stability. The competing memories of Vietnam vied with each other. As senators invoked various aspects of Vietnam and its analogical power, Senator Kennedy even referring to 'George Bush's Vietnam', the president repeated the now familiar mantra on resolve, strength and the US will.[75] Yet, Iraqification, though intended to provide the necessary light at the end of the proverbial tunnel in the approach to the US presidential campaign of 2004, immediately drew parallels to Vietnamization and intuition of defeat. The Vietnam veteran, Senator John McCain, pointed out in November 2003, 'When the United States announces a schedule for training and deploying Iraqi security officers, then announces the acceleration of that schedule, then accelerates it again, it sends a signal of desperation, not certitude'.[76] Through to 2006 Iraqification appeared as though it were designed more for domestic reasons rather than tactical or even strategic considerations. It seemed to echo the earlier process. In September 1970, K. Wayne Smith of the National Security Council informed Henry Kissinger that 'no analysis has ever been provided to show that the logic of Vietnamization has proven correct'. There was no evidence of effective RVNAF (Armed Forces of South Vietnam) gains, or of pacification, or that enemy strength had declined significantly to permit US redeployment. 'No one in DOD or MACV [Military Assistance Command/Vietnam] has devised an analytical basis for examining redeployment alternatives. In essence, we are withdrawing from Vietnam the same way we went in: blind'.[77]

Avoiding casualties was essential to successful strategy. Yet Americans were likely to tolerate some casualties as long as the potential for success was high. If occupations or operations were considered impossible or counterproductive casualty, phobia became more apparent. Between the end of the Cold War and 9/11, casualty aversion was even more pronounced because there was no internal US consensus on the various 'humanitarian' interventions during the 1990s.[78]

Though Bush's support was initially high even while the initial stages of the invasion were taking place, opinion began to shift as the US weighed the costs of the war and considered the casualties. That overall decline in support was more or less steady as time went on.[79] Administration officials were well aware of the strategic implications of such concerns. As the insurgency demonstrated its staying power over the wary months of 2003, US military officials attempted to belittle their impact; Lt. Gen. Ricardo Sanchez, the top commander in Iraq, described the attacks as 'strategically and operationally insignificant'. The White House simultaneously confirmed their intent to stay; its spokesman, Trent Duffy, told reporters that the attacks were designed to get the Americans to run and undermine US resolve and determination, but he asserted that 'our will and our resolve are unshakable'. Despite such protest, the deeper impact of the attacks was becoming more and more obvious. A former US Army Colonel teaching at Georgetown University in Washington, DC pointed out presciently, 'Every single one of these attacks challenges American will, and American will is the center of gravity in this campaign'. Moreover, the US position was increasingly questioned by former US commanders; Wesley Clark, who oversaw US operations in Kosovo, argued that the US position was increasingly desperate, that the administration did not have a plan and had no answer to the ongoing attacks.[80]

How the Bush administration addressed the issue became increasingly difficult. Insurgents were determined to continue attacks that not only killed the Iraqis 'collaborating' with the United States, but also enough Americans to demonstrate that the United States would not be leaving the country as a viable project in the near future. The point was to cause doubt within the United States. Bush was increasingly accused of avoiding the issue of US casualties. He faced the most acute dilemma. If he addressed each instance of casualties he would remind the public of the ongoing death and destruction with little positive news to convey. If the flag draped coffins were allowed to be screened too, Americans would be even more aware of the human costs of the war. Bush could not selectively choose which memorial services or funerals to attend, and he certainly could not attend all of them. He had to find a balance between expressions of sympathy and drawing attention to US caualties without undermining US resolve. Moreover, reports indicated that he did not want to become trapped in the daily body counts that had haunted the LBJ White House.[81]

The Vietnam analogy was pervasive. Bush early on tried to side-step the issue when asked directly in 2002 whether initial US involvement might eventually draw in more US forces and commitment. He argued that he thought the second phase of the war was more akin to World War II than to Vietnam, 'this is a war in which we fight for the liberties and freedom of our country'. Few believed him. And as he and his deputies issued positive accounts of US efforts, echoes of the 'credibility gap' rekindled the spectre of Vietnam. President Johnson eventually bowed out of the presidential race after his poor performance in New Hampshire in 1968; his positive accounts of the war jarred with the media depictions. The Tet Offensive changed elite opinion in early 1968, following the general change of US public opinion from earlier in the war. And then, in 2004, the Tet analogy returned. There were hundreds of stories in the Western media that mentioned Tet that year. Finally in June Donald Rumsfeld indicated that he was in no doubt that the insurgents had learned from Tet, 'and the fact that if they make a big enough splash, even though they get a lot of people killed and we pound them, they end up winning psychologically'.[82]

The psychology both in Iraq and in the States was imperative, because Iraq was not just about the immediate concerns of the post-9/11 period or even the articulation of the concerns on Iraq advanced by the Project for the New American Century, it was also about the deep psychological wound that had developed amongst some US strategists.[83] That plot line jarred with national narratives, in which victory was seen as habitual.

When the discourse linking Iraq to Vietnam almost became overwhelming, and threatened to become the 'tipping point' in the battle for hearts and minds, when there was increasing reference to it on Capitol Hill and amongst US opponents in Iraq, President Bush addressed the nation during prime time to bolster resolve and counter the Vietnam analogy and accusations on his credibility. He pointed out that the US commitment was firm, that he had no intention of leaving in the near term. He reminded the people who had lost relatives in Iraq that 'we will finish the work of the fallen'; that 'if additional forces are needed, I will send them'. Except by late in the year it was clear the US forces were experiencing considerable difficulty recruiting to the armed forces. Earlier, in 1970, Dr Irving Greenberg testified to the Senate Foreign Relations Committee that the momentum of human sacrifice seemed to be guiding US policy to sustain the war rather than admit error: 'This was the moral weakness of a Vietnamization policy designed to purchase time and not admit failure of the dead but cost many more lives in the interim'.[84] That war persisted well beyond the realisation of failure.

Bush was committed to Iraq. He indicated that while:

we will continue taking the greatest care to prevent harm to innocent civilians … we will not permit the spread of chaos and violence. I have directed our military commanders to make every preparation to use decisive force, if necessary, to maintain order and to protect our troops.

The schedule for democratisation would be kept: elections, the constitution and the formation of government. Bush argued this was not just about Iraq:

The success of free government in Iraq is vital for many reasons. A free Iraq is vital because 25 million Iraqis have as much right to live in freedom as we do. A free Iraq will stand as an example to reformers across the Middle East. A free Iraq will show that America is on the side of Muslims who wish to live in peace, as we have already shown in Kuwait and Kosovo, Bosnia and Afghanistan. A free Iraq will confirm to a watching world that America's word, once given, can be relied upon, even in the toughest times.

And:

Above all, the defeat of violence and terror in Iraq is vital to the defeat of violence and terror elsewhere; and vital, therefore, to the safety of the American people. Now is the time, and Iraq is the place, in which the enemies of the civilized world are testing the will of the civilized world. We must not waver.[85]

However, US tactics and use of overwhelming force on the ground and from the air was counterproductive. Moreover, recruitment became difficult. Rumsfeld was forced to announce that the rotation of US troops might be delayed, as reports indicated widespread low morale and enumerated suicide rates amongst US soldiers. Such were the concerns that a report commissioned by Ricardo Sanchez was delayed for three months before release. The moderate Shia senior cleric, Ayatollah Ali al-Sistani, refused to condemn Moqtada al-Sadr; instead he criticised 'the methods used by occupation forces in the current escalating situation in Iraq ...'. Nevertheless, Sanchez indicated their force would be 'robust', powerful and deliberate and that US forces would not be deterred, and the streets of Falluja were soon targeted by airpower. Widespread casualties brought further criticism and resentment. Mohammed Hassan al-Balwa, head of Falluja's city council, argued that the US tactics were making more and more people sympathetic to the resistance and 'this behaviour of the Americans will make everyone seek revenge. Falluja has become a symbol for those who reject the occupation'.[86]

After Vietnam, domestic support was largely predicated on the conduct of intervention through short, sharp operations with a demonstration of a decisive use of force,[87] by proxy forces if the operations were sustained, or through airpower with the eventual introduction of US ground troops. This experience and Bush administration ambitions challenged these assumptions and the accumulated lessons after Vietnam; in turn the administration would be challenged by a declining US support for the war, sustained resistance in Iraq and a loss of credibility globally. To echo Congressional testimony from 1970, the United States would be 'tempered by tragedy'.[88]

130

Exit strategy

An exit strategy was the last of the main criteria that needed consideration; extracting the United States without damage to its credibility was essential. The strategy could not appear as hasty as in Vietnamization where the emphasis was more on exit than strategy. Leaving Iraq precipitously would deepen the Vietnam syndrome. After the 'catastrophic victory', the Bush administration was grappling with the exit strategy as things started to go awry. Leaving Iraq would not be easy given that the United States basically took action on a unilateral basis, the Blair government and other contributions not withstanding. Washington had to consider the exit based on the transfer of power at the political level, 'Iraqification' at the military level and it had to consider what it leaves behind in terms of the long-term struggle for the 'hearts and minds' of the people of Iraq, the United States, and for US credibility elsewhere. By May 2005 a report by the International Institute of Strategic Studies (IISS) concluded that 'best estimates suggest that it will take up to five years to create anything close to an effective indigenous force able to impose and guarantee order across the country'. Iraqification was constantly challenged by the violence of the insurgencies. The intervention was the proverbial elephant in the living room. From al Qaeda's point of view, Bush's Iraq policies have arguably produced a confluence of propitious circumstances: a strategically bogged down America, hated by much of the Islamic world, and regarded warily even by its allies. Iraq offered al Qaeda a recruitment and proving ground for the next generation of its members.[89]

Strange that an administration filled with such experienced politicians chose to ignore the accumulated lessons on intervention since Vietnam, lessons which in the past they had partly helped to construct. Primarily Washington did not have an exit strategy. They had no clear idea of what the endgame would look like, beyond broad visions. Their credibility was badly damaged by the manner in which the pre-intervention diplomacy was conducted; the high handed and determined administration chose not to listen to or accept limits suggested by its allies. The coalition of the willing would not be allowed to shape the mission; Bush's mission shaped the coalition and few joined. When troubles descended it was obvious that the EU, NATO or the UN would be unlikely to sign up to help. Iraq was not just about Iraq, it was also about transatlantic relations and a balance of global power. Critics of Bush in the US Senate went so far as to point out the lessons that his father had cited on trying to occupy Iraq or of moving into Baghdad. Bush senior had predicted the quagmire that Iraq would become when he justified the need to avoid involvement: 'To occupy Iraq would instantly shatter our coalition, turning the whole Arab world against us …. It would have taken us way beyond the imprimatur of international law bestowed by the resolution of the Security Council …'. US soldiers would become involved in urban guerrilla warfare and 'plunge that part of the world into even greater instability and destroy the credibility we were working so hard to re-establish'.[90]

Instead, Bush junior and his administration chose war intoxicated with visions of their own success and omnipotence. Their credibility was damaged through the arrogance of their diplomacy, the inability to discover weapons of mass destruction, the lack of a widespread welcome of US troops, the abuses at Abu Ghraib and elsewhere, and the continued insurgency. They had failed to ask the most basic questions of the exit strategy. What happens when they take Baghdad? What happens when Saddam Hussein falls? Who will govern the country and how? Would the state remain viable or split up into mini-states that could destabilise the entire region as each mini-state sought regional alliances for their own protection? Would a free, democratic Iraq necessarily produce the results in elections that comported with US strategies or desires? The thinking was a mess. As one commentator concluded, 'The failure to answer this question at the start set back US efforts in Iraq in such a way that the US has not recovered and may never do so'.[91]

US Congressional Representative, Jim McDermott, pointed out the series of failures that the administration had engaged in for over a year while US casualties were mounting. 'Iraq has been a mistake from the beginning', he noted. It was not 'a test. Iraq is not a laboratory. They are shooting real bullets, and we keep pretending we have a policy. Some say Iraq is not like Vietnam. Iraq looks more and more like Vietnam every day', he informed the House. Analysts moved through the 11 reasons former Secretary of Defense, Robert McNamara, cited for the US failure in Vietnam and also concluded that though the countries could not be directly compared, too many of the mistakes were repeated, from not informing the public fully, not having an adequate domestic debate that was honest and straightforward, relying on false and fabricated or attractive intelligence, the tendency to exaggerate the dangers to the United States and so forth.[92]

The shape of the exit strategy remained undetermined. The elections in early 2005 produced a government heavily dominated by the Shia as the Sunni sectors mostly boycotted the process. Despite the protestation of commitment and resolve, Washington faced another acute dilemma. They could leave and leave a weak state to prevail over seemingly insurmountable chaos. They could stay; see out their commitments, perhaps exacerbating the tensions through their continued heavy-handed tactics. But by staying they faced another domestic crisis as recruitment to US forces dried up. Volunteers were few and far between; recruitment targets were not met. Bringing back the draft threatened a domestic backlash; extending tours of duty provoked disgruntlement and unrest. Why at this point would the other multilateral agencies come onboard? Washington had largely ignored them in 2002, shunned them in 2003 and excluded them from the lucrative contracts after that. The costs of engagement were too steep without any potential reward. There was no good option for Washington.[93]

The exit strategy was hugely problematical. The political transfer had not been resolved effectively. Iraqification was a mess and unlikely to produce a smooth transfer without severely disrupting US credibility. And what the US left behind, primarily in Iraq but also throughout the world, was further aggravation, disorder and animosity. US power was sundered by the desire to move beyond rivals and use Iraq as a test case. Vietnam haunted such thinking and strategies.

In the absence of legitimacy Washington increasingly became embroiled in the dilemmas of Empire and the dialectics of violence which could both enhance and sunder its standing. The dilemma of empire became quite obvious early after 9/11. It is perhaps a myopic irony of tragic proportions that the Bush administration did not learn from its own history or even that of other empires. That as US power extended across the 'Third World' after World War II or even across Central America and East Asia in the early decades of the twentieth century, there was increasing resistance. The US narratives of benevolence and security that perhaps legitimated their own behaviour were not shared by many others and nationalist resistance was widespread. Moreover, Washington was merely the latest to fall into such a dilemma. As Edward Said wrote, 'it was the case nearly everywhere in the non-European world that the coming of the white man brought forth some sort of resistance'.[94]

While the US response to 9/11 in Afghanistan was widely seen as legitimate, its wont to empire in Iraq was widely perceived as illegitimate and was not sanctioned by the United Nations. There was widespread diplomatic resistance that was played out most acutely over the autumn of 2002 and spring of 2003. There was widespread popular distaste often expressed in various forms of anti-Americanism and of course after the overthrow of Hussein there was widespread resistance. It seemed that in the minds of many US strategists the only way that the United States could overcome its strategic dilemma that the loss in Vietnam presented was to demonstrate through decisive military power that it could achieve certain ends. Given the massive and disproportionate size of the US military might there was little doubt that they would not achieve their short-term objectives. This very overwhelming power simultaneously undermined it. Perhaps Bush senior might have added a fairly accurate historical addendum to his inaugural message that no great nation could be sundered by a memory, that all exercises of preponderance produce resistance, and that great power could be sundered by amnesia.

Any exit strategy by the United States would enhance the maladies of Vietnam: Washington would either be seen to retreat in the face of the insurgency or attempts to eliminate insurgent bases or facilities with widespread casualties would generate further, deeper animosities. The NSC lesson of May 1975 remains in poignant irony:

> The American people now appear to have quite different, and more limited, visions of our proper role in the world and our ability to influence events. In a sense, a control mechanism has evolved within our society which is likely to prevent for the foreseeable future any repetition of a Viet-Nam style involvement.[95]

In the attempt to overcome the impact of the Vietnam syndrome, the discussion of Vietnam has rarely been more prevalent. It was as if the tendons of the Achilles heel had been rediscovered in the 'American mind'.

Notes

1 I would like to acknowledge the support of the British Academy for funding research trips to the Nixon Project, and the Ford, Carter and Reagan Presidential Libraries. The College of Arts, Social Sciences and Celtic Studies, University College Cork, is also gratefully acknowledged for their continued support toward research. I would also like to thank Lloyd Gardner and John Dumbrell for comments on an earlier draft.

2 See Mikkel Vedby Rasmussen, 'The History of a Lesson: Versailles, Munich and the Social Construction of the Past', *Review of International Studies*, 29, 2003, pp. 499–519; see for instance CNN Time, Madeleine Albright, http://www.cnn.com/ALLPOLITICS/1997/gen/resources/players/albright/.

3 See Jeffrey Record, *Making War, Thinking History: Munich, Vietnam, and Presidential Uses of Force from Korea to Kosovo*, Annapolis, MD: Naval Institute Press, 2002.

4 Ronald Reagan, 'Text of Address on Central America', April 27, 1983, *Congressional Quarterly*, 41(17), April 30, 1983, pp. 853–6; President Ronald Reagan, Veterans Day Ceremony, Arlington Cemetery, November 11, 1985, Presidential Handwriting File: Presidential Speeches, folder 403, box 21, Reagan Presidential Library.

5 Gary R. Hess, *Presidential Decisions for War: Korea, Vietnam and the Persian Gulf*, Baltimore, MD: The Johns Hopkins University Press, 2001, p. 221.

6 Robert Jay Lifton, *Superpower Syndrome: America's Apocalyptic Confrontation with the World*, New York: Nation Books, 2003, p. 49.

7 Edward W. Said, *Culture and Imperialism*, London: Chatto and Windus, 1993.

8 Robert J. McMahon, 'Credibility and World Power: Exploring the Psychological Dimension in Postwar American Diplomacy', *Diplomatic History*, 15(3), Fall 1991, p. 455.

9 Melvyn Leffler, *A Preponderance of Power: National Security, the Truman Administration, and the Cold War*, Stanford, CA: Stanford University Press, 1992.

10 John J. Mearsheimer, *The Tragedy of Great Power Politics*, New York: W. W. Norton, 2001, p. 3.

11 Lloyd C. Gardner, *Pay Any Price: Lyndon Johnson and the Wars for Vietnam*, Chicago, IL: Ivan R. Dee, 1995.

12 Michael Ignatieff, *Virtual War: Kosovo and Beyond*, New York: Picador, 2000, p. 163.

13 Robert Singh, 'The Bush Doctrine', in Mary Buckley and Robert Singh (eds) *The Bush Doctrine and the War on Terrorism: Global Responses, Global Consequences*, London: Routledge, 2006, p. 23.

14 Andrew J. Bacevich, *The New American Militarism: How Americans are Seduced by War*, New York: Oxford University Press, 2005, pp. 157–8.

15 Hess, op. cit.; Richard E. Neustadt and Ernest R. May, *Thinking in Time: The Uses of History for Decision Makers*, New York, Free Press, 1986.

16 Record, op. cit., p. 17.

17 Francis Fukuyama, *After the Neocons: America at the Crossroads*, London: Profile, 2006, pp. 48–50.

18 Francis Fukuyama, *The End of History and the Last Man*, London: Penguin, 1992, p. xi.

19 Allen Hunter (ed.), *Rethinking the Cold War*, Philadelphia, PA: Temple University Press, 1998.

20 President George H. W. Bush, Inaugural Address, West Front of the US Capitol, January 20, 1989, http://www.yale.edu/lawweb/avalon/presiden/inaug/bush.htm.

21 Tom Engelhardt, *The End of Victory Culture: Cold War America and the Disillusioning of a Generation*, Amherst, MA: University of Massachusetts Press, 1995; Wolfgang Schivelbusch, *The Culture of Defeat: On National Trauma, Mourning, and Recovery*, New York: Henry Holt, 2003.

22 See Arnold R. Isaacs, *Vietnam Shadows: The War, Its Ghosts, and Its Legacy*, Baltimore, MD: The Johns Hopkins University Press, 1997, p. 76.

23 Anthony Swafford, *Jarhead: A Soldier's Story of Modern* War, London: Scribner, 2003; and *Jarhead*, dir. Sam Mendes, 2005.

24 Schivelbusch, op. cit., p. 294.

25 Michael Cox, 'American Power Before and After 11 September: Dizzy with Success?' *International Affairs*, 78(2), 2002, p. 275 n. 48.

26 Lifton, op. cit., p. 166.

27 Rory Carroll, 'US Troops Launch Big Iraq Offensive', *The Guardian* (London), June 18, 2005.

28 Toby Dodge, *Iraq's Future: The Aftermath of Regime Change*, Adelphi Paper 372, Oxford: Routledge, 2005; see also Richard Loch-Pullan's chapter in this book.

29 Rasmussen, op. cit., pp. 499–519.

30 John Lewis Gaddis, 'A Grand Strategy of Transformation', *Foreign Policy*, November/ December, 2002, p. 54.

31 The White House, The National Security Strategy of the United States of America, September 2002, http://www.whitehouse.gov/nsc/nss.html.

32 Ibid.

33 Patrick Tyler, 'U.S. Strategy Plan Calls for Insuring No Rivals Develop', *New York Times*, March 8, 1992; David Ryan, *US Foreign Policy in World History*, London: Routledge, 2000, p. 190.

34 US National Security Strategy, and accompanying papers, April 1982, document 8290283 (NSDD 32) System II, NSC Records, the Reagan Presidential Library.

35 Peter Kornbluh, 'The US Role in the Counterrevolution', in Thomas W. Walker (ed.) *Revolution and Counterrevolution in Nicaragua*, Boulder, CO: Westview Press, 1991, p. 325.

36 See Fred Halliday, *Cold War, Third World*, London: Hutchinson Radius, 1989.

37 Noam Chomsky, testimony, 'Causes, Origins, and Lessons of the Vietnam War', hearings before the Committee on Foreign Relations, United States Senate, 92nd Congress, 2nd session, May 9, 1972, pp. 85, 99.

38 Greg Morsbach, 'Venezuela Aims for Biggest Military Reserve in Americas', *The Guardian* (London), March 4, 2006; Julian Borger, 'Chávez vows to Resist US "Inoculation Strategy"', *The Guardian* (London), February 18, 2006.

39 George W. Bush, address to the nation, Fort Bragg, North Carolina, June 28, 2005, www.whitehouse.gov/news/releases/2005/06/print/20050628-7.html.

40 Richard V. Allen to Ed Meese and James Baker, 'Why El Salvador Isn't Vietnam', February 25, 1981, El Salvador, volume 1, OA 91363, the Reagan Presidential Library.

41 Barry Rubin, 'The Real Roots of Arab Anti-Americanism', *Foreign Affairs*, 81(6), November/December 2002, p. 80.

42 The Glaspie Transcript, July 25, 1990, in Micah L. Sifry and Christopher Cerf (eds) *The Gulf War Reader: History, Documents, Opinions*, New York: Random House, 1991, p. 125.

43 Ewen MacAskill, 'Blair Gives Strongest Hint Yet on Taking War to Iraq', *The Guardian* (London), March 4, 2002.

44 Brian Whitaker, 'Iraq Plans Urban Warfare to Thwart US', *The Guardian* (London), August 9, 2002.

45 Rory McCarthy, '22 Killed as Troops Clash With Shias', *The Guardian* (London), April 5, 2004; Rory McCarthy, 'Chaos Killing and Kidnap', *The Guardian* (London), April 9, 2004; Jonathan Steele and Ewen MacAskill, 'Battles Rage from North to South', *The Guardian* (London), April 8, 2004; Rory McCarthy and Julian Borger, 'Death Toll Hits 600 in Bloody Siege of Falluja', *The Guardian* (London), April 12, 2004.

46 Mark Danner, 'The Battlefield in the American Mind', *The New York Times*, October 16, 2001.
47 Maureen Dowd, *New York Times*, February 23, 1991.
48 Quoted in Bob Woodward, *The Commanders*, New York: Simon and Schuster, 1991, p. 339.
49 Dowd, op. cit.
50 George W. Bush, President Commemorates Veterans Day, Tobyhanna, Pennsylvania, November 11, 2005, http://www.whitehouse.gov/news/releases/2005/11/20051111-1.html.
51 Leslie H. Gelb, testimony, 'Causes, Origins, and Lessons of the Vietnam War', hearings before the Committee on Foreign Relations, United States Senate, 92nd Congress, 2nd session, May 9, 1972, pp. 3–4.
52 President Richard Nixon in conversation May 12, 1969, editorial note, document 23, *Foundations of Foreign Policy, 1969–1972, Foreign Relations of the United States*, Vol. 1 (2003)Washington, DC: GPO, pp. 80–1.
53 Fredrik Logevall, *Choosing War: The Lost Chance for Peace and the Escalation of War in Vietnam*, Berkeley, CA: University of California Press, 1999, pp. 412–13.
54 Schivelbusch, op. cit., pp. 10–11.
55 Fukuyama, *After the Neocons*, op. cit., p. 50.
56 Secretary Henry A. Kissinger, memorandum for the President, 'Lessons of Vietnam', May 12, 1975, NSA, Presidential Country Files for East Asia and the Pacific. Country File: Vietnam, Vietnam (23), box 20, Gerald R. Ford Library.
57 Jeffrey Record and W. Andrew Terrill, *Iraq and Vietnam: Differences, Similarities, and Insights*, Carlisle, PA: Strategic Studies Institute, 2004, pp. 4ff.
58 W. R. Smyser memorandum to Secretary Kissinger, 'Lessons of Vietnam', May 12, 1975, NSA, Presidential Country Files for East Asia and the Pacific, Country File: Vietnam, Vietnam (23), box 20, Gerald R. Ford Library.
59 Secretary Henry A. Kissinger, memorandum for the President, Lessons of Vietnam, May 12, 1975, NSA, Presidential Country Files for East Asia and the Pacific. Country File: Vietnam, Vietnam (23), box 20, Gerald R. Ford Library.
60 Thom Shanker, 'Rumsfeld Favors Forceful Actions to Foil an Attack', *New York Times*, October 14, 2002; see also Donald H. Rumsfeld, 'Transforming the Military', *Foreign Affairs*, 81(3), May/June 2002, pp. 30–2.
61 See Richard A. Melanson, *American Foreign Policy since the Vietnam War: The Search for Consensus from Richard Nixon to George W. Bush*, 4th edn, Armonk, NY: M. E. Sharpe, 2005, pp. 3–42.
62 President George Bush, Remarks at National Day of Prayer and Remembrance, The National Cathedral, September 14, 2001, The White House, www.whitehouse.gov/news/releases/2001/09/20010914-21.html; President George Bush, Address to a Joint Session of Congress and the American People, September 20, 2001, the White House, www.whitehouse.gov/news/releases/2001/09/20010920-8.html.
63 Simon Tisdall and Ewen MacAskill, 'America's Long War', *The Guardian* (London), February 15, 2006.
64 Bob Woodward and Dan Balz, 'We Will Rally the World', *Washington Post*, January 28, 2002, www.washingtonpost.com/wp-dyn/articles/A46879-2002Jan27.html; Eric Schmitt and Thom Shanker, 'Administration Considers Broader, More Powerful Options for Potential Retaliation', *New York Times*, September 13, 2001.
65 David Ryan, 'Ten Days in September: The Creeping Irrelevance of Transatlantic Allies', *Journal of Transatlantic Studies*, 1, special edition, Spring 2003; David Ryan, 'Americanisation and Anti-Americanism at the Periphery: Nicaragua and the Sandinistas', *European Journal of American Culture*, 23(2), 2004, pp. 20–36.
66 'Pew, Mistrust of America in Europe Even Higher, Muslim Anger Persists', Pew Research Center for the People and the Press, March 16, 2004.

67 Maureen Dowd, 'I'm with Dick. Let's make War!' *The Guardian* (London), August 29, 2002.

68 See Lock-Pullan in this collection.

69 Ed Vulliamy, 'Get Ready for War, Bush Tells America', *The Observer* (London), September 16, 2001.

70 Toby Dodge, 'Iraqi Army is Tougher than US believes', *The Guardian* (London), November 16, 2002; Barry R. Posen, 'Foreseeing a Bloody Siege in Baghdad', *New York Times*, October 13, 2002; Michael R. Gordon, 'Iraq Said to Plan Tangling the U.S. in Street Fighting', *New York Times*, August 26, 2002.

71 John F. Burns, 'Iraq Leader Exhorts His People to Draw Arms Against Invaders', *New York Times*, March 20, 2003; John F. Burns, 'As Allies Race North, Iraq Warns of Fierce Fight', *New York Times*, March 24, 2003; R. W. Apple, 'Bush Moves to Prepare Public for a Harder War', *New York Times*, March 24, 2003; Robert Pape, 'Wars Can't Be Won Only From Above', *New York Times*, March 21, 2003; Robert Fisk, '"America Will Have to Fight Street by Street"', *The Independent on Sunday* (London), March 9, 2003.

72 Martin Woolacott, 'War is Only Feasible Because Iraq Isn't a Threat to the US', *The Guardian* (London), September 20, 2002.

73 See Douglas Kellner, *The Persian Gulf TV War*, Boulder, CO: Westview Press, 1992; Philip M. Taylor, *War and the Media: Propaganda and Persuasion in the Gulf War*, Manchester: Manchester University Press, 1992; W. Lance Bennett and David L. Paletz (eds), *Taken By Storm: The Media, Public Opinion, and U.S. Foreign Policy in the Gulf War*, Chicago, IL: University of Chicago Press, 1994.

74 See for instance the tracking of approval, Pew Research Center for the People and the Press, Presidential Approval, http://pewresearch.org/datatrends/?NumberID=12.

75 Julian Borger, 'Uprising in Iraq Could Derail Bush', *The Guardian* (London), April 7, 2004.

76 Suzanne Goldenberg, '"Iraqification" key to return of US troops', *The Guardian* (London), November 8, 2003.

77 K. Wayne Smith, memorandum for Dr Kissinger, 'U.S. Troop Redeployments', September 2, 1970, Nixon Project Materials, NSDM, Box H-215, NSDM 52.

78 Mark Burgess, 'Averting Casualty Aversion', Weekly Defense Monitor, Center for Defense Information, March 14, 2002, www.cdi.org/weekly/2002/issue05.html.

79 Adam Nagourney and Janet Elder, 'Opinions Begin to Shift as Public Weighs War Costs', *New York Times*, March 26, 2003.

80 Richard W. Stevenson, 'Public Doubt vs. Bush Vows', *New York Times*, November 3, 2003.

81 William Safire, 'Iraq War III', *New York Times,* November 3, 2003; Maureen Dowd, 'Death Be Not Loud', *New York Times*, November 6, 2003; Elisabeth Bumiller, 'Issue for Bush: How to Speak of Casualties?', *New York Times*, November 5, 2003; Giles Tremlett and Duncan Campbell, 'Body Bag Count puts Strains on Coalition', *The Guardian* (London), December 1, 2003.

82 President George Bush, press conference, March 13, 2002 http://www.whitehouse.gov/news/releases/2002/03/20020313-8.html; Don Oberdorfer, 'Tet: Who Won?' *Smithsonian Magazine*, November 2004, www.smithsonianmag.com/issues/2004/november/index.php.

83 See generally, Lifton, op. cit.; Alex Callinicos, *The New Mandarins of American Power*, Cambridge: Polity, 2003; Walden Bello, *Dilemmas of Domination: The Unmaking of the American Empire*, New York: Henry Holt, 2005, pp.41–7.

84 Irving Greenberg, testimony, 'Moral and Military Aspects of the War in Southeast Asia', Committee on Foreign Relations, United States Senate, 91st Congress, 2nd session, May 7 and 12, 1970, p. 12.

85 President George W. Bush, address to the nation, the White House, April 7, 2004, www.whitehouse.gov/news/releases/2004/04, April 13, 2004; Colonel Daniel Smith,

'The Psychology of War', *Foreign Policy in Focus*; Representative Owens, House of Representatives, April 21, 2004, http://thomas.loc.gov.

86 Rory McCarthy, '22 Killed as Troops Clash with Shias', *The Guardian* (London), April 5, 2004; Rory McCarthy, 'Chaos Killing and Kidnap', *The Guardian* (London), April 9, 2004; Jonathan Steele and Ewen MacAskill, 'Battles Rage from North to South', *The Guardian* (London), April 8, 2004; Rory McCarthy and Julian Borger, 'Death Toll Hits 600 in Bloody Siege of Falluja', *The Guardian* (London), April 12, 2004.

87 Trevor B. McCrisken, *American Exceptionalism and the Legacy of Vietnam: US Foreign Policy Since 1974*, Basingstoke: Palgrave Macmillan, 2003.

88 Greenberg, op. cit., p. 12.

89 Richard Norton-Taylor and Michael Howard, 'Peace in Iraq "Will Take at Least Five Years to Impose"', *The Guardian* (London), May 25, 2005.

90 George Bush and Brent Scowcroft, from *A World Transformed*, cited by Senator Carl Levin, 'US Policy in Iraq', United States Senate, floor, October 11, 2004.

91 Peter W. Galbraith, 'How to Get Out of Iraq', *The New York Review of Books*, 51(8), May 13, 2004.

92 Jim McDermott, 'The Iraq War Just Keeps Getting Worse', House of Representatives, May 4, 2004; Lawrence J. Korb, '11-Step Program for Iraq Failure: The Bush Team is Repeating the Mistakes the US Made in Vietnam', *Eye on Iraq*, Center for Defense Information, May 3, 2004, www.cdi.org.

93 Galbraith, op. cit.

94 Edward W. Said, *Culture and Imperialism*, London: Chatto and Windus, 1993, p. xii.

95 W. R. Smyser memorandum to State Department, 'Lessons of Vietnam', May 12, 1975, NSA, Presidential Country Files for East Asia and the Pacific, Country File: Vietnam, Vietnam (23), box 20, Gerald R. Ford Library.

7

EUROPE'S VIETNAM SYNDROME

America and the quagmire of Iraq

Jon Roper

The President of the United States is encountering domestic and international opposition to an unpopular war. He faces an upcoming election campaign. In successive months, leaders from Germany, France and finally Great Britain go to Washington for talks. After the President has been re-elected, his closest foreign policy adviser, now his Secretary of State, recalls the visits and reflects that at the time:

> European public opinion, at least as represented by the media, opposed the war. But European leaders registered no objection. During the entire period of the war I recall no criticism by a European leader in even the most private conversation. They seemed paralysed by the same dilemma we faced. They wanted the war ended quickly … But they also wanted American credibility unimpaired.[1]

In his memoirs, *White House Years* (1979), Henry Kissinger thus writes about the meetings of the three Europeans, Willy Brandt, Georges Pompidou and Harold Wilson, with Richard Nixon in the early months of 1970.

Kissinger also claims that 'strangely, Vietnam played a minor role' in the discussions between the European leaders and the American President in Washington.[2] He was being typically disingenuous. It is not so peculiar given the context of the times. During the Cold War, the potential use of nuclear weapons – weapons of mass destruction – concentrated the minds of politicians everywhere. The governments of West Germany, France and the United Kingdom, in line with public opinion in those countries, did not commit military resources to what became America's 'mission impossible' in Southeast Asia and may have disagreed with Nixon's continued prosecution of the war after his election in 1968. But Europe still needed to maintain the unity of the transatlantic alliance. Diplomatic deference demanded that any public criticism of the President's foreign policy should remain muted.

Nowadays the tone of the conversation between European leaders and the American President has changed from that of the Nixon era. Critical of the contemporary influence of neo-conservatism in the formation of American foreign policy, particularly as it has shaped George W. Bush's commitment to America's 'War on Terror', politicians from – in Donald Rumsfeld's provocative characterisation – 'Old' Europe, notably Germany and France, have objected to American military action overseas. Indeed, this, coupled with the widespread hostility shown by much of European public opinion towards America's pre-emptive strike on Iraq and its dysfunctional aftermath, has been taken as a sign that the tectonic plates of the transatlantic relationship have shifted permanently.

It is not the first time that this alliance has been politically transformed as a result of military conflict in the Middle East. In 1956, the Suez crisis moulded attitudes for a generation. Philip Gordon argues that it had 'a lasting impact on French and British national strategic cultures and would end up affecting their policies nearly 50 years later'. When the United States, working in association with the United Nations, refused to support the British and French invasion of Suez, the European powers, both retreating from empire, drew very different conclusions. For the French, the lesson was that America could not be relied upon, and that France should be prepared to develop its foreign policy independently from that of the United States, as was to happen after Charles de Gaulle became President of the Fifth Republic. In Britain, a concern developed not to jeopardise unnecessarily the so-called 'special relationship' with the United States that had been and would remain the cornerstone of its post-war foreign policy, even if this in turn called into question its future within the developing European community. For Gordon, 'those contrasting conclusions played out in British and French policy during the Iraq crisis of 2003'.[3]

Yet European opposition to America's prosecution of the 'War on Terror' in Iraq is not simply explained as a legacy of an earlier disagreement about intervention in the Middle East. It is also the result of a principle and a perception. The principle is that the American President should not take pre-emptive – and largely unilateral – military action in potential defiance of the supra-national institution of the United Nations and worldwide public opinion. The perception, deriving from Europe's own historical experience, is that political problems do not always prove tractable to military solutions. What is relevant in terms of the relationship between recent events in Iraq and those over 30 years ago in Southeast Asia is that such views are similar to those wrapped up in the expression that defines the legacy of that American foreign policy debacle, the impact of which has been at least as great upon the United States as that of Suez was upon Britain and France. 'Old' Europe's opposition to the American President's pre-emptive military action in Iraq is thus in effect another manifestation of the Vietnam Syndrome.

The Vietnam War symbolises the ascendancy of the 'Imperial Presidency' and its capacity to commit American military forces overseas without a formal Congressional Declaration of War. The precepts of the Truman Doctrine and its related foreign policy framework of containment and the domino theory meant that such executive action could be taken if necessary without international support. After Vietnam, however, this power to act unilaterally as Commander in Chief was pre-emptively curtailed by Congress and by domestic public opinion. Nixon's immediate successors, Gerald Ford, Jimmy Carter and Ronald Reagan, did not involve the United States directly in large scale and sustained military action abroad. Following the end of the Cold War, however, America has committed its troops in three major conflicts overseas – at the President's behest but still without Congressional Declarations of War – in the Gulf, in Afghanistan and in Iraq, either with the approval of the United Nations, or in association with coalitions of those nations willing (or sometimes not so willing) to lend their support. Seen through the lens of domestic American politics, each of these conflicts has been in part about the rehabilitation of the President's war making power after Vietnam. For contemporary neo-conservatives in the United States, indeed, this is essential to the successful conduct of American foreign policy. However, it is a power that has proven contentious, not least because if a war is perceived as unsuccessful – as was the case in Vietnam – the President's credibility is called into question. This has been reflected in the widespread European and American opposition to the dubious conduct of the conflict in Iraq.

Neo-conservatives have interpreted European criticism of the President's use of military force in support of contemporary American foreign policy as confirmation of the declining power of one continent and the ascendancy of another. In Europe, sympathy for George W. Bush's foreign policy evaporated during the year following the 9/11 attacks, and in the face of criticism, as Garry Dorrien has observed, the *Weekly Standard*, one of neo-conservatism's most influential journals, characteristically 'blasted European complaints about American arrogance and unilateralism, calling Europe the "axis of rudeness"'. For Americans like Robert Kagan, then living in Europe, as Dorrien suggests, it appeared that 'during the Cold War European anti-Americanism was counterbalanced by anticommunism, but now it wasn't counterbalanced by anything'.[4] Kagan's response, in *Paradise and Power* (2003), was both controversial and outspoken. It was, he argued, 'time to stop pretending that Europeans and Americans share a common view of the world, or even that they occupy the same world'. Instead Europeans viewed international relations from the perspective of Kant's philosophy, while Americans believed that the world was best seen through the eyes of Thomas Hobbes. They lived on different planets: Europeans on Venus, Americans on Mars. Yet in suggesting such generalisations, neo-conservatism tried to endorse a unity of ideological outlook on either side of the Atlantic that transparently did not exist.

Kagan's thesis is that:

> on the all-important question of power – the efficacy of power, the morality of power, the desirability of power – American and European perspectives are diverging. Europe is turning away from power ... It is entering a post-historical paradise of peace and relative prosperity. ... Meanwhile the United States remains mired in history ... where international laws and rules are unreliable, and where true security and the defense and promotion of a liberal order still depend on the possession and use of military might.[5]

141

But if this is the case, it begs a further question. Who, within the constitutional framework of America, should deploy that 'military might'? For neo-conservatives the all-important actor is the President. And the problem for them is that his power as Commander in Chief to commit American forces overseas has been, and, particularly since Vietnam, still is, contested. It is only through overcoming the Vietnam Syndrome that the way is cleared for America's international relations to be based upon a power morality that, despite Kagan's analysis, seems more reminiscent of Nietzsche's philosophy than of Hobbes' political thought.

This chapter discusses the development, the erosion and the attempted rehabilitation of the President's capacity to use military force during the past 50 years, both before and after Vietnam. It argues that the impact of the Vietnam Syndrome upon the Presidency was initially felt in Congressional attempts to curb the executive's assumption of a war making power. However, as the Gulf War of 1991 demonstrated, at a time of international crisis, the legislature still comes under intense political pressure to support executive-led military action. Moreover, the new existential threat of the 'War on Terror' has led to a renegotiation of the constitutional contract between the executive and legislature along the lines of that which it established 50 years ago. The remaining force of the Syndrome thus lies institutionally in the check that may be offered by the United Nations on this exercise of Presidential power, and its influence on domestic and international public opinion. It is this that the controversy over the Iraq war has highlighted. European opposition to the war and the refusal of some of its leaders to defer to the President's desire to prosecute it is a rallying point for those Americans who still oppose aggressive interventionism overseas. This is a problem for neo-conservatives, for whom the rehabilitation of the power of the Presidency remains a paramount concern.

In *Paradise and Power*, Kagan mentions Vietnam three times. He argues variously that in the immediate post-Vietnam period, America was more inclined to seek diplomatic than military solutions to international problems because its leaders thought that – like Europe in its deference to American power – they 'were working from a position of weakness'. Elsewhere he suggests that: 'a setback in Iraq or "another Vietnam"' would not be 'a military ... calamity great enough' to pose a threat to the 'long era of American hegemony' that is in the making. Finally, he concludes that the 'lesson of Vietnam' – the dangers of military interventionism – was briefly significant before the enduring 'lesson of Munich' (and indeed of Pearl Harbor) reasserted itself: that American strategic involvement with the world should be based upon its military supremacy. In other words, the impact of Vietnam on American politics was short-term, and now it should be business as usual.[6]

But there are two more enduring 'lessons of Vietnam'. The first is familiar enough to the former imperial powers of Europe. It is that military action does not lead necessarily to the solutiobn of political problems. Indeed, it may make such problems worse. The second is that when the American President, acting as Commander in Chief, assumes the primary responsibility for committing

American military forces overseas in pursuit of foreign policy goals, the political prestige and the credibility of the office is shaped by the outcome of the war.

By glossing over these 'lessons of Vietnam', Kagan avoids a continuing debate, on both sides of the Atlantic, about the efficacy of Presidential military action. The last war formally declared by Congress was in response to Pearl Harbor. Since then, and the list is not exhaustive, the five most significant American military interventions overseas – Korea, Vietnam, the first Gulf War, Afghanistan and now Iraq – have been undertaken as a result of Presidential initiatives. If Korea ended as a stalemate and the first Gulf War as a stand-off, and if the long-term political effects of the campaigns thus far undertaken in the 'War on Terror' are as yet unknown, Vietnam still remains as the foreign policy debacle that destroyed a presidency (Johnson's), and contributed to the political climate in which Nixon's conduct during Watergate left the credibility of the institution itself damaged. The division between Europe and America, and within the United States itself, can thus be focused on the issue of the political legitimacy and the potential efficacy of the President's use of military power. In other words, the argument continues one that in America both pre-dates and follows the end of the Vietnam War but which in its aftermath has found its most cogent expression in that conflict's eponymous Syndrome.

In the United States, it made its political debut soon after the last American helicopters had clattered away from the roof of the nation's embassy in Saigon, as South Vietnam was finally invaded from the North. It was then a simple, compelling idea, apparently suited to the times. As Michael Klare put it, the Vietnam Syndrome represented 'the American public's disinclination to engage in further military interventions in internal third world conflicts'. Furthermore, it 'had both institutional and subjective manifestations'.[7] The most significant institutional response to Vietnam was the War Powers Act, the Congressional attempt to check and balance the President's capacity to deploy American military forces which has had limited success in preventing such action. However, the subjective perceptions wrapped up in the Syndrome have proven more difficult to resolve. Differing attitudes towards Presidential military interventions overseas thus symbolise an ideological and political divide within America that is reflected in Europe as well.

For those in the United States – neo-conservatives, abetted by leading 'offensive realists' like Secretary of Defense Donald Rumsfeld – who believe that a 'strong America' is best personified by a 'strong President', the Vietnam Syndrome is a problem. To the extent that it acts as a check on the President's capacity to use American military power in support of his foreign policy objectives, it diminishes the national and international standing of the office. The history of the Syndrome can thus be seen in terms of attempts in America to overcome it by dramatic demonstrations of the efficacy of military power in the face of increasing resistance, not least from 'Old' Europe.

Formosa to the Gulf of Tonkin: Congress and the President's war making power

Existential fear fuels existential conflict. Assumed rather than declared, the Cold War was fought against an ideology. This contemporary American world view was shared by its allies in Western Europe, but support amongst them for American-led military action in third world nations was always less than enthusiastic: in Korea and notably in Vietnam. Although both Britain and France contributed military resources to the conflict in Korea, fighting under the auspices of the United Nations but effectively seconded to support American forces, the war effort there was overwhelmingly that of the United States. The relationship between French and American involvement in Vietnam was more complex, but after France's defeat at the battle of Dien Bien Phu in 1954 ended its colonial adventure there, it took no further part when, a decade later, the United States escalated its military commitment in Southeast Asia. Similarly, Britain resisted the suggestion that, in the immediate aftermath of the French defeat, it should embark on joint action with the United States against the Vietminh: a policy of non-involvement which was to remain unchanged, and which at the time, helped to persuade Eisenhower not to seek Congressional approval for American military intervention in Vietnam in the wake of the French withdrawal from its former colony.[8]

At the same time, the exercise of military options by the United States became inextricably linked with executive power, driving the development of the 'Imperial Presidency'. As the Cold War evolved the President was able to negotiate his way around Congress's constitutional responsibility to declare war by appealing in times of crisis to his own constitutional powers as Commander in Chief of the nation's armed forces. Korea and Vietnam were both wars to which America was committed by its executive rather than its legislature.

In the interval between them, the relationship between President and Congress with respect to the use of American military power was progressively redefined in response to an atmosphere of continuing Cold War crisis and the perceived threat from international communism. The executive and the legislature repeatedly renegotiated a Cold War contract between the constitutional framework on the one hand, and the desire to suggest consensus between the separated institutions sharing powers, in the interests of maintaining national security, on the other. Presidential initiatives that potentially committed American forces abroad without formal Congressional declarations of war – even though the interventions did not take place – had the cumulative effect of setting precedents for unilateral executive action in Vietnam.

During the 1950s and 1960s, therefore, as William Gibbons observes, Congress passed a series of resolutions 'which approved or authorized Presidential use of the armed forces to protect a country or countries, or declared U.S. determination to defend a country or an area'.[9] The first of these, the Formosa resolution, passed in 1955, gave the President power to take pre-emptive military action. It was a 'predated declaration of war' that was not implemented, but, at the time, Congress accepted that such a resolution was 'an effective way of achieving national unity and supporting national policy'.[10] With communist China threatening to invade islands under the control of the nationalist government in the Formosa Straits, President Eisenhower wanted the bi-partisan support of Congress should he decide on a military response. The President pushed at an open door. As the then Democrat Majority Leader in the Senate, Lyndon Johnson, put it: 'We are not going to take the responsibility out of the hands of the constitutional leader and try to arrogate it to ourselves'.[11]

In 1956, it was the unilateral action by European nations in Suez that led to the President asking Congress again to endorse the potential deployment of military force overseas if he thought it necessary. One outcome of that crisis was the 'Eisenhower Doctrine', which addressed what in the President's view had become 'the existing vacuum in the Middle East'. In a meeting with Congressional leaders on December 31, 1956, he argued that this should be 'filled by the United States before it is filled by Russia'.[12] In support of this position, Eisenhower pressed for another Congressional resolution (the Middle East Resolution of 1957). This time, however, rather than explicitly authorising the President's use of pre-emptive military force, Congress was less permissive and more equivocal in its attitude towards the President's possible use of military power.

The resolution was carefully worded:

> ...if the President determines the necessity thereof, the United States is prepared to use armed forces to assist any nation or group of such nations requesting assistance against armed aggression from any country controlled by international communism: *Provided* That such employment shall be consonant ... with the Constitution of the United States.

In the discussion in the Senate Foreign Relations Committee over the substitution of this formulation of words for the simple 'authorization' of executive action, John F. Kennedy asked if the resolution meant that 'we are granting the President the right to use the Armed Forces without coming again to Congress'. His fellow Senator, Mike Mansfield, replied that 'we are not granting him the right. We are in effect reasserting or reaffirming his right ...'.[13] Such a discussion indicates the Cold War tightrope that the executive and the legislature were walking: while the President's overriding priority was national security, and to have the power to respond militarily to perceived international crises if necessary, Congress was concerned to check and balance this within the framework of a Constitution which gave it alone the authority to declare war.

John F. Kennedy's first foreign policy adventure as President is illustrative of this theme. The Bay of Pigs debacle came about as a result of the President's refusal to commit American military forces in support of the CIA trained exiles who attempted to invade Cuba in April 1961. Had he done so, it is clear that he would not have been able to rely on the earlier Congressional authorisations for his action: the Formosa resolution was specific to that area of the world, and the Middle East resolution only applied to nations requesting help against communist aggression, not to a brigade intent on toppling a revolutionary regime.

Whether the potential reaction of Congress impinged on Kennedy's thinking at the time is open to debate. However, in the aftermath of the disaster he was aware, as he said to Allen Dulles, that 'under a parliamentary system of government it is I who would be leaving office' (in America, it was the President who was requesting that the Director of the CIA resign). Congress refrained from any concerted criticism of the new President. The Bay of Pigs led to an increase in Kennedy's popular support. Yet his often quoted response to his newfound popularity ('It's just like Eisenhower. The worse I do, the more popular I get') glosses over the fact that the Gallup poll which showed 61 per cent of Americans approving of his 'handling of the situation in Cuba', also indicated that 65 per cent opposed committing 'our armed forces ... to help overthrow Castro'.[14] It was a sign that public opinion, as much as Congressional oversight, could have an impact on the President's capacity to commit American military power overseas.

David Halberstam suggests that 'it would be said of John Kennedy and Lyndon Johnson that both had their Bay of Pigs, that the former's lasted four days and the latter's lasted four years'.[15] Given the brevity of the event and the prevailing need to maintain the transatlantic alliance, Western European reaction to the President's 'Caribbean Suez' was muted, but the political aftershocks of the events in Cuba were nevertheless felt two months later when Kennedy met with Khrushchev in Vienna. According to Halberstam, following his meeting with the Soviet leader, the President told the journalist James Reston that Khrushchev had assessed him in the light of what had happened in Cuba.

> I think he thought that anyone who was so young and inexperienced as to get into that mess could be taken, and anyone who got into it, and didn't see it through, had no guts. So he just beat the hell out of me. So I've got a terrible problem. If he thinks I'm inexperienced and have no guts, until we remove those ideas we won't get anywhere with him. So we have to act.

Moreover, 'now we have a problem in trying to make our power credible, and Vietnam looks like the place'.[16] That issue of credibility, which is at the core of contemporary neo-conservative thinking, would re-occur for Presidents in office during and after America's military intervention in Southeast Asia.

As Kennedy's foreign policy developed after the Bay of Pigs, Congress remained concerned to endorse his actions even if the President's interpretation of his power to commit American forces abroad did not require him formally to seek its approval. In the defining month of his Presidency, October 1962, the legislature approved a resolution on Cuba that sanctioned the use of military force if necessary. Passed in the build-up to the missile crisis, it came despite, as Theodore Sorensen observes, the President's polite indication at a September news conference – calling to mind his question in the Senate in 1957 – that 'a Congressional resolution on the matter, while not unwelcome, was not necessary for the exercise of his authority'.[17] It had become an accepted political reality that the President's assumption of leadership in matters of national security implied either Congressional support or deference to his action as Commander in Chief.

It was the Tonkin Gulf Resolution, passed in 1964 in the early stages of America's escalating military involvement in Vietnam, which came to symbolise the legislature's final acquiescence in giving the executive a 'blank cheque' for the exercise of a war making power. The incidents involving American and North Vietnamese naval vessels that took place early in August 1964 are as controversial as the war of which they are a part. But in their aftermath, once more the executive sought the legislature's approval to commit American military forces abroad if such action was deemed necessary. In his special message to Congress on August 5, 1964, President Johnson suggested it consider a resolution 'based on similar resolutions enacted … in the past' and cited the precedents of Formosa, the Middle East and Cuba. The Tonkin Gulf Resolution of August 7, which was passed unanimously by the House of Representatives, and with only two Senators voting against it, enabled the President 'to take all necessary measures to repel any armed attack against the forces of the United States and to prevent further aggression' and 'to take all necessary steps, including the use of armed force' to defend South Vietnam. In signing it, Johnson argued that: 'this resolution stands squarely within the four corners of the Constitution of the United States. … [it] confirms and reinforces powers of the Presidency'.[18] Yet as Robert McNamara came to see, it was not so much the fact of the resolution itself that would cause controversy, but the uses to which it was put in the developing American war in Southeast Asia. In this way, he suggests, 'the problem was not that Congress did not grasp the resolution's potential but that it did not grasp the war's potential and how the administration would respond in the face of it'.[19]

Vietnam saw the first large-scale and sustained commitment of American military forces overseas since Korea. A fundamental difference between the two wars is that in the first the United States acted through the United Nations and with the support of European allies. In the second it did not. By passing the Tonkin Gulf resolution, Congress acted according to precedents it had set at times of previous international crises. Even though the consequences might not have been what it intended – and indeed Congress became a focal point for opposition to the war during the hearings of the Foreign Relations Committee under Senator Fulbright – it had nevertheless effectively colluded in the development of the Imperial Presidency's war making capacity. On the other hand – as Europe's leaders at the time also realised – the war was thus the President's problem. It became successively 'Lyndon Johnson's War' and 'Richard Nixon's War' with devastating impact on both their Presidencies and upon the institution to which they were elected. As Vietnam unravelled, for the President, as John F. Kennedy realised after Vienna, and for the nation, as Henry Kissinger later suggested in his memoirs, the problem was one of credibility. Johnson and Nixon bequeathed to their successors the potential of the 'credibility gap': a tipping point when domestic political support for the President drains away as public opinion recognises a disjunction between his perception of the efficacy of his actions as Commander in Chief and their interpretation of the reality of war.

JON ROPER

Overcoming the Syndrome: the Gulf War

In the aftermath of Vietnam, in 1973, and in response to the feeling that Lyndon Johnson had bamboozled it nine years previously, Congress passed – over Richard Nixon's veto – the War Powers Act. Since then, all Presidents have taken the position that what they consistently prefer to call a 'resolution' is an unconstitutional infringement of executive authority; but it remains as a Congressional talisman in its attempt to regain some control of America's war making power. Yet the War Powers Act does nothing to prohibit the executive from taking the initiative as Commander in Chief. It does not restrain the potential for the President to commit America's military overseas. All it demands is greater accountability. Under its terms the President has the statutory authority to commit American forces to military action without necessarily referring to Congress, provided the conflict does not last longer than 90 days. The contemporary President thus retains what his predecessors had acquired through precedent, practice, and the legislature's acceptance of political realities: a war making initiative that can be exercised independently from Congress and, according to those critical of this development, despite the constitutional intent of the Founders. The War Powers Act as the institutional manifestation of the Vietnam Syndrome is in effect less dramatic than it may first appear. The legislative reassertion of Congressional war powers following the Vietnam War has proved very problematic, not least because of the political difficulties faced by Members of Congress who have sought to challenge executive calls to arms. So the remaining strength of the Syndrome as a restraint on Presidential action lies more in the subjective realm. After Vietnam, the question was whether the President could act in such a way again, particularly if the court of national and international opinion was against him.

During President Jimmy Carter's administration, the United States and its allies in Western Europe were broadly in agreement. The Vietnam Syndrome was a self-denying ordinance for a President who might otherwise seek to pursue an activist foreign policy that required military action. In the era of Cold War containment this implied self-discipline: a realisation that military power was not the only solution to foreign policy problems. Carter appreciated this. Speaking at Notre Dame University on May 22, 1977, he argued that:

> for too many years we've been willing to adopt the flawed and erroneous principles and tactics of our adversaries, sometimes abandoning our own values for theirs. We've fought fire with fire, never thinking that fire is better quenched with water. This approach failed, with Vietnam the best example of its intellectual and moral poverty'.[20]

But the American President could still rattle a sabre. In his State of the Union Address on January 23, 1980, and in response to the Soviet invasion of Afghanistan, he announced the 'Carter Doctrine'. Like the 'Eisenhower Doctrine' it was framed in the context of the perceived Soviet threat to American interests in the Middle East. The President was unequivocal:

148

Let our position be absolutely clear: An attempt by any outside force to gain control of the Persian Gulf region will be regarded as an assault on the vital interests of the United States of America, and such an assault will be repelled by any means necessary, including military force.[21]

Yet Carter's belligerence should be seen in context: not only of the election year in which he made his speech, but also in terms of the continuing implosion of his administration. In July 1979, after a much publicised process of public consultation and Presidential soul-searching, he had addressed the nation on the subject – which his speech did not explicitly name – of the 'national malaise'. He identified a sense of spiritual unrest and psychological disturbance caused by the political traumas of the preceding two decades. Four months later American hostages were taken at its embassy in Teheran. That crisis in Iran, coupled with the ineffective military response to it – the failed rescue attempt – effectively ejected Carter from the White House. His Presidency became associated with a period of relative national weakness in world affairs. In its subjective manifestation, the Vietnam Syndrome had thus assumed a significance in American political debate which transcended the immediate aftermath of the war for which it was named. It was invested with a psychological meaning.

Ronald Reagan once famously remarked: 'I didn't leave the Democratic party. The Democratic Party left me'. During the 1980s, a number of those who became his supporters had undergone a similar political conversion. Their titular leader within the Democrats had been Senator Henry 'Scoop' Jackson, from Washington State, who had supported Lyndon Johnson's policy in Vietnam to its disastrous end, and who had campaigned for the party's nomination in 1972 and 1976. As the Democrats settled on Presidential candidates such as George McGovern, Jimmy Carter, Walter Mondale and Michael Dukakis, before re-inventing themselves anew with Bill Clinton, these converts, among them Richard Perle and Paul Wolfowitz, became neo-conservative advocates of American power symbolised by a strong executive who could take, if necessary, decisive military action as Commander in Chief. Gradually they moved into positions of influence in Republican administrations.

For neo-conservatives, the domestic reluctance to support military commitments necessary to maintain a policy of Cold War containment, preserving American influence abroad, was a sign of international impotence. The Syndrome inhibited Presidential action and undermined Presidential power. It was not so much a restraint as a constraint. It was something to be overcome, but this was not to be achieved quickly. Indeed, despite the re-building of the American executive's self-confidence in the 1980s, supported by Ronald Reagan's breezy, optimistic, and at times bellicose, rhetoric, the President did not risk large-scale military interventionism overseas that required sustained national or international support. The administration's commitment of troops briefly in Grenada can be juxtaposed with the withdrawal of forces from Lebanon.

The continuing constraint of the Syndrome was further demonstrated in the Iran-Contra affair. This effective privatisation of American foreign policy came about as a result of Congress's refusal to fund what the President wanted: a military campaign against the elected government of Nicaragua. Reagan could not presume the freedom of action as Commander in Chief that had been assumed by some of his predecessors. If, by the time he left office, the executive had been rhetorically strengthened, neo-conservatives realised that it was still politically weak.

This contemporary condition of the Presidency was dramatised during the 1988 Presidential election campaign. On October 19, 1987, during the week that George Bush announced his candidacy, the cover story in *Newsweek* was headlined 'Fighting the Wimp Factor'. It argued that the then Vice-President lacked the political character to emerge from Reagan's shadow and assert strong leadership in the White House. Underlying this criticism was the assumption that the American President should be able to project an image of power, nationally and internationally, if necessary through his actions as Commander in Chief. Ironically, in this regard, Bush was helped in the campaign by the unfortunate photograph of his opponent, Michael Dukakis, in the driving seat of a tank while disobeying one of John F. Kennedy's maxims: politicians should never be photographed wearing hats. The Democrat's oversized helmet only added to the image of a candidate out of his depth, dwarfed by the military equipment he hoped one day to control.

The Vietnam Syndrome thus remained an issue for the Commander in Chief. In his inaugural address, George Bush argued for 'a statute of limitations' on the political divisions caused by the Vietnam War. But the legacy remained. Writing after the new President had taken office, William Westmoreland, the former commander of American forces in Southeast Asia, directly addressed the Syndrome's psychological dimension. He argued that:

> Vietnam was a war that continues to have an impact on politics. I fear that one of the big losses, in fact, probably the most serious loss of that war, is what I refer to as the Vietnam psychosis. Any time anybody brings up the thought that military forces might be needed, you hear the old hue and cry 'another Vietnam, another Vietnam'. That can be a real liability to us as we look to the future.[22]

The President would have agreed. Once in the White House, therefore, George Bush's wish to eviscerate the 'wimp factor' would be expressed in his attempt to overcome the Vietnam Syndrome through a decisive and successful use of American military power, with national and international support. He was able to capitalise on the two events that defined his presidency: the end of the Cold War and Iraq's invasion of Kuwait. To demonstrate that as President he could exercise power as Commander in Chief, George Bush took the opportunity of Iraq's invasion of Kuwait to fight the first full-scale war involving American military forces since Vietnam.

In so doing, the President re-opened the question of his constitutional powers to commit American forces overseas. He confronted memories of Vietnam and also the War Powers Act. During the build-up of American forces in the Gulf, and prior to war breaking out, Bush, working with the support of the UN, claimed that he was 'anxious to see and would certainly welcome a [Congressional] resolution that says we are going to implement the United Nations resolutions to a tee'. Nevertheless, when he was asked whether he needed Congress to endorse his actions with a resolution, his reply called to mind John F. Kennedy's response to a similar question in October 1962. 'I … feel that I have the constitutional authority – many attorneys having so advised me'.[23] Subsequently, when signing the congressional resolution that authorised the use of military force against Iraq, Bush nevertheless insisted that:

> my request for congressional support did not, and my signing of this resolution does not, constitute any change in the long-standing positions of the executive branch on either the President's constitutional authority to use the Armed Forces to defend vital U.S. interests or the constitutionality of the War Powers Resolution.[24]

But he had achieved Congressional backing for military action on a scale not seen since Vietnam.

The Gulf War remained overwhelmingly an American enterprise. For Colin Powell, the President's principal military adviser, moreover, the military action there was framed in the context of his analysis of what had gone wrong for America in Southeast Asia. The 'Powell Doctrine', applied in the Gulf, evolved from his experience in Vietnam. So:

> if force was to be used, it should be overwhelming, and its application should be decisive and preferably short. Military intervention should not be undertaken unless the outcome was all but guaranteed. The aims in using force needed to be precisely defined beforehand, and as soon as they were achieved American forces should be quickly extracted, lest the Pentagon risk sliding into a quagmire. American casualties had to be held to a minimum.[25]

The war was thus fought with these 'lessons of Vietnam' very much in mind. The American military, which, prior to Vietnam, had been consistently supportive of Presidential military action overseas – and indeed had advocated it during key Cold War events such as the Cuban Missile Crisis, when civilian leaders had proven, wisely, more restrained – now counselled caution: another institutional manifestation of the Syndrome.

Indeed, for Lawrence Freedman and Efraim Karsh, the experience of Vietnam shaped a new American way of war in the Gulf:

> Key actors in the American political process were determined not to repeat the mistakes of the 1960s: the administration was resolved not to get trapped in an unwinnable war; the military would not allow civilians to impose artificial restrictions that would deny them the possibility of decisive victory; Congress refused to be railroaded into giving the executive *carte blanche* to

wage war; and the diplomats did not wish to find themselves supporting a military campaign in isolation from natural allies.[26]

President Bush was careful to build an international coalition and to keep European support for America's action in the implementation of United Nations resolutions requiring Iraq to quit Kuwait. France and Britain deployed troops in the Gulf, and Germany contributed military equipment. The result was the quick fix of a high technology campaign with few American and allied casualties. But for America, did it consign the legacy of defeat in Southeast Asia to history?

Despite the President's assertions, military success in the Gulf War did not mean that America had 'kicked the Vietnam syndrome once and for all'.[27] On the contrary, Saddam Hussein remained in power because of the Syndrome: the President was not prepared to see domestic admiration for his military leadership drain away, and at the same time expose the fragility of his international coalition by continuing the war in the Middle East. The war, fought according to the precepts of the 'Powell Doctrine', was not prolonged. Although there had been domestic and international support for the American President's military action in response to Iraq's invasion of Kuwait, it was, like American – and European – endorsement for his war making power, qualified and conditional. The Vietnam Syndrome thus continued to be a forceful restraint on the President's use of military force. At the same time George W. Bush's actions confirmed to neo-conservatives in America that the Syndrome remained a constraint on the President's freedom of military and political manoeuvre.

For those who identified American power with Presidential power, the final years of the twentieth century – Henry Luce's 'American Century' – endorsed this continuing legacy of Vietnam and its impact on the executive's capacity to act as Commander in Chief.[28] In 1993, the Clinton administration's inability to persuade European leaders to support a policy of lifting the arms embargo against Serbia's opponents in Bosnia and using airpower to attempt to resolve the conflict in the Balkans was another demonstration of the President's comparative political weakness. Richard Perle, by then a former assistant Secretary of Defense, commented that when Clinton sent his Secretary of State to Europe for what was supposed to be an 'exchange of views' on Bosnia, 'it was an exchange all right: Warren Christopher went to Europe with an American policy and came back with a European one'. When America suffered a military debacle in Mogadishu, it was not just neo-conservatives who felt the blow. Richard Holbrooke, a member of Clinton's administration, referred to a 'Vietmalia Syndrome': the American public's rapid rejection of a military presence overseas if its altruistic purpose was undermined by images of defeat.[29] The Clinton administration gradually found its feet in terms of foreign policy, and undertook military interventionism in the Balkans with the support of its European allies. However, for neo-conservatives and 'offensive realists', not much had changed since the Carter years. America remained weak to the extent that its President did not enjoy complete freedom of political action backed by potential use of military force.

George W. Bush, Europe and Iraq

In February 2004, in his lecture at the American Enterprise Institute, the neo-conservative Charles Krauthammer argued that a foreign policy based on what he called 'democratic realism' justifies interventionism wherever 'there is a strategic necessity – meaning, places central to the larger war against the existential enemy, the enemy that poses a global mortal threat to freedom'. More specifically, the 'new existential enemy' is 'the Arab-Islamic totalitarianism that has threatened us in both its secular and religious forms for the quarter-century since the Khomeini revolution of 1979'. In other words, this is an enemy that the United States, constrained by the Vietnam Syndrome, has, until now, failed to confront. For Krauthammer, indeed, after Vietnam, liberal internationalism, 'the foreign policy of the Democratic Party', had been 'transmuted into an ideology of passivity, acquiescence and almost reflexive anti-interventionism' except during the Clinton years in cases that were 'morally pristine enough to justify the use of force' but were 'devoid of raw national interest'.[30]

Since September 11, 2001, however, within the United States, the President has been able to capitalise on America's existential fear to frame a new existential war fought to advance the neo-conservative view of that 'raw national interest'. Moreover, George W. Bush, in unilaterally declaring his 'War on Terror', re-created the circumstances of the Cold War, in which Presidential military initiatives in support of the broader campaign became battles in that war. Indeed, his time in the White House was to be defined by his role as Commander in Chief in committing American forces abroad. After 9/11, Congress acquiesced in two major overseas military engagements: Afghanistan and Iraq. The legislature has been confronted with a dilemma familiar from the Cold War era but now articulated in the vocabulary of the new war. It is difficult to deny the President Congressional support if the premise of his argument is accepted: that military action is necessary to pre-empt the threat to national security from global terrorism. Once troops are committed, Congress finds it equally hard not to rally to the President's cause. If Congress's constitutional power to declare war is again nullified then the President has once more checkmated the Constitution. The desire for forceful executive action in support of an aggressive American foreign policy holds sway.

Indeed in the immediate aftermath of 9/11, Congress, anxious to demonstrate national unity in a way reminiscent of its Cold War sensibilities, passed another resolution. Entitled 'Authorization for Use of Military Force' and signed into law a week after the attacks, it passed both Houses of Congress with only one dissenting vote. It authorised the President:

> to use all necessary and appropriate force against those nations, organizations, or persons he determines planned, authorized, committed, or aided the terrorist attacks that occurred on September 11, 2001, or harbored such organizations or persons, in order to prevent any future acts of international terrorism against the United States by such nations, organizations or persons.

The President congratulated Congress for acting 'wisely, decisively, and in the finest traditions of our country'. He also took the opportunity to point out, in similar language to that used by his father a decade previously, that 'in signing this resolution, I maintain the longstanding position of the executive branch regarding the President's constitutional authority to use force ... and regarding the constitutionality of the War Powers Resolution'. Irrespective of the constitutional quarrelling, Congress had once again cleared the way for the President to commit military forces overseas. The executive and the legislature had found 'a legislative vehicle around which both branches could unite to support the President's response to the terrorist attacks on the United States'.[31] Three weeks later, America invaded Afghanistan.

What is apparent, therefore, is that in the initial military campaigns in the 'War on Terror', in Afghanistan and subsequently in Iraq, the President has been able to gain Congressional support for his actions, within the framework implied by the War Powers Act. This has allowed him to implement his powers as Commander in Chief. So the Vietnam Syndrome no longer precludes the President's institutional use of military power. Such influence as it retains, remains at the subjective level.

In the Gulf War of 1991, the speed of the military campaign, the low level of American casualties, and the President's ability to construct an international coalition in favour of the action demonstrated that George Bush had picked the right fight. In his 'War on Terror', thus far, in terms of the swiftness of the initial campaigns, his son also gambled successfully. Short-term military objectives were achieved. In Afghanistan, the Taliban's regime was destroyed, but Osama Bin Laden, whom Clinton's National Security Adviser Sandy Berger had told Dick Cheney and Condoleezza Rice represented 'an existential threat' to the United States, remained at large.[32] In Iraq, Saddam Hussein was overthrown and subsequently captured. However, the reconstruction of Afghan and Iraqi society has proven a less clear-cut process.

Another 'lesson of Vietnam', contained in its Syndrome, which is familiar enough to many European nations, has prompted debate even among neo-conservatives in America. It is that military power does not necessarily solve political problems. As Francis Fukuyama argued, in a critique of the address to the American Enterprise Institute, if Charles Krauthammer had 'listened carefully to what many Europeans were actually saying' prior to the invasion of Iraq, he would have learnt that their 'objection to the war' was in fact 'a prudential one having to do with the overall wisdom of attacking Iraq'. In particular, Fukuyama observed, 'on the question of the manageability of postwar Iraq, the more sceptical European position was almost certainly right; the Bush administration went into Iraq with enormous illusions about how easy the postwar situation would be'. The United States ignored its experience of around 18 attempts at nation-building over the past century or so, in which only three – Germany, Japan and South Korea – might be deemed successful. In all the others, 'the U.S. either left nothing behind in terms of self-sustaining institutions, or else made things worse'.[33] Vietnam remains a case in point.

It was America's misfortune to underestimate its opposition in Vietnam. The Vietnamese defied American rational expectations that they would submit to overwhelming force and superior military technology. The Vietnam Syndrome was the product of the fact not only that America lost its war in Southeast Asia but also that the means it attempted to use in pursuit of its goal manifestly did not work. The resolve of those prepared to defy it is the great unknown for any nation contemplating military action overseas: a fact that European nations have learnt from their own imperial past.

In 1961, when President Charles de Gaulle was asked by President John F. Kennedy for advice on intervention in Vietnam, he predicted that if America deepened its military commitment there, 'you will, step by step, be sucked into a bottomless military and political quagmire'.[34] It is an early use of the metaphor that has come to define America's war in Vietnam in the popular imagination. During the 'War on Terror', those European leaders who refused to become fellow-travellers in the quest for weapons of mass destruction in Iraq might have had de Gaulle's warning in mind. The opposition to America's military intervention in Iraq demonstrated that a European formulation of the Vietnam Syndrome as an unwillingness to condone the American President's use of military power to further his foreign policy goals, particularly when the efficacy of the action is doubtful, remains intact. European support for the brief campaigns in the first Gulf War and Afghanistan become limiting cases in a default position that remains wary of an American President who defines himself through his actions as Commander in Chief in an existential war.

The exception to test this rule among the contemporary leaders of Germany, France and Britain is, of course, Tony Blair. In the case of Iraq, the British Prime Minister stepped outside the recent traditions of his party to become at the least a 'Scoop' Jackson Democrat, if not a quasi-neo-conservative in his support for the American President. In the Korean War, it is true that Labour's leader and then Prime Minister, Clement Attlee, had accepted that 'we'll have to support the Yanks', but on a visit to Washington in December 1950 he tried to persuade President Truman to consider a ceasefire and the withdrawal of UN troops.[35] During the Vietnam War, Harold Wilson, Labour's first Prime Minister after an interval of 13 years, was asked by Lyndon Johnson to send a 'token force' to support the American commitment. According to Wilson, Johnson was desperate: 'a platoon of bagpipers would be sufficient; it was the British flag that was wanted'.[36] The Prime Minister refused the President's request and, like Attlee during Korea, later tried to mediate in America's war. Elements of the Labour party have a history of opposing American military adventurism, and for many of its members, support for George W. Bush's policy in Iraq was a political litmus test that Blair failed.

Conclusion

What, then, of the future in terms of the Vietnam Syndrome and the 'War on Terror'? At the height of the Cold War, McGeorge Bundy, John F. Kennedy's National Security Adviser, put forward the concept of existential deterrence as a strategic option for the control of nuclear weapons. In any calculus as to whether to use nuclear force, the decision should be informed with an awareness of the likely consequences: if a nuclear first-strike would produce a response that would inevitably mean that the aggressor would also suffer a nuclear attack, then a rational calculus would be to avoid such a strike and its devastating outcome. Existential deterrence operates as a restraint on what may be militarily appealing but politically impossible.

It is a useful analogy. In a time of existential war, if constitutional checks have been eroded, the President is still accountable for taking the nation to war. In seeking an existential deterrent that might inhibit unilateral executive military action, the subjective manifestations of the Vietnam Syndrome – domestic opposition and lack of international support, expressed through the United Nations – are potentially important restraints. If in the brief incursion into Afghanistan, the existential fears wrapped up in George W. Bush's 'War on Terror' were strong enough to overcome the Syndrome, in Iraq, recollections of the experience of Vietnam have had more force in shaping democratic opinion both in America and in Europe.

Whereas Richard Nixon, meeting European leaders during the Cold War, could anticipate a certain degree of deference framed in the context of anxieties about the threat from weapons of mass destruction, America's military campaigns in its latest existential war have led to fewer political inhibitions among those European leaders prepared to express their disagreements with George W. Bush. If, in the rhetorical run-up to future pre-emptive military missions, Britain leaves another *ad hoc* 'coalition of the willing', international as well as domestic opinion may act as a critical restraint upon future Presidential actions that would be increasingly seen as unilateral. Iraq snapped French and German patience with the neo-conservative worldview embraced by the current administration in America. It stretched the limits of political tolerance in Britain. What Vietnam demonstrated is that if the American President is isolated, domestically and internationally, in an unpopular war, the political consequences for the individual (Johnson, Nixon) and the office (the future restraint or constraint of the Syndrome) are far-reaching. In this regard, 'Old' and 'New' Europe's commitment, or lack of it, to the American President's actions as Commander in Chief is critical. For unlike Richard Nixon and his Secretary of State, who found European leaders unwilling to take issue with them over Vietnam, George W. Bush and Condoleezza Rice have felt already the force of European criticism impacting upon the existential deterrence of American public opinion and its increasing opposition to the continuing American military presence in Iraq.

'Democratic realism' has re-created a quagmire. European reaction to the war in Iraq serves to focus attention once again on the significance of the Vietnam Syndrome and the issue of Presidential credibility in insisting that political problems are tractable to military solutions. It also implies a recurrence of a neo-conservative nightmare in which the legacy of 'George W. Bush's War' constrains his successor's future capacity to act as Commander in Chief. Overcoming that problem may then require a more mature consideration of the efficacy, the morality and indeed the desirability of Presidential power.

Notes

1 Henry Kissinger, *White House Years*, Boston, MA: Little, Brown and Company, 1979, p. 424

2 Ibid., p. 424

3 Philip Gordon, 'Trading Places: America and Europe in the Middle East', *Survival*, 2005, vol. 47, pp. 87–100, 95–6.

4 Garry Dorrien, *Imperial Design: Neoconservatism and the New Pax Americana*, New York: Routledge, 2004, pp. 163–4.

5 Robert Kagan, *Paradise and Power*, London: Atlantic Books, 2003, p. 3.

6 Ibid., pp. 28, 88, 91.

7 Michael T. Klare, *Beyond the 'Vietnam Syndrome': U.S. Interventionism in the 1980s*, Washington, DC: Institute for Policy Studies, 1981, pp. 1–2.

8 See Anthony Short, *The Origins of the Vietnam War*, London: Longman, 1989, pp. 137–44.

9 William Gibbons, *The U.S. Government and the Vietnam War*, Princeton, NJ: Princeton University Press, 1986, part 1, p. 278.

10 Ibid., p. 281.

11 Quoted in Dorothy Schaffter and Dorothy M. Mathews, *The Powers of the President as Commander in Chief of the Army and Navy of the United States*, New York: Da Capo Press, 1974, p. 98.

12 Peter Lyon, *Eisenhower*, Boston, MA: Little, Brown & Company, 1974, pp. 727–8.

13 Gibbons, *The U.S. Government and the Vietnam War*, part 1, pp. 347–8.

14 Robert Dallek, *An Unfinished Life: John F. Kennedy, 1917–1963*, Boston, MA: Little, Brown & Company, 2003, pp. 365–6, 370–1.

15 David Halberstam, *The Best and the Brightest*, London: Pan, 1973, p. 84.

16 Ibid., p. 96.

17 Theodore Sorensen, *Kennedy*, New York: Harper & Row, 1965, p. 672.

18 'Special Message to the Congress on U.S. Policy in Southeast Asia', August 5, 1964 and 'Remarks Upon Signing Joint Resolution of the Maintenance of Peace and Security in Southeast Asia', August 10, 1964, in *Public Papers of the Presidents of the United States: Lyndon B. Johnson*, Washington, DC: United States Government Printing Office, 1965, 1963–4, Book II, pp. 931, 947.

19 Robert McNamara, *In Retrospect: The Tragedy and the Lessons of Vietnam*, New York: Random House, 1995, p. 141.

20 Quoted in R. McMahon (ed.), *Major Problems in the History of the Vietnam War*, Lexington, MA: D. C. Heath & Co., 1990, p. 600.

21 Quoted in Klare, *Beyond the Vietnam Syndrome*, op. cit., p. 37.

22 William Westmoreland, 'Vietnam in Perspective', in P. J. Hearden (ed.) *Vietnam: Four American Perspectives*, Indiana: Purdue University Press, 1990, p. 45.

23 'The President's News Conference on the Persian Gulf Crisis', January 9, 1991, http://bushlibrary.tamu.edu/research/papers/1991/91010903.html.

24 'Statement on Signing the Resolution Authorizing the Use of Military Force Against Iraq', January 14, 1991, http://bushlibrary.tamu.edu/research/papers/1991/91011400.html.

25 M. Gordon and B. Trainor, *The Generals' War: The Inside Story of the Conflict in the Gulf*, Boston, MA: Little, Brown and Company, 1990, preface p. viii.

26 L. Freedman & E. Karsh, 'How Kuwait Was Won: Strategy in the Gulf War', *International Security*, 1991, pp. 5–41, 15–16.

27 'Remarks to the American Legislative Exchange Council', March 1, 1991, http://bushlibrary.tamu.edu/research/papers/1991/91030102.html.

28 Henry Luce characterised it as such in his editorial for *Life Magazine*, February 7, 1941, advocating America's entry into World War II. It is a theme reprised by those

neo-conservatives who in 1997 established the 'Project for the New American Century'.

29 Quoted in David Halberstam, *War in a Time of Peace*, London: Bloomsbury, 2002, pp. 229, 265.

30 Charles Krauthammer, 'Democratic Realism: An American Foreign Policy for a Unipolar World', Washington, DC: The AEI Press, 2004 http://www.aei.org/publications/pubID.19912,filter.all/pub_detail.asp.

31 See Congressional Research Service [CRS] Reports, RL32267: 'The War Powers Resolution: After Thirty Years', March 2004, http://www.fas.org/man/crs/RL32267.html#_1_26.

32 Quoted in Sydney Blumenthal, *The Clinton Wars*, London: Viking, 2003, p. 796.

33 Francis Fukuyama, 'The Neoconservative Moment', *The National Interest*, Summer 2004, http://www.tacitus.org/story/2004/8/15/163930/722.

34 Quoted in Michael Maclear, *Vietnam: The 10,000 Day War*, London: Eyre Methuen, 1981, p. 59.

35 Kenneth Harris, *Attlee*, London: Weidenfeld & Nicolson, 1982, pp. 454, 464.

36 Harold Wilson, *The Labour Government 1964–1970*, London: Weidenfeld & Nicolson and Michael Joseph, 1971, p. 264.

8

NO MORE VIETNAMS

Iraq and the analogy conundrum

Trevor B. McCrisken[1]

At the conclusion of the Gulf War in 1991, a jubilant President George H. W. Bush declared, 'By God, we've kicked the Vietnam syndrome once and for all'.[2] Bush's optimism that the United States had finally left behind the legacy of defeat in the Vietnam War was misplaced. Some fifteen years later the 'Vietnam analogy' is still being used in popular and elite discourse in an attempt to understand, explain and critique the US intervention in Iraq. As the military and political situation in Iraq worsens, critics of the Bush administration's policy assert that the United States is becoming 'bogged down' in an increasingly complex, unending occupation that is developing into a 'Vietnam-style quagmire'. Those who support the US war effort, however, claim that Iraq is nothing like Vietnam and that the analogy is misplaced. This chapter argues that Vietnam is generally not an appropriate analogy to interpret the course of events in Iraq due to differences in the international context of the two conflicts; the objectives and tactics of the United States; the strength of nationalism; and the nature of the insurgency. The analogy cannot be dismissed entirely, however, as it does provide a guide to understanding the sustainability of US public support; the conflict's impact on US credibility; the likely nature of a US withdrawal; and the long-term effects of the war on US foreign policy.

Analogies and foreign policy

The use of analogies in foreign policy-making is relatively commonplace. Policymakers, and indeed the public at large, often attempt to make sense of current situations by drawing on perceived 'lessons' of the past. One of the most widely used analogies is that of 'Munich' which became a dominant influence on US foreign policy-making after World War II. The commonly perceived lesson of the ill-fated Anglo-French agreement with Hitler and Mussolini on September 29, 1938 is that the appeasement of aggressors must never again be allowed. This analogy informed the thinking of, for example, Harry Truman and his advisors over Korea; the Eisenhower, Kennedy, and Johnson administrations over Vietnam; and President George W. Bush's father after Iraq invaded Kuwait in 1990.[3]

This last case is particularly instructive. Announcing the deployment of US forces to Saudi Arabia in August 1990, President Bush declared that 'if history teaches us anything, it is that we must resist aggression or it will destroy our freedoms. Appeasement does not work. As was the case in the 1930s, we see in Saddam Hussein an aggressive dictator threatening his neighbors'.[4] Bush and his advisors consistently gave the imperative of resisting aggression as one of the main strategic reasons for intervening on behalf of Kuwait. Bush also made repeated comparisons between Saddam Hussein and Hitler, despite the unease among advisors such as Colin Powell and Brent Scowcroft and the claims of critics that he was over-personalising the conflict.[5] The Munich analogy was not the only historical legacy, however, upon which Americans drew in the debate over whether the US-led coalition should intervene militarily to drive Iraqi forces from Kuwait. Opponents of using force frequently referred to the apparent lessons of the Vietnam War. Senator Bob Kerrey, for example, opposed military intervention because, he argued, like Vietnam it would entail 'thousands of [US] casualties without military necessity, moral justification, or public endorsement'.[6] Ironically, the Bush administration itself drew upon the Vietnam analogy to justify its decision to halt the 1991 war short of deposing Saddam Hussein. Bush 'firmly believed that we should not march into Baghdad' because that would entangle the US in 'an unwinnable urban guerrilla war'.[7] As another administration official put it, in words that now seem rather prophetic:

> We decided early on that if there was anything that could turn this into a Vietnam conflict it was going into densely populated areas and getting twelve soldiers a day killed by snipers. The main reason was that if we went in to overthrow [Saddam Hussein], how would we get out? If we set up a puppet government, how would we disentangle?[8]

The impact of analogous thinking on US policy making in 1990–1 is clear: while the Munich analogy had convinced the administration to use force against Iraq, it was the Vietnam analogy that contributed to the decision not to pursue the war beyond the stated objective of liberating Kuwait.

The use of analogies by presidents and their foreign policy advisors is something of a minefield. While ignoring or discounting history and experience can be naïve, the misapplication of historical analogies can also be detrimental to policy. As Ernest May observes: 'policy-makers ordinarily use history badly'.[9] A major problem is that the two situations being compared are rarely, if ever, entirely alike. What worked or failed in the earlier instance, therefore, is unlikely to provide clear guidelines for how a policymaker should deal with the current situation. Moreover, the perceived lessons of the earlier episode can become distorted over time and are susceptible to misperception and political or ideological bias. Analogous thinking can also be extremely limiting, placing perceptual constraints on decision makers once they have decided the lessons of say 'Munich' or 'Vietnam' are appropriate. Since the Vietnam War, successive US administrations have found their willingness to employ the use of force severely limited by the imperative of avoiding 'another Vietnam'. US policymakers considering the use of force in places as distinct as Iran, Lebanon, Grenada, Nicaragua, Libya, Panama, Kuwait, Iraq, Bosnia, Somalia, Rwanda, Kosovo and Afghanistan struggled with the often conflicting lessons of the 'Vietnam syndrome'. Whether they have tried to work within or overcome the perceived lessons of the earlier conflict, they have tended not to employ force unless they are confident that the intervention has clear, attainable objectives that can be swiftly achieved while minimising casualties.[10]

The Vietnam analogy and Iraq

President George W. Bush has used often tenuous historical analogies in attempts to justify rhetorically his foreign policies. He has repeatedly compared the 'war on terror', for example, to the challenges posed by both World War II and the Cold War. He insists that 'we must not forget the lessons of the past' and has claimed that the threat posed by 'evil Islamic radicalism', 'militant Jihadism' or 'Islamo-fascism' is equivalent to that posed in the twentieth century by first fascism and then communism. His conclusion is that the US must go on the offensive to defeat this latest 'totalitarian empire' and that the sacrifices being made by US forces in Iraq are the moral equivalent of those made in the earlier conflicts.[11] Bush and his supporters deny, however, that the war in Iraq has become analogous to the failed US intervention in Vietnam. Nevertheless, it is the Vietnam analogy that has become increasingly commonplace in the arguments of those critical of Bush's approach to the war from both sides of the political divide in the US. It is used particularly by those who believe the United States should withdraw from the conflict. In April 2004, for example, Democratic Senator Edward Kennedy, one of the administration's most vocal opponents, condemned the war and declared starkly that 'Iraq is George Bush's Vietnam'.[12] Senator Chuck Hagel, a senior Republican member of the Senate Foreign Relations Committee and a Vietnam veteran, has also raised the analogy in his critiques of policy in Iraq, concluding in August 2005: 'We are locked into a bogged down problem not unsimilar, dissimilar [sic] to where we were in Vietnam'.[13] Even the Iraqi insurgents are aware of the analogy. As he roused an uprising against coalition forces in 2004, the Shiite cleric and militia leader Moqtada al-Sadr warned that 'Iraq will be another Vietnam for America and the occupiers'.[14]

The Vietnam analogy is being used, therefore, by different political actors in different contexts and with different objectives in mind. But how appropriate is the analogy? To what degree can lessons be drawn from the US experience of the Vietnam War and be applied to the situation in Iraq? Are there sufficient similarities between the two conflicts and the reactions to them to warrant such an endeavour? To begin with, it is clear that there are several significant differences that make the Vietnam and Iraq wars incomparable and undermine the analogy.

The international context

One of the most marked differences between the Vietnam and Iraq wars is that the international context has been transformed by the ending of the Cold War. The global system is extremely different from what it was in the 1960s. The Vietnam conflict was a product of the Cold War, fought by the United States in an effort to contain the spread of Soviet Communism. The imperatives of the Cold War inhibited the ability of the United States to prosecute the war in Vietnam. US objectives and actions were limited by the fear of escalation due to the real threat of Chinese or Soviet direct intervention, particularly during the main period of American escalation up to 1968. The Vietnamese Communists were also significantly bolstered by external support for their war effort. Military and economic aid came in huge quantities from both the Soviet Union and China, even late in the conflict as détente and rapprochement unfolded. The Soviets supplied modern weaponry such as tanks, jet fighters and surface-to-air-missiles as well as several thousand technicians, while China sent food, clothing and small arms together with some 320,000 engineering and artillery troops to assist with the building and repair of infrastructure. Hanoi became adept at exploiting the differences between Moscow and Beijing in order to maximise the aid from both allies.[15] The US also had only limited allied support in Vietnam where even Britain, Washington's closest ally in the Iraq campaign, and her other NATO partners refused to aid the US effort.[16]

With the United States now the only superpower, the Bush administration has not had to face the prospect of major power foreign intervention or aid on the side of the Iraqi insurgents, nor does it appear likely that it will. Washington did go to war in Iraq despite strong opposition from most other leading powers including Germany, France, Russia and China.[17] The lack of significant coalition partners, aside from Britain, has been damaging politically and militarily. The perceived lack of legitimacy it affords the intervention has also increased the difficulty to some degree of winning Iraqi 'hearts and minds'. But unlike Vietnam, none of the major powers that opposed the US-led invasion of Iraq have any inclination to aid those fighting against US occupation. The White House has made much of the 'foreign Islamist fighters' and members of al-Qaeda who are allegedly stirring up or even orchestrating the insurgency.[18] Their actual numbers are very small, however, with US experts and Iraqi officials admitting in November 2005 that at least 90 per cent of the insurgents are Iraqi and that the percentage could be as high as 96 per cent. Official sources also showed that only 3.8 per cent of the 13,300 detainees within Iraq by October 2005 were foreign.[19] There have been accusations by the United States and Britain of Iran supplying and training Iraqi insurgents and of supplies crossing both the Iranian and Syrian borders.[20] Any such efforts are incomparable, however, to the levels of foreign assistance enjoyed by Hanoi and the South Vietnamese Communists and do not amount to a sophisticated supply network along the lines of the Ho Chi Minh Trail. In fact, there is no shortage of small arms and explosives already within Iraq since thousands of soldiers returned to their homes fully armed when Saddam Hussein's regime collapsed. There has also always been a great deal of private gun ownership in Iraq and most adult males have had military training and seen active duty, thus making the need for outside help in these matters far from necessary. The impact of foreign fighters, and particularly suicide bombers, does have serious consequences and should not be discounted entirely, but as Toby Dodge has concluded, they are neither 'the main or most important forces sustaining the insurgency' which is very much 'a home-grown phenomenon'.[21]

US objectives and methods

The objectives of the United States in Iraq and the methods being used to achieve them are very different from those in Vietnam. The express objective in the earlier conflict was to maintain the status quo by containing Communism in North Vietnam while ensuring the survival of anti-Communist rule in South Vietnam. At no time did Washington actively pursue the overthrow of Communism in the North; its focus was on counter-revolution in the South.[22] By contrast, the United States has been the revolutionary force in Iraq. The central objective from the beginning of the Iraq War was the overthrow of the existing regime and its replacement with some manner of democratic government. Indeed, the so-called neo-conservatives influencing the administration saw the Iraq campaign as the beginning of a democratic revolution that would extend throughout the Middle East, an agenda effectively taken up by the administration in its 'forward strategy of freedom in the Middle East'.[23]

The nature of fighting in the two wars is also significantly different. Vietnam began as a counterinsurgency effort for the US military and then developed into a largely conventional war.[24] Conversely, the Iraq campaign began as a short conventional war and then developed into a counterinsurgency. The initial campaign, which resulted in the collapse of the Ba'athist regime, lasted little more than a month from the opening of hostilities on March 20, 2003 to President Bush's declaration on May 1 that major combat operations were over. Operation Iraqi Freedom, as it was dubbed in Washington, entailed the so-called 'shock and awe' air-led campaign that targeted the regime's political, military and communications infrastructure coupled with a rapid ground assault to capture Baghdad and other major Iraqi cities.[25] When Ba'athist rule collapsed, coalition forces found their role transformed into one of providing basic security and of suppressing a burgeoning insurgency, roles for which they were ill-prepared. Bush's advisors had expected the US to be welcomed with opened arms by the Iraqi population who would be grateful that Saddam Hussein's regime was no more. Deputy Secretary of Defense Paul Wolfowitz, for example, was confident before the war began that: 'The Iraqi people understand what this crisis is about. Like the people of France in the 1940s, they view us as their hoped-for liberator'.[26] Instead, the US has had to lead coalition forces in a sustained counterinsurgency effort throughout much of Iraq for more than three years.

The tactics employed in this effort also contrast in many ways with those used in Vietnam. Air power was a dominant factor in the Vietnam War with extensive bombing campaigns against targets in North and South Vietnam as well as Cambodia and Laos coupled with bombing pauses designed to cajole peace negotiations. The 7.8 million tons of bombs used totalled more than the amount dropped by all aircraft during World War II.[27] Although the use of air support in the campaign against alleged insurgency strongholds near the Syrian border intensified toward the end of 2005, sustained strategic bombing campaigns were employed only in the initial phase of the Iraq War.[28] There is also a marked difference in the US force strength between the two conflicts. At the peak of

Washington's commitment to South Vietnam in April 1969, US forces numbered 543,000. The US deployment was complemented by 65,000 allied forces and 820,000 South Vietnamese troops by the end of 1968, the latter rising to over a million by 1972.[29] The forces deployed in Iraq are much smaller despite the Pentagon's initial war plan envisioning a similar force of 500,000 being deployed to overthrow Saddam Hussein's regime. When the US invaded Iraq in March 2003, there were 241,516 US military personnel in the region with a further 41,000 from the United Kingdom, 2,000 from Australia and 200 from Poland. By early April, with the Ba'ath regime about to fall, only 116,000 of the US troops available in the region were actually operating inside Iraq.[30] At its peak around the December 2005 Iraqi elections, US forces in Iraq totalled 160,000 together with a total of 23,000 coalition troops. The total number of Iraqi Security Forces by the end of 2005 was 227,800, although the proportion of these 'trained and ready' is a matter of some debate. [31] The scale disparity is still greater when the strength of enemy forces is considered. Communist troops in North and South Vietnam numbered 300,000 in 1963, 700,000 in 1966, and approaching a million by 1973.[32] The insurgency in Iraq is miniscule by comparison with numbers estimated between 15,000 and 20,000 by the end of 2005.[33]

Nationalism and insurgency

Despite divisions within Vietnamese society, the Vietnamese Communists were adept at tapping into an intensely strong nationalist movement among the people who had a long history of unified resistance to foreign intervention, going back to the Trung Sisters who led a rebellion against Chinese rule in the first century AD. The Communists enjoyed high levels of legitimacy; they had fought against French colonialism and Japanese occupation, and had declared Vietnam's national independence before the country was artificially divided between North and South in 1954. The 'genius' of the Communist Party was, according to historian William Duiker, their ability to 'combine patriotic and economic themes in an artful way to win the allegiance of a broad spectrum of the Vietnamese people'.[34] There is a relatively nascent Iraqi nationalism, forged partly by resistance to the wars fought against Iran and the US and its allies in recent years, and also due to the loyalty imposed through a complex system of violence and patronage by thirty-five years of Ba'athist rule. This sense of Iraqi nationalism helps to explain, for example, why resistance to coalition forces in Umm Qasr and Nassiriyah was stronger than expected in March 2003.[35] Nonetheless, ever since its creation after World War I, Iraq has been characterised by 'the exacerbation and re-creation by the state of communal and ethnic divisions as a strategy of rule'.[36] The Iraqi population is predominantly Arab with a significant Kurdish minority of around 20 per cent and a further 5 per cent who are Turkoman, Assyrian and other groups. The largest group in Iraq are Shias making up around 60 per cent of the population compared with some 35 per cent who are Sunni. It is the latter, however, that have always dominated Iraqi government.[37] The Ba'ath Party, which took control of Iraq in 1968, was Sunni Muslim and ensured that the Shia majority was 'grossly underrepresented in the upper echelons of the military, police, and intelligence, as well as the Baathist and governmental hierarchy'.[38] The Kurdish minority, meanwhile, suffered much oppression and violence under Ba'athist rule including the levelling of Kurdish villages and the use of chemical weapons against unarmed civilians during the Iran–Iraq War.[39] Sectarian and ethnic divisions and their exploitation are significantly more pronounced in Iraq than they were in Vietnam. Indeed, these divisions were reflected in the results of the December 2005 Iraqi elections and look set to continue to complicate the situation in Iraq for the US and its coalition partners.[40]

The differing levels of societal and patriotic cohesion in Vietnam and Iraq are reflected in the nature of their respective insurgencies. In Vietnam, the Communists waged a centrally directed, carefully planned strategy of revolutionary war complete with detailed economic and social programmes designed to maximise popular support. The Communists also had clear and consistent objectives: to expel the United States; remove the Saigon government; and reunify Vietnam under Communist rule.[41]

By contrast, the Iraqi insurgency is the work of dozens of disparate groups and lacks the unity of purpose that drove the Vietnamese Communists. The insurgency is made up of a 'hybrid' of organised criminal gangs; disaffected members of the Ba'ath regime and security forces; Iraqi Islamist groups, both Sunni and Shia; and a number of foreign fighters allegedly under the sway of al-Qaeda.[42] Although an end to foreign occupation appears an implicitly shared objective, the insurgents have no clearly declared agenda, and lack ideological and organisational cohesiveness. The Bush administration has placed much emphasis on the influence of some key individuals such as Moqtada al-Sadr and the Jordanian Islamist and alleged al-Qaeda leader Musab al-Zarqawi. The Iraqi insurgency lacks the leadership, however, of a unifying central figure such as Ho Chi Minh or General Vo Nguyen Giap. The divisions within the insurgency are rife with some 74 different groups vying for influence and attention. Indeed, much of the worst insurgency violence is not directed at the US or Iraqi security forces but is sectarian in nature.[43] Increasingly, analysts of the situation in Iraq are concluding that the sectarian nature of much of the insurgency is bringing the country ever closer to a civil war quite unlike that experienced in Vietnam.

There are, then, significant differences in the international context, the objectives and tactics of the United States, the strength of nationalism and the nature of the insurgencies that make comparisons between the Vietnam and Iraq wars difficult. However, the Vietnam analogy cannot be dismissed entirely. There are some key areas in which policymakers can draw valuable lessons and we can make useful comparisons.

Sustainability of support

There is an overriding 'lesson' of the Vietnam conflict that applies to policymakers today irrespective of the differences between the US engagements in Vietnam and

Iraq. It is that US public support for a long-term military commitment abroad cannot be sustained unless:

* the objectives are compelling, clear and attainable;
* there is demonstrable progress in achieving those objectives; and
* the costs in terms of lives and matériel are kept to an acceptable level.[44]

The main reason why the Vietnam War became so unpopular domestically, and thus unsustainable, was not simply the high casualty rate. Between 1965 and 1972, the years of major US combat in Vietnam, 55,750 Americans were killed and a further 292,000 were wounded at a rate of almost 7,000 dead per year, an average of 19 killed every day. These rates were lower, however, than World War I (108 killed per day), World War II (305 per day) and the Korean War (48 per day).[45] The main reason for opposition to the war in Vietnam was not casualty sensitivity alone, but the growing belief that the war was not worth the sacrifices being made. The Korean War had also become deeply unpopular but the visibility and impact of the opposition was tempered by the fact that the Cold War consensus was firmer in the early 1950s than it would be by the late 1960s. The two World Wars also indicate that if the US public perceives the cause to be compelling enough, it will be willing to accept high numbers of US casualties. Opposition to the war in Vietnam solidified as the objectives became unclear over time, progress was difficult to measure, and an increasing credibility gap developed between the progress US officials said was being made and the realities on the ground. The longer the war continued, the less compelling the original objectives appeared, and the less willing the US populace became to continue to make the sacrifices necessary to pursue those objectives.

In this respect, the situation in Iraq does appear increasingly analogous with the Vietnam experience. The percentage of the US populace that believes the war in Iraq was worth fighting has fallen to 44 per cent, some 20 percentage points lower than after Bush declared major combat operations at an end in 2003.[46] The initially high approval ratings for the war were largely due to the objectives appearing clear, compelling and attainable: defeat Iraq's military forces and depose the Ba'ath leadership to end the alleged threat of Iraqi weapons of mass destruction. Indeed, President Bush had assured journalists at a press conference shortly before hostilities began that Iraq would not become another Vietnam, effectively because the administration would be following the tenets of the Vietnam syndrome:

> Our mission is clear in Iraq: ... disarmament. And in order to disarm it would mean regime change. I'm confident we'll be able to achieve that objective, in a way that minimizes the loss of life. ... And our mission won't change. ... We have got a plan that will achieve that mission.[47]

After Bush declared these goals achieved on May 1, 2003, however, the military objectives did shift. Once Saddam Hussein's regime was deposed, the objectives were not only redefined but expanded to include attempts to bring domestic order and stability which would help facilitate reconstruction; putting down continued 'pockets of resistance'; and capturing or killing the remnants of the regime, including Saddam himself who was subsequently seized on December 14, 2003. Most of these objectives, however, have proven less clearly attainable and more prone to frustration. US efforts at bringing stability and order to Iraq have not only been marred by escalating violence but also undermined by a host of other problems that seem likely to continue for some time: 'official and unofficial corruption, sporadic vigilantism, police misconduct, militia feuding, political backstabbing, economic travail, regional separatism, government incompetence, rampant criminality, religious conflict, and posturing by political entrepreneurs spouting anti-American and anti-Israel rhetoric'.[48] The failure of successive South Vietnamese governments to establish political legitimacy for themselves or provide for the security of their state holds sage warnings for current US policymakers. The Saigon government was established by the French and subsequently supported by the United States, making it difficult to escape the perception that it was a 'puppet regime'. This lack of legitimacy was compounded by corruption, ineptitude, and an inability to establish long-term security without a considerable US military presence. The new Iraqi government will have to strive to avoid being tainted by close association with Washington. This may prove difficult, however, given the continued large US military presence in the country deemed necessary to maintain security.

The corrupting effects of the war in Vietnam were felt most keenly on the home front. Lyndon Johnson had lied to Congress about the course of the war from the outset. The justifications for escalating the Vietnam War were based on dubious premises, and the sense that Americans could not trust their leaders grew as wide as the credibility gap between official pronouncements of progress in the war and the reports from the fighting in Vietnam.[49] Parallels can certainly be drawn with the Iraq campaign with support for the war declining as it became increasingly obvious that Iraq did not possess weapons of mass destruction and accusations of deception and misinformation concerning pre-war intelligence became more serious.

Another element in the unease about Iraq finds similarities with the growth of opposition to Vietnam. The revelations of abuse from Abu Ghraib prison and the use of force against civilians (such as the bombing of a wedding party at Makr al-Deeb, a desert hamlet near the Syrian border) have raised questions about the morality of US actions in Iraq.[50] One of the main sources of opposition to the war in Vietnam was that the United States was widely perceived to be 'using its immense power in ways inconsistent with the principles, the values, the ethical standards of the American people'.[51] The bombing of non-military targets, the use of 'body counts' and 'kill ratios' to measure progress, the dropping of napalm and nerve agents, and the massacring of civilians, most notoriously at My Lai, all demonstrated the low value that Washington seemed to place on the lives of the Vietnamese. They also undermined claims that the United States was fighting to protect the freedom of the Vietnamese populace.[52] Similarly in Iraq, US claims that the coalition is fighting to establish a free, democratic society are being undermined by some of the ways in which force is being deployed. The failures in the efforts to win the 'hearts and minds' of the Vietnamese should prove instructive to US officials seeking similar goals in Iraq. These questions of legitimacy and morality have contributed to the opposition to the war and the growing sense that the Iraq War is increasingly less worthy of the sacrifices being asked of the American people.

A widely held assumption is that the more deadly and frequent attacks on US targets in Iraq become the more likely it is that public opinion will turn against continued US involvement. Compared with earlier conflicts, including Vietnam, the US casualty rate in Iraq is actually very low. By February 12, 2006 there had been 2,270 US fatalities and 16,653 wounded.[53] This amounts on average to just over 2 US deaths per day, 17 less than in Vietnam and far fewer than in Korea or the World Wars. The number of US military wounded in Iraq (15 per day) is also considerably lower than in Vietnam (114 per day). It is often argued by critics of the war that US public opinion will call for an immediate withdrawal from Iraq should there be a significant increase in these casualty rates or if there is a major attack that causes heavy loss of US lives. Conventional wisdom holds that the Tet Offensive – the massive, countrywide assault by Vietnamese Communist forces in January 1968 – turned a majority of US citizens against the war in Vietnam and brought an end to US involvement. Some critics of the Iraq intervention, therefore, look for a similar watershed event to precipitate a US withdrawal. However, the impact of Tet is often misunderstood: it was elite and official opinion, rather than public opinion, that took a significant turn against the Vietnam War as a result of the Tet Offensive.[54]

By 1968, as John Mueller argues, 'public support for and opposition to the war in Vietnam [had] hardened ... to the point where events were less likely to make much of an impression'.[55] Instead, it was influential opinion leaders within the Johnson administration, in Congress, the media, the business world, in education and elsewhere who concluded that continued effort in Vietnam would be futile and no longer worth the sacrifice.[56] There is some evidence that a similar phenomenon is occurring over Iraq: high-ranking legislators from both parties and other influential opinion leaders have become increasingly critical, although administration officials are remaining firm that the continued commitment to Iraq is absolutely essential. Public support for the war in Iraq, meanwhile, eroded much more quickly than it did in the earlier unpopular wars of Korea and Vietnam.[57] Approval of Bush's handling of the situation in Iraq fell below 50 per cent for the first time just four months after he had declared the end of major combat. There has been a relatively steady decline since, reaching a low of 36 per cent in November 2005.[58] Major events, whether positive such as the capture of Saddam Hussein or the holding of elections, or negative such as the revelations of abuse at Abu Ghraib prison, have caused only temporary shifts of approval up or down.[59] Most telling, perhaps, are a series of polls taken over the last six months of 2005 that show consistently a near 50–50 split between those who 'think the US should keep military troops in Iraq until the situation has stabilized' and those who 'think the US should bring its troops home as soon as possible'.[60] As with Vietnam, it seems unlikely that even a major insurgency assault on US targets would now cause a precipitous decline in support or opposition to the war since approval and disapproval appear to have consolidated around a hard core. Even if such an event did occur, however, it does not necessarily follow that a rapid withdrawal from Iraq would be the result. It should be remembered that the Tet Offensive did not end the Vietnam War. US involvement continued for a further five years at great cost in lives and matériel.

The examples of Lebanon in 1982–3 and Somalia in 1993–4 are also cited as evidence that a concerted effort on the part of the Iraqi insurgency to inflict higher casualty figures on US forces would cause such public and congressional outcry that the White House would be forced to withdraw from Iraq. In October 1983, 241 US Marines were killed in a suicide bomb attack on their barracks in Beirut. Subsequently the US public and Congress appeared unwilling to give continued support to an intervention with no tangible rewards in a situation of which they had little knowledge or understanding. Nonetheless, withdrawal was not immediate – the euphemistic 'redeployment offshore' did not come until the following February. Public opinion was also difficult to gauge, since the highly popular invasion of Grenada took place two days after the barracks bombing.[61] There are significant differences, however, between the impact of the Beirut bombing and the likely outcome of any similar attack in Iraq. Most significantly, the level of US commitment and responsibility in Lebanon was far lower than it is in Iraq. US forces were in Beirut as part of a multinational peacekeeping force under UN auspices rather than being an occupying force in a country the White House decided to invade with only a few allies. The stakes have been set much higher in Iraq than they were in Lebanon, making withdrawal a much more difficult prospect for George W. Bush than it was from Lebanon for Ronald Reagan.

The other example of a debacle leading to a collapse of public support for an intervention and a precipitous US withdrawal is the case of Somalia in 1993–4. However, this case is rather more complicated than conventional wisdom would have it and in fact can be read as evidence that major, deadly attacks on US forces can actually harden public resolve and support for the president, at least in the short run. Many legislators and other opinion leaders reacted strongly to the killing of 18 US Army Rangers on the streets of Mogadishu in October 1993, calling for immediate withdrawal because they believed the public would not support further engagement. As Representative Jim Ramstad of Minnesota put it, 'the President had better get his foreign policy act together before Somalia becomes another Vietnam'. The US was 'getting bogged down in a prolonged and deadly operation' that he described as 'the height of foreign policy folly'.[62] President Clinton responded to the incident by actually reinforcing the existing troop deployment in Somalia rather than withdrawing them immediately, though he did pledge that all US forces would be withdrawn and replaced with other UN forces by March 31, 1994.[63]

Opinion polling reveals that, rather than reflecting congressional calls for an immediate withdrawal, sizeable public majorities supported Clinton's decision to reinforce US troops in Somalia followed by a gradual withdrawal. Legislators and other critics of the administration seem to have misread the public mood. Although there were clear majorities in favour of a withdrawal from Somalia, an ABC News poll found only 37 per cent of respondents wanted the troops to pull out immediately. A CNN/*USA Today* survey also found a minority of 43 per cent seeking immediate withdrawal. Indeed, these and other polls found majorities of between 55 and 61 per cent supportive of President Clinton's decision to increase the US troop commitment to Somalia in the short term followed by a gradual withdrawal. Most tellingly, ABC found 75 per cent of respondents favouring the use of a 'major military attack' if negotiations failed to secure the release of American prisoners taken in the October firefight. Contrary to the conventional wisdom, as Michael MacKinnon has observed, 'there was no overwhelming outcry by the public to pull out of Somalia. Rather it appears as though many members of Congress either overestimated the public's reaction, or simply presumed what it would be'.[64] The example of Somalia suggests that policymakers themselves are more sensitive to Vietnam analogies than the public at large.

The Bush administration's political and military commitment to Iraq has now reached beyond the point that a 'Somalia-style' loss of life could precipitate a more rapid US withdrawal. Similar numbers to the 18 US personnel killed in the 'Battle of Mogadishu' have already been lost in single attacks in Iraq. A bomb attack on a US military base in Mosul killed 19 Americans and wounded more than 60 on December 21, 2004. Almost a year later, on December 1, 2005, a roadside bomb claimed 10 US Marines near Fallujah. These attacks refocused media attention on the substantial public disapproval of the war and gave some greater force to the vocal elements of those opposed to the war. Neither event, however, caused underlying popular approval and disapproval for the war to shift significantly enough to either rouse greater congressional opposition or to force the administration's hand on the issue of withdrawal. Bush and his foreign policy team remain adamant, in fact, that success in Iraq is the crucial element in their foreign policy. The administration made concerted efforts as 2005 drew to a close, for example, to persuade the US public that progress is being made in Iraq; and that maintaining the commitment will bring positive results and secure greater stability in the region and increased security for the United States.[65] This is why the Iraqi elections are so crucial for the Bush team. If the results are accepted as legitimate and a government is formed successfully it will strengthen the president's argument that the expenditure of lives and materiel in Iraq has been necessary and rewarding. If the elections come to be perceived as a failure, and the loss of US lives intensifies, elite and public opinion will be severely tested and calls for a more rapid withdrawal will grow in strength.

US credibility in Vietnam and Iraq

Successive US presidents regarded defending South Vietnam from Communism as a test of the credibility of US power and resolve in the Cold War. Vietnam was perceived as a crucial domino that must be prevented from falling if Washington was to contain Communism in Asia. Each president from Harry Truman to

Lyndon Johnson gradually intensified US involvement in Vietnam as a result.[66] By the time Richard Nixon was elected president in 1968, Washington had already expended billions of dollars and thousands of lives in Vietnam. Although Nixon campaigned on a pledge to end the war, he was not interested in doing so immediately. He insisted that any withdrawal must be 'honourable' because simply abandoning South Vietnam would be out of character with US traditions of defending 'free peoples' and, more importantly, would undermine US credibility. Immediate withdrawal would not only jeopardise the Saigon government but also, he argued, seriously undermine the credibility of US strength and resolve in the eyes of not only enemies and rivals, but also allies.[67] Nixon believed that 'this first defeat in our Nation's history would result in a collapse of confidence in American leadership, not only in Asia but throughout the world'.[68] National Security Advisor Henry Kissinger shared his president's concerns: 'However we got into Vietnam ... whatever the judgment of our actions, ending the war honorably is essential for the peace of the world. Any other solution may unloose forces that would complicate the prospects for international order'.[69] Nixon therefore kept the United States in Vietnam for a further four years, gradually reducing the size of the troop commitment until he was confident that Saigon could defend itself, at least for a 'decent interval'.

The stakes in Iraq have also been set high by the Bush administration. Iraq has long held strategic value for the United States, particularly as a buffer to Iranian ambitions in the region since 1979. Even at the end of the 1991 Gulf War, part of the US calculation not to remove Saddam Hussein's regime was based on the perceived need to maintain a relatively strong Iraq as a 'threat and counterweight to Iran'.[70] The establishment of a stable, ordered Iraq is now a priority for the United States in order to help forestall increased instability in the wider Middle East and provide a renewed stalwart against Iran. However, a stable, ordered, yet authoritarian Iraq is no longer an acceptable option to Washington. Iraq, more than Afghanistan, has become regarded as a test case for US ambitions to extend the reach of democracy in the world. Since his second inaugural address in January 2005, this appears to be the key organising principle of Bush's second term foreign policy.[71] The long-term US goal of spreading democracy and freedom will be widely perceived, both domestically and internationally, as suffering a major setback should Iraq fail to fulfil the requirements of democratisation.

The degree to which Iraq matters in US foreign policy is so high, however, largely because Bush has stated consistently that US success in Iraq is imperative. In September 2003, with the Iraqi insurgency in its infancy, Bush declared that Iraq was now 'the central front' in the war on terror. Bush admitted that securing success in Iraq would 'take time and require sacrifice' but he vowed that 'we will do what is necessary, we will spend what is necessary, to achieve this essential victory in the war on terror'.[72] The president's determination has barely faltered since with speech after speech reiterating how crucial to his foreign policy and the war on terror success in Iraq remains. He has insisted repeatedly that US troops will not leave Iraq until the country has stabilised and is able to defend itself. This approach has raised the stakes by making success in the country not only a test of the president's own credibility, but also the United States as a world power. Much like Nixon before him, Bush has declared that 'immediate withdrawal from Iraq would be a mistake' that would 'weaken the United States'.[73] If the US were to cut its losses and leave Iraq, Bush argues:

> We would abandon our Iraqi friends and signal to the world that America cannot be trusted to keep its word. ... We would cause the tyrants in the Middle East to laugh at our failed resolve, and tighten their repressive grip. We would hand Iraq over to enemies who have pledged to attack us and the global terrorist movement would be emboldened and more dangerous than ever before. To retreat before victory would be an act of recklessness and dishonor, and I will not allow it.[74]

Bush has made clear, therefore, that the administration's 'military strategy is straightforward: As Iraqis stand up, Americans will stand down'.[75]

The withdrawal analogy

Consistently setting the stakes so high makes it increasingly difficult for the Bush administration and potentially its successors to withdraw US forces, or even substantially scale them down, without compelling evidence that a stable political system is in place and that the Iraqis can provide adequately for their own security. As with Vietnam, therefore, the maintenance of US credibility will require the withdrawal of US troops from Iraq to be a gradual one. Pronouncements by US generals and also the US Ambassador to Iraq in August 2005 suggested possible reductions of about 20,000 to 30,000 troops during 2006 provided the political and security situation has improved and Iraqi security forces are proving more effective.[76] Such reductions are not the same as withdrawal, however, and would still leave a substantial US force in Iraq for some time to come. Indeed, in the same month that force reductions were being suggested, General Peter Schoomaker made clear that the US Army is preparing to keep more than 100,000 troops in Iraq for a further four years or more, if necessary, to ensure stability and security. President Bush has himself ruled out a precise timetable for withdrawal, stating instead that 'I will make decisions based on the progress we see on the ground'.[77] The gradual scaling back of US force numbers coupled with increases in the number of indigenous security forces was exactly the process undertaken in Vietnam. President Nixon announced the beginning of troop withdrawals under his policy of 'Vietnamization' in May 1969 but by year's end only 68,200 of the half a million US forces in Vietnam had pulled out. The US commitment was then slowly reduced to 334,600 by the end of 1970, to 156,800 by the end of 1971, to 47,000 by June 1972, and finally to complete withdrawal in March 1973, while at the same time South Vietnamese armed forces numbers were bolstered until they totalled beyond one million.[78] Although Bush has insisted that, 'So long as I'm the President, we will stay, we will fight, and we will win the war on terror',[79] his preference will nonetheless be for a substantial scaling back of US force numbers in Iraq before the end of his presidency. Bush's legacy will be deeply affected by the state of the situation in Iraq when he leaves office in January 2009. His administration will need to strike a delicate balance between satisfying US domestic calls for troop reductions and retaining sufficient force levels to facilitate political and security progress in Iraq. Withdrawal by stages similar to Nixon's process of Vietnamization is the most likely scenario over the next three to four years.

As with Nixon's policy, however, such a withdrawal will have consequences. Those critics pessimistic about the chances of a stable, functioning democracy becoming established in Iraq will point to the ultimate failure of US objectives in Vietnam despite the efforts to bolster Saigon's power as US forces were reduced. Nixon's 'peace with honor' provided merely a pause in the ongoing struggle for control of Vietnam. It extricated the United States but it did little to ensure enduring peace and security for South Vietnam with the 'decent interval' between US withdrawal and the fall of Saigon to Communist forces lasting only two years.[80] Contemporary critics fear similarly that civil war will come to Iraq upon a US withdrawal whether it is in 2006 or in four years' time.

The costs of Nixon's strategy should also give pause for thought to those concerned about the potential consequences of a longer-term US military commitment to Iraq. Over a third of the total US casualties in the war occurred while Nixon sought peace with honour. Between 1969 and 1973, 20,553 American, 107,504 South Vietnamese, and more than half a million North Vietnamese and NLF (National Liberation Front) personnel were killed. Civilian casualties for the period were also very substantial, although there is no official record of the number.[81] Nixon also expanded the conflict into neighbouring Cambodia and Laos even while he was winding down the US involvement. Similarly, the longer the US remains in Iraq casualty figures will continue to grow and the potential for an expansion of the area of conflict beyond Iraq's borders into Syria or Iran may become more likely.

Vietnam legacies – Iraq legacies

As with the defeat of US objectives in Vietnam some 30 years ago, perceived failure in Iraq could prove a highly chastening experience for the United States. The undermining of US credibility and accompanying decline in self-confidence and resolve would constrain Washington's ability to motivate, persuade, and coerce others to do its bidding. It would also make it more difficult for the United States to sidestep international organisations and the norms of international behaviour without facing still greater opposition and admonishment than it has over Iraq. The rapid overthrow of Saddam Hussein's regime demonstrated US military prowess. The destruction of the regime's rule, following the defeat of the Taliban in Afghanistan, was held up as an example to other potential adversaries that the United States could act successfully on its desires for regime change in 'rogue' states. However, the inability of US forces to stabilise Iraq and put down insurgents has diminished the impact of the original 'victory' and undermined the threat potential of US military force. Ultimate failure by Washington to secure

Iraq would only embolden further those states and non-state actors who oppose or ignore US will or threaten US interests globally.

If there is an ultimate lesson of the Iraq War it is that it reiterates one of the central lessons of the Vietnam War: there are limits to the power of the United States, particularly in terms of the utility of the use of force. Successive post-Vietnam US administrations attempted to initially work within those limits and then more recently to work around them. Bush's doctrine of pre-emption was the most forthright attempt to show the world that Washington had banished the 'ghosts of Vietnam' and was now willing to utilise its massive military might whenever and wherever it saw fit, with or without international approval. The Iraq experience, however, has made further use of pre-emptive action far less likely due to the over-commitment of US forces and the fear of initiating another long-term entanglement. While there are clearly problems with some aspects of the Vietnam analogy when applied to Iraq, the one lasting connection that the two conflicts are likely to have is that the experience in Iraq will reinforce the Vietnam syndrome and return the US to the post-Vietnam norm of using force only in short, sharp interventions designed to secure clear and attainable objectives as swiftly as possible using massive force while minimising the risk of casualties.

Notes

1 I would like to thank Andrew Hammond, Tom Wales and Robert K. McMahon for their helpful comments on early drafts of this chapter.

2 George H. W. Bush, 'Remarks to the American Legislative Exchange Council, March 1, 1991', *Public Papers of the Presidents of the United States: George Bush, 1991*, http://bushlibrary.tamu.edu/research/papers/1991.

3 See Ernest R. May, *'Lessons' of the Past: The Use and Misuse of History in American Foreign Policy*, Oxford: Oxford University Press, 1975; Robert Jervis, *Perception and Misperception in International Politics*, Princeton, NJ: Princeton University Press, 1976; Richard E. Neustadt and Ernest R. May, *Thinking in Time: The Uses of History for Decision Makers*, New York: Free Press, 1986; Yuen Foong Khong, *Analogies at War: Korea, Munich, Dien Bien Phu and the Vietnam Decisions of 1965*, Princeton: Princeton University Press, 1992; Jeffrey Record, *Making War, Thinking History: Munich, Vietnam and Presidential Uses of Force from Korea to Kosovo*, Annapolis, MD: Naval Institute Press, 2002; Stanley A. Renshon and Deborah Welch Larson (eds) *Good Judgment in Foreign Policy: Theory and Application*, Lanham, MD: Rowman & Littlefield, 2003.

4 George H. W. Bush, 'Address to the Nation Announcing the Deployment of United States Armed Forces to Saudi Arabia, August 8, 1990', *Public Papers of the Presidents of the United States: George Bush, 1990*, http://bushlibrary.tamu.edu/research/papers/1990/90080800.html.

5 Colin L. Powell with Joseph E. Persico, *My American Journey*, New York: Random House, 1995 p. 491; George Bush and Brent Scowcroft, *A World Transformed*, New York: Alfred A. Knopf, 1998, p. 389; Trevor B. McCrisken, *American Exceptionalism and the Legacy of Vietnam: US Foreign Policy Since 1974*, Basingstoke: Palgrave Macmillan, 2003, pp. 142–3.

6 Quoted in Howard Schuman and Cheryl Rieger, 'Historical Analogies, Generational Effects, and Attitudes Toward War', *American Sociological Review*, 1992, vol. 57, pp. 301–21, 316.

7 Bush and Scowcroft, op. cit., p. 464.
8 Quoted in Robert W. Tucker and David C. Hendrickson, *The Imperial Temptation: The New World Order and America's Purpose*, New York: Council on Foreign Relations Press, 1992, p. 146.
9 May, op. cit., p. xi.
10 McCrisken, op. cit.
11 See, for example, George W. Bush, 'President Commemorates 60th Anniversary of V-J Day, August 30, 2005', White House Office of the Press Secretary, Press Release; George W. Bush, 'President Discusses War on Terror at National Endowment for Democracy, October 6, 2005', White House Office of the Press Secretary, Press Release. All Bush administration press releases are available online on the White House website at www.whitehouse.gov/news/index.html.
12 Edward M. Kennedy, 'Speech Delivered at the Brookings Institution, April 5, 2004', Brookings Institution, Washington, DC, Press Release, http://www.brookings.edu/comm/events/20040405kennedy.pdf.
13 Quoted in Brian Knowlton, 'US Army Planning for Longer Stay in Iraq', *International Herald Tribune*, August 22, 2005, http://www.iht.com/articles/2005/08/21/news/troops.php.
14 Quoted in Jonathan Steele and Ewen MacAskill, 'Battles Rage from North to South', *The Guardian* (London), April 8, 2004 http://www.guardian.co.uk/international/story/0,,1188103,00.html.
15 George C. Herring, *America's Longest War: The United States and Vietnam, 1950–1975*, 3rd edn, New York: McGraw-Hill, 1996, pp. 163–4, 274; Gabriel Kolko, *Vietnam: Anatomy of a War, 1940–1975*, London: Allen & Unwin, 1986, pp. 156–8, 372, 404–6, 429–30, 433, 473–5; Gerard J. DeGroot, *A Noble Cause: America and the Vietnam War*, Harlow: Longman, 2000, pp. 225–7; Jeffrey Record and W. Andrew Terrill, *Iraq and Vietnam: Differences, Similarities, and Insights*, Carlisle, PA: Strategic Studies Institute, 2004, pp. 5–6.
16 Sylvia Ellis, *Britain, America and the Vietnam War*, Westport, CT: Greenwood Press, 2004; Herring, *America's Longest War*, op. cit., pp. 166–7, 304; William S. Turley, *The Second Indochina War: A Short Political and Military History, 1954–1975*, New York: Mentor, 1986, p. 202; Peter King (ed.), *Australia's Vietnam: Australia in the Second Indochina War*, Sydney: Allen & Unwin, 1983; Roberto Rabel, *New Zealand and the Vietnam War: Politics and Diplomacy*, Auckland: Auckland University Press, 2005.
17 Philip H. Gordon and Jeremy Shapiro, *Allies at War: America, Europe and the Crisis Over Iraq*, New York: McGraw Hill, 2004; Bob Woodward, *Plan of Attack*, New York: Simon & Schuster, 2004; William Shawcross, *Allies: US, Britain, Europe and the War in Iraq*, London: Atlantic, 2003; Michael Clarke, 'The Diplomacy that Led to War in Iraq', in Paul Cornish (ed.) *The Conflict in Iraq, 2003*, Basingstoke: Palgrave Macmillan, 2004.
18 See George W. Bush, 'President Outlines Strategy for Victory in Iraq, November 30, 2005', White House Press Release, http://www.whitehouse.gov/news/releases/2005/11/20051130–2.html; *National Strategy for Victory in Iraq*, Washington, DC: National Security Council, November 2005.
19 Anthony H. Cordesman, *Iraq and Foreign Volunteers*, Washington, DC: Center for Strategic and International Studies, 2005, pp. 2–3.
20 Tony Blair, 'Joint Press Conference with Iraqi President Jalal Talabani, October 6, 2005', *10 Downing Street Website*, http://www.pm.gov.uk/output/Page8272.asp; Mark Oliver, 'Iranian Troops "Training Iraqi Insurgents"', *The Guardian* (London), October 12, 2005, http://www.guardian.co.uk/international/story/0,,1590455,00.html.
21 Toby Dodge, *Iraq's Future: The Aftermath of Regime Change*, Adelphi Paper 372, Abingdon and New York: Routledge, 2005, pp. 12, 18–19.
22 Record and Terrill, op. cit., pp. 6–7.

23 Stefan Halper and Jonathan Clarke, *America Alone: The Neo-Conservatives and the Global Order*, Cambridge: Cambridge University Press, 2004; George W. Bush, 'Remarks by the President at the 20th Anniversary of the National Endowment for Democracy, November 6, 2003', White House Office of the Press Secretary, Press Release, http://www.whitehouse.gov/news/releases/2003/11/20031106–3.html.

24 D. Michael Shafer, *Deadly Paradigms: The Failure of US Counterinsurgency Policy*, Leicester: Leicester University Press, 1988; Turley, op. cit.; Neil Sheehan, *A Bright Shining Lie: John Paul Vann and America in Vietnam*, New York: Vintage, 1989; Record and Terrill, op. cit., pp. 8–9.

25 Philip Wilkinson and Tim Garden, 'Military Concepts and Planning' and 'Campaign Analysis: Ground and Air Forces', in Cornish, op. cit., pp. 107–19, 120–33.

26 Paul Wolfowitz, 'Remarks as delivered to Veterans of Foreign Wars, Omni Shoreham Hotel, Washington, DC, March 11, 2003', United States Department of Defense, Press Release, http://www.dod.mil/speeches/2003/sp20030311–depsecdef 0082.html.

27 Turley, op. cit., p. 89.

28 Bradley Graham, 'Military Confirms Surge in Airstrikes', *Washington Post*, December 24, 2005, p. A14.

29 Record and Terrill, op. cit., pp. 9–10. Allied forces in Vietnam were drawn from South Korea, Australia, New Zealand, the Philippines and Thailand.

30 Woodward, op. cit., pp. 8, 36–7, 401, 406.

31 Iraqi Security Forces include Police, National Guard, Armed Forces and Border Patrol. *Iraq Index: Tracking Variables of Reconstruction and Security in Post-Saddam Iraq*, February 13, 2006, Washington, DC: Brookings Institution, 2006, pp. 20, 25, http://www.brookings.org/fp/saban/iraq/index.pdf.

32 Record and Terrill, op. cit., p. 10.

33 *Iraq Index*, p. 18.

34 William J. Duiker, *Sacred War: Nationalism and Revolution in a Divided Vietnam*, New York: McGraw Hill, 1995, p. 252. See also Frances FitzGerald, *Fire in the Lake: The Vietnamese and the Americans in Vietnam*, New York: Vintage, 1972; William J. Duiker, *The Communist Road to Power in Vietnam*, 2nd edn, Boulder, CO: Westview Press, 1996.

35 See Toby Dodge, *Inventing Iraq: The Failure of Nation Building and a History Denied*, London: Hurst, 2003 pp. 159–64.

36 Ibid., p. 169.

37 Ibid.; Dilip Hiro, *Iraq: A Report from the Inside*, London: Granta, 2003; Andrew Cockburn and Patrick Coburn, *Saddam Hussein: An American Obsession*, London: Verso, 2002, pp. 58–67; Geoff Simons, *Iraq: From Sumer to Post-Saddam*, 3rd edn, Basingstoke: Palgrave Macmillan, 2004; Dodge, *Iraq's Future*, op. cit. Most of the Kurdish population is also Sunni Muslim.

38 Hiro, op. cit., p. 27.

39 Ibid., pp. 73–5; Simons, op. cit., pp. 297–305, 316.

40 Jonathan Steele, 'Religious Parties Deal Blow to US Hopes in Iraq', *The Guardian* (London), December 21, 2005, http://www.guardian.co.uk/print/0,3858,5360406–103681,00.html; Brian Whitaker, 'Ruling Shia Coalition Won Election, Results Confirm', *The Guardian* (London), February 11, 2006, http://www.guardian.co.uk/international/story/0,,1707467,00.html.

41 Duiker, *Sacred War*, op. cit.; FitzGerald, op. cit.; Duiker, *Communist Road to Power*, op. cit.; Record and Terrill, op. cit., p. 8.

42 Dodge, *Iraq's Future*, op. cit., pp. 14–19.

43 See, for example, Nelson Hernandez and Hassan Shammari, 'Attack on Iraqi Funeral Kills at Least 42', *Washington Post*, January 5, 2006, p. A10; Richard A. Oppell, Jr, 'Carnage: Up to 130 Killed in Iraq, Drawing a Shiite Warning', *New York Times*, January 6, 2006, p. A1; Dodge, *Iraq's Future*, op. cit, pp. 13–14.

44 See McCrisken, op. cit.

45 Record and Terrill, op. cit., pp. 11–12.
46 ABC News/*Washington Post* Poll on Iraq, January 23–26, 2006, reproduced at http:// www.pollingreport.com/iraq.htm.
47 George W. Bush, 'President George Bush Discusses Iraq in National Press Conference, March 6, 2003', White House Office of the Press Secretary, Press Release, http:// www.whitehouse.gov/news/releases/2003/03/20030306–8.html.
48 John Mueller, 'The Iraq Syndrome', *Foreign Affairs*, November/December 2005, http://www.foreignaffairs.org/20051101faessay84605/john-mueller/the-iraq-syndrome.html.
49 McCrisken, op. cit. p. 29.
50 See Seymour M. Hersh, *Chain of Command: The Road from 9/11 to Abu Ghraib*, London: Allen Lane, 2004.
51 David W. Levy, *The Debate Over Vietnam*, 2nd edn, Baltimore, MD: Johns Hopkins University Press, 1995, p. 46.
52 McCrisken, op. cit., pp. 28–9.
53 *Iraq Index*, pp. 4–7.
54 McCrisken, op. cit., pp. 30–1.
55 John E. Mueller, *War, Presidents, and Public Opinion*, New York: John Wiley & Sons, 1973, pp. 54–7.
56 Stanley Karnow, *Vietnam: A History*, New York: Viking Press, 1983, pp. 546–7.
57 Mueller, 'The Iraq Syndrome', op. cit.
58 See ABC News/*Washington Post* poll on Iraq, January 23–26, 2006, http://www. pollingreport.com/iraq.htm.
59 Mueller, 'The Iraq Syndrome', op. cit.
60 Pew Research Center for the People and the Press Survey, February 1–5, 2006, http:// www.pollingreport.com/iraq.htm.
61 See McCrisken, op. cit., pp. 110–12; Lou Cannon, *President Reagan: The Role of a Lifetime*, New York: Touchstone, 1991; George P. Shultz, *Turmoil and Triumph: My Years as Secretary of State*, New York: Charles Scribner's Sons, 1993, pp. 43–116; Caspar Weinberger, *Fighting for Peace: Seven Critical Years in the Pentagon*, London: Michael Joseph, 1990.
62 'Withdraw United States Troops From Somalia Now', House of Representatives, October 5, 1993 *Congressional Record*, 139(133), p. H7382.
63 McCrisken, op. cit., pp. 166–7.
64 Michael G. MacKinnon, *The Evolution of US Peacekeeping Policy Under Clinton: A Fairweather Friend*, London: Frank Cass, 2000, pp. 79–80.
65 George W. Bush, 'President Outlines Strategy for Victory in Iraq, November 30, 2005'; Bush, 'President Discusses War on Terror and Rebuilding Iraq, December 7, 2005'; Bush, 'President Discusses War on Terror and Upcoming Iraqi Elections, December 12, 2005'; Bush, 'President Discusses Iraqi Elections, Victory in the War on Terror, December 14, 2005'; Bush, 'President's Address to the Nation, December 18, 2005', White House Office of the Press Secretary, Press Releases, http://www.whitehouse. gov/news.
66 See Leslie H. Gelb with Richard K. Betts, *The Irony of Vietnam: The System Worked*, Washington, DC: Brookings Institution, 1979; Larry Berman, *Planning a Tragedy: The Americanization of the War in Vietnam*, New York: W. W. Norton, 1984; Fredrik Logevall, *Choosing War: The Lost Chance for Peace and the Escalation of the War in Vietnam*, Berkeley, CA: University of California Press, 1999; David Kaiser, *American Tragedy: Kennedy, Johnson, and the Origins of the Vietnam War*, Cambridge, MA: Belknap Press, 2000.
67 McCrisken, op. cit., p. 31.
68 Richard M. Nixon, 'Address to the Nation on the War in Vietnam, November 3, 1969', *Public Papers of the Presidents of the United States: Richard M. Nixon, 1969*, Washington, DC: United States Government Printing Office, 1971, p. 902.

69 Quoted in Herring, op. cit., p. 245.
70 Powell, op. cit., p. 490.
71 George W. Bush, 'President Sworn-In to Second Term, January 20, 2005'; Bush, 'National Endowment for Democracy, October 6, 2005', White House Office of the Press Secretary, Press Releases, http://whitehouse.gov/news.
72 George W. Bush, 'President Addresses the Nation, September 7, 2003', White House Office of the Press Secretary, Press Release, http://whitehouse.gov/news.
73 George W. Bush, 'President Discusses Iraqi Constitution with Press Pool, August 23, 2005', White House Office of the Press Secretary, Press Release, http://whitehouse.gov/news.
74 George W. Bush, 'President's Address to the Nation, December 18, 2005', op. cit.
75 George W. Bush, 'President Honors Veterans of Foreign Wars at National Convention, August 22, 2005', White House Office of the Press Secretary, Press Release, http://whitehouse.gov/news.
76 Rory Carroll, 'US Hopes to Withdraw 30,000 Troops', *The Guardian* (London), August 8, 2005, http://www.guardian.co.uk/international/story/0,1544491,00.html.
77 Bush, 'President's Address to the Nation, December 18, 2005', op. cit.
78 Turley, op. cit., pp. 148, 156, 215, 217.
79 George W. Bush, 'President Addresses Military Families, Discusses War on Terror, August 24, 2005', White House Office of the Press Secretary, Press Release, http://whitehouse.gov/news.
80 McCrisken, op. cit., p. 33.
81 Herring, op. cit., pp. 282–3.

9

VIETNAM AND IRAQ
Strategy, exit and Syndrome

John Mueller

I would like to assess three aspects of the American war in Vietnam and then compare them to what may be similar elements in the current war in Iraq. These are the strategy applied by the United States, the process by which it exited, and the longer-term international consequences of the events.

Vietnam

By 1965 the Hanoi-backed communist insurgents appeared to be on the verge of victory against American-supported forces in South Vietnam, and it seemed that the only way to rescue the situation was to send American troops to take over the counter-insurgency effort. A consensus existed both within and outside the administration that it was very important to keep South Vietnam out of communist hands. As future war critic David Halberstam asserted at the time, Vietnam was a 'strategic country in a key area, it is perhaps one of only five or six nations in the world that is truly vital to U.S. interests'.[1]

Vietnam was seen to be an important testing ground of the efficacy of wars of national liberation. Throughout the world, Defense Secretary Robert McNamara observed, the conflict was regarded as 'a test case of U.S. capacity to help a nation meet a Communist "war of liberation"', and North Vietnamese leaders agreed, 'South Vietnam is the model of the national liberation movement of our time. If the special warfare that the United States imperialists are testing in South Vietnam is overcome, then it can be defeated anywhere in the world', while the Chinese were arguing that 'the whole cause of world revolution hinges' on such 'revolutionary struggles' in the third world.[2] Vietnam also seemed vital because of the threat China seemed to present in the area, both by itself and by its increasingly close ties to the huge island republic of Indonesia, then led by the mercurial Sukarno who had embarked on a clamorous policy of hostility toward the West and toward his Western-oriented neighbours.[3]

South Vietnam thus seemed to be wedged strategically between the glowering Chinese threat from the north and the clamorous Indonesian threat from the south. In his autobiography, President Lyndon Johnson describes the phenomenon as

'Communist pincers'.[4] For *New York Times* editorial columnist C. L. Sulzberger, the situation resembled a 'vast nutcracker'.[5]

Strategy

To defeat the communist insurgency in Vietnam, the United States initially adopted a strategy of attrition. The basic idea was to send over large numbers of American troops to 'seize the initiative' and to carry the war to the enemy through relentless 'search and destroy' operations. It was assumed that the enemy would eventually reach its breaking point: it would become 'convinced that military victory was impossible and then would not be willing to endure further punishment', as the general in charge, William Westmoreland, put it at the time.[6]

There were at least three ways the American strategy might have been successful. All had encouraging historical precedents.

One of these was the 'fade away' thesis. As the State Department's Walt Rostow put it at the time, if the communists failed to win, then they might 'finally give up in discouragement' as they had in Greece, Malaya, and the Philippines.[7] So weakened, McNamara hoped, they 'would choose to reduce their efforts in the South and try to salvage their resources for another day'.[8]

Another possible path to success would have been through a deft combination of military effectiveness and diplomatic manoeuvre. Denied military victory, the communists might have tried to cut a deal. After all, when their military efforts in Korea were stalemated, the communists had negotiated an agreement to return to pre-war boundaries. Moreover, the communists in Indochina in 1954 and in Laos in 1961 had been willing to accept compromise settlements rather than continue the war. To be sure, the Indochina agreements were basically face-saving devices for Western countries to withdraw, but they did show the willingness of the communists to accept partitions and at least temporary cease-fires rather than continue to pursue a costly war.

A third possibility was that the Soviet Union, an important North Vietnamese ally and supplier, might become discouraged. Wooed by the benefits of *detente* and wary of the costs and escalatory dangers of wars of national liberation, the Soviets might be able to pressure their little client into a more accommodating stance. As presidential aide Bill Moyers recalled, 'The President—well, most of us shared this at the White House—we felt that he could reason with the Russians and they would deliver'.[9]

American policymakers, then, did have some plans for success in the war. The idea was to push the North Vietnamese communists until they broke; as Leslie Gelb and Richard Betts characterize the thinking of the time, 'How could a tiny, backward Asian country *not* have a breaking point?'.[10]

Expectations varied about where that breaking point might be. Some in the administration were fairly confident of early victory once American might and 'can do' inventiveness were properly applied against what Johnson called 'a raggedy-ass little fourth-rate country'.[11] Moyers says, 'There was a confidence—it was never bragged about, it was just there—a residue perhaps of the confrontation of missiles over Cuba–that when the chips were really down, the other people would fold'.[12] An atmosphere of self-confidence – even of omnipotence – was also fostered by Johnson's spectacular re-election triumph of 1964.

In their calculations, American decision makers made one crucial mistake: as Secretary of State Dean Rusk observed in 1971, they 'underestimated the resistance and determination of the North Vietnamese'.[13] But experience suggests that this mis-estimation, however unfortunate, was quite reasonable. As it happens, the willingness of the North Vietnamese communists and their southern allies, the Vietcong, to accept punishment in Vietnam was virtually unprecedented in the history of modern warfare. If the battle death rate as a percentage of pre-war population is calculated for each of the hundreds of countries that have participated in international and colonial wars since 1816, it is apparent that Vietnam was an extreme case. Even discounting heavily for exaggerations in the 'body count', the communist side was willing to accept battle death rates that were about twice as high as those accepted by the fanatical, often suicidal, Japanese in World War II. Furthermore, the few combatants who did take losses as high as the Vietnamese communists were mainly those like the Germans and Soviets in World War II who were fighting to the death for their national existence – not merely for expansion, like North Vietnam. This extraordinary communist tenacity could not have been confidently anticipated. Evidence from the French Indochina War certainly was of little help: in their major battles in the war against the Americans and South Vietnamese the communists suffered tens of thousands of battle deaths, while in the massed battle against the French at Dien Bien Phu in 1954 they had lost about 7,900 men – and apparently had been pushed to the limits of collapse as a result.[14]

The failure of American decision makers to appreciate the fanaticism of the enemy may be regrettable, but it can hardly be judged unreasonable. In Vietnam, it seems, the United States was up against an incredibly well functioning organization – firmly disciplined, tenaciously led, and largely free from corruption or enervating self-indulgence. To a degree that was virtually unprecedented, the organization was able to enforce upon itself an almost religious devotion to duty, sacrifice, loyalty, and fatalistic patience. Although the communists often experienced massive military setbacks and periods of stress and exhaustion, they were always able to refit themselves, re-arm, and come back for more. It may well be that, as one American general put it, 'they were in fact the best enemy we have faced in our history'.[15]

Exit

After the Tet Offensive of 1968, in which the communists seemed to demonstrate that the end of the war was likely to be a long way off, the Johnson administration re-evaluated its strategy. As a result of this exercise, it essentially decided to cease the American escalation and to begin to turn the war over to the South Vietnamese.[16] Once in office in 1969, Richard Nixon continued Johnson's policy of Vietnamization and of reducing the American casualty rate by decreasing

American combat activity. He tried to keep the military pressure on, especially by bombing, and he continued to hope that the communists could be made to cave in.[17] Reluctantly and under substantial pressure, Nixon also eventually began to withdraw American troops even as peace talks with the enemy, started in Johnson's final year, dragged on.

By the 1970s the United States still continued its association with the war in large measure because the North Vietnamese held some American prisoners. Although it may not make a great deal of sense to continue a war costing thousands of lives in order to gain the return of a few hundred prisoners, it is difficult to exaggerate the potency of the prisoner of war issue. In May 1971, 68 percent of those surveyed on a public opinion poll agreed that all US troops should be brought home from Vietnam by the end of the year. However, when asked if they would favour withdrawal 'if it threatened [not *cost*] the lives and safety of United States POWs held by North Vietnam', support dropped to 11 percent.[18] Henry Kissinger, the chief American representative at the Vietnam peace talks, was well aware of the political imperative. In reviewing American options, he concluded that unilateral withdrawal and Vietnamization would not 'do the trick' because they 'would not return our prisoners'.[19] Apparently, the option of ending the war without the return of the prisoners was not even a hypothetical consideration.

Finally in January 1973, Nixon and Kissinger were able to cut a deal with the communists: the United States withdrew its substantially reduced direct military participation in the war, communist troops were allowed to remain poised for action in the south under a cease-fire arrangement, and the Americans got their prisoners back. Nixon, echoing Neville Chamberlain's unfortunate slogan of 1938, perhaps unconsciously, called the deal 'peace with honor', and Kissinger received the Nobel Peace Prize for his efforts. As virtually everyone else expected, furious war eventually broke out again – in 1975. The South Vietnamese lost ignominiously.

The precipitous collapse of South Vietnam in 1975 and with it the whole American position in that country represented quite possibly the greatest foreign policy debacle in American history. During the war, fears were often voiced that a loss in Vietnam would have severe domestic political consequences in the US – as the rise of the McCarthy era was commonly said to have had its roots in the loss of China to communism in 1949. (An imperfect analogy, however: the reaction in the early 1950s was not simply to the communist success in China in 1949, but to the fact that a year later the United States found itself at war with communist China in Korea.) In stark contrast to these dire anticipations, defeat – indeed, utter rout – in Vietnam was accepted with remarkable equanimity.

There were at least three reasons for this.

First, to a considerable degree the war had become decoupled from American sensibilities by the settlement of January 1973; that is, there had been a 'decent interval' of two years during which the war had seemingly been given back to the Vietnamese. Important to this development was the return in early 1973 of the 500 American prisoners of war held by North Vietnam. It is often suggested that Vietnam differed from other wars in that there was never a glorious homecoming for the returning soldier-heroes. But for this small group of men there was an emotional and well-publicized return, and that constituted a highly visible end to the war for the public. (Actually, it is rather curious that Americans have so readily accepted Vietnam as a defeat for the United States. The decent interval phenomenon leaves an easy way out: we did our job, got things under control, turned things over to the South Vietnamese who then blew it. But, rather surprisingly, this point of view is rarely expressed.)

Second, the perceived Cold War importance of South Vietnam had been diminishing for years due, particularly, to an anti-communist coup and bloodbath in once communist-leaning Indonesia, and to the rise of the Cultural Revolution in China during which that country turned inward. Thus, the chief reason to re-insert US troops into the war in 1975 would have been to save or to defend the South Vietnamese. But poll evidence demonstrates that the American public viewed the South Vietnamese with considerable disrespect, even contempt, and the public had long been prepared to abandon them if they could not effectively fight for themselves. This could be seen as early as 1966. At that time some 15 to 35 percent of the public favoured withdrawal from Vietnam; but this percentage jumped to 54 percent when the poll question was phrased to include the condition 'suppose the South Vietnamese start fighting among themselves', and to 72 percent when it included the phrase, 'if the South Vietnamese government decides to stop fighting'. Other polls suggest the commitment to the South Vietnamese and fears of a post-war bloodbath in Vietnam were relatively minor elements in popular support for the war.[20]

Third, the collapse in Indochina was probably made easier to accept by an ancillary, if essentially insignificant, event: the capture in 1975 of the American ship *Mayaguez* and its crew by Cambodian communists and its subsequent daring recapture by American troops. Although about as many lives were lost in the rescue attempt as there were sailors aboard, the drama and macho derring-do of the venture probably served to mollify American anguish. It was possible to believe that, while the communists could defeat America's erstwhile allies in Southeast Asia, they were impotent against true American might.

The chief initial reaction to debacle was to try to forget about it.[21] Few were even interested in finding out if those who had anticipated a bloodbath in the wake of an American withdrawal were going to be correct. As it happened, they were. After taking control of South Vietnam, the communists executed at least 65,000 people and systematically destroyed the economy, impelling masses of people to flee, and tens, or possibly hundreds of thousands died in the process.[22] In neighbouring Cambodia, the communist victors caused some one or two million of Cambodia's eight million people to die by execution, starvation, or disease – in proportion, probably the most savage genocide in history. However, this cataclysmic event was studiously ignored, in part from fears that paying attention might dangerously lead to the conclusion that American troops should be sent over to rectify the disaster: over most of its course the three network news telecasts devoted a total of 29 minutes to the cataclysm.[23]

Moreover, foreign policy was the great non-issue of the subsequent presidential campaign in 1976. Indeed, far from engendering a debate over 'who lost Vietnam', the debacle was actually cited by the man who presided over it, Gerald Ford, as a point in his *favour* in his re-election efforts. When he came into office, he observed, 'we were still deeply involved in the problems of Vietnam;' but now 'we are at peace. Not a single young American is fighting or dying on any foreign soil'.[24]

Syndrome

After Vietnam, there was a strong desire – usually called the Vietnam Syndrome – not to do that again. And, in fact, there never were other Vietnams for the United States during the Cold War. Due to fears of 'another Vietnam', the administration was kept by Congress even from rather modest anti-communist ventures in Africa and, to a lesser extent, in Latin America (though there was bipartisan support for aiding the anti-Soviet insurgency in Afghanistan).

But from a Cold War perspective, it all eventually came out rather well. A common image during Vietnam was of toppling dominoes: Vietnam needed to be held, it was argued, because its loss would have a cascading effect as a set of other countries followed suit. To a degree, something of a domino effect did take place after Vietnam, but it ended up working to the advantage of the West and helped bring about a non-violent end to the Cold War.

In 1975 three countries – Cambodia, South Vietnam, and Laos – toppled into the communist camp. Partly out of fear of repeating the Vietnam experience, the United States went into a sort of containment funk – the Vietnam Syndrome – and watched from the sidelines as the Soviet Union, in what seems in retrospect to have been remarkably like a fit of absent-mindedness, opportunistically gathered a set of third world countries into its imperial embrace: Angola in 1976, Mozambique and Ethiopia in 1977, South Yemen and Afghanistan in 1978, and Grenada and Nicaragua in 1979. The Soviets at first were quite gleeful about these acquisitions – the 'correlation of forces', they concluded, had magically and decisively shifted in their direction.[25]

However, far from whetting their appetite for more, these gains ultimately not only satiated their appetite for expansion but, given the special properties of the morsels they happened to consume, served to give the ravenous expanders a troubling case of indigestion. For almost all the new acquisitions soon became economic and political basket cases, fraught with dissension, financial mismanagement, and civil warfare. In 1979 the situation in neighbouring Afghanistan had so deteriorated that the Soviets found it necessary to send in troops, and they then descended into a long period of enervating warfare there. Also in 1979, the Soviet dependency in Vietnam invaded Cambodia and toppled the even more brutal communist government there. With Soviet aid, they continued their occupation despite lingering guerrilla opposition – 'Vietnam's Vietnam', some called it – and despite a punitive attack across their northern border by the Chinese, who were angered at what they took to be Vietnamese imperialism in Cambodia.

As each member of their newly expanded empire turned toward the Soviet Union for maternal warmth and sustenance and absorbed increasing amounts of Soviet treasure and, in the case of Afghanistan, blood, many Soviets began to wonder about the wisdom of the ventures. Perhaps, it began to seem, they would have been better off contained.

It took 40 years but, plagued by such costly economic, social, and military disasters, the Soviets finally began to embrace grim reality, adopt serious reform, and, especially, rise above ideology. And this eventually led to its abandonment of the Cold War.[26]

Insofar as the policy of containment was devised to force the Soviets to confront their inherent contradictions, the result of this process suggests a curious paradox. George Kennan and the other early containment theorists were correct to conclude that Soviet communism was a singularly undesirable and fundamentally flawed form of government, and they were right to anticipate that it would inevitably have to mellow when it could no longer avoid confronting its inherent contradictions. But Soviet communism might have reached this painful point somewhat earlier if its natural propensity to expand had been tolerated rather than contained.

Iraq

The winner of the 2000 presidential election in the United States, George W. Bush, came into office suggesting that the United States ought to develop a 'humble' foreign policy, and, along with some of his foreign policy advisers, such as Condoleezza Rice, he expressed an aversion to 'nation-building'.[27] However, after international terrorists shockingly flew airliners into New York's World Trade Center and Washington's Pentagon on September 11, 2001, Bush instantly shucked off that perspective and proclaimed that he was taking on the distinctly unhumble responsibility to 'rid the world of evil'.[28] The first stage of that campaign was to intervene very forcefully in an ongoing civil war in Afghanistan in an effort to attack a group of international terrorists based in that country. The American venture enjoyed a considerable amount of international support. It also proved to be remarkably successful and was unexpectedly easy.

The easy success in Afghanistan was encouraging – not, perhaps, unlike the sense of can-do self-confidence that, as Moyers noted, affected American foreign policy after the Cuban Missile Crisis and that helped in turn to inspire the notion that the US military would succeed reasonably handily in Vietnam. Accordingly, the Bush administration now set its sights on the Saddam Hussein regime in Iraq.

Strategy

It was anticipated that a military invasion by an effective army could eliminate the regime, and it seemed entirely possible that Iraq's ill-led and demoralized army, which fought almost not at all when challenged in the 1991 Gulf War, would put up little armed resistance to such an invasion.[29] There were efforts to tie Iraq to international terrorism, and fears that the dictatorial and unstable Saddam could develop weapons of mass destruction remained high, now embellished by the argument that he might palm them off on dedicated terrorists to explode in distant lands. These arguments enjoyed quite a bit of support with the American public and Congress, still reeling from the September 11 attacks, but Bush's only notable foreign ally on the issue was Tony Blair's United Kingdom. Determined to see it out, Bush and Blair shrugged off international disapproval and launched naked aggression against Iraq. As expected, the Iraqi military disintegrated under the onslaught and seems to have lacked any semblance of a coherent strategy of resistance.[30]

The invaders quickly and easily toppled a regime held in wide contempt – though not much urgent fear – around the world. But to achieve success, the invaders would have had quickly to establish a stable, acceptable, effective, moderate government there, and it would have been highly desirable as well to uncover convincing links between the Iraqi regime and global terrorism while seizing sizable caches of the much touted weapons of mass destruction that they expected to find. With that, the venture likely would eventually have achieved a considerable degree of (probably somewhat grudging) international legitimacy, and it might have encouraged further American ventures elsewhere.

Neither convincing terrorist links nor WMD were found in Iraq, however, and efforts quickly to establish an effective, acceptable government there failed utterly. Moreover, the foreign occupiers soon found that they were stretched thin in their efforts to rebuild a nation out of the rubble that remained after Saddam, American and British enforced international economic sanctions and the war, had taken their toll. It had been hoped that the Iraqis would greet the conquerors by dancing happily in the streets and somehow coordinate themselves into a coherent and appreciative government, rather as in previous ventures in Panama and East Timor and maybe in Bosnia and Kosovo. But, although many were glad to see Saddam's tyranny ended, the invaders often found the population resentful and humiliated, rather than gleeful and grateful. Moreover, bringing order to the situation was vastly complicated by the fact that the government-toppling invasion had effectively created a failed state which permitted widespread criminality and looting.[31] In addition, some people – including some foreign terrorists drawn opportunistically to the area – were dedicated to sabotaging the victors' peace and to killing the policing forces.

In Iraq, as in Vietnam, the United States (and in the case of Iraq, Britain too) face an armed opposition that is dedicated, resourceful, capable of replenishing its ranks after losses, and seemingly determined to fight forever if necessary. In Vietnam, as noted, the hope was that after suffering enough punishment the enemy would reach its 'breaking point' and then either fade away or seek accommodation. Great punishment was inflicted, but the enemy never broke; instead it was the United States that faded away after signing a face-saving agreement. Whether the insurgency in Iraq has the same determination and fortitude is yet to be seen, but the signs thus far are not very encouraging: it does not appear to be weakening.

Exit

As in Vietnam, it is difficult to see how the insurgents in Iraq can be defeated at a tolerable cost in American and British lives: the insurgents are variously motivated, but they seem likely, despite tactical setbacks, to be willing and able to continue their activities at least until the hated invaders leave. Accordingly, the policy of Vietnamization has been updated and applied to Iraq – Iraqification, some are calling it, if possible an even uglier word. As in Vietnam, responsibility for policing the resistance is increasingly being handed over to a shaky, patched-together government, army, and police force; tactics seem to be in the process of being shifted to reduce casualties and troops will probably gradually begin to be removed; and support for the locals will increasingly be limited to economic aid and encouraging words.

The local government and military in Vietnam collapsed to the communist insurgents a couple of years later, but the enemy they were up against possessed a massive military force backed by, indeed centred in, North Vietnam. The insurgency in Iraq, albeit deadly and dedicated, represents a much smaller and less well organized force and would likely have far more difficulty taking over the country. Moreover, many of the insurgents are probably fighting simply to get the United States out of the country and can be expected to cease doing so when the Americans leave – as happened to some of the insurgents when the Soviets left Afghanistan in 1989 and when the Israelis left southern Lebanon in 2000.[32] To that degree, the insurgency might become more manageable without the American presence there though there could still be a determined effort by at least some of the rebels to go after the remaining, American-fabricated government consisting, in their eyes, of quislings and collaborators.

As there were fears of a bloodbath in Vietnam after the Americans left, there are understandable and somewhat comparable concerns this time around that Iraq could devolve into a civil war after the Americans leave. By 2006 it began to seem like a civil war had begun in Iraq even with American and British troops still present in the country. For the most part, it seems, the Shiites do not see the insurgents merely as representative of the Sunni population. Also to be feared would be what happened in Afghanistan among those combatants who remained in the fray – a cruel, scrabbling conflict between warlord groups, many of them essentially criminal.[33] Images of the lengthy and incredibly chaotic civil war in Lebanon also come to mind.

It is often argued, including by Bush and Blair, that a too-hasty exit from Iraq will be exhilarating to international terrorists who will see it as an even greater victory than the one over the Soviets in Afghanistan. Osama bin Laden's theory that the Americans can be defeated, or at least productively inconvenienced, by inflicting comparatively small, but continuously draining, casualties on them will achieve apparent confirmation. Thus, a venture designed and sold in part as a blow against international terrorists will end up emboldening and energizing them.

The dilemma is that almost any exit from Iraq will have this effect. People like bin Laden believe that America invaded Iraq as part of its plan to control the oil in the Middle East. But the United States does not intend to do that (at least not in the direct sense bin Laden and others doubtless consider to be its goal), nor does it seek to destroy Islam as many others around the world also bitterly assert. Thus just about any kind of American withdrawal will be seen by such people as a victory for the harassing terrorist insurgents, who, they will believe, are due primary credit for forcing the United States to leave without accomplishing what they take to be America's key objectives. Thus even an orderly retreat from Iraq will likely be taken by international terrorists as a great victory, even greater than the one against the Soviet Union in Afghanistan or the one against Israel in southern Lebanon. Iraq has also become something of a terrorist training – or perhaps inspiration – zone.

In some important respects, therefore, depending on the continued resilience of the insurgency, Iraq could be shaping up to be a major debacle, rather like Vietnam. However, on the brighter side for the administration, unless failure in Iraq leads directly to terrorism in the US, the experience with Vietnam suggests that the American people are quite capable of taking debacle in their stride. Moreover, they supported the decision to withdraw policing US troops from Lebanon in 1984 after a terrorist bomb killed 241 of them in the civil war there, and the man who presided over the debacle, Ronald Reagan, readily won re-election a few months later. Something similar happened to Bill Clinton when he withdrew policing troops from Somalia in 1994: by the time the next election rolled around, people had largely forgotten the whole episode. Americans have not proven to be terribly 'defeat phobic', as some have maintained. In addition, even if disaster follows in Iraq after American withdrawal – as it did in Lebanon, Somalia, and Vietnam – the people dying will be Iraqis, not Americans. And the deaths of foreigners are not what move the public.[34]

In one important respect, withdrawal from Vietnam was much more difficult politically than it would be from Iraq. North Vietnam held 500 Americans – including John McCain – prisoner in Hanoi, and leaving Vietnam without getting those prisoners back, as noted earlier, seems to have been a political non-starter. There is no comparable problem in Iraq.

As in Vietnam, it is likely that financial support for the local, fabricated government will decline significantly after withdrawal. The American Congress finds it necessary to support American troops abroad, but has always been able to contain its enthusiasm for enterprises that seem like foreign aid. After all, Iraqis, like South Vietnamese, do not vote in American elections.

Syndrome

There are likely to be important consequences of the Iraq experience. Indeed, no matter how the war there comes out, an 'Iraq Syndrome' seems likely: 'No more Vietnams' will be replaced, or updated, by 'No more Iraqs'. A poll in relatively war-approving Alabama conducted in 2005 asked whether America should be prepared to send troops back to establish order if full-scale civil war erupted in Iraq after a US withdrawal. Only a third of the respondents favoured doing so.[35]

The experience will probably change American foreign policy and further deflate the already-limited willingness of developed states to apply military force to police the world.[36] There will likely also be notable decreases in the acceptance of a number of beliefs. Among these are the notions that the United States should take unilateral military action to correct situations or regimes it considers reprehensible but which present no very direct and very immediate threat to it; that it should and can forcibly bring democracy to nations not now so blessed; that it has the duty to bring order to the Middle East; that having by far the largest defence budget in the world is necessary and mostly brings benefits; that international cooperation is of only very limited value; and that Europeans and other well-meaning foreigners are naive and decadent wimps. There may also be new pressures to reduce the military budget, and the country is more likely to seek international cooperation, sometimes possibly even showing perceptible signs of humility. Among the casualties for American policy therefore could be the Bush Doctrine, empire, unilateralism, pre-emption (actually, preventive war), last-remaining-superpowerdom, and indispensable-nationhood. Indeed, these once-fashionable (and sometimes self-infatuated) concepts are already picking up a patina of quaintness.

The chief beneficiaries of the Iraq War are likely to be the rogue/axis-of-evil (or devil *du jour*) states of Iran and North Korea. In part because of American military and financial overextension in Iraq (and Afghanistan), the likelihood of any coherent application of military action or even of focused military threat against these two unpleasant entities has substantially diminished, as it has against what at one time seemed to be the American administration's next targets: Syria especially, as well as Libya, Saudi Arabia, Egypt, and Lebanon (not to mention France and the State Department).[37]

The Iraq Syndrome suggests that any intelligence determining such states to be threatening will be deeply questioned, that any moves to apply military force to them will be met with widespread dismay and opposition unless there is severe provocation, and that any additional persecution by such regimes of their own people will be wistfully tolerated and ignored. In 1994, the United States seems to have been just about ready to go to war with North Korea spurred by a contested intelligence conclusion that there was 'a better than even' chance that North Korea had the makings of a small nuclear bomb.[38] By contrast, when that country abruptly declared in February 2005 that it now actually possessed nuclear weapons, the announcement was officially characterized as 'unfortunate' and as 'rhetoric we've heard before'.[39] Iran has already become defiant, and its newly elected president has actually had the temerity to suggest – surely, the unkindest cut – that he does not consider the United States to be the least bit indispensable.

As argued earlier, the Vietnam Syndrome proved beneficial in the long term for the United States. Perhaps, the Iraq Syndrome will as well.

It seems clear in hindsight that the United States persistently and often vastly exaggerated both the international and domestic capacity of communism to inflict damage in carrying out its threatening revolutionary goals and its willingness to accept risk to do so. Moreover, the policies designed to deal with the threat turned out to be overly militaristic, were far too expensive, and, ultimately, were probably unnecessary. Cold War anxieties about the capacity of the enemies within – domestic communists and their sympathizers – also proved to be much inflated. As suggested above, international communism principally died as a consequence of its own weight, not of Western policy.

Fears of terrorism and of Muslim extremism – which underlay much of the momentum toward the war in Iraq – may prove to be similarly misguided. Although prominent politicians and pundits profess to see the threat as a major, even an existential, one, it is unlikely that the tiny bands of violent extremists have, or will have, the capacity to inflict sustained major damage or to take over a significant country.[40]

When history is on one's side – as I think it is for the prosperous, free capitalist states of the West – the best policy often is to let it take its course. Dedicated meddling is unnecessary and can be costly and counterproductive. That appears to have been a central lesson of the Vietnam experience. It may well also hold for Iraq.

Notes

1 David Halberstam, *The Making of a Quagmire*, New York: Random House, 1965, p. 15. Oddly, this passage and other similar ones are omitted in the 1988 reprint edition of the book.

2 Robert McNamara, *Pentagon Papers*, Senator Gravel Edition, Boston, MA: Beacon, 1971, vol. 3, p. 500; see also pp. 50–1. North Vietnam: Vo Nguyen Giap quoted by Maxwell Taylor in J. William Fulbright, *The Vietnam Hearings*, New York: Vintage, 1966, p. 169. Chinese: Lin Biao, 'Long Live the Victory of People's War!', September 3, 1965, in K. Fan (ed.) *Mao Tse-Tung and Lin Pao: Post-Revolutionary Writings*, Garden City, NY: Anchor, 1972, p. 396.

3 Roger Hilsman, *To Move a Nation: The Politics of Foreign Policy in the Administration of John F. Kennedy*, New York: Delta, 1967, part 8.

4 Lyndon Baines Johnson, *The Vantage Point: Perspectives of the Presidency 1963–1969*, New York: Holt, Rinehart and Winston, 1971, p. 606.

5 C. L. Sulzberger, 'Foreign Affairs: The Nutcracker Suite', *New York Times*, 10 April 1966, p. E8.

6 *Pentagon Papers*, op. cit., vol. 3, pp. 482–3. Or, as Westmoreland put it in 1967: 'We'll just go on bleeding them until Hanoi wakes up to the fact that they have bled their country to the point of national disaster for generations' (Guenter Lewy, *America in Vietnam*, New York: Oxford University Press, 1978, p. 73).

7 *Pentagon Papers*, op. cit., vol. 3, pp. 381–2.

8 *Pentagon Papers*, op. cit., vol. 4, p. 624. Some military leaders apparently felt the North Vietnamese supply of fighting-age men could be severely depleted, a calculation Defense Department analysts found to be physically impossible: Lewy, op. cit., pp. 82–4; Alain C. Enthoven and K. Wayne Smith, *How Much is Enough?*, New York: Harper Colophon, 1971, pp. 295–300.

9 Bill Moyers, 'Bill Moyers Talks About the War and LBJ', in Robert Manning and Michael Janeway (eds) *Who We Are: An Atlantic Chronicle of the United States and Vietnam*, Boston, MA: Little, Brown and Company, 1969, p. 270.

10 Leslie H. Gelb with Richard K. Betts, *The Irony of Vietnam: The System Worked*, Washington, DC: Brookings Institute, 1979, p. 343, emphasis in the original.

11 Barbara Tuchman, *The March of Folly: From Troy to Vietnam*, New York: Knopf, 1984, p. 321.

12 Moyers, op. cit., p. 262.

13 Dean Rusk, Interview on NBC-TV, July 2, 1971.

14 For a full treatment of this analysis, see John Mueller, 'The Search for the "Breaking Point" in Vietnam: The Statistics of a Deadly Quarrel', *International Studies Quarterly*,1980, vol. 24, pp. 497–519.

15 Quoted in Douglas Kinnard, *The War Managers*, Hanover, NH: University Press of New England, 1977, p. 67. As Westmoreland put it tersely, 'Any American commander who took the same vast losses ... would have been sacked overnight' (*A Soldier Reports*, Garden City, NY: Doubleday, 1976, pp. 251–2). On this issue, see also Mueller, 'Search', op. cit., pp. 511–15. Worth questioning in this regard, then, are the decisions of the Vietnamese communists who continued to send thousands upon thousands of young men to the south to be ground up by the American war machine and who willingly accepted virtually unprecedented losses for a goal that was far from central to their survival as a nation and that could have been pursued in far less costly ways.

16 On these decisions, see Herbert Y. Schandler, *The Unmaking of a President: Lyndon Johnson and Vietnam*, Princeton, NJ: Princeton University Press, 1977.

17 For example, Nixon's adviser Kissinger often observed that 'North Vietnam could not be the only country in the world without a breaking point' (Allan E. Goodman, *The Lost Peace: America's Search for a Negotiated Settlement of the Vietnam War*, Stanford, CA: Hoover, 1978, p. 96).

18 John Mueller, *War, Presidents and Public Opinion*, New York: Wiley, 1973, pp. 97–8.

19 Henry A. Kissinger, *White House Years*, Boston, MA: Little, Brown and Company, 1979, pp. 1011, 1039.

20 Mueller, *War, President and Public Opinion*, op. cit., pp. 49, 86.

21 There had been a similar reaction after the American Civil War. See Gerald F. Linderman, *Embattled Courage: The Experience of Combat in the Civil War*, New York: Free Press, 1987.

22 Jacqueline Desbarats and Karl D. Jackson, 'Research Among Vietnam Refugees Reveals a Blood Bath', *Wall Street Journal*, April 22, 1985, p. 29.

23 William C. Adams and Michael Joblove, 'The Unnewsworthy Holocaust: TV News and Terror in Cambodia', in William C. Adams (ed.) *Television Coverage of International Affairs*, Norwood, NJ: Ablex Publishing, 1982, pp. 217–25.

24 Sidney Kraus, *The Great Debates: Carter vs. Ford, 1976*, Bloomington, IN: Indiana University Press, 1979, pp. 538–9.

25 George W. Breslauer, 'Ideology and Learning in Soviet Third World Policy', *World Politics*, vol. 17, April 1987, pp. 429–41, 436–7.

26 On this issue, see John Mueller, 'What Was the Cold War About? Evidence from Its Ending', *Political Science Quarterly*, vol. 119, Winter 2004–5, pp. 609–31.

27 See, in particular, Rice's article in the January/February 2000 issue of *Foreign Affairs*, in which she observes that 'the military is a special instrument. It is lethal, and is meant to be. It is not a civilian police force. It is not a political referee. And it is most certainly not designed to build a civilian society.... Using the American armed forces as the world's "911" will degrade capabilities, bog soldiers down in peacekeeping roles, and fuel concern among other great powers that the United States has decided to enforce notions of "limited sovereignty" worldwide in the name of humanitarianism' (C. Rice, 'Campaign 2000: Promoting the National Interest', *Foreign Affairs*, 2000, vol. 79, pp. 46–56, 53–4).

28 Memorial Service speech at the National Cathedral, 14 September 2001.

29 On the pathetic capacities of the Iraq army in 1991, see John Mueller, 'The Perfect Enemy: Assessing the Gulf War', *Security Studies*, 1995, vol. 5, pp. 77–117.

30 See, for example, George C. Wilson, 'Why Didn't Saddam Defend His Country?', *National Journal*, April 19, 2003, p. 1222.

31 The homicide rate in Baghdad seems to have reached some 90 or 100 per 100,000 (www.brookings.edu/iraqindex). This would make it among the highest ever recorded in the history of the human race.

32 See also Nir Rosen, 'If America Left Iraq', *Atlantic*, December 2005, pp. 42–6.

33 Ahmed Rashid, *Taliban: Militant Islam, Oil and Fundamentalism in Central Asia*, New Haven, CT: Yale University Press, 2000.

34 On these issues, see John Mueller, 'The Iraq Syndrome', *Foreign Affairs*, 2005, vol. 73, pp. 44–54.

35 Sean Reilly, 'Poll Shows Alabamians Still Support President', *Mobile Register*, May 22, 2005.

36 On this process, see John Mueller, *The Remnants of War*, Ithaca, NY: Cornell University Press, 2004, chapters 7–8.

37 See, for example, Norman Podhoretz, 'In Praise of the Bush Doctrine', *Commentary*, September 2002, pp. 19–28.

38 Don Oberdorfer, *The Two Koreas: A Contemporary History*, revised edn, New York: Basic Books, 2001, p. 307.

39 Sonni Efron and Bruce Wallace, 'North Korea Escalates Its Nuclear Threat', *Los Angeles Times*, February 11, 2005, p. A1.

40 For a development of these issues, see John Mueller, 'Simplicity and Spook: Terrorism and the Dynamics of Threat Exaggeration', *International Studies Perspectives*, 2005, vol. 6, pp. 155–73.

10

FALLING DOMINOES

The United States, Vietnam and the war in Iraq

Matthew Masur[1]

When the United States went to war in Iraq in March 2003, many Americans looked to past events to understand the conflict. Both supporters and critics of the war selectively used American history to buttress their arguments. As with any American military intervention since 1975, critics warned that Iraq would become another Vietnam. They argued that the United States was simply repeating the disastrous mistakes of the 1960s and cautioned that Iraq, like Vietnam, would become a quagmire for the United States.

Supporters of the war, including members of the Bush administration, preferred to glean different lessons from American history. According to Bush and his advisors, the war in Iraq was more akin to America's noble struggles against totalitarianism during World War II and the Cold War. As with those earlier struggles, the justness of America's cause legitimated the fight and guaranteed eventual victory.

Both of these positions vastly oversimplify the connections between Iraq and earlier American military struggles. They also raise legitimate questions about the war in Iraq. What can American history tell us about the current conflict? Does the Vietnam War provide lessons that can be applied to Iraq? And finally, how has Iraq changed the lessons that Americans take from Vietnam?

Domino theories: from Saigon to Baghdad

In May 1965, historian George Kahin and political scientist Robert Scalapino met in Washington DC to debate America's escalating involvement in Vietnam. The debate was part of a nationwide teach-in, modelled on the teach-ins held at Michigan and other universities earlier in the spring. Kahin had originally been scheduled to debate McGeorge Bundy, but Bundy had to withdraw from the proceedings to attend to the crisis in the Dominican Republic. Scalapino, Bundy's replacement, began his remarks by noting that:

> [T]he Viet-Nam crisis constitutes one of the most complex and serious crises faced by the United States since World War II. There are no easy answers. Probably, very few individuals in this audience concur specifically upon

every detail relating to the crisis, or upon the most logical steps to be taken in attempting to resolve it.[2]

Scalapino's description of the intellectual climate in 1965 holds true today. The war in Iraq has ignited a contentious public debate about American foreign policy. Americans, we are told, are more divided than they have been since the 1960s. Thoughtful observers sharply disagree over every element of the war in Iraq. If there is one common belief, however, it is that American history offers lessons that can illuminate the current conflict.

Since the terrorist attacks on September 11, 2001, President Bush and his advisors have regularly cited American history to defend or justify American foreign policy. In an address before the Philippine Congress in 2003, for example, Bush's characterization of Philippine history seemed to support America's current policy in Iraq. 'America is proud of its part in the great story of the Filipino people', Bush stated. 'Together our soldiers liberated the Philippines from colonial rule. Together we rescued the islands from invasion and occupation'.[3] He went on to praise the Philippines for its commitment to freedom and democracy.

The subtext was clear: the United States and the Iraqi people have similarly liberated Iraq. Iraq, like the Philippines, will become a key American ally and a bastion of freedom and democracy. Bush seemed to refer to both the Spanish–American War in 1898 and also to World War II. But Bush failed to note America's occupation of the Philippine Islands, nor did he mention that nearly 50 years passed between the end of Spanish rule in the Philippines and Philippine independence in 1946. It is hard to imagine that the Spanish–American War and the brutal fight against the Filipino insurgency are the historical antecedents Bush would like to repeat during the current bloodshed in Iraq.

On May 7, 2005, President Bush ignited a small historical debate after delivering a speech in Riga, Latvia. In the address, Bush criticized the agreement at Yalta for sacrificing 'the freedom of small nations' and leading to 'one of the greatest wrongs of history'. Bush's controversial characterization prompted several historians, notably Arthur Schlesinger, Jr, to defend President Roosevelt's negotiations in early 1945.[4]

Bush's words at Riga were noteworthy because they reflect a common theme in his administration's historical references. In his most important speeches dealing with American foreign policy, Bush has regularly cited America's twentieth century struggles against fascism and communism. In his commencement address at West Point in 2002, Bush stated that the war against terror:

> is similar to the cold war. Now, as then, our enemies are totalitarians, holding a creed of power with no place for human dignity. Now, as then, they seek to impose a joyless conformity, to control every life and all of life.[5]

In an address a year after the September 11 attacks, he declared that 'the great struggles of the twentieth century between liberty and totalitarianism ended with a decisive victory for the forces of freedom'.[6]

These analogies have not been exclusive to the president. Former Homeland Security head Tom Ridge declared that 'America and her friends have stared down the daunting armies of Hitler and the oppression of communism. ... Today, we stare down the callous soldiers of hate and the horrific reality of global terrorism'.[7] In August 2003, Condoleezza Rice and Donald Rumsfeld compared the occupation of Iraq to the occupation of Germany after World War II. They suggested that the dangers faced by American soldiers should not discourage the public. The reward for remaining steadfast is a reformed and rehabilitated Iraq, which, like West Germany during the Cold War, can serve as a model of freedom and democracy. Although the occupation of Iraq may exact a heavy toll, it is for a worthy cause.[8]

The president's repeated references to World War II and the Cold War are meant to evoke images of American altruism and sacrifice. Americans, of course, view World War II as a noble struggle against fascism and militarism. After defeating the Axis powers, the United States stood up to the equally dangerous threat of communism. In Bush's narrative, World War II and the Cold War demonstrate America's commitment to freedom for all people. As Bush explained in the 2003 State of the Union Address,

> America's duty is familiar. Throughout the 20th century, small groups of men seized control of great nations, built armies and arsenals, and set out to dominate the weak and intimidate the world. In each case, their ambitions of cruelty and murder had no limit. In each case, the ambitions of Hitlerism, militarism, and communism were defeated by the will of free peoples, by the strength of great alliances, and by the might of the United States of America.[9]

For Bush, the liberation of the Philippines, the victory in World War II, the occupation of West Germany, and the Cold War all provide historical models that justify current American foreign policy. America's success in these areas, according to the administration, supports Bush's decision to take action in Iraq.

Missing from this list is the Vietnam War. The reasons for this omission are rather obvious. At every stage of the war in Iraq, opponents have compared American policy in Iraq to the failed war in Vietnam. Within days of the start of the Iraq War in 2003, the Bush administration had to fight the perception that the United States was becoming embroiled in a quagmire. The failure to find weapons of mass destruction or to demonstrate a definitive link between Saddam Hussein and the September 11 attacks have drawn comparisons to the Tonkin Gulf incident as misleading justifications for war. And America's ongoing fight against Iraqi insurgents has fostered a renewed interest in counterinsurgency tactics used in the 1960s and 1970s.

For most Americans, the Vietnam War offers lessons of how *not* to fight a war. It is not surprising, then, that Bush has been reluctant to cite the Vietnam War as a positive example for the war in Iraq. Indeed, Bush has admitted that his administration could learn from the mistakes of Vietnam. '[O]ne lesson [from Vietnam] is that there be a clear objective that everybody understands' Bush told an interviewer for the *New York Times* in early 2005. It was also important, he continued, that Americans understand 'the connection between that goal and our future'.[10]

Bush's speeches and policy documents show, however, that Vietnam is more than an example of past mistakes. The president's rhetoric indicates that he and his advisors have applied a modified version of the 'domino theory' to the political situation in the Middle East. They believe that the fall of a government – or, in contemporary parlance, regime change – is contagious. In Vietnam, Americans worried that the fall of South Vietnam would inevitably lead to the spread of communism in Asia. The Bush administration holds the optimistic belief that freedom and democracy, once established in Iraq, will take root throughout the Middle East. In his 2005 State of the Union Address, Bush explained that 'the advance of freedom will lead to peace' and that the advance 'has great momentum in our time'.[11] In his speech at West Point, he explained that a fundamental goal of American foreign policy is to 'extend the peace by encouraging free and open societies on every continent'.[12]

Supporters of the war in Iraq have come to describe this as a 'democratic domino' or 'reverse domino' theory. With the failure to find weapons of mass destruction or to establish a link between Saddam Hussein and the September 11 attacks, this became the preferred explanation for the war in Iraq. Critics of the war tend to dismiss the administration's statements about the march of freedom in the Middle East. Supporters point to any positive developments in the Middle East or elsewhere as evidence that Bush's policy is working.

Bush's use of the domino theory makes more sense when viewed with his other historical references. The domino theory, although applied to the Cold War, has its roots in American policy in World War II. If there was a single lesson from World War II, it was, of course, that one should never appease an aggressor. The domino theory was simply an updated version of this lesson. Failing to stop communism would allow it to spread, unhindered, much as Hitler did before World War II. If the domino theory itself was discredited in Vietnam, the earlier lesson – never appease an aggressor – was not. Just as Eisenhower updated the Munich analogy for use in Vietnam, Bush has modified the domino theory for use in Iraq.

Historians see the domino theory as a disappointing example of American policymakers' tendency to simplify foreign affairs and to learn the wrong lessons from past events. Using the context of World War I, American officials in the mid-1930s misjudged the threat of German Nazism. American isolationism was a vivid example of misapplying the lessons of the past, and with great consequences. Similarly, most historians believe that the domino theory was an improper application of past mistakes – mostly the appeasement of Hitler – to new conditions. The irony, of course, is that the domino theory was intended to *correct* the errors of appeasement. The United States, unlike Britain and France in the 1930s, would not remain idle while a dictatorial and tyrannical system threatened world peace and stability.

The *provenance* of the domino theory may explain the neo-conservative affinity for using a similar concept in describing American policy in the Middle

East. In the administration's view, the domino theory is not a discredited relic of America's misguided intervention in Vietnam. Instead, it places Iraq in the tradition of America's noble and righteous fight in what Bush calls 'a conflict between good and evil'.[13] This adapted version of the domino theory helps to explain Bush's ironic lesson from Vietnam. The modified theory lets Bush elide difficult questions about American Cold War foreign policy while characterizing American goals in the starkest terms. While some Americans might harbour doubts about Vietnam, who would oppose a war to promote good and banish evil?

It is important, then, to look more closely at the consequences of the domino theory in the 1950s. The clearest explanation of the domino theory came from President Eisenhower. As he explained, 'you have a row of dominoes set up, you knock over the first one, and what will happen to the last one is the certainty that it will go over very quickly'.[14] The fall of Indochina, Eisenhower explained, could lead to the spread of communism to Thailand, Burma, and Indonesia, which would threaten the Philippines, Japan, Taiwan, Australia, and New Zealand.

The appeal of the domino theory as a justification for intervention in Vietnam was its simplicity. The image of a falling row of dominoes was a vivid metaphor for the spread of communism in Southeast Asia. After the establishment of a communist government in China and the outbreak of the Korean War, the belief that communism was marching across Asia was especially convincing.

Policymakers were not alone in promoting the domino theory. In the early 1950s, the *New York Times* echoed Eisenhower's rhetoric:

> The defense of the Associated States of Indo-China is vital not merely to France but to the whole of the free world. In fact, this defense is less important to France, as such, than it is to Southeast Asia, to Britain and the United States, and to the entire cause of freedom ... . If Indo-China falls, the way is open to Thailand, Malaya, Burma, and eventually Indonesia and India.[15]

The domino theory offered the possibility that the United States could take steps to halt the spread of communism. If the fall of South Vietnam might lead to the spread of communism across the Pacific, then the United States could stop communism in its tracks by successfully defending South Vietnam. The domino theory provided the United States with a 'front line' in its global struggle to defeat communism. Instead of fighting the spread of an idea at points around the world, the United States could focus on a particular front in the battle.

The domino theory and its modern counterpart supplied basic justifications for intervention in Vietnam and Iraq. In both instances, American success hinged on successfully creating a functioning democratic state, either as a bulwark against communism (South Vietnam) or as a beachhead of freedom (Iraq). In both cases, Americans initially ignored the challenges of nation-building. Only after the conflicts dragged on did Americans truly appreciate the scope of the interventions.

Nation-building in the 1950s: contemporary echoes

Contemporary discussions of nation-building in Vietnam show a striking resemblance to prescriptions for American policy in Iraq. Even before the end of French colonialism in 1954, a number of articles in American papers noted that the path to a French victory was through training and equipping more native soldiers and officers. The creation of an effective Vietnamese army would symbolize 'the real transfer of sovereign authority' to the local government; it would also be 'a powerful means of establishing popular confidence'.[16] *Newsweek* asked when native troops would be able to halt the 'Reds' in Indochina and responded that 'a big, lightly armed, highly mobile native force ... can lick the Red guerrillas at their own game'.[17] In 1953 and 1954, *U.S. News and World Report* repeatedly argued that native troops were the solution to French military set-backs.[18]

Even more widespread were assertions that France had to grant Vietnam independence in order to undercut the Viet Minh. The *New York Times* asserted that, in order to be successful, France had to give more authority to the Vietnamese government. *U.S. News and World Report* proposed that the United Nations direct the war in Indochina, thereby taking the question of independence out of the hands of the French. By guaranteeing independence from France, the UN would give the Vietnamese an incentive to fight the communists.[19] One magazine explained that independence would give the Vietnamese 'something to fight for other than a watered-down French colonialism'. Another editorial declared the United States should promote the establishment of a free and independent government in accordance with the wishes of the Indochinese. In 1951, a *Commonweal* columnist wrote that the primary goal of most Vietnamese was for political independence; if France relinquished its colony the Viet Minh would lose much of its support.[20]

According to the *New York Times*, because of the American willingness to defend Indochina, the Vietnamese '[had] their chance to emerge as free peoples in a free world'.[21] This free world took on decidedly Americanized qualities. The *Times* glowingly described a free, national election in 1953 as 'the start of real government by consent. It still has a long way to go but the direction has been established'. This was offered in direct contrast to the communists, who 'opposed and attempted to sabotage the election'. The need for the US to defend the ideals of democracy was manifest: 'Vietnam must be defended. The hope of independence and freedom is explicit in just such an election as this. There would be no such hope if the Communists were allowed to win'.[22]

These articles illuminate the information on which many Americans based their assessments of the French War in Indochina in the 1950s. Of the critiques of French policy in the region, those suggesting broad social and economic reforms were scarce. Many articles, on the other hand, supported training more native troops as a potentially effective policy to defeat the Viet Minh. Although presumably requiring a large economic commitment, this would not have been nearly as demanding as sponsoring fundamental social and economic reforms. The most common suggestion, however, was to give the Associated States more independence. Throughout the 1950s, articles decried French colonialism in

Indochina and mocked Bao Dai as a puppet leader. Independence, either immediate or gradual, was often presented as the necessary and sufficient condition for defeating the Viet Minh. Significantly, by promoting the panacea of Indochinese sovereignty, magazines and newspapers communicated to Americans that stopping communism in Vietnam would not entail a particularly heavy burden for the US. In other words, once colonialism was replaced with freedom and democracy, the Viet Minh would collapse and the communist threat would be averted.

These articles bolstered the argument that most Vietnamese were not committed communists. Their support for the communists was either pragmatic or, more likely, based on deceit, but never the result of a true belief in communism. Americans in the 1950s, just like many Americans today, did not try to explore the true motivations of the nations' enemies. Finally, they suggested simple solutions to what were, in fact, intractable problems. As the United States soon learned, the training of native troops was not a simple endeavour, and the creation of the Army of the Republic of Vietnam (ARVN) did not guarantee the survival of South Vietnam. Similarly, holding free and democratic elections raised the possibility that an unacceptable candidate would win public office. While the United States supported elections in South Vietnam, it was only under certain controlled circumstances.

The United States, of course, decided to prevent the falling dominoes by intervening in Vietnam. America's efforts to establish a bastion against communist expansion in South Vietnam are well known. Beginning in 1954, the United States implemented a series of nation-building programmes to strengthen the South Vietnamese government. The United States offered generous economic support to the South Vietnamese military, helped to train South Vietnamese civil servants, and contributed to rural development.[23] The United States has initiated a similar effort in Iraq, though the basic chronology has been reversed. The failure of nation-building programmes in Vietnam led to full-scale military intervention in 1965; in Iraq, America's military victory in 2003 was followed by efforts to build a functioning Iraqi nation. In each case, the US initiated propaganda campaigns to buttress the nation-building effort. Although these efforts in Vietnam have been mostly overlooked, their failure should serve as a cautionary tale for the Bush administration in Iraq.

American attempts to strengthen South Vietnam also included an extensive programme of information and propaganda.[24] After 1954, South Vietnam was one of the most important locations for United States Information Agency programming. In the decade before the 'Americanization' of the war in 1965, the United States implemented a variety of techniques in the hopes of spreading the ideas of freedom, democracy, and free market capitalism to South Vietnam. Although these efforts ultimately failed, the United States can learn from these mistakes. In particular, the results of American propaganda and information campaigns in South Vietnam highlight the fact that simply promoting the values of freedom and democracy is not enough. American policy has to match the rhetoric.

In the late 1950s, US Information Agency programmes throughout the world publicized the values of freedom and economic progress. Freedom was, in the words of United States Information Agency director George Allen, 'the solid rock on which American ideals were founded'.[25] According to USIA programmes, freedom was more than an abstraction. The United States had put the ideals of freedom in action in a society founded on democratic participation. In 1959, USIA materials juxtaposed 'the bright world of free choice' with 'Communist enticements, subversion, and enslavement'.[26]

In 1956 and 1960, the Agency used American presidential elections to show democracy in action. In 1956, 'peoples overseas were given a comprehensive picture of how Americans express their free choice in naming a President of the United States'.[27] Four years later, 'USIA undertook to achieve maximum understanding around the world of the Presidential elections, as a means of illustrating democracy in action'.[28] Another USIA pamphlet noted that 'displays featuring American trade unions [and] American voters going to the polls ... have been widely popular abroad'.[29]

In Vietnam, American information programmes were formulated to balance 'support of the Diem government with material explaining US policies, culture, and way of life'.[30] One USIA report lamented that even after the French withdrawal in 1954, French culture retained a strong presence in Vietnam and Vietnamese people had only a 'spotty' picture of the United States. The report asserted that there was 'an urgent need for establishing ... [a] rapport between our two peoples which will obviate misunderstanding, prejudice, resentment, and criticism and promote mutual esteem, confidence, appreciation and friendship'.[31]

During the Vietnam War, American policymakers believed that no one would willingly choose to live under communist tyranny. Presented with accurate and objective information about the United States, the Vietnamese would inevitably abandon their support for Ho Chi Minh and the communist cause. An extensive information and propaganda programme was meant to fulfil this goal in Vietnam. The United States used all varieties of information techniques – magazines, mobile displays, language classes, and radio broadcasts – to explain American values and American policies in Vietnam. These programmes had limited success, at least in part because the South Vietnamese government did not embody the American messages of freedom and democracy.

America's attempts to use informational programmes to win support for Ngo Dinh Diem and his administration failed. The goals of USIA programmes in South Vietnam were simply incompatible with Diem's actions as president. While the United States preached freedom, democracy, and the benefits of capitalism, Vietnamese faced a repressive regime and an increasingly unequal distribution of wealth. One American Public Affairs Officer explained Diem's decline in the 1960s:

> I think we did manage to inculcate the Vietnamese with some ideas about how the United States worked, particularly in the media area, and in some measure: democracy [sic]. Now, Ngo Dinh Diem himself was not a democrat by any means. He was about as autocratic and dictatorial as anybody could be ... . Our principal problem ... was to present our concepts of democracy

and political and economic theory and practice in the face of the dictatorial oppression that Diem laid on his people.[32]

American policymakers in the 1950s had complete confidence in the universal appeal of freedom and democracy, values embodied in the American political system. As one historian of Vietnam explained, US foreign policy was predicated on 'the belief that no people truly exercising self-determination will choose communism or authoritarianism because all people desire representative political institutions'.[33] These attitudes have re-emerged in George Bush's rhetoric. President Bush opened his National Security Strategy with powerful words from his post-September 11 speech:

> People everywhere want to be able to speak freely; choose who will govern them; worship as they please; educate their children—male and female; own property; and enjoy the benefits of labor. These values of freedom are right and true for every person, in every society—and the duty of protecting these values against their enemies is the common calling of freedom-loving people across the globe and across the ages.[34]

Bush has repeated these themes throughout his presidency. His National Security Strategy clearly states that

> the United States must defend liberty and justice because these principles are right and true for all people everywhere … . No people on earth yearn to be oppressed, aspire to servitude, or eagerly await the midnight knock of the secret police.

Later, the document suggests that the United States needs to adopt a 'more comprehensive approach to public information efforts that can help people around the world learn about and understand America … . This is a struggle of ideas and this is an area where America must excel'.[35]

The United States has incorporated these ideas into American nation-building efforts in the Middle East, much as it did in Vietnam. The National Security Strategy issued after September 11 stated that the United States would 'wage a war of ideas to win the battle against international terrorism'. As part of this effort, the United States will use 'effective public diplomacy to promote the free flow of information and ideas to kindle the hopes and aspirations of freedom of those in societies ruled by the sponsors of global terrorism'.[36] In 2005, Bush nominated Karen Hughes, one of his closest advisors, to serve as Under Secretary of State for Public Diplomacy and Public Affairs (since 1999 the State Department has been responsible for American informational activities).

Information programmes constitute an important part of what he described as America's 'forward strategy of freedom in the greater Middle East'. Bush announced in the 2004 State of the Union Address that the Voice of America and other broadcast services would be expanding their Arabic and Persian programming in the Middle East. The US also launched Al-Hurra, an Arabic-language television station meant to compete with Al-Jazeera and Al-Arabiya. Details on other aspects of America's information programmes are necessarily sketchy. A contractor paid by the Pentagon has planted pro-American stories in the Iraqi press. It also appears that the same contractor has hired influential Iraqi clerics to help craft America's propaganda message.

These efforts, Bush declared, will 'cut through the barriers of hateful propaganda' in the Middle East. Bush appears confident that these programmes will bear fruit for the US because he believes in the universal applicability of freedom and democracy. As Bush explained, 'God has planted in every human heart the desire to live in freedom'.[37]

Whether Bush is correct that people everywhere want the same things, it does not follow that they will interpret the United States as the power most likely to bring these benefits. Many Iraqis clearly do not believe that the United States is intent on bringing freedom: some are under the impression that the United States has replaced one form of tyranny with another. Similarly, when policymakers in the 1950s expressed similar sentiments, their platitudes did not begin to describe the complex political situation in Vietnam. Many Vietnamese were sceptical of American intentions. This is not surprising, considering that the United States supported anti-democratic regimes in South Vietnam. Dismissing Ho Chi Minh and the Vietnamese communists as enemies of freedom was not an effective strategy as long as the United States raised doubts about its own commitment to freedom in Vietnam. The same can be said for Iraq: President Bush must do more than attack the insurgents as enemies of freedom. He must convince the Iraqi people that the United States has their best interests in mind.

The subsequent history of the domino theory in Southeast Asia, and the popularity of certain American values, can provide ammunition for both supporters and opponents of Bush's policy in Iraq. Cambodia and Laos did install communist governments in the 1970s, seemingly vindicating the belief that the fall of Vietnam would set the stage for communism to spread to the rest of Indochina. At the same time, fears of the inexorable march of communism were greatly exaggerated. Many historians have shown that greater attention to Vietnamese culture and history could have raised serious doubts about the domino theory. Vietnam's history of warfare with the Chinese and with the Khmer should have created more scepticism about the feasibility of communism unifying such different countries. By the end of the 1970s, Vietnam was at war with both Cambodia and China.

But the Bush administration may want to consider further ramifications of its belief in the inevitable spread of democracy and freedom. If democracy can, indeed, breed democracy, then what explains the victory of North Vietnam in the Vietnam War? And why does Vietnam remain communist today? There are many possible answers to these questions, some of which are not likely to be viewed kindly by the Bush administration. Perhaps the Republic of Vietnam was not truly a free and democratic state, thus precluding the spread of these values in the region. Or, perhaps, the influence of the Soviet Union and China prevented the Vietnamese from having the opportunity to choose a truly free and democratic government. Supporters and opponents of the war in Iraq need to engage these difficult questions, because it is unlikely that the administration will do so.

Does the outcome of the Vietnam War provide any insight for the future of the 'democratic domino' in the Middle East? The reality in the Middle East may be neither as rosy as the Bush administration reports nor as dire as the president's critics believe. Presidential elections in Iraq and the ratification of the Iraqi Constitution were undoubtedly successes for democracy in the region, though not unqualified ones. Even many critics of the war agree that the elections held in January and in December 2005, whatever their flaws, were a considerable improvement over conditions in Iraq under Saddam Hussein. Historians should not hesitate, whatever their political leanings, to recognize signs of progress in the Middle East.

At the same time, the Bush administration and supporters of the war should not claim that any move toward democracy since 2003 is the direct result of America's war against Iraq. The Bush administration, for example, has suggested that Libya's recent concessions to international demands should be attributed to America's aggressive efforts to spread democracy. This ignores the fact that Libya had been working to rejoin the international system long before the US went to war in Afghanistan or Iraq. After a decade of crippling UN and American sanctions, Qaddafi recognized that he would benefit from caving to international demands that he turn over suspects in the Lockerbie bombing and pay reparations to the victims' families. By early 2001, Qaddafi had already taken steps toward fulfilling these requirements. Historians must ensure that the Bush administration does not wrongfully take credit for this and other events. It is too early to tell, for example, if the recent steps toward political liberalization in the Middle East will continue. What is apparent, however, is that the Bush administration will latch on to any signs of democratization in the Middle East, much as Bush officials have latched on to any events in America's history that may drum up support for US policies.

Vietnam revisionism and the conflict in Iraq

In his interpretation of the domino theory and the spread of American values abroad, Bush has failed to learn the lessons of Vietnam. At the same time, some supporters of the war are using the war in Iraq to change the lessons of Vietnam. Rather than look at the Vietnam War as a failed enterprise that should not be repeated, they draw attention to America's successes in Vietnam.

The Bush administration is not alone in countering conventional interpretations of the war in Vietnam. Some supporters of the war in Iraq have used current events to question and revise the basic lessons that Americans gleaned from the Vietnam conflict. Like Bush, these revisionists do not claim that intervention in Vietnam was a mistake.[38] While many Americans press for a withdrawal from Iraq to prevent another quagmire, revisionists caution that the United States should not lose its will, as it did in the early 1970s. Further, they suggest that the United

States can adopt successful counterinsurgency strategies that were used at the end of the Vietnam War. As with Bush's adaptation of Vietnam-era ideas, their reassessment should be examined critically.

Revisionist accounts of the Vietnam War are not new. Although most early studies of American involvement in Vietnam were quite critical, some historians and commentators characterized the war as a just cause and concluded that the United States could have been victorious in Southeast Asia.[39] These accounts were usually marginalized – prevailing academic and public attitudes about Vietnam have generally held that it was a military and foreign policy disaster. But there has been a renewed interest in revisionist accounts of Vietnam, and the war in Iraq is at least one explanation for this intellectual trend.

Lewis Sorley's *A Better War* offers an explanation of this revisionist view of the war in Vietnam.[40] According to Sorley, the United States finally figured out the most effective way to fight the war in Vietnam in the late 1960s and early 1970s. By abandoning General William Westmoreland's attrition strategy in favour of counterinsurgency tactics, the United States and the South Vietnam effectively defeated the National Liberation Front (NLF) and the North Vietnamese Army by 1972. Sorley concludes that, if the United States had continued to support the South Vietnam after 1973, it could have survived as an independent and non-communist state.

Although Sorley's book was written before the war in Iraq, the current struggle has generated increased attention to his work. For many supporters of the war, Sorley's book offers a blueprint for Iraq. Based on his study, they suggest that the United States should focus more heavily on counterinsurgency techniques. They also note that eroding public support in the 1970s precluded ongoing American assistance for South Vietnam. Therefore it is important that the Bush administration retains public support for the war in Iraq and prevents the war from dragging on for too long.[41]

Sorley's work is not alone in suggesting that Americans have misunderstood the true lessons of Vietnam. Keith Taylor, a historian of ancient Vietnam, has recently ignited a historiographical debate with his discussions about the Vietnam War.[42] Taylor has stated that historical accounts of the Vietnam War support three basic 'axioms' about the struggle: '[t]hese are that there was never a legitimate non-communist government in Saigon, that the U.S. had no legitimate reason to be involved in Vietnamese affairs, and that the U.S. could not have won the war under any circumstances'.

These three axioms, Taylor states, were created by the antiwar movement in the 1960s and have been accepted as fact ever since. Taylor concludes, however, that each of these axioms is false. His arguments are not entirely novel. Other scholars, including Sorley, have come to similar conclusions. It is worth noting, however, the degree to which current events seem to influence Taylor's assertions, or at least his rhetoric. While Taylor does not directly address American policy in Iraq, it is almost impossible to read his essay without thinking about current foreign policy:

I believe that global power in the hands of the United States should be taken as a responsibility, not something about which we need to be apologetic. If the United States fails to use this power for the general good of the people in this world, then it will lose not only its power but also the good that it has accumulated; the liberties that have thrived in the shade of American power will then be endangered. I am not a self-hating American who, shrinking from responsibility, would rather indulge in guilt for mistakes made than in daring to work against the global entropy of suffering and chaos.

Writing in the first person and in the present tense, Taylor continues:

I invite you to look around the world for an acceptable alternative to the democratic practices championed, however imperfectly, by the United States today. I see no such alternative ... I have come to realize that it is time to speak up. The youth of this country deserve better than to be taught cynicism and hatred of what is still the best hope for humankind.[43]

A handful of other prominent scholars, officials, and journalists have more explicitly looked to Vietnam as a blueprint for success in Iraq, rather than a roadmap to failure. Melvin Laird, Richard Nixon's Secretary of Defense, contributed an article to *Foreign Affairs* that echoed Sorley's and Taylor's arguments. In it, Laird admits that '[i]t is time for a reasonable look at both Vietnam and Iraq—and what the former can teach us about the latter'. But he cautioned that Americans should not simply label Vietnam a 'bad idea': Vietnam was 'a complex ... mixture of good and evil from which there are many valuable lessons to be learned'.[44]

Laird suggested that the United States should learn from the successes of 1970s counterinsurgency tactics in Vietnam, an idea that has gained currency with other supporters of the war in Iraq. Andrew Krepinevich, Jr recently argued that counterinsurgency tactics, modelled in part on Vietnam-era strategies, were the key to winning the war in Iraq.[45] David Ignatius has stated that high-ranking civilian and military officials are reading Sorley's book with an eye toward strategies in Iraq.[46]

The recent nostalgia for Vietnam-era foreign policy is a bit surprising. As David Ignatius himself noted, '[p]erhaps it's a measure of how bad things are going in Iraq that the strategists are looking to Vietnam for models of success'.[47] But the current popularity of these views stems not so much from their academic credibility as their political usefulness. The popularity of these revisionist arguments rests in part on the fact that they offer an antidote to the 'Vietnam syndrome' that has plagued American foreign policy since the mid-1970s. For the last 30 years, opponents of American military interventions have held a monopoly on the lessons of Vietnam. With these reinterpretations, hawks have found a response to the repeated demands for 'no more Vietnams'.

These revisionist accounts have much to say about Vietnam that is valuable. Taylor questions some of the basic assumptions that have dominated scholarship on the Vietnam War for 30 years. In particular, he suggests that historians pay greater attention to the Republic of Vietnam as a state with at least as much legitimacy as North Vietnam in the 1960s. Sorley draws attention to the war after 1968, a period that is often treated superficially in many histories of the war. But they should not necessarily be used to justify the war in Iraq or suggest a winning strategy in the Middle East. In fact, some scholars have already raised specific doubts about Sorley's characterization of the success of counterinsurgency tactics in the early 1970s.[48]

As these examples show, we should be careful of the way we use the history of the Vietnam War to explain America's ultimate goals in the Middle East. At the same time, we should be aware of the ways that the war in Iraq is exerting a noticeable influence on interpretations of the Vietnam War. The end result of these trends is that Americans will come to believe that the Vietnam War provides a clear example of successful nation-building that will inevitably lead to the spread of American values in the Middle East.

In the mid-1950s, Graham Greene used the domino theory as the basis for a discussion in *The Quiet American* between Pyle, the titular character, and Fowler, the British journalist. While stranded in a French watchtower, Pyle begins to explain the stakes in the fight against communism. 'If Indochina goes...', he starts to say. Fowler interrupts him, 'I know the record. Siam goes. Malaya goes. Indonesia goes. What does "go" mean?'[49] Americans may want to employ the same healthy scepticism when judging the historical analogies used in debates over the war in Iraq.

Notes

1 This chapter began as a conference paper at the 2005 meeting of the Society for Historians of American Foreign Relations. I thank Robert K. Brigham, Luu Doan Huynh, Edward G. Miller, and Jennifer Walton for their valuable comments on this chapter.

2 Marcus G. Raskin and Bernard B. Fall (eds), *The Viet-Nam Reader: Articles and Documents on American Foreign Policy and the Viet-Nam Crisis*, New York: Vintage Books, 1965, p. 296.

3 George W. Bush, 'Remarks by the President to the Philippine Congress', October 18, 2003, http://www.whitehouse.gov/news/releases/2003/10/20031018–12.html. See also David E. Sanger, 'Bush Cites Philippines as Model in Rebuilding Iraq', *New York Times*, October 19, 2003, pp. 1, 20.

4 George W. Bush speech in Riga, Latvia, May 7, 2005, http://www.whitehouse.gov/news/releases/2005/05/20050507–8.html. For Schlesinger's response, see http://www.huffingtonpost.com/theblog/archive/2005/05/yalta-delusions.html.

5 'Commencement Address at the United States Military Academy in West Point, New York', June 1, 2002, *Public Papers of the Presidents of the Untied States: George W. Bush, 2002* (Book 2), Washington, DC: United States Government Printing Office, 2004, p. 920. See also Elisabeth Bumiller, 'U.S. Must Act First to Battle Terror, Bush Tells Cadets', *New York Times*, June 2, 2002, pp. 1, 6.

6 George W. Bush speech at the White House, September 17, 2002, http://www.whitehouse.gov/nsc/nssintro.html.

7 Tom Ridge, remarks at the Transatlantic Homeland Security Conference, September 13, 2004, http://www.whitehouse.gov/news/releases/2004/09/20040915.html.

8   Condoleezza Rice, Remarks to Veterans of Foreign Wars, August 25, 2003, http://www.whitehouse.gov/news/releases/2003/08/20030825–1.html.

9   'President's State of the Union Message to Congress and the Nation', *New York Times*, January 29, 2003, pp. A12–A13.

10 Todd S. Purdum, 'Flashback to the 60s: A Sinking Sensation of Parallels between Iraq and Vietnam', *New York Times*, January 29, 2005, p. 12.

11 Bush 2005 State of the Union Address, February 2, 2005, http://www.whitehouse.gov/news/releases/2005/02/20050202–11.html.

12 George W. Bush speech at the White House, September 17, 2002, http://www.whitehouse.gov/nsc/nssintro.html.

13 Bush speech at West Point, June 1, 2002. *Public Papers of the Presidents of the United States: George W. Bush, 2002* (Book 2), Washington: United States Government Printing Office, 2004, p. 920.

14 The President's News Conference of April 7, 1954. *Public Papers of the Presidents of the United States: Dwight D. Eisenhower 1954*, Washington, DC: US Government Printing Office, 1960, p. 383.

15 'The "Why" of Indo-China', *New York Times*, March 28, 1953, p. 16.

16 'Help for Vietnam and Laos', *New York Times*, April 28, 1953, p. 26; Edward S. Skillin, 'The War in Indo-China', *The Commonweal*, March 23, 1951, p. 585.

17 'Can Native Troops Halt the Reds in Indo-China?', *Newsweek*, May 4, 1953, p. 48.

18 See, for example, 'Indochina: It Looks Safe Now', March 6, 1953, pp. 44–6; 'One Foot in a New War', February 12, 1954, pp. 20–1; 'Is U.S. Heading into a New War?' April 23, 1954, pp. 17–19; 'What Comes After Dienbienphu', May 7, 1954, pp. 21–23; 'How French Could Still Win', June 18, 1954, pp. 30–2.

19 C. L. Sulzberger, 'Indo-China Settlement Poses Tough Problems', *New York Times*, June 14, 1953, Section 4, p. E3; 'One Foot in a New War', op. cit., p. 21; 'Is U.S. Heading into a New War?', op. cit., p. 17.

20 Vincent S. Kearney, 'Developing Crisis in Southeast Asia', *America*, May 16, 1953, p. 187; 'A United States Policy for Asia', *Christianity and Crisis*, October 16, 1950, p. 135; 'The War in Indo-China', op. cit., pp. 584–5.

21 'The "Why" of Indo-China', op. cit., p. 16.

22 'Election in Vietnam', *The New York Times*, January 26, 1953, p. 18.

23 See, for example, David L. Anderson, *Trapped by Success: The Eisenhower Administration and Vietnam, 1953–1961*, New York: Columbia University Press, 1991; Joseph Buttinger, *Vietnam: A Political History*, New York: Frederick A. Praeger, 1968; Philip Caton, *Diem's Final Failure: Prelude to America's War in Vietnam*, Lawrence, KS: University of Kansas Press, 2000; George McT. Kahin, *Intervention: How America Became Involved in Vietnam*, New York: Dial Press, 1986; Stanley Karnow, *Vietnam: A History*, New York: The Viking Press, 1983; A. J. Langguth, *Our Vietnam: The War, 1954–1975*, New York: Simon and Schuster, 2000; John D. Montgomery, *The Politics of Foreign Aid: American Experience in Southeast Asia*, New York: Frederick A. Praeger, 1962; Robert Scigliano, *South Vietnam: Nation Under Stress*, Boston, MA: Houghton Mifflin Company, 1963.

24 See Matthew B. Masur, *Hearts and Minds: Cultural Nation-Building in South Vietnam, 1954–1963*, unpublished PhD dissertation, The Ohio State University, 2004.

25 United States Information Agency, *14th Review of Operations*, Washington, DC: US Government Printing Office, 1960.

26 United States Information Agency, *17th Report to Congress*, Washington, DC: US Government Printing Office, 1961, p. 1.

27 United States Information Agency, *7th Review of Operations*, Washington, DC: US Government Printing Office, 1956, p. 4.

28 United States Information Agency, *15th Report to Congress*, Washington, DC: US Government Printing Office, 1960, p. 9.

29 United States Information Agency, *16th Report to Congress*, Washington, DC: US Government Printing Office, 1961, pp. 10–11.

30 'Annual USIS Assessment Report for Period October 1, 1956 through September 30, 1957', p. 1, October 12, 1957. Foreign Service Despatches, Asia, Records of the United States Information Agency (RG 306), United States National Archives II, College Park, Maryland (hereafter NAII).

31 John J. Slocum, 'Inspection Report: USIS Vietnam', March 8–31, 1956, pp. 2–3. Special Reports, 1953–63, Office of Research, Records of the United States Information Agency (RG 306), NAII.

32 Oral history interview with John M. Anspacher, March 22, 1988, p. 30. Foreign Affairs Oral History Project, Special Collections Division, Georgetown University Library, Washington, DC.

33 Andrew Rotter, *The Path to Vietnam: Origins of the American Commitment to Southeast Asia*, Ithaca, NY: Cornell University Press, 1989, p. 3.

34 Bush, speech at the White House, September 17, 2002, http://www.whitehouse.gov/nsc/nssintro.html.

35 Bush, National Security Statement, p. 3, 19, http://www.whitehouse.gov/nsc/nssall.html.

36 Bush, National Security Statement, p. 5, http://www.whitehouse.gov/nsc/nssall.html.

37 'President's State of the Union Message to Congress and the Nation', *The New York Times*, January 21, 2004, pp. A18–A19.

38 I do not use the term 'revisionist' in the derogatory sense of fabricated (like 'holocaust revisionist'). Rather, I use it in the sense that historians sometimes used to describe historical interpretations that question some elements of the orthodox historiography.

39 For a discussion of the historiography of the Vietnam War, see Gary R. Hess, 'The Unending Debate: Historians and the Vietnam War', in Michael Hogan (ed.) *America and the World*, Cambridge: Cambridge University Press, 1995.

40 Lewis Sorley, *A Better War: The Unexamined Victories and Final Tragedy of America's Last Years in Vietnam*, New York: Harvest, 1999.

41 Matt Steinglass, 'Vietnam and Victory', *The Boston Globe*, December 18, 2005, pp. K1, K5.

42 K. W. Taylor, 'How I Began to Teach about the Vietnam War', *Michigan Quarterly Review*, 2004, vol. 43, pp. 637–47.

43 Ibid., p. 647.

44 Melvin Laird, 'Iraq: Learning the Lessons of Vietnam', *Foreign Affairs,* 2005, 84(6), pp. 31–43.

45 Andrew F. Krepinevich, Jr, 'How to Win in Iraq', *Foreign Affairs*, 2005, 84(5), pp. 87–104.

46 David Ignatius, 'A Better Strategy for Iraq', *Washington Post*, November 5, 2005, p. A23.

47 Ibid.

48 Steinglass, 'Vietnam and Victory', op. cit., pp. K1, K5.

49 Graham Greene, *The Quiet American*, New York: Penguin Classics Deluxe Edition, 2004, p. 86.

11

THE IRAQ AND VIETNAM WARS

Some parallels and connections

John Dumbrell

All post-1973 US wars and military interventions have been played out in the shadow of the Vietnam conflict. In 1986, Mark Hatfield, the anti-war Republican Senator from Oregon, described President Reagan's Central American policies as follows: 'Here we go again, old men creating a monster for young men to destroy'.[1] During the Senate debate preceding the 1991 Gulf War, Senator Edward Kennedy predicted even higher American casualties than in Vietnam.[2] The 'givens' of much recent American foreign policy – the Powell Doctrine, the 'pretty prudent public', worries about nation-building and 'foreign policy as social work', military caution, and the 'Vietnam syndrome' itself – thread their way inexorably back to the earlier conflict.

When Bill Clinton stood for Presidential office in 1992, he declared that his election, the election of a former opponent of the war, would 'finally close the book on Vietnam'.[3] The book remains stubbornly open. For this, there are some overarching reasons – reasons why memories of the war (to use President Bush Senior's 1991 phrase) have not yet been 'kicked'.[4] The 'Vietnam generation', Clinton's and Bush Junior's generation, is now essentially the generation enjoying political leadership in the US. Dan Quayle in 1980 was only the first of many candidates for executive office to find their war record the subject of severe scrutiny. More important still, the war was the key divisive and defining issue in recent American social, political and military history. All American institutions – churches, political parties, labour unions, and families – were riven by the war. Along with civil rights, the war defined a generation. It sharpened the 'culture wars', under-girded lifetime political orientations, and determined military doctrine. Little wonder that Vietnam's open book still influences perceptions of the current conflict in Iraq, as well as (at least to some degree) the conduct of the war itself. Unquestionably, the invasion of Iraq in 2003 was the most controversial American international action since the 1970 Cambodian invasion. We are pre-programmed to look for parallels and connections.

At least at the level of rather unreflective intuition, such parallels and connections are not difficult to find. The confident Kennedy liberals of the 1960s – Halberstam's 'best and brightest'[5] – call to mind George W. Bush's confident neo-conservatives and offensive realists. Nation-building, problems of local support, cultural insensitivity, a tendency to view local issues through global spectacles:

possible links between US policy in Vietnam and Iraq seem endless. The fact that the later war was consciously waged with the (often rather ambiguous) 'lessons of Vietnam' to the fore seems only to add poignancy and irony to the parallels. Policymakers have to strive to learn Vietnam's lessons without succumbing to inappropriate analogies. The horrors of Abu Ghraib call to mind the cages of Saigon. Can the US military nation-build in Iraq any more successfully in the Middle East than it did in Indochina? Should it try to nation-build at all? After 'Vietnamization', we now encounter 'Iraqification'. A debate in *The National Interest* in 2004 between Morton Abramowitz and David Rivkin made many of these connections explicit, with Rivkin arguing in true Vietnam-era style that the real prize in Iraq was American international credibility.[6] The Iraqi elections of early 2005 were dismissed by numerous opponents of the war as a mere replay of the September 1967 elections in South Vietnam. One could continue. The accusations of political misuse of intelligence levied at the George W. Bush administration were foreshadowed in the Johnson and Nixon years. The generational dimension to views on both conflicts was sharply apparent (though, in the Iraq case, this was probably more pronounced in Europe than in the United States). International hostility to the Iraq conflict was, if anything, even more intense than towards US involvement in Vietnam. Jacques Chirac is the Charles de Gaulle for our times. In both conflicts, the USA was accused of international lawbreaking, and of achieving results directly counter to stated objectives: supporting dictators in the name of freedom in Southeast Asia; in the Middle East, acting as foolish and arrogant *de facto* allies of the Al Qaeda. Anatol Lieven discerns a strong tendency during both wars to 'homogenize' the enemy: 'communists' in Vietnam, 'terrorists' in Iraq.[7] A related debate concerns the extent to which either Vietnam or Iraq involved exceptional and untypical use of American power. John Lewis Gaddis, for example, has argued that the Iraq invasion partook of a defensive and, in terms of the entire sweep of US foreign policy history, predictable response to the 9/11 attacks.[8]

The putative Vietnam–Iraq closeness is magnified by explicit connections and by conscious evocations in the later war of memories of the former. As will be noted later, memories of LBJ's 1964 Tonkin Gulf 'blank cheque' loomed large in Congressional debates in 2002–3. At times the 2004 Presidential election seemed more concerned with Vietnam than with Iraq. Key figures from the earlier era strode forth to declare that history was indeed repeating itself. Walter Cronkite, anchor of the CBS Evening News and celebrated commentator in the 1968 Tet Offensive, declared in 2003: 'I see a very close parallel … we are facing an intensifying guerrilla war, and it is taking a great deal of our people and treasury'.[9] Daniel Ellsberg, leaker of the Pentagon Papers, foresaw in October 2003: 'This war could go on forever, no matter how unpopular it gets. That's very like Vietnam: a stale, hopeless occupation'. America was being 'lied into a war again'.[10]

The putative parallels and connections between Vietnam and Iraq are many and various. For purposes of stimulating discussion, this chapter will briefly explore just two dimensions: US domestic politics (particularly the role of Congress in 2002–4, parallels to the Gulf of Tonkin Resolution and the echoes of the Vietnam

War in the 2004 Presidential election campaign); and US–UK relations. Before embarking on these discussions, however, it is worth making the limits of comparison clear.

The Vietnam War was a limited conflict in which some key aspects of American power – notably nuclear weapons and the ability to invade North Vietnam – were not applied. Nevertheless, the Vietnam War saw over 58,000 US fatalities. Estimates of Vietnamese deaths vary greatly, but a figure of over one million is probably a very conservative estimate. Even now, some Vietnam War casualty statistics – such as the over 25,000 ARVN (South Vietnamese government army) personnel who died in 1973, the year of the 'peace' agreement – have a capacity to shock. At its height in 1968–9, the US had over half a million troops deployed. The war lasted, at least by some estimates, 25 years (longer, of course, if we are considering the whole history of conflict associated with Vietnamese nationalism). Between LBJ's 1964– 5 Americanization and escalation, and the 1973 withdrawal, the US experienced at least six years of intense fighting: a period, by anyone's calculation, longer than US involvement in either twentieth-century world war. The Iraq involvement, at least to date, is not a conflict of a similar order. At the height of the fighting and post-conflict disorder in 2003, the US had around 130,000 personnel in Iraq, with 150,000 deployed at the time of the January 2005 elections. The 2005 Pentagon forecasts for 2006 were reported as envisaging a continuing deployment level of around 120,000. One major inhibition on massive deployment in Iraq, of course, is the political unwillingness to reinstate the draft – itself a legacy of the earlier conflict. In Vietnam, even with the draft and with huge troop deployments, the US did not have enough soldiers on the ground to satisfy the demands of its 'non-enclave' strategy: US ground forces were too often over-exposed by 'search and destroy' missions across territory which could not realistically be held even in the medium term. In Iraq, a combination of over-confidence, and Secretary Donald Rumsfeld's adherence to the 'revolution in military affairs' concept of lean engagement, led to a disastrous under-commitment of manpower, a mistake which the swift disbandment of Saddamist security forces following the invasion compounded.[11]

The Iraq conflict, despite the lower level of troop commitment, has nevertheless been hugely expensive. By February 2006, the cost of the conflict to the United States was estimated as drawing level to the 330 billion approximate cost of the Korean War in 2006 dollars. (At one stage in the run-up to the Iraq invasion, Secretary Rumsfeld estimated the cost at just $50 billion). The overall cost of the War on Terror, including the Iraq conflict, was estimated at nearly half a trillion dollars, nearing Vietnam War totals. The most pessimistic estimate of the cost of the Iraq conflict is that given by Linda Bilmes and Joseph Stiglitz: $2.24 trillion through 2015. An American Enterprise Institute-Brookings joint estimate in 2006 put the likely Iraq cost at $540–670 billion. Perhaps all that can be concluded is that the Iraq engagement is likely to be protracted – President Bush has defused expectations of an American exit by the November 2008 elections – and, in money terms, at least of the same kind of order of expense as Vietnam. The profound global inflationary effects of Vietnam spending are less likely to be replicated. At the time of writing, US fatalities were above 2,000. Estimates of Iraqi casualties vary, and also raise the question of how Iraqi victims of the insurrection should be incorporated into the totals. Yet even the most pessimistic estimates of Iraqi fatality numbers do not approach commonly accepted totals for Vietnamese deaths in the earlier conflict.[12]

Public opinion on the Vietnam War was structurally complex, with a majority opposing immediate withdrawal even into the early 1970s. However, anti-war protest was intense and unprecedented. In regard to Iraq, public opinion was also complex. The 2003 invasion, however, was more popular than any period or episode in the US involvement in Vietnam.[13] Approval ratings for the invasion, and for US policy in Iraq, declined significantly in late 2003–4, revived at the time of the Iraqi elections, only to slide back subsequently. Anti-Iraqi War protest has been occasionally intense, but has not reached Vietnam era proportions. Several commentators noted how major protests in American cities in 2006 to oppose tighter immigration laws dwarfed anti-war activities. In this respect Iraq has more in common with the Korean than with the Vietnam War. John Mueller argues that generalised public opposition to the war effort 'has little to do with whether or not there is an active antiwar movement at home'.[14]

If the sheer scale of the Vietnam involvement (except to some degree in a narrow financial sense) dwarfed that of the US commitment to date in Iraq, seekers of parallels and connections between the two wars should also take account of the radically divergent international conditions. The Vietnam War was fought out on the basis of anti-communist containment doctrines. The Iraq War, despite Washington's failure to establish links between 9/11 and Baghdad, was fought as part of the War on Terror, under conditions of global unipolarity. By 2003, the US was vulnerable to asymmetric terrorist threat, not to the countervailing force of any nation state.

One early, though very thorough, effort to consider Iraq/Vietnam parallels concluded that differences greatly outweighed similarities. Differences identified by Record and Terrill included the arguments about scale and international strategic environment discussed above. Vietnam had a long, unified national history and culture; Iraq is an ancient civilization – indeed arguably *the* most ancient – but is a young, artificial, culturally disunited state. The conflict in Vietnam developed from a guerrilla to a conventional war; in Iraq, the development was in the opposite direction. American goals in Vietnam were counter-revolutionary; in Iraq, they are (at least according to Record and Terrill) revolutionary.[15] The neo-conservative doctrine of imposing democracy in one Middle Eastern state, and hoping for a kind of osmotic multiplier effect in the whole region, represents (as Matthew Masur argues elsewhere in this book) a species of counter-domino theory, a raising-up of the democratic dominoes.

Some Vietnam/Iraq differences are attributable to conscious efforts to avoid repeating earlier mistakes and miscalculations (recall General Tommy Franks' 'we don't do body counts'). 'Shock and awe' air tactics presumably derive to some degree from the 'lessons of Vietnam'. In Vietnam, the air war accounted for around half of all US military expenditure; in Iraq, following the initial bombardment, and despite the subsequent air assaults on Fallujah, the air war has not assumed similar proportions. In Iraq, the insurgency – a mixture of foreign fighters, Sunni resisters, Ba'athists, some Shia militants and Iraqi nationalists – is more various, and, despite the existence of non-communist opposition to the regimes in Saigon, less centrally directed than in Vietnam. The Iraq insurgency has external help, but no external sponsor to match China or Russia. The single biggest US post-invasion mistake in Iraq was Paul Bremer's policy of disbanding the Iraqi army and civil service; the decision has no obvious Indochinese parallel (though failure to build the ARVN into a reliable security partner was a damaging feature of 1960s US policy in Vietnam). Last but not least, Vietnam had no oil reserves. Considering all the similarities and differences between the two conflicts, James I. Matray in 2004 cited Mark Twain: 'History doesn't repeat itself; at best it rhymes'.[16] As promised, we now turn to two particular dimensions of the Vietnam/Iraq conundrum.

Congress, the Gulf of Tonkin Resolution and the 2004 presidential election

The Vietnam War escalation decisions of 1964–5 were taken at the high-water mark of the Cold War consensus, with its central tenets that politics should stop at the water's edge, and that the President knows best. LBJ did involve some key legislative leaders, notably Senator Mike Mansfield, in his administration's deliberations over escalation. The key war authorisation, the 1964 Gulf of Tonkin Resolution, passed easily, with only Senators Morse and Gruening famously standing opposed. Significant Congressional challenge, however, did emerge, and well before the February 1968 Tet Offensive: notably in the form of Senator J. William Fulbright and his various Senate Foreign Relations Committee hearings. The televised hearings beginning in January 1966 provided a degree of national education in the debates surrounding the war, as well as (increasingly, as Fulbright himself assumed more of an anti-war stance) a platform for war doubters and opponents. The Congressional temper changed significantly after Tet, with prominent Senators increasingly identifying themselves with the anti-war cause. The wind was taken from legislative anti-war sails to some extent by President Nixon's policy of Vietnamization, but Congressional criticism was re-energised in the wake of the invasion of Cambodia. In the Nixon era, Congress acted to investigate prisoner abuses in South Vietnam. Senate doves publicised and furthered the anti-war case. Congressional protest hastened the US exit from Cambodia, and arguably set limits, along with public opinion and anti-war protest generally, on Nixon's freedom of action. The administration's post-Cambodian invasion policy in Vietnam operated in the shadow of Congressional restrictions, along with the encroachment of a legislatively imposed timetable for withdrawal.

Looking to the Iraq conflict, we are immediately struck by contrasts. We must, of course, be careful to compare like with like. US military involvement in a conflict centred on Iraq may, indeed, stretch far into the future. In such circumstances, legislative resurgence, and incursion into areas previously reserved to executive discretion, may be anticipated. We do not have to look as far back as the Vietnam War to find Congress using its financial authority to restrict and terminate US military action; this occurred in Africa in the early 1990s. However, even comparing pre-2005 policy in Iraq with pre-1968 Vietnam policy, large differences appear. Above all there was no Vietnam equivalent to 9/11: no central, unambiguous event – the dubious Gulf of Tonkin 'attacks' were certainly no parallel – which galvanised policy and attitudes.

Various Congressional figures emerged as putative leaders of the legislative surge against the Iraq conflict. Media attention inevitably focused on the opinions of Vietnam veterans. Congressman John Murtha of Pennsylvania, the first Vietnam combat veteran to be elected to the Congress, voted for the original Iraq War Resolution, and attracted enormous publicity when he eventually moved to a position of support for timetabled withdrawal. The nearest equivalent to Senator Fulbright, however, probably has been Senator Robert C. Byrd, Democrat of West Virginia, who centred his opposition on constitutional grounds, and is a senior member of Appropriations, rather than of the Senate Foreign Relations Committee. Fulbright's old committee contains moderate Republicans (notably Chairman Richard Lugar and Senator Chuck Hagel) who, along with leading Democrats like Joe Biden, were, from the early days of the conflict, very willing to issue criticism, especially over the lack of post-invasion planning. According to Biden in March 2003: 'The truth of the matter is that the theoretical notion of the check and balance on the administration through the purse strings in war is ephemeral; it doesn't exist'.[17] The ranking Senate Foreign Relations Committee Democrat's generalisation applied also, of course, to the Vietnam War, at least before 1970. It might also be added that the 1973 War Powers Resolution, explicitly designed to prevent 'more Vietnams', had little impact on the Iraq conflict. My main point here, however, is that, in the case of Iraq (2002–5), pro-war consensus and Congressional reluctance to assert its authority, were greater than in the case of Vietnam, even in the post-Tonkin Gulf, pre-Tet Offensive period.

The main parallels that have been drawn in relation to Vietnam/Iraq legislative assertion involve the comparison between the 1964 Gulf of Tonkin Resolution and the October 2002 Iraq force authorisation. Congressional opponents of the rush to war repeatedly invoked the events of August 1964, not only in relation to the October 2002 authorisation but also regarding various post-9/11 grants of authority to the President. Representative Barbara Lee (Democrat, California), the only Member of Congress to vote against Senate Joint Resolution 23 (the immediate post-9/11 authorisation), compared herself to Morse and Gruening. Congress, according to Lee, was 'repeating the mistake it made in 1964', when it 'abandoned its own constitutional responsibilities and launched our country into years of undeclared war in Vietnam'.[18]

During the October 2002 force authorisation debate, Robert Byrd made several telling parallels with 1964. As with the Gulf of Tonkin, argued Byrd, Congress was being asked to take information on trust. Congress was 'again being asked to vote on the use of force without hard evidence that the country [Iraq] poses an immediate threat to the national security of the United States'. Once again,

Congress (in 2002, as in the Presidential election year of 1964) was being asked to vote against the background of looming legislative elections.[19]

According to Byrd, Senate Joint Resolution 46 (the 2002 force authorisation measure) was actually even more sweeping than the famous 'blank cheque' of 1964. The 2002 Resolution was based on discretionary Presidential authority under the pre-emption doctrine (outlined in President Bush's June 2002 West Point address, and in the National Security Strategy of September 2002). Byrd further argued that the 1964 Resolution, unlike S. J. Resolution 46, was concomitant with the United Nations Charter. Moreover: 'With the Tonkin Gulf Resolution, *Congress* could "terminate" military action. With S. J. Resolution 46, only the *president* can terminate military action'.[20] The Gulf of Tonkin Resolution was also frequently invoked in the immediate pre-invasion legislative debates of March/April 2003. Some liberal Democrats, for example, sought to bring anti-war lawsuits based on Vietnam-era decisions, which had declared the 1964 Resolution invalid.[21]

Vietnam-era echoes in the 2004 US Presidential election campaign at times almost threatened to drown out serious debate over Iraq. Swift Boat Veterans (high-profile critics of candidate Senator John Kerry's war record), Kerry's three Vietnam Purple Hearts, Bush's apparent neglect of his National Guard duties in 1972: these debates generated far more heat than light, but they illustrated forcefully the extent to which the new Middle Eastern conflict had re-ignited memories of the earlier Indochinese one.

John Kerry's decision (notably at the Democratic nominating convention) to foreground his Vietnam record – a record of opposition to war as well as involvement in it – was designed, of course, to damage Bush by raising questions about how the future President had conducted himself in the Vietnam years. It also represented a responsible and forceful effort squarely to address the national security agenda within the campaign. In retrospect the decision can be seen to have damaged Kerry: not merely in calling forth demons represented by the Swift Boat Veterans, but in distracting attention from domestic issues which might have favoured the Democrat. Kerry, and key figures (like Senator Joe Biden and Richard Holbrooke) associated with his foreign policy campaign, also began warning about a revival of the 'Vietnam syndrome' in post-Iraq invasion conditions. In this line of thinking, American internationalism itself could be a casualty of the war in Iraq.[22]

Other Vietnam-era reverberations may briefly be summarised. The 2004 Presidential election, like that of 1968, held foreign policy issues at its centre.[23] In opening-out the anti-war agenda and giving John Kerry room to move beyond 'Bush lite' positions, Howard Dean played the role of Eugene McCarthy to Kerry's Bobby Kennedy. Ralph Nader's campaign threatened at one point to damage Kerry in the way that George Wallace had taken Southern Democrat votes in 1968. Both 1968 and 2004 were preoccupied with the possibility of an 'October surprise' (in 2004, the surprise turned out to be not the capture of bin Laden, but rather the Al Qaeda leader's taped intervention). Once again, however, we are struck as much by 1968/2004 differences as parallels: the lower level in 2004 of domestic political violence, the relatively harmonious Democratic convention, and the lack of a real equivalent to the Tet Offensive.

Despite important Vietnam- and Iraq-era differences, the US domestic debate between 2002 and 2005 was little exercised by issues of legislative prerogatives and presidential accountability. John Kerry certainly did not dwell on such issues to any great degree in the 2004 campaign. At times, Senator Robert Byrd seemed as out of tune with the presidentialist temper of the times as had Senators Morse and Gruening in 1964. If Members of Congress have a clear interest in maintaining the powers and prerogatives of the national legislature, they also have an interest in not exposing themselves to charges of unpatriotic irresponsibility. In the early stages of both the Vietnam and the Iraq conflicts, the latter interest clearly outweighed the former.

US–UK relations

Prime Minister Harold Wilson's refusal to send British troops to Vietnam severely interrupted the dynamics and working practices of US–UK Cold War 'special relations'. Wilson's refusal derived less from personal conviction than from his appreciation of the political damage that would have been involved in a decision to despatch British forces to an unpopular war, which large sections of British Labour Party opinion condemned as imperialist and counter-revolutionary. Wilson attempted to lessen the offence given to the Johnson Administration by deploying a range of arguments to 'excuse' London's refusal to send troops. Wilson argued that Britain, as co-chairman of the Geneva Conference, had a special usefulness to the US as a potential mediator in Vietnam. Military involvement would simply compromise British credibility. (Wilson made several efforts to start a credible British mediation effort, most famously in the Phase A/Phase B negotiations of February 1967 with Soviet leader Aleksei Kosygin. These efforts all collapsed due to a mixture of Wilsonian unrealism, American backsliding and failure to take Wilson seriously, along with the intrinsic difficulties of finding positive ground for diplomatic progress.) Wilson also argued, even less convincingly, that the British effort in Malaya – a conflict that was actually coming to a conclusion by 1965 – represented an adequate British commitment to Far Eastern security.

President Johnson and his advisers consciously considered unleashing on Britain what came to be called the 'Hessian option': the use of US economic power effectively to force British troops into Vietnam. LBJ seems to have vetoed this course of action. He was sensitive to Wilson's economic and political difficulties (though, of course, famously incredulous that Britain could not even muster a 'platoon of bagpipers'). Washington was also cautious about repeating the heavy-handed economic pressure associated with the 1956 Suez crisis. Also of significance was Wilson's implied threat to move to rapid and destabilising devaluation of the pound if Washington attempted to force his hand. In the event, London backed the war with words, with (often disguised) arms sales, with intelligence information from Hong Kong, and with a modest and covert deployment of some British special forces. At various points, most famously in May–June 1966 when the US undertook intensive bombing of Hanoi and Haiphong, London verbally 'dissociated' itself from American action.[24]

Fast-forwarding to the twenty-first century, we find another Labour Prime Minister, Tony Blair, standing four-square behind post-9/11 American foreign policy, and committing British forces to Iraq not only in the face of intense Labour opposition, but also following what was (in February 2003) probably the largest anti-war demonstration in British history. At the start of the invasion, Saddam Hussein and President George W. Bush were competing neck-and-neck in British public opinion polls for the title of the 'greatest threat to world peace'.[25] No other British leader before Blair ever took a comparable political risk on behalf of the 'Special Relationship' and British allied loyalty to the US. The only remotely comparable action in recent history – Anthony Eden at Suez – was, of course, taken in the teeth of American opposition.

Why did Wilson and Blair behave so differently? In the case of US–UK relations, history manifestly did not repeat itself. Let us look first to changes in international circumstances. Here, the logic of the changed Anglo-American relationship appeared to point towards Blair having more freedom of action than Wilson. In 2003, after all, Britain was a power with a history of 30 years membership in a European community, whose leading founder-members, France and Germany, opposed the Iraq invasion. In the mid-1960s, Britain, with a sinking pound, declining economy and overstretched global commitments, was in receipt of a series of large American loans. By 2003, the UK was far less economically dependent on the US (though, of course, fear of American economic power cannot be ruled out as a possible cause of Blair's decision to support the invasion). Most importantly, the Cold War glue that had fixed the US–UK 'Special Relationship' for so long had ended over a decade before. The post-Cold War period had been filled by predictions that the era of 'special relations' between London and Washington was over.[26] To be sure, close defence and intelligence inter-linkages between the two allies remained; but, if anything, to a weaker degree than in the Wilson era.

A glance at the comparable political circumstances and difficulties of Wilson and Blair perhaps explains things a little further. Wilson seems to have felt that his own political survival, and that of his government, was at risk if he sent troops to the unpopular war. There certainly would have been Cabinet resignations, backbench rebellions and mass demonstrations. Yet such phenomena also attached themselves to Blair's decision – and Blair actually survived, albeit with his leadership damaged. He went on to win in May 2005 what would have been regarded by Wilson as a very valuable parliamentary majority. Perhaps Wilson could also have survived? Clearly, we have to throw into the explanatory pot the fact that Blair enjoyed before 2005 a far larger majority than did Wilson, even following the 1966 General Election. (The 1964 election had given Wilson an effective overall majority of just five; after March 1966, the figure was 97.) Blair's New Labour lacked that degree of sympathy for America's opponents in the conflict, which had existed in its 1960s counterpart. Again, we must also take account of the differing scale of the two wars. Despite its ugly and prolonged aftermath, the relatively rapid fall of Saddam Hussein's government took some of the intensity away from Blair's predicament. Lastly, the support given to Blair by his main Labour rival, Chancellor Gordon Brown, was a major asset to the Prime Minister in his drive for survival. Given the ideological composition of the Labour Party in the 1960s, along with the intrinsic scale and intensity of the Vietnam War, Wilson's survival might – no stronger term is appropriate – have been less likely than Blair's.

A factor that assumes enormous importance in explaining the Wilson–Blair variations is that of personal leader belief. Wilson, despite his leftist past, was a fence-sitter; Blair, at least in the international arena, is a conviction politician. Blair's support for the invasion needs to be assessed and explained in terms of his personal convictions, both regarding the 'Special Relationship' itself, and about the deeper purposes of international politics.

Blair's beliefs about the US–UK 'Special Relationship' are traditionalistic. They involve a melding, and reworking for the post-Cold War era of integrating Europeanism, of Prime Minister Harold Macmillan's old 'Greeks and Romans' paradigm and of the concept of the UK as the 'Atlantic bridge'. In this view, US–European economic disputes stand separate from foreign and, especially, defence policy Atlanticism. Britain's interest, and the interests of the international community generally, are best served by positioning London close to Washington, more or less regardless of who is in charge of the White House. Public support for US military action in particular should be balanced by private candour. To quote David Manning, Blair adviser and subsequent UK Ambassador to the US: 'At the best of times, Britain's influence on the US is limited. But the only way we exercise that influence is by attaching ourselves firmly to them and avoiding public criticism wherever possible'.[27] London, according to 'Greeks and Romans' thinking, should whisper civilising sentiments into the Emperor's ear. Thus may the US be wooed away from its endemic propensity to impetuosity, and from its imperial and self-defeating tendency to treat valuable allies with contempt. If acting as latter-day 'Greeks' to the new 'Romans' also brings practical benefits (such as US support for the retention of Britain's seat in the UN Security Council, or even the acquisition of post-war reconstruction contracts in Iraq), then so much the better.[28]

Blair's understanding of the 'Special Relationship', and of the UK's role as 'Atlantic bridge' does go some way towards explaining his decision to send troops to Iraq. The problem for our question about Vietnam/Iraq comparisons, however, is that Harold Wilson would broadly have shared that understanding. The 'Greeks and Romans'/'Atlantic bridge' paradigm has (with the possible exception of Prime Minister Edward Heath) been a prominent feature of all Cold War and post-Cold War Prime Ministerial belief systems. What explains the Wilson–Blair divergence is, to some extent, the different rational calculations in either case of the chances of political survival following troop commitment. More profoundly, however, Blair – most emphatically unlike Wilson – actually believed in the rightness of the cause. Regime change in Iraq presented itself as an outgrowth of the 'post-Westphalian' doctrine of ethical interventionism that Blair had famously championed in his Chicago speech of April 1999. It reflected his own reaction to 9/11 as an event which impelled the enemies of terrorism and disorder to 'reorder the world around us'.[29] As Blair was reported to have responded to a query in February 2003 about his excessive and dangerous loyalty to the post-9/11 American international project: 'It's worse than you think, I believe in it'.[30]

Conclusion

Memories of the Vietnam War fade neither for Americans, America's enemies nor America's allies. Before the Iraq invasion, Tariq Aziz warned the US of a new 'quagmire'. A putative 'Iraq syndrome' became an articulated feature not only of the John Kerry 2004 election campaign, but a prominent aspect of widespread commentary on the future trajectory of US foreign policy. At the thirtieth anniversary of the end of the Vietnam War, commentators linked the issue of the 'abandonment' of South Vietnam (and, indeed, of Indochina, including Cambodia) to the possible consequences of 'abandoning' Iraq.

In conclusion, it seems appropriate to consider the case for the Iraq invasion, and for British involvement in it, made by Christopher Hitchens, the UK journalist working in the US. Reasonably enough, Hitchens, the former opponent of American policy in Vietnam, emphasises the murderous and destabilising nature of the regime of Saddam Hussein. The Iraqi insurgents were dismissed by Hitchens in early 2005 as 'dismal riff-raff', even in comparison with 'the dogmatic Communists in Malaya in the 1940s, organised principally among the Chinese majority', much less when compared to the anti-American Vietnamese. If anyone in Indochina deserves to be compared to the Iraqi insurgents, it is (for Hitchens) the Khmer Rouge, not Ho Chi Minh's authentic avatars of Vietnamese nationalism. The 'Vietnam/Iraq babble is, from any point of view, a busted flush'.[31]

As Hitchens and others argue, Vietnam–Iraq differences outweigh the similarities. However, Hitchens protests too much. The Vietnamese communists and nationalists had a certain authenticity, but eventually erected a Stalinist state in Vietnam. Among the Iraqi insurgents, there are, no doubt, 'authentic' nationalists as well as brutal Saddamists and outside extremists and terrorists. Neither conflict can reasonably be reduced to simple sloganeering. The most important parallel, surely, is that the Vietnam War and the Iraq invasion were both unnecessary and (particularly if we factor in the inadequate and flawed post-conflict planning in Iraq) unwise uses of military power. In neither instance were immediate questions of US national security, much less national survival, involved. As military figures like James Gavin, in the Vietnam instance, and Anthony Zinni, in the case of Iraq, have pointed out, reckless and unnecessary wars – especially those fought a long way from home – risk losing the support of the US Congress, the US public, US allies and perhaps even of the US military itself.

Notes

1 See T. G. Paterson, 'Historical Memory and Illusive Victory: Vietnam and Central America', *Diplomatic History*, 1988, vol. 12, pp. 1–18, 18.
2 *Congressional Record* (1991), p. 5272.

3 See *Time*, November 16, 1992, p. 50.

4 See R. W. Tucker and D. C. Hendrickson, *The Imperial Temptation*, New York: Council on Foreign Relations, 1992, p. 152.

5 David Halberstam, *The Best and the Brightest*, New York: Random House, 1972.

6 Morton Abramowitz, 'Does Iraq Matter?', *The National Interest*, 2004, vol. 27, pp. 27–41; David B. Rivkin, 'Averting an Iraq Syndrome', *The National Interest*, 2004, vol. 27, pp. 97–109. For different perspectives on 'Vietnamization' *versus* 'Iraqification', see Melvin Laird, 'Iraq: Learning the Lessons of Vietnam', *Foreign Affairs*, 2005, 84(6), pp. 22–43; Stephen Biddle, 'Seeing Baghdad, Thinking Saigon', *Foreign Affairs*, 2006, 85(2), pp. 2–14.

7 Anatol Lieven, *America Right or Wrong*, New York: HarperCollins, 2004, p. 71.

8 J. L. Gaddis, *Surprise, Security and the American Experience*, Cambridge MA: Harvard University Press, 2004.

9 'Truthout: Walter Cronkite Draws Parallels between Iraq, Vietnam', www.truthout. org/cgi-bin/artman/exec/view.cgi/6/3580 (acessed July, 2 2006).

10 'Ellsberg sees Iraq, Vietnam Parallels', www.aberdeennews.com/mld/twincities/ news/7055717.htm (accessed 5 February 2005).

11 See Michael Gordon and Bernard Trainor, *Cobra II: The Inside Story of the Invasion and Occupation of Iraq*, London: Atlantic Books, 2006.

12 J. Borger, 'Cost of War Soars to 440bn [dollars] for US', *The Guardian* (London), 4 February 2006, p. 17; 'Blood and Treasure: Paying for Iraq', *The Economist*, 8 April 2006, pp. 53–4; J. Sloboda and H. Dardagan, 'The Iraq Body Count Project: Civil Society and the Democratic Deficit', in A. Danchev and J. Macmillan (eds) *The Iraq War and Democratic Politics*, London: Routledge, 2005, pp. 219–37.

13 See Chester Pach, 'The Past has Another Pattern: Vietnam and Iraq', *Passport*, December 2004, pp. 15–17.

14 J. Mueller, 'The Iraq Syndrome', *Foreign Affairs*, 2005, 84, pp. 44–54, 46.

15 J. Record and W. A. Terrill, *Iraq and Vietnam: Differences, Similarities, and Insights*, Carlisle, PA: Strategic Studies Institute (US Army), May 2004.

16 I. Matray, 'The Iraq War in Historical Perspective', *Passport*, December 2004, pp. 13–14.

17 *Congressional Quarterly Weekly Report*, March 1, 2003, p. 251.

18 Quoted in R. C. Cohen, 'The Past as Prologue', *National Journal*, September 29, 2003, p. 3001.

19 See R. C. Byrd, 'A Lesson from History', in R. C. Byrd *Losing America: Confronting a Reckless and Arrogant Presidency*, New York: Norton, 2004, pp. 230–35.

20 See *Congressional Quarterly Weekly Report*, March 22, 2003, p. 317. For fuller accounts of the Congressional debates on the Iraq invasion, see J. Dumbrell, 'The Bush Doctrine', in George C. Edwards and Philip J. Davies (eds) *New Challenges for the American Presidency*, New York: Pearson Longman, 2004, pp. 229–45; J. Dumbrell, 'Bush's War', in Alex Danchev and John Macmillan (eds) *The Iraq War and Democratic Politics*, London: Routledge, 2005, pp. 35–46.

21 See *Congressional Quarterly Weekly Report*, February 22, 2003, p. 454.

22 See J. Dumbrell, 'President Kerry's Foreign Policy: Continuity and Discontinuity in Contemporary American Foreign Policy', in I. Morgan and P. Davies (eds) *Right On? Political Change and Continuity in George W. Bush's America*, London: Institute for the Study of the Americas, 2006, pp. 59–74; Paul Starobin, 'John Kerry: Leader of the Free World', *National Journal*, September 18, 2004, p. 1281.

23 See Melvin Small, 'The Election of 1968', *Diplomatic History*, 2004, 28, pp. 513–28.

24 For an account of Wilson and Vietnam, see J. Dumbrell, *A Special Relationship: Anglo–American Relations in the Cold War and After*, London: Palgrave, 2001, ch. 7. Much academic dispute revolves around putative US–UK 'deals' over the pound and support for the US in Vietnam.

25 See *The Sunday Times*, February 16, 2003, p. 14.
26 See John Dickie, *'Special No More': Anglo-American Relations: Rhetoric and Reality*, London: Weidenfeld and Nicolson, 1994.
27 Quoted in John Kampfner, *Blair's Wars*, London: Simon and Schuster, 2003, p. 117.
28 On Blair's view of the 'Special Relationship', see J. Dumbrell, 'The US–UK "Special Relationship" in a World Twice Transformed', *Cambridge Review of International Affairs*, 17, 2004, pp. 437–50.
29 Quoted in Peter Riddell, *Hug Them Close: Blair, Clinton, Bush and the 'Special Relationship'*, London: Politico's, 2003, p. 145.
30 Quoted in Kampfner, op. cit., p. 279.
31 C. Hitchens, 'Beating a Dead Parrot: Why Iraq and Vietnam have Nothing Whatsoever in Common', http://slate.msn-com/id/2112895/ (posted January 31, 2005; accessed February 3, 2005). See also C. Hitchens, *Regime Change*, London: Penguin, 2003; C. Hitchens, *Love, Poverty and War*, New York: Nation Books, 2004.

BIBLIOGRAPHY

Anderson, David L., *Trapped By Success: The Eisenhower Administration and Vietnam, 1953–1961*, New York: Columbia University Press, 1991.

Arendt, Hannah, *On Violence*, New York: Harcourt Brace, 1970.

Arnove, Anthony (ed.), *Iraq Under Siege: The Deadly Impact of Sanctions and War*, Cambridge, MA: South End Press, 2000.

Avant, D., *Political Institutions and Military Change: Lessons From Peripheral Wars*, Ithaca, NY: Cornell University Press, 1994.

Bacevich, Andrew J., *The New American Militarism: How Americans are Seduced by War*, New York: Oxford University Press, 2005.

Bacevich, Andrew and E. Cohen, (eds), *War Over Kosovo: Politics and Strategy in a Global Age*, New York: Columbia University Press, 2001.

Bamford, James, *A Pretext for War: 9/11, Iraq, and the Abuse of America's Intelligence Agencies*, New York: Doubleday, 2004.

Bello, Walden, *Dilemmas of Domination: The Unmaking of the American Empire*, New York: Henry Holt, 2005.

Berman, Larry, *Planning a Tragedy: The Americanization of the War in Vietnam*, New York: W. W. Norton, 1984.

Betts, R., *Soldiers, Statesmen, and Cold War Crises*, Cambridge, MA: Harvard University Press, 1977.

Blumenthal, Sydney, *The Clinton Wars*, London: Viking, 2003.

Brandes, Stuart D., *Warhogs: A History of War Profits in America*, Lexington, KY: The University Press of Kentucky, 1997.

Bush, George and Brent Scowcroft, *A World Transformed*, New York: Alfred A. Knopf, 1998.

Buzzanco, Robert, *Masters of War: Military Dissent and Politics in the Vietnam Era*, Cambridge: Cambridge University Press, 1996.

Byrd, Robert C., *Losing America: Confronting a Reckless and Arrogant Presidency*, New York: Norton, 2004.

Callinicos, Alex, *The New Mandarins of American Power*, Cambridge: Polity, 2003.

Callwell, C., *Small Wars: Their Principles and Practice*, 3rd edn, Lincoln, NB and London, University of Nebraska and HMSO, 1996.

Campbell, Kurt M. and Celeste Johnson Ward, 'New Battle Stations?', *Foreign Affairs*, vol. 82, no. 5, September/October 2003.

Carter, James M. 'Inventing Vietnam: The United States and State-making in Southeast Asia', Dissertation, University of Houston, 2004.

222

Clark, W., 'Gradualism and American Military Strategy', *Military Review*, vol. 60, no. 9, 1975.

Clarke, Michael, 'The Diplomacy that Led to War in Iraq', in Paul Cornish, (ed.), *The Conflict in Iraq, 2003*, Basingstoke: Palgrave Macmillan, 2004.

Clarke, Richard, *Against All Enemies: Inside America's War on Terror*, New York: The Free Press, 2004.

Cockburn, Andrew and Patrick Coburn, *Saddam Hussein: An American Obsession*, London: Verso, 2002.

Cohen, E., 'Dynamics of Military Intervention', in A. Levite, B. Jentleson and L. Berman, (eds), *Foreign Military Intervention*, New York: Columbia University Press, 1992.

Coleman, Penny, *Flashback: Posttraumatic Stress Disorder, Suicide, and the Lessons of War*, Boston, MA: Beacon Press, 2006.

Collins, J. Jr, *The Development and Training of the South Vietnamese Army 1950–1972. Vietnam Studies*, Washington, DC: GPO, 1975.

Cordesman, Anthony H., *The Iraq War: Strategy, Tactics, and Military Lessons*, Washington, DC: CSIS Press, 2003.

—— *Iraq and Foreign Volunteers*, Washington, DC: Center for Strategic and International Studies, 2005.

Cox, Michael, 'American Power Before and After 11 September: Dizzy with Success?', *International Affairs*, vol. 78, no. 2, 2002.

Crabb, Cecil V. Jr, and Pat M. Holt, *Invitation to Struggle: Congress, the President, and Foreign Policy*, 2nd edn, Washington, DC: Congressional Quarterly Press, 1984.

Crocker, B., 'Iraq: Going it Alone, Gone Wrong', in R. Orr, (ed.), *Winning the Peace: An American Strategy for Post-Conflict Reconstruction*, Washington, DC: Center for Strategic and International Studies, 2004.

Daalder, Ivo H. and James M. Lindsay, *America Unbound: The Bush Revolution in Foreign Policy*, Washington, DC: Brookings Institution Press, 2003.

Daggett, S., 'Government and the Military Establishment', P. Schraeder, (ed.), *Intervention into the 1990's: U.S. Foreign Policy in the Third World*, 2nd edn, Boulder, CO: Lynne Rienner, 1992.

Dallek, Robert, *An Unfinished Life: John F. Kennedy, 1917–1963*, Boston, MA: Little, Brown & Company, 2003.

Danchev, Alex and J. Macmillan (eds), *The Iraq War and Democratic Politics*, London: Routledge, 2005.

DeGroot, Gerard J., *A Noble Cause: America and the Vietnam War*, Harlow: Longman, 2000.

Department of Defense, *National Military Strategy of the United States of America*, Washington, DC: GPO, 1997.

Department of the Army, *A Study of Strategic Lessons Learned in Vietnam*. 8 Vols. McLean, VA: BDM Corporation, 1979.

DePuy, W., 'Infantry Combat', in L. Gilmore, and C. Conway, (eds), *Selected Papers of General William E. DePuy*, Fort Leavenworth, KS: Combat Studies Institute, 1994.

Dickie, John, *'Special No More': Anglo-American Relations: Rhetoric and Reality*, London: Weidenfeld and Nicolson, 1994.

Dobbins, James, John G. McGinn, Keith Crane and Seth G. Jones, *America's Role in Nation Building from Germany to Iraq*, Santa Monica, CA: Rand Corporation, 2003.

Dodge, Toby, *Inventing Iraq: The Failure of Nation Building and a History Denied*, London: Hurst, 2003.

—— *Iraq's Future: The Aftermath of Regime Change*, Adelphi Paper 372, Oxford: Routledge, 2005.

Dorrien, Garry, *Imperial Design: Neoconservatism and the New Pax Americana*, New York: Routledge, 2004.

Downie, R., *Learning From Conflict: The U.S. Military in Vietnam, El Salvador, and the Drug War*, Westport, CT: Praeger, 1998.

Duiker, William J., *Sacred War: Nationalism and Revolution in a Divided Vietnam*, New York: McGraw Hill, 1995.

—— *The Communist Road to Power in Vietnam*, 2nd edn, Boulder, CO: Westview Press, 1996.

Dumbrell, John, *A Special Relationship: Anglo-American Relations in the Cold War and After*, London: Palgrave, 2001.

—— 'The Bush Doctrine', in George C. Edwards and Philip J. Davies, (eds.) *New Challenges for the American Presidency*, New York: Pearson Longman, 2004.

_____ 'The US–UK "Special Relationship" in a World Twice Transformed', *Cambridge Review of International Affairs*, vol. 17, 2004.

_____ 'Bush's War', in Alex Danchev and John Macmillan, (eds), *The Iraq War and Democratic Politics*, London: Routledge, 2005.

—— 'President Kerry's Foreign Policy: Continuity and Discontinuity in Contemporary American Foreign Policy', in I. Morgan and P. Davies, (eds), *Right On? Political Change and Continuity in George W. Bush's America*, London: Institute for the Study of the Americas, 2006.

Dunn, Carroll H., *Base Development in South Vietnam, 1965–1970*, Washington, DC: Department of the Army, 1972.

Ellis, Sylvia, *Britain, America and the Vietnam War*, Westport, CT: Greenwood Press, 2004.

Engelhardt, Tom, *The End of Victory Culture: Cold War America and the Disillusioning of a Generation*, Amherst, MA: University of Massachusetts Press, 1995.

Ernst, John, *Forging a Fateful Alliance: Michigan State University and the Vietnam War, East*, Lansing, MI: Michigan State University Press, 1998.

Ewell J. and I. Hunt, Jr, *Sharpening the Combat Edge: The Use of Analysis to Reinforce Military Judgment*, Vietnam Studies, Washington, DC: GPO, 1974.

FitzGerald, Frances, *Fire in the Lake: The Vietnamese and the Americans in Vietnam*, New York: Vintage, 1972.

Foong Khong, Yuen, *Analogies at War: Korea, Munich, Dien Bien Phu and the Vietnam Decisions of 1965*, Princeton, NJ: Princeton University Press, 1992.

Freedman, Lawrence, 'Escalators and Quagmires: Expectations and the Use of Force', *International Affairs*, vol. 67, no. 1, 1991.

—— *The Revolution in Strategic Affairs. Adelphi Paper 318*, London: Oxford University Press/ RIIA, 1998.

Freedman, Lawrence and Efraim Karsh, 'How Kuwait Was Won: Strategy in the Gulf War', *International Security*, vol. 6, no. 2, Fall 1991.

Fukuyama, Francis, 'The End of History', *The National Interest*, Summer 1989.

—— *The End of History and the Last Man*, London: Penguin, 1992.

—— 'The Neoconservative Moment', *The National Interest*, Summer 2004.

—— *After the Neocons: America at the Crossroads*, London: Profile, 2006.

Fussell, Paul, *The Great War and Modern Memory*, New York: Oxford University Press, 2000.

Gacek, C., *The Logic of Force: The Dilemma of Limited War in American Foreign Policy*, New York: Columbia University Press, 1994.

Gaddis, John Lewis, 'A Grand Strategy of Transformation', *Foreign Policy*, November/December 2002.

—— *Surprise, Security and the American Experience*, Cambridge, MA: Harvard University Press, 2004.

Gardner, Lloyd C., *Pay Any Price: Lyndon Johnson and the Wars for Vietnam*, Chicago, IL: Ivan R. Dee, 1995.

Gardner, Lloyd and Marilyn B. Young (eds), *The New American Empire*, New York: The New Press, 2005.

Gelb, Lesley H. and Richard K. Betts, *The Irony of Vietnam: The System Worked*, Washington, DC: Brookings Institution, 1979.

George, A., and W. Simons, (eds), *The Limits of Coercive Diplomacy*, 2nd edn, Boulder, CO: Westview Press, 1994.

Gibbons, William, *The U.S. Government and the Vietnam War*, Princeton, NJ: Princeton University Press, 1986.

Gibson, J., *The Perfect War: Technowar in Vietnam*, Boston, MA: Atlantic Monthly, 1986.

Gordon, Michael and Bernard Trainor, *The Generals' War: The Inside Story of the Conflict in the Gulf*, Boston, MA: Little, Brown and Company, 1990.

—— *Cobra II: The Inside Story of the Invasion and Occupation of Iraq*, London: Atlantic Books, 2006.

Gordon, Philip H. and Jeremy Shapiro, *Allies at War: America, Europe and the Crisis Over Iraq*, New York: McGraw Hill, 2004.

Gray, C., *Postmodern War: The New Politics of Conflict*, London: Routledge, 1997.

Halberstam, David, *The Making of a Quagmire*, New York: Random House, 1965.

—— *The Best and the Brightest*, New York: Random House, 1972.

—— *War in a Time of Peace*, London: Bloomsbury, 2002.

Halliday, Fred, *Cold War, Third World*, London: Hutchinson Radius,1989.

Halper, Stephan and Jonathan Clarke, *America Alone: The Neo-conservatives and the Global Order*, Cambridge: Cambridge University Press, 2004.

Helms, R., *The Persian Gulf Crisis: Power in the Post-Cold War World*, Westport, CT: Praeger, 1993.

Herring, George, *America's Longest War: The United States and Vietnam, 1950–1975*, 4th edn, New York: McGraw Hill, 2002.

Hersh, Seymour M., *Chain of Command: The Road from 9/11 to Abu Ghraib*, New York: HarperCollins, 2004.

Hess, Gary R., 'The Unending Debate: Historians and the Vietnam War', in Michael Hogan, (ed.), *America and the World*, Cambridge: Cambridge University Press, 1995.

—— *Presidential Decisions for War: Korea, Vietnam and the Persian Gulf*, Baltimore, MD: The Johns Hopkins University Press, 2001.

Hills, A., *Future War In Cities: Rethinking a Liberal Dilemma*, London: Frank Cass, 2004.

Hilsman, Roger, *To Move a Nation: The Politics of Foreign Policy in the Administration of John F. Kennedy*, New York: Delta, 1967.

Hiro, Dilip, *Iraq: A Report from the Inside*, London: Granta, 2003.

Hitchens, Christopher, *Love, Poverty and War*, New York: Nation Books, 2004.

Hoffman, F., *Decisive Force: The New American Way of War*, London: Praeger, 1996.

Hunter, Allen (ed.), *Rethinking the Cold War*, Philadelphia, PA: Temple University Press, 1998.

Ignatieff, Michael, *Virtual War: Kosovo and Beyond*, New York: Picador, 2000.

Isaacs, Arnold R., *Vietnam Shadows: The War, Its Ghosts, and Its Legacy*, Baltimore, MD: The Johns Hopkins University Press, 1997.

Jervis, Robert, *Perception and Misperception in International Politics*, Princeton, NJ: Princeton University Press, 1976.

Johnson, Chalmers, *The Sorrows of Empire: Militarism, Secrecy, and the End of the Republic*, New York: Henry Holt & Company, 2004.

Johnson, Lyndon Baines, *The Vantage Point: Perspectives of the Presidency 1963–1969*, New York: Holt, Rinehart and Winston, 1971.

Joint Chiefs of Staff, *Joint Pub 1: Joint Warfare of the US Armed Forces*, Washington, DC: GPO, 1991.

Kagan, Robert, *Paradise and Power*, London: Atlantic Books, 2003.

Kaiser, David, *American Tragedy: Kennedy, Johnson, and the Origins of the Vietnam War*, Cambridge, MA: Belknap Press, 2000.

Kampfner, John, *Blair's Wars*, London: Simon and Schuster, 2003.

Kaplan, R., *Imperial Grunts: The American Military on the Ground*, New York: RandomHouse, 2005.

Karnow, Stanley, *Vietnam: A History*, New York: Viking Press, 1983.

Kaufman, Richard, *The War Profiteers*, New York: The Bobbs-Merrill Company, Inc., 1970.

King, Peter (ed.), *Australia's Vietnam: Australia in the Second Indochina War*, Sydney: Allen & Unwin, 1983.

Kinnard, D., *The War Managers*, Wayne, NJ: Avery, 1985.

Kissinger, Henry, *White House Years*, Boston, MA: Little, Brown and Company, 1979.

Klare, Michael T., *Beyond the 'Vietnam Syndrome': U.S. Interventionism in the 1980s*, Washington, DC: Institute for Policy Studies, 1981.

Kolko, Gabriel, *Vietnam: Anatomy of a War, 1940–1975*, London: Allen & Unwin, 1986.

Krauthammer, Charles, *Democratic Realism: An American Foreign Policy for a Unipolar World*, Washington, DC: AEI Press, 2004.

Krepinevich, Andrew F. Jr, *The Army and Vietnam*, Baltimore, MD: John Hopkins University Press, 1986.

—— 'How to Win in Iraq', *Foreign Affairs*, vol. 84, no. 5, September/October 2005.

Laird, Melvin, 'Iraq: Learning the Lessons of Vietnam', *Foreign Affairs*, vol. 84, no. 6, 2005.

Latham, A., 'Re-Imagining Warfare: The "Revolution in Military Affairs"', in C. Synder, (ed.), *Contemporary Security and Strategy*, London: Macmillan Press, 1999.

Leffler, Melvyn, *A Preponderance of Power: National Security, the Truman Administration, and the Cold War*, Stanford, CA: Stanford University Press, 1992.

Levy, David W., *The Debate Over Vietnam*, 2nd edn, Baltimore, MD: Johns Hopkins University Press, 1995.

Lieven, Anatol, *America Right or Wrong*, New York: HarperCollins, 2004.

Lifton, Robert Jay, *Superpower Syndrome: America's Apocalyptic Confrontation with the World*, New York: Nation Books, 2003.

Lock-Pullan, Richard, '"An Inward Looking Time": the US Army 1973–7', *Journal of Military History*, vol. 67, no. 2, 2003.

—— *US Intervention Policy and Army Innovation: From Vietnam to Iraq*, London: Routledge, 2006.

Logevall, Fredrik, *Choosing War: The Lost Chance for Peace and the Escalation of War in Vietnam*, Berkeley, CA: University of California Press, 1999.

Luttwak, Edward, 'Where Are the Great Powers? At Home with the Kids', *Foreign Affairs*, vol. 73, no. 4, 1994.

——— 'A Post-Heroic Military Policy', *Foreign Affairs*, vol. 75, no. 4, 1996.

MacDonald, P., *Giap: The Victor in Vietnam*, London: Fourth Estate, 1993.

Macgregor, D., *Transformation Under Fire: Revolutionizing How America Fights*, Westport, CT: Praeger, 2003.

MacKinnon, Michael G., *The Evolution of US Peacekeeping Policy Under Clinton: A Fairweather Friend*, London: Frank Cass, 2000.

Masur, Matthew B., *Hearts and Minds: Cultural Nation-Building in South Vietnam, 1954–1963*, unpublished PhD dissertation, The Ohio State University, 2004.

May, Ernest R., *'Lessons' of the Past: The Use and Misuse of History in American Foreign Policy*, Oxford: Oxford University Press, 1975.

McCrisken, Trevor B., *American Exceptionalism and the Legacy of Vietnam: US Foreign Policy Since 1974*, Basingstoke: Palgrave Macmillan, 2003.

McMahon, Robert J., 'Credibility and World Power: Exploring the Psychological Dimension in Postwar American Diplomacy', *Diplomatic History*, vol. 15, no. 3, Fall 1991.

McMaster, H., *Dereliction of Duty: Lyndon Johnson, Robert McNamara, The Joint Chiefs of Staff, and The Lies That Led to Vietnam*, New York: HarperCollins, 1997.

McNamara, Robert, *In Retrospect: The Tragedy and the Lessons of Vietnam*, New York: Random House, 1995.

Mearsheimer, John J., *The Tragedy of Great Power Politics*, New York: W. W. Norton, 2001.

Melanson, Richard A., *American Foreign Policy since the Vietnam War: The Search for Consensus from Richard Nixon to George W. Bush*, 4th edn, Armonk, NY: M. E. Sharpe, 2005.

Melman, Seymour, *Pentagon Capitalism: The Political Economy of War*, New York: McGraw-Hill Company, 1970.

Millet, Allen R., and Peter Maslowski, *For the Common Defense: A Military History of the United States of America*, New York: The Free Press, 1994.

Mueller, John, *War, Presidents, and Public Opinion*, New York: John Wiley, 1973.

——— 'The Search for the "Breaking Point" in Vietnam: The Statistics of a Deadly Quarrel', *International Studies Quarterly*, December 1980.

——— 'The Perfect Enemy: Assessing the Gulf War', *Security Studies*, Autumn 1995.

——— *The Remnants of War*, Ithaca, NY: Cornell University Press, 2004.

——— 'What Was the Cold War About? Evidence from Its Ending', *Political Science Quarterly*, Winter 2004–5.

——— 'Simplicity and Spook: Terrorism and the Dynamics of Threat Exaggeration', *International Studies Perspectives*, May 2005.

——— 'The Iraq Syndrome', *Foreign Affairs*, November–December 2005.

Murray W. and R. Scales, Jr, *The Iraq War: A Military History*, London: Belknap/Harvard University Press, 2003.

Nagl, J., *Learning to Eat Soup with a Knife: Counterinsurgency Lessons from Malaya and Vietnam*, Chicago, IL: University of Chicago Press, 2005.

Neustadt, Richard E. and Ernest R. May, *Thinking in Time: The Uses of History for Decision Makers*, New York: Free Press, 1986.

Palmer, B., Jr, *The 25 Year War: America's Military Role in Vietnam*, New York: Da Capo, 1984.

Paterson, Thomas G., 'Historical Memory and Illusive Victory: Vietnam and Central America', *Diplomatic History*, vol. 12, 1988.

Peters, P., *Fighting for the Future: Will America Triumph?*, Mechanicsburg, PA: Stackpole Books, 1999.

Peterson, M., *The Combined Action Platoons: The U.S. Marines' Other War In Vietnam*, Westport, CT: Praeger, 1989.

Phillips, David L., *Losing Iraq: Inside the Postwar Reconstruction Fiasco*, Boulder, CO: Westview Press, 2005.

Powell, Colin L. with Joseph E. Persico, *My American Journey*, New York: Random House, 1995.

Rabel, Roberto, *New Zealand and the Vietnam War: Politics and Diplomacy*, Auckland: Auckland University Press, 2005.

Rashid, Ahmed, *Taliban: Militant Islam, Oil and Fundamentalism in Central Asia*, New Haven, CT: Yale University Press, 2000.

Raskin, Marcus G. and Bernard B. Fall (eds), *The Viet-Nam Reader: Articles and Documents on American Foreign Policy and the Viet-Nam Crisis*, New York: Vintage Books, 1965.

Rasmussen, Mikkel Vedby, 'The History of a Lesson: Versailles, Munich and the Social Construction of the Past', *Review of International Studies*, vol. 29, 2003.

Record, Jeffrey, *Making War, Thinking History: Munich, Vietnam and Presidential Uses of Force from Korea to Kosovo*, Annapolis, MD: Naval Institute Press, 2002.

Record, Jeffrey and W. Andrew Terrill, *Iraq and Vietnam: Differences, Similarities, and Insights*, Carlisle: Strategic Studies Institute, May 2004.

Renshon, Stanley A. and Deborah Welch Larson (eds), *Good Judgment in Foreign Policy: Theory and Application*, Lanham, MD: Rowman & Littlefield, 2003.

Rosen, S., 'New Ways of War: Understanding Military Innovation', *International Security*, vol. 13, no. 1, 1988.

Roth, D., *Sacred Honor: The Authorised Biography of General Sir Colin Powell*, London: HarperCollins, 1994.

Rotter, Andrew, *The Path to Vietnam: Origins of the American Commitment to Southeast Asia*, Ithaca, NY: Cornell University Press, 1989.

Rubin, Barry, 'The Real Roots of Arab Anti-Americanism', *Foreign Affairs*, vol. 81, no. 6, November/December 2002.

Rumsfeld, Donald, 'Transforming the Military', *Foreign Affairs*, vol. 81, no. 3, May–June 2002.

Ryan, David, *US Foreign Policy in World History*, London: Routledge, 2000.

—— 'Ten Days in September: The Creeping Irrelevance of Transatlantic Allies', *Journal of Transatlantic Studies*, vol. 1, special edition, Spring 2003.

Said, Edward W., *Culture and Imperialism*, London: Chatto and Windus, 1993.

Sarkesian, S., J. Williams and F. Bryant, *Soldiers, Society and National Security*, London: Lynne Rienner, 1995.

Scarborough, Rowan, *Rumsfeld's War: The Untold Story of America's Anti-Terrorist Commander*, Washington, DC: Regency Publishing Company, 2004.

Schandler, Herbert Y. *The Unmaking of a President: Lyndon Johnson and Vietnam*, Princeton, NJ: Princeton University Press, 1977.

Schivelbusch, Wolfgang, *The Culture of Defeat: On National Trauma, Mourning, and Recovery*, New York: Henry Holt, 2003.

Schneider, William, 'Public Opinion', in Joseph S. Nye, Jr., (ed.), *The Making of America's Soviet Policy*, New Haven, CT: Yale University Press, 1984.

Schraeder, P. (ed.), *Intervention into the 1990's: U.S. Foreign Policy in the Third World*, 2nd edn, Boulder, CO: Lynne Rienner, 1992.

Schuman, Howard and Cheryl Rieger, 'Historical Analogies, Generational Effects, and Attitudes Toward War', *American Sociological Review*, vol. 57, 1992.

Scigliano, Robert, *South Vietnam: Nation Under Stress*, Boston, MA: Houghton-Mifflin Company, 1963.

Shafer, D. Michael, *Deadly Paradigms: The Failure of US Counterinsurgency Policy*, Leicester: Leicester University Press, 1988.

Shawcross, William, *Allies: US, Britain, Europe and the War in Iraq*, London: Atlantic, 2003.

Sheehan, Neil, *A Bright Shining Lie: John Paul Vann and America in Vietnam*, New York: Vintage, 1989.

Short, Anthony, *The Origins of the Vietnam War*, London: Longman, 1989.

Shultz, George, *Turmoil and Triumph: My Years as Secretary of State*, New York: Macmillan, 1993.

Sifry, Micah L. and Christopher Cerf (eds), *The Gulf War Reader: History, Documents, Opinions*, New York: Random House, 1991.

—— *The Iraq War Reader: History, Documents, Opinions*, New York: Simon & Schuster, 2003.

Simons, Geoff, *Iraq: From Sumer to Post-Saddam*, 3rd edn, Basingstoke: Palgrave Macmillan, 2004.

Simons, W., 'U.S. Coercive Pressure on North Vietnam, Early 1965', in A. George and W. Simons, (eds), *The Limits of Coercive Diplomacy*, 2nd edn, Boulder, CO: Westview, 1994.

Singer, P. W., *Corporate Warriors: The Rise of the Privatized Military Industry*, Ithaca, NY: Cornell University Press, 2003.

—— 'War, Profits, and the Vacuum of Law: Privatized Military Firms and International Law', *Columbia Journal of Transnational Law*, vol. 24, no. 2, Spring 2004.

Singh, Robert, 'The Bush Doctrine', in Mary Buckley and Robert Singh, (eds), *The Bush Doctrine and the War on Terrorism: Global Responses, Global Consequences*, London: Routledge, 2006.

Sorensen, Theodore, *Kennedy*, New York: Harper & Row, 1965.

Sorley, Lewis, *A Better War: The Unexamined Victories and Final Tragedy of America's Last Years in Vietnam*, New York: Harvest, 1999.

Spector, R., 'U.S. Army Strategy in the Vietnam War', *International Security*, vol. 11, no. 4, 1987.

—— *After Tet: The Bloodiest Year in Vietnam*, New York: Free Press, 1993.

Summers, Harry Jr, *On Strategy: A Critical Analysis of the Vietnam War*, Novato, CA: Presidio, 1982.

—— *On Strategy II: A Critical Analysis of the Gulf War*, New York: Dell, 1992.

Suskind, Ron, *The Price of Loyalty: George W. Bush, the White House, and the Education of Paul O'Neill*, New York: Simon & Schuster, 2004.

Swafford, Anthony, *Jarhead: A Soldier's Story of Modern War*, London: Scribner, 2003.

Sweeney, J. (ed.), *A Handbook of American Military History: From the Revolutionary War to the Present*, Boulder, CO: Westview, 1996.

Tuchman, Barbara, *The March of Folly: From Troy to Vietnam*, New York: Knopf, 1984.

Tucker, Robert W. and David C. Hendrickson, *The Imperial Temptation: The New World Order and America's Purpose*, New York: Council on Foreign Relations Press, 1992.

Turley, William S., *The Second Indochina War: A Short Political and Military History, 1954–1975*, New York: Mentor, 1986.

Vickers, M., 'Revolution Deferred: Kosovo and the Transformation of War', in A. Bacevich and E. Cohen, (eds), *War Over Kosovo: Politics and Strategy in a Global Age*, New York: Columbia University Press, 2001.

Weinberger, Caspar, *Fighting for Peace: Seven Critical Years in the Pentagon*, New York: Warner, 1990.

Westmoreland, William, *A Soldier Reports*, New York: Dell, 1976.

Wittkopf, Eugene R., *Faces of Internationalism: Public Opinion and American Foreign Policy*, Durham, NC: Duke University Press, 1991.

Woodward, Bob, *The Commanders*, New York: Simon & Schuster, 1991.

—— *Plan of Attack*, New York: Simon & Schuster, 2004.

Young, Marilyn B., *The Vietnam Wars, 1945–1990*, New York: HarperCollins ,1991.

—— 'Imperial Language', in Lloyd Gardner and Marilyn B. Young, (eds), *The New American Empire*, New York: The New Press, 2005.

INDEX

torture policies 63; and use of executive
power 153–4; and use of historical
references 161, 194, 195; withdrawal
strategy 169, 170, 171–3, 187
Butler, Richard 14
Byrd, Robert 26, 214–15

CACI International 90
Callwell, Charles 80
Cambodia 183, 184, 202, 213
Camp David 19, 23
Carter Doctrine 148–9
Carter, Jimmy 2, 6, 12, 114, 121, 122, 141,
148, 148–9
Casteel, Steve 34
Caterpillar Tractor Company 94
CBS 210
Center for Public Integrity 87
Central Intelligence Agency (CIA) 11, 12,
13, 17, 19–20, 23, 56, 58, 79, 121
CH2M Hill 88
Chain of Command: A Thriller
(Weinberger and Schweizer) 26
Chalabi, Ahmad 10–11, 13, 58
Chávez, Hugo 118
Cheney, Richard 11, 17, 19, 22–3, 56, 86,
88, 89, 154
Chicago Council on Foreign Relations
(CCFR) 50, 51
Chile 24
China 8, 182, 183, 202
Chirac, Jacques 210
Chomsky, Noam 117
Choosing War (Logevall) 2
Christopher, Warren 152
Civil Operations and Rural Development
Programme (CORDS) 78–9
Clark, Wesley 71, 128
Clausewitz, K.M. von 67
Cleland, Max 39
Clinton, Bill 12, 13, 14, 56, 111, 112, 113,
149, 152, 154, 170, 188, 209
CNN 18
CNN/*USA Today* survey 170
Coalition Provisional Authority (CPA) 60,
90
Coalition of the Willing 24, 131, 156
Cold War 70; accommodationists
50–1; axioms of 48–9; and casualty
aversion post-Cold War 128; and
conflation of nationalism/communism
124; consensus in 3, 166, 213; and
containment policy 148; contrast with
War on Terrorism 66; and credibility
111; cultural 49–52; effect of Vietnam
War on 51–2; end of 9, 184, 185;

and European anti-Americanism/
anticommunism 141; followership
model/structure of public opinion
50–1, 64(n7); hardliners 50; and
ideology 144; imperatives of 161–2;
and importance of South Vietnam 183;
isolationism 50; likened to fight against
radical Islam 63; and the nuclear family
52; origins of 114; policies 8, 197; and
presidential power 145; presidential
references to 195; and private firms
post-Cold War 86, 102; procedural
49; tectonic shifts since 16; traditional
internationalists 51; and US national
unity 153; US position in 11; and
US–UK Special Relationship 218; and
use of nuclear weapons 139
Combined Action Platoons (CAP) 78
Command and General Staff College 42
Command and General Staff College
(CGSC) 67
Commodity Import Program (CIP) 98
communism 197, 198–200
Congressional Declarations of War 140,
141
Conrad, Joseph 37
counter-insurgency (COIN), and hunting/
killing insurgents 36; ignoring of 69;
learning from 205; and limits of US
power 118; members of 162, 213, 219;
nature of 164–5; number of attacks 35,
91; and politics 81; strength of 186; and
suicide bombings 59; understanding of
66, 75, 77, 79–80; US reaction to 40,
41–2, 45(n31), 46(n50), 128; Vietnam–
Iraq comparison 75
Cronkite, Walter 39, 210
Cuba 145–6, 147, 151, 181, 185
Custer-Battles 90

Da Nang 93
Daily Telegraph 38
Dean, Howard 215
'Defence Planning Guidance' 11, 13, 117
democracy 1–2, 116–17, 121, 171, 194–5,
199, 201–3, 205
Democrats 1, 25, 55, 149, 150, 215
Department of Homeland Security 53, 54
*Dereliction of Duty: Lyndon Johnson,
Robert McNamara, Joint Chiefs of
Staff, and the Lies that Led to Vietnam*
38
Desert Fox 14
Desert Storm 11
détente 9, 12
Dien Bien Phu 144, 181

CONTEMPORARY SECURITY STUDIES

NATO'S SECRET ARMY
Operation Gladio and Terrorism in Western Europe
Daniel Ganser

THE US, NATO AND MILITARY BURDEN-SHARING
Peter Kent Forster and Stephen J. Cimbala

RUSSIAN GOVERNANCE IN THE TWENTY-FIRST CENTURY
Geo-strategy, geopolitics and new governance
Irina Isakova

THE FOREIGN OFFICE AND FINLAND 1938–1940
Diplomatic sideshow
Craig Gerrard

RETHINKING THE NATURE OF WAR
Isabelle Duyvesteyn and Jan Angstrom (eds)

PERCEPTION AND REALITY IN THE MODERN YUGOSLAV
CONFLICT
Myth, falsehood and deceit 1991–1995
Brendan O'Shea

THE POLITICAL ECONOMY OF PEACEBUILDING IN POST-
DAYTON BOSNIA
Tim Donais

THE DISTRACTED EAGLE
The rift between America and Old Europe
Peter H. Merkl

THE IRAQ WAR
European perspectives on politics, strategy, and operations
Jan Hallenberg and Håkan Karlsson (eds)

STRATEGIC CONTEST
Weapons proliferation and war in the Greater Middle East
Richard L. Russell

PROPAGANDA, THE PRESS AND CONFLICT
The Gulf War and Kosovo
David R. Willcox

MISSILE DEFENCE
International, regional and national implications
Bertel Heurlin and Sten Rynning (eds)

GLOBALISING JUSTICE FOR MASS ATROCITIES
A revolution in accountability
Chandra Lekha Sriram

ETHNIC CONFLICT AND TERRORISM
The origins and dynamics of civil wars
Joseph L. Soeters

GLOBALISATION AND THE FUTURE OF TERRORISM
Patterns and predictions
Brynjar Lia

NUCLEAR WEAPONS AND STRATEGY
The evolution of American nuclear policy
Stephen J. Cimbala

NASSER AND THE MISSILE AGE IN THE MIDDLE EAST
Owen L. Sirrs

WAR AS RISK MANAGEMENT
Strategy and conflict in an age of globalised risks
Yee-Kuang Heng

MILITARY NANOTECHNOLOGY
Potential applications and preventive arms control
Jurgen Altmann

NATO AND WEAPONS OF MASS DESTRUCTION
Regional alliance, global threats
Eric R. Terzuolo

EUROPEANISATION OF NATIONAL SECURITY IDENTITY
The EU and the changing security identities of the Nordic states
Pernille Rieker